MW00966042

RELIGION AND CANADIAN SOCIETY

RELIGION AND CANADIAN SOCIETY:

Traditions, Transitions, and Innovations

LORI G. BEAMAN

Religion and Canadian Society: Traditions, Transitions, and Innovations
Edited by Lori G. Beaman

First published in 2006 by
Canadian Scholars' Press Inc.
180 Bloor Street West, Suite 801
Toronto, Ontario
M5S 2V6

www.cspi.org

Copyright © 2006 Lori G. Beaman, the contributing authors, and Canadian Scholars' Press Inc. All rights reserved. No part of this publication may be photocopied, reproduced, stored in a retrieval system, or transmitted, in any form or by any means, electronic, mechanical, or otherwise, without the written permission of Canadian Scholars' Press Inc., except for brief passages quoted for review purposes. In the case of photocopying, a licence may be obtained from Access Copyright: One Yonge Street, Suite 1900, Toronto, Ontario, M5E 1E5, (416) 868-1620, fax (416) 868-1621, toll-free 1-800-893-5777, www.accesscopyright.ca.

Every reasonable effort has been made to identify copyright holders. CSPI would be pleased to have any errors or omissions brought to its attention.

Canadian Scholars' Press gratefully acknowledges financial support for our publishing activities from the Government of Canada through the Book Publishing Industry Development Program (BPIDP) and the Government of Ontario through the Ontario Book Publishing Tax Credit Program.

Library and Archives Canada Cataloguing in Publication

Religion and Canadian society : traditions, transitions, and innovations / [edited by] Lori G. Beaman.

Includes bibliographical references.

ISBN 1-55130-306-X

1. Religion and sociology—Canada—Textbooks. 2. Canada—Religion—Textbooks.

I. Beaman, Lori G. (Lori Gail), 1963–

BL2530.C3R39 2006   306.6'0971   C2006-900052-2

Cover photograph: "Shadow of Man in Front of Stain" by Selma Yalazi from stock.xchng website: http://www.sxc.hu. Copyright © Selma Yalazi, 2005. Reprinted with permission of Selma Yalazi/stock.xchng. Text and cover design: Susan Thomas / Digital Zone

06   07   08   09   10   5   4   3   2   1

Printed and bound in Canada by Marquis Book Printing Inc.

TABLE OF CONTENTS

PREFACE

Several years ago when I was preparing to teach a sociology of religion course I explored the available texts and was shocked to find that almost none focused on sociology of religion in Canada. The best edited collection had gone out of print, and in any event was now somewhat dated. Much has changed in the sociology of religion since that volume was written. Theoretical debates have shifted, demographics have changed, and the role of religion in the world generally is being taken more seriously by scholars. This is a critical moment in history in terms of understanding the religion–society relationship, and yet it seems that we are not particularly well equipped to study it. This book is a beginning attempt to remedy that by pulling together work by some of the key scholars working in the sub-discipline of sociology of religion in Canada.

We don't pretend that this book covers every topic that is important in the field. Nor does it review the "founding fathers" in any great detail. The creation of any edited collection necessitates some difficult decisions, and this collection is no exception. In some instances there simply didn't exist work that covered certain areas we wanted to include. This is a clear signal that in this field there is much to be studied that has thus far been left untouched. In addition, some scholars who have made important contributions to the sociological study of religion in Canada have been left out. Sometimes their work was too specialized for a collection such as this one that aims to cover a broad range of topics. Some of these scholars and their work is mentioned in Further Readings at the end of each part. We encourage readers to explore more fully those areas that are of particular interest to them.

No book comes into being without the co-operation and collaboration of many people. Thank you to the authors of the chapters. You have each made important contributions to the field, and have persisted in studying an area that receives limited recognition by the broader academic community. Thanks also to the reviewers of the proposal for valuable suggestions and encouraging comments. Thank you to research assistant Nicole Saunders for brainstorming with me on discussion questions, and for a keen eye for editorial detail. Thank you to research assistant Lisa Smith, particularly for the terrific suggestions on key concepts. Thank you also to Megan Mueller for her invaluable suggestions and openness to my ideas.

Finally, a note about the chapters: As editor I was extremely reluctant to make any significant changes to the content of wording of these works, which had almost all been previously published elsewhere. Thus, there are occasionally references to events as though they are current or to time, like "we are now at the end of the twentieth century."

A NOTE FROM THE PUBLISHER

Thank you for selecting *Religion and Canadian Society: Traditions, Transitions, and Innovations,* edited by Lori G. Beaman. The editor and publisher have devoted considerable time and careful development (including meticulous peer reviews) to this book. We appreciate your recognition of this effort and accomplishment.

TEACHING FEATURES

This volume distinguishes itself on the market in many ways. One key feature is the book's well-written and comprehensive part openers, which help to make the readings all the more accessible to undergraduate students. The part openers add cohesion to the section and to the whole book. The themes of the book are clearly presented in these openers.

The general editor, Lori G. Beaman, has also greatly enhanced the book by adding pedagogy. Each part ends with Critical Thinking questions pertaining to each reading as well as detailed, annotated recommended readings.

INTRODUCTION

The aim of this reader is to offer a selection of readings that represent an overview of some of the key issues in sociology of religion from a Canadian perspective. The reader moves through three thematic cornerstones: traditions, transitions, and innovations. Subthemes run throughout, including the definition of religion, the secularization debate, the challenge of diversity, and the gendered aspects of religious experience. The works in this collection are intended to raise theoretical, empirical, and methodological questions.

My description of myself as a religious "none" is always the source of confusion in my classes, as most students hear "nun" and look at me with a bit of unbelieving astonishment. Two things always strike me about this moment: first, their preconceived notions about how a nun should look. One of the tasks of sociological exploration is to open a window onto understanding. Sociology can enter the world of religion, and into the world of the religious nun, or the religious none, and help to explicate an ethnography of that self, as well as to explain the social and cultural context of the religious participant.

The second insight from the "nun" story is this: single-category descriptions are woefully inadequate to describe religious experience and religiosity. Religious experience is many layered, situated in ever-changing cultural and social context, and develops with the life course of the individual believer. Exploration of the life course reveals different types of encounters with religion—perhaps childhood attendance in a traditional church, leaving during adolescence, exploration of different spiritual practices throughout adulthood, perhaps a return to the church of origin, or a combination of traditional and "alternative" religious and spiritual practices. As social scientists, how do we account for this diversity of experience?

METHOD AND METHODOLOGY

Integral to the social scientific study of religion is a consideration of methodological quandaries and issues of method. Not all sociological research involves fieldwork or face-to-face contact with members of religious groups, but such methods are central to the exploration of religion in society. Methodologically, key questions include these: From whose perspective is the research to be undertaken? How much disclosure of one's own religious life history is necessary or desirable? A number of the chapters in this volume deal with these issues, including William Shaffir's exploration of an Orthodox Jewish community; Siân Reid's reflexive examination of being a Witch studying a Wiccan community; and Susan Palmer's foray into the worlds of new religious groups.

Methods questions are endless—to use a life history approach, conduct a survey, or engage in participant observation? Each will produce a different type of story. Reginald Bibby, for example, makes extensive use of survey methods, creating a snapshot of religiosity in Canada. Susan Palmer uses participant observation and in-depth interviewing, as well as content analysis to offer detailed insight into the specific groups she studies. Nancy Nason-Clark uses triangulated research methods, combining survey methods, focus groups, and in-depth interviews to explicate the response of organized religion to violence against women. Samuel Reimer uses comparison to illuminate the differences between religiosity in Canada and the United States.

Probably the most important point in all of this is that no one method offers the "truth" about religion and society or a particular group. Religion is a lived phenomenon, and as such is dynamic and shifting as practitioners weave their beliefs through their day-to-day lives. The key is to be aware of choices of method and methodological implications, and to be open to alternative ways of exploring sociological questions about religious life.

TRADITIONS, TRANSITIONS, AND INNOVATIONS

The first part of this book, "Traditions," is designed to introduce the reader to a broad overview of religion in Canada, including demographic information and important debates. The traditions we focus on in this part are not so much religious traditions as the theoretical and methodological traditions in the sociology of religion. This part begins with the work of Roger O'Toole to provide a historical context for the examination of contemporary issues. Reginald Bibby's work offers an overview of the contemporary situation in Canada, and David Seljak's chapter is an important caveat to the notion of a singular Canadian picture, presenting some of the unique aspects of religion in Quebec. Samuel Reimer focuses on the differences in culture to explore and compare the degree to which people are "religious" in Canada and the United States. The section ends with Peter Beyer's exploration of the current theoretical debates in sociology of religion, particularly those around secularization and rational-choice theory.

"Transitions" will explore some of the ways in which traditional beliefs about religion are challenged, as well as look at the reshaping of traditional religions in contemporary society. In addition, the notion of boundaries will be examined, as religious groups must negotiate their way through their identities in the context of society. By virtue of its being a lived phenomenon, religion does not remain static. This part will attempt to capture some of the transitions that occur in the process. Nason-Clark's chapter examines the response of organized religion to violence against women. William Closson James's work challenges received wisdom on "religious" experience, pushing us to reconsider definitions of religion. This part also explores some of the debates that have an impact on these transitions, from the religion–science tension explicated by William Stahl to the question of who is "really" religious as it is discussed by Reimer in his comparison of Canadian and

U.S. religious behaviour. William Shaffir's work gives an ethnographic close-up of the transitions that are part of boundary maintenance in a Jewish community. And Sîân Reid's work captures two aspects of "transitions": the Wiccan community and the variety of shapes it takes, and the sociologist as researcher of religion.

"Innovations," the third part, picks up on current issues in the sociology of religion: despite their relatively low numbers, new religious movements (NRMs) attract a great deal of attention. This section includes the work of two researchers in new religious movements. Dawson and Hennebry's work addresses the question of whether and how new religious movements are using the Internet to disseminate information and attract members. Susan Palmer takes us on a backstage journey as a researcher of new religious movements. The issue of religious freedom has moved to centre stage post-September 11, 2001, and Beaman's chapter examines the ways in which religious freedom is defined in law using Aboriginal spirituality as a case study. Hoodfar's work teases out some of the debates around religious freedom and religious symbols by using the veil as a case study. Each of these works illustrates the complexity of the issues surrounding the construction of meaning from the perspective of "insiders" and of those in the broader society. Eaton's work brings together a variety of disciplinary perspectives to work through the issues of religion and the environment, specifically the intersection of ecofeminism and liberation theologies.

THE DYNAMIC NATURE OF RELIGION AND SOCIETY

In recognizing that religious life is always shifting, are there changes to which we should pay particular attention? We know that immigration is playing an important role in the religious landscape of Canada, bringing together larger populations of groups who have traditionally had a presence in Canada, such as Sikhs, Muslims, and Buddhists. Research into the demographic shifts is important, but equally critical is an understanding of how the texture of religious life is changing. New religious groups are also under-studied, and while their growth is not as dramatic as popular media might have us believe, they are an important part of the story of religion in Canada. Also marginalized in the sociological study of religion have been First Nations peoples and their spiritualities. The complex history of colonization, attempted destruction of Aboriginal culture, and denial of spiritual traditions are intertwined in the picture of religion in Canada today, but, with the exception of the discipline of Aboriginal Studies, rarely are the focus of sociological research on religion.

Another "missing" element of the picture of religion in Canada from a sociological perspective is the ways in which rural communities contrast with urban centres. For often pragmatic reasons much of the research on religion and society is done in urban centres. This gives us a particular view of the religious dynamic in Canada, but fails to convey a sense of the religious life of rural inhabitants.

Another vector in the religion–society relationship is the fundamentalism we see infiltrating public policy south of the border. Happenings in the United States have an impact on our religious landscape as well. This doesn't necessarily mean that we follow the same trends; indeed we may be inspired to head in the opposite direction. Nonetheless, given the local and global impact of religious trends in the United States it is certainly a good idea to pay attention to how they play out.

Whether the blending of traditions is something new, or has simply moved closer to the forefront of interest for sociologists of religion, it is a fascinating phenomenon, particularly given the rather closed categories previously used to explore religious life in Canada. Whether we are thinking about hockey as religion, about the First Nations person who blends traditional ways of knowing with Roman Catholicism, or about the religious practitioner who sporadically attends a traditional church, engages in meditation, attends a spiritual growth retreat, and uses Aboriginal rituals, religious life is much more complex and rich than a simple measure of church affiliation would indicate.

Finally, the interaction between religion and law is central to understanding religious diversity in Canada. Here we see that religious freedom is not as easily defined as we might think, and that there is a surprising adherence to mainstream ideas about what religion looks like. Moreover, we see polygamists defending their right to defy the law, Jehovah's Witness youth refusing blood transfusions, evangelical universities defending their policies on gays and lesbians, and churches dividing over the legalization of same-sex marriage. Law's role in relation to religion is complicated and, like the very definition of religion, is ever-shifting.

On the one hand, then, we have a picture of religion in Canada that captures a stable religious market, with Canadians plodding along on their religious course, little different from past generations. On the other, we have a picture of a multiplicity of religions with tensions and conflict over the definition of religion and the ability to engage in religious practices. Which picture is correct? Both, it would seem, and we will explore this complexity through the readings that follow.

PART I: TRADITIONS

The past few years have seen religion making the news headlines with great frequency: the Raelian cloning experiments, the bombing of a Jewish school in Montreal, a young Jehovah's Witness woman refusing blood transfusions as part of her cancer treatment, head scarves and prayer space for Muslim students, same-sex marriage and gay clergy, and so on. Religious beliefs prompt action, or are used by the media to frame action, whether the actor intends this or not. Understanding religion in society allows us to see past the rhetoric of the media, and to move beyond simplistic causal explanations that lack nuance.

As social scientists we are well equipped to think about religion and society with conceptual tools that other disciplines do not use, and, at least in Canada, a critical history that brings a unique edge to our sociological toolbox. Unfortunately, the study of religion has generally not occupied a central place in social science, and so we find ourselves in a world in which religion is playing a central role with a limited ability to draw on social scientific research and insights. In Canada a variety of reasons explain this, including our strong roots in Marxist sociology. This has given us a rich critical tradition, but has also resulted in a simplistic dismissal of religion as unimportant to the study of society, an approach with which Marx himself surely would have disagreed.

As a sociologist of religion I have been met with looks of amusement, puzzlement, and sometimes what borders on hostility—why would I want to devote so much of my professional life to the study of religion? I am joined in this book by some of Canada's best sociologists who do just that. Their work offers a solid foundation on which to build a sociology of religion that can offer insight into this country's rich, vibrant religious diversity.

One of the greatest challenges in preparing this book has been to try to reflect an accurate picture of the religious landscape in Canada. At the heart of this challenge is the fact that we are in a moment of transition: population growth in Canada is currently being achieved through immigration and those who are coming to this country often bring with them religious traditions that are outside of, or on the margins of, those traditionally dominant in Canada. This shift means that understanding our religious history is an important component of the genealogy of religion. Only if we attempt to understand the nature of religious hegemony can we begin to grasp the implications of the ways in which the religious make-up of Canada is changing. In a country that touts multiculturalism and diversity as symbolic markers of our civility, exploration of religious life offers a window onto power relations and struggles over the meaning of religion in contemporary culture. Thus it is that we have a *Charter of Rights and Freedoms* that emphasizes the multicultural fabric of the nation while pronouncing the supremacy of God. In short, the religious landscape is complex and multi-faceted. How is it possible for social scientists to capture this?

One of the challenges is the tendency to focus on population percentages: Christians make up x percentage, Hindus y percentage, and "other" z percentage. The problem is this: if we focus only on quantitative measures of narrow categories we will miss an important opportunity to explore the full texture of religious life. We may also miss significant trends in religion and society. For example, when we talk about x percentage of Muslims in Canada and their numeric presence among the religious population, we gain one piece of information, but we learn relatively little about how Muslims live out their faith on a daily basis. The texture of Muslim identity and the complexity of belief are absent from conclusions gleaned from surveys. Our studies should explicate the differences between Muslims, as well as the similarities. How do Muslim women negotiate their identities? How do Muslim youth understand the role of faith in their lives?

The texture issue takes on a different dimension moving from one region of the country to the other. I grew up in New Brunswick, a province that largely was, and remains, one of the "Bible belts" of Canada. I have also lived in southern Alberta, which was the home of a significant "other" Christian group, the Church of Jesus Christ of Latter-day Saints, popularly known as Mormons. I currently live in Montreal, which is diverse and multicultural and presents a multiplicity of religious and spiritual opportunities. The varieties of religious life in each of these areas is quite different. Our sociological perspective must be able to explore critically the complex and multi-faceted religious and spiritual aspects of this nation.

I've touched on two of the key issues in the social scientific study of religion—cultural and social context and the idea of Christian hegemony. The most significant debate in the sociology of religion, one that has had wide discussion and has shaped much of the literature in this field, is most commonly known as the "secularization debate." This debate begins with some theorists arguing that with modernity has come the demise of religion. Put another way, proponents of the secularization thesis have argued that religion has gradually lost its influence at the individual, institutional, and societal levels. Religion, argued Peter Berger, is no longer a sacred canopy of meaning (he has since shifted his position on secularization).[1] Other theorists have countered, arguing that while religion's influence has shifted, religion is not disappearing. They maintain that cultural context must be considered, and that over time religion waxes and wanes, and, moreover, that secularization itself is multi-faceted and textured in ways that make it difficult to assess and measure.

Why has this debate occupied so much space in the sociology of religion? Partially, because it shapes the very reason to study religion. If religion is no longer relevant, why spend time and energy studying it? The beginning place on the secularization debate also has profound effects on the how and why of studying religion and society. For example, if we accept the secularization thesis, then we will consider religious freedom as it is guaranteed under the *Charter of Rights and Freedoms* from a different perspective than if we argue that religion has an impact on our interpretation of law, and our definition of religion. When judges say "we live in a secular society," what are they saying? Secularization is, in some measure, a reifying myth whose restatement obscures the power struggles around the definition of religion. In some senses mainstream Christianity forms the backdrop for social processes. This is not to say mainstream Christianity goes unchallenged, but in many ways it remains unquestioned. As sociologists we need to "make strange" this religious backdrop in order to better study its impact.

Religion has not, however, remained static in Canadian society, and nowhere is this more dramatically observed than in Quebec. The Quiet Revolution brought a dramatic change in church attendance in Quebec, which has led some to argue that it is the most secular province in Canada. However, even though church attendance is low, the level of affiliation with the dominant religion of that province, Roman Catholicism, remains high. The shift experienced in Quebec has been outwardly profound, and yet the steadfast refusal of Quebecers to completely disassociate from the traditional church is an interesting puzzle that has implications not only for understanding the province, but for better understanding religion in Canada.

How can we make sense of such seemingly dramatic changes? Does the secularization thesis help us to understand broad patterns of participation in organized religion? The picture of religious participation is constantly changing, and indeed is not one picture, but many. Robert Orsi argues that lived religion is the most important site of study, allowing us to see how people live out their religious beliefs on a day-to-day basis.[2] Measurements of church attendance and adherence to ritual and knowledge of key teachings are of limited use to an approach that focuses on lived religion. This does not mean, however, that power and structural influences are ignored; in other words, focusing on lived religion does not mean using a purely descriptive approach. Rather, social structure and power dynamics are connected to living religious practice that is dynamic and rich. This approach allows us to avoid conceptualizing the past as a religious monolith, in which all were churched and devoted, and the present as devoid of religion. A focus on lived religion encourages us to see religion in its present as ever dynamic, moving with social, cultural, and individual life histories. The challenge of this view is that it is very difficult to hit a moving target.

What is missing from the sociological study of religion? Theorizing that does not consider the experiences of religious groups on the margins, other than simply to position them there, mention them in passing, and then move on, will be inadequate to help us to make sense of religious life in Canada. Perhaps because of its numeric predominance Christianity has had a brighter spotlight than other religions, but even so I would argue that we don't know as much about even Christian religious life as we ought to. Moreover, the sociological study of religion is in need of a revamping that accounts for the sophisticated manner in which people engage in religious participation. To be sure, there are those who participate in more traditional ways—regular church attendance or participation in a synagogue, for example. But to measure and assess religion on the basis of institutional participation leaves out important religious practices and beliefs: what of Wiccans who are sole practitioners, or who are participants in covens that fall outside of our observational tools? What of the person who attends the once-a-month labyrinth walk at the neighbourhood United church, knows the clergy person by name, but never attends the church? What of the candle-lighting ritual of the women's group, whose members have both traditional affiliations and not? To use the words of Orsi, how are people bridging the gap, or creating relationships between heaven and earth?

Much of this part of the book seeks to understand "traditions," within historical context. This is essential to making sense of the places from which we arrived at the current situation, and to understanding ideas like the "Supremacy of God" in the *Canadian Charter of Rights and Freedoms*, but conspicuous in its absence in these chapters is any detailed examination of religious groups or traditions outside of a relatively narrow Christian mainstream. Does this mean there were in Canada's past no groups that weren't Christian? First Nations spiritual rituals were the focus of the purging efforts of white colonizers; the religious practices of Chinese and Japanese immigrants were also seen as a threat; Sikhs, Muslims, and Hindus each have a long history of presence in Canada, and so on. While these and many other religious minority groups are part of Canada's religious heritage, sociological explanation and exploration is conspicuous in its absence. We invite you as reader to remember this gap in knowledge as you consider the sociology of religion in Canada—its past, its present, and its future.

In this section, Roger O'Toole offers an overview of religion in Canada, situating its present contours in historical context. O'Toole points out the dominance of Christianity, the parameters of secularization, and the differences between Canadian and U.S. culture and religiosity. He notes the unique shape of religion in Quebec, and the place of mainline religion in Canada. O'Toole draws our attention to the difference between affiliation and involvement. Tensions exist not only between religious groups and society as they struggle over boundaries, but also within denominations as well, as they grapple with social issues that divide "conservative" and "liberal" forces. O'Toole also highlights the importance of the "new religions" (many of which actually have a long history in Canada) in the contemporary Canadian religious scene. O'Toole's whirlwind tour of religion in Canada gives us much to think about, including the need for more sociological analysis of the religion–society dynamic.

Reginald W. Bibby focuses on denominational loyalty, giving us a close-up look at one facet of secularization. Bibby documents the relatively stable affiliation patterns of Canadians, noting that even when people switch denominations they do so within denominational families. He argues that in general those raised within the traditional religions tend to remain within them, and even those who identify as "nones" are unlikely to turn to "outside" groups. Bibby's work explores in some detail the affiliation–involvement dichotomy identified by O'Toole. The bottom line is that while Canadians are much less inclined to participate actively in the religions with which they identify than they were a generation ago, they are still affiliated with those religions. In summary, they aren't going anywhere; they just aren't participating in denominational life.

Bibby's foundational work gives us a picture of a fairly stable religious "market" in Canada. His chapter raises some interesting possibilities for future research. Much of our sociological research energy has been devoted to studying Christian groups, but what about other religious traditions that have a long history in Canada—for example,

Japanese Buddhism; Sikhism on the west coast in particular, and Judaism. While numerically these groups are relatively small, they are an important part of the Canadian religious mosaic. Who are the religious "others" we see in survey results? Another important question, currently being researched by Peter Beyer and his research team, is the degree to which so-called immigrant religions are being transmitted intergenerationally. Finally, while we have a sense of a lack of participation in organized and traditional religions, what are Canadians up to in their spiritual lives? What beliefs and practices are not being explored by traditional measures? Can social scientists find ways to explicate spiritual and religious behaviours that take place outside of institutional boundaries?

David Seljak provides another piece of the Canadian religious puzzle in his chapter on Quebec. Although many regional variations on religious texture exist, Quebec is distinct from the rest of Canada in its religious past and present. Seljak's chapter reflects on the interface of religion and politics, drawing out some key ideas to examine the specifics in Quebec. Seljak raises the interesting possibility that Quebec in fact *had* a civil religion, a concept that is discussed more fully in Reimer's chapter. Another important idea in the Seljak discussion is the public–private dichotomy and its usefulness in thinking about religion in Quebec. What is especially apparent is the absolute necessity of considering cultural specificities when studying the religion–society relationship. The intertwining of language, the separatist movement, liberalism, religious history, social justice, and religious present makes for an intriguing story specific to Quebec. Yet, from its uniqueness we need to pay close attention to what we can learn, including the fact that there is no monolithic or unified voice on any one of these points of intersection. Perhaps an important step in sociology of religion is to use the Quebec case as a lens through which to view the peculiarities of the religion–society relationship in other regions.

While Quebec is an interesting internal point of comparison, the United States is an intriguing point of external contrast. Sam Reimer works through the notion of religiosity by comparing Canada and the United States. Reimer identifies "culture-religion" as a factor in the high degree of religiosity of Americans. He points out that there is a blurring of the sacred and the secular in the United States (something that is perhaps even more the case now than when Reimer wrote his article a few years ago). Culture-religion, or civil religion, is a concept that has little meaning in the Canadian context. Its absence, and in the United States its presence, are rendered more visible by the comparative approach employed by Reimer. More broadly, Reimer's chapter highlights the importance of cultural context in studying the meaning of religious participation. Keeping in mind that the data used by Reimer employ Christian-centred and rather narrow categorical measures of religiosity, it would be interesting to think about how his conclusions might be expanded if religiosity were more broadly cast. Is the Canadian mosaic more receptive to diverse religious expression than the U.S. melting pot?

We end this part with the work of Peter Beyer, who attempts to reconcile what are sometimes seen as two competing perspectives—the rational choice/religious market approach and the secularization thesis. As Beyer points out, this battle is in part regionally located as one between the United States and Europe, with Canada (as it frequently does) falling somewhere in between. Beyer takes an interesting position in that, unlike most of his contemporaries, he is able to make sense of these two perspectives, and indeed to attempt a reconciliation, suggesting that they can be used to correct each other. Like O'Toole, Beyer is careful to situate his discussion in the unique historical streams of Canadian religious life. Beyer's article draws out the nuance of the theories; for example, he notes that secularization theorists focus not just on the decline of influence of religion, but on the "differentiation of religion from other spheres of life." In other words, as some like to put it, religion has been privatized. More broadly, Beyer's chapter raises some key issues, the first being the importance of theoretical perspectives in thinking about religion and society. The second is that multiple theoretical perspectives can fill in gaps in knowledge and help us to see in new ways. It is the rare sociologist who is able to transcend theoretical boundaries as Beyer does. As we move through the remainder of the book, keep in mind that the theoretical perspective employed by a researcher means that she explores issues in a particular way. In other words, theoretical stances determine both what is included and what is excluded in the process of framing the research question.

NOTES

[1] Peter L. Berger, *The Sacred Canopy: Elements of a Sociological Theory of Religion*, Garden City: Doubleday, 1967.

[2] Robert A. Orsi, "Is the Study of Lived Religion Irrelevant to the World We Live In? Special Presidential Plenary Address," *Journal for the Scientific Study of Religion* 42(2) (2003): 169-174.

RELIGION IN CANADA:
ITS DEVELOPMENT AND CONTEMPORARY SITUATION

Roger O'Toole

INTRODUCTION

In 1873, the British social reformer Florence Nightingale inquired: "What will be our religion in 1999?" (Schwartz, 1990:270) Subject to their usual interpretive diversity, sociologists will shortly be in a position to answer her question. On the eve of a new millennium, there is an inevitable inclination to engage in cultural stock-taking. In true *fin-de-siècle* spirit, therefore, the following discussion sketches the main outlines of the religious situation in Canada at a juncture where the arithmetic of time predisposes us to peer, Janus-like, both backward and forward.

THE CANADIAN CONTEXT

Canada is a vast and physically diverse country but its small population of 29 million clusters in the shadow of that "longest undefended border in the world" which separates it from the approximately 260 million inhabitants of the United States. A constitutional monarchy confederated in 1867 under the religiously inspired title of "dominion," this nation originates in the political fusion of "two founding races," though it now embraces a far broader mosaic of indigenous and immigrant groups. Tracing its ancestry to France, Britain and the United States, Canada has, for much of its history, incorporated "two solitudes" of a linguistic, religious and cultural character, a situation only partly mitigated by official bilingualism, relentless secularization and rampant Americanization respectively. While a depiction of Canada as "two nations warring in the bosom of the same state" is a profound exaggeration, the contemporary political significance of Francophone and Anglophone differences requires no elaboration (Guindon, 1988:125). While Canada is now less prone to a garrison mentality inspired by its powerful southern neighbour, its citizens, both Anglophone and Francophone, retain a deep-seated ambivalence towards Americans and "the American way of life." This wariness persists despite the numerous political, economic, legal and cultural changes which, in recent decades, have notably intensified Canadians' resemblance to their U.S. counterparts (Lipset, 1990).

For three decades, Canadian political and cultural life has been intermittently dominated by evolving permutations of Quebec separatism, regional disaffection, constitutional reform and the quest for a distinctive national identity. Preoccupation with such matters, however, has neither lessened ordinary Canadians' desire for the more prosaic and tangible rewards of high income and an enviable quality of life nor, until recently, has it markedly diminished their ability to achieve them. *La révolution tranquille* which occurred in the province of Quebec was by no means the only quiet revolution affecting the transformation of Canada from the 1960s to the 1990s. During this period, overall prosperity combined with massive expansion of the welfare state, liberalized immigration policy and an official federal goal of multiculturalism to change the national social profile fundamentally. Another quiet revolution, a decade old, is still in process as painfully prolonged economic recession, massive government debt, privatization of state-run enterprises, high unemployment, business restructuring and reduction of social services all conspire to lower Canadians' expectations and dampen their traditionally optimistic assessments of the future. In common with other countries in the Western world, the predominant mood of Canada at the end of the millennium is one of insecurity, anxiety and trepidation.

DOMINION AND DENOMINATION: THE RELIGIOUS LANDSCAPE

A product of the unique geography and history of the land and its peoples, Canadian religion exhibits its own characteristic features at the same time as it manifests many of the typical patterns associated with the religious activities of contemporary post-industrial societies. In similar vein, while sharing much in common with the religious life of its nearest neighbour, Canada boasts significant national and regional deviation from the U.S. norm. More generally, of course, the drama of Canadian religiosity is enacted, as elsewhere, against a familiar backdrop of disenchantment and secularization: the grand narrative which has preoccupied sociology from its very beginnings.

Although the importance of Canadian religion has been, with few exceptions, greatly underestimated by both sociologists and historians, its crucial role in the nation's development now appears, if somewhat belatedly, to have attained more widespread recognition (McGowan, 1990). If it is acknowledged that "Canada from the beginning has been a strongly religious nation," it follows that "no real understanding of the forms and values of Canadian society is possible without a knowledge of the diverse religious convictions, organizations and experience that have substantially shaped this society." No attempt to map the contours of contemporary Canadian religion can avoid noting many stark contrasts with the nineteenth-century religious panorama. Nor, indeed, can it escape innumerable encounters with the Victorian religious legacy whether in sacred or secular contexts. In the broadest sense, the vitality of Victorian Christianity has profoundly shaped the character or identity of the nation. Thus, many features of modern Canadian life, including the political party system, the welfare state, foreign policy goals and a distinct "law and order" bias arguably originate, at least in part, in religious ideas, attitudes and structures which are now quite unfamiliar to contemporary Canadian Christians (O'Toole, 1982).

Perhaps the most enduring bequest of Victorian Christianity to its religiously committed descendants has been in the realm of form rather than content. The nineteenth-century "churching of Canada" differed significantly from the corresponding process witnessed in the United States (Finke and Stark, 1992) and, as a consequence, the anatomy of contemporary Canadian religion bears less resemblance to its U.S. correlative than might initially or superficially be supposed. In this respect, the evolution of Canadian religion has followed a European rather than a U.S. model, in keeping with a characteristic Canadian reluctance, both French and English, to abandon the ties of ancestral authority in a revolutionary American manner. Steeped in the heroic mythology of religious dissent and constitutionally celebrating the separation of church and state, the United States has long accommodated the sect as its predominant and paradigmatic mode of religious organization. In contrast, Canadian religion boasts manifestly establishmentarian roots. Though sectarianism has undoubtedly played a vital and vigorous minor role, it has been large churches with strong links to powerful political, business and cultural elites which have dominated Canadian religious experience since their importation. Thus, while acknowledging its religious diversity, one scholar has described Canada as "a society where Christian traditions with historical roots in Britain and Western Europe dominate the demography of religious identity from Newfoundland to British Columbia" (Simpson, 1988:351).

Translation of these differences into the terms of the currently fashionable sub-disciplinary market paradigm (Warner, 1993; Beyer, 1994) produces an image of the United States as an arena of religious free-competition. North of the border, however, all indicators proclaim a condition of protracted religious oligopoly in the nation as a whole while the province of Quebec displays near-monopoly in the religious realm. If "much of the history of religion in Canada is the story of conflict, competition and accommodation between Roman Catholics, the United Church of Canada … and the Anglicans," the "domination of churches and denominations," especially the so-called "big three," is still arguably the paramount characteristic of organized religion in this country (Simpson, 1988:351; Nock, 1993:47–53). Approximately two-thirds of Canadians identify themselves with one or other of these bodies and, while this proportion has diminished slightly over the last three decades, it remains, nonetheless, a singularly striking statistic.

The justifiable scrutiny so far accorded the distinctive form and intriguing demographics of Canadian denominationalism should not be allowed to distract attention entirely from a fact so obvious that it appears almost redundant: the Canadian Christian heritage itself. For, despite the inroads of secularization, an evident crisis of religious commitment and an expanding non-European presence in its population, Canada undoubtedly remains remarkably Christian in a broad sense of that term (Statistics Canada, 1993; Maclean's, 1993). Although less than a third of Canadians regularly attend religious services, an overwhelming number describe themselves as Christians while significant majorities subscribe in varying degrees to specific doctrinal beliefs and articles of the Christian faith. While clearly important in itself, a recent expansion in the numbers of those embracing religions other than Christianity, together with an increase of those professing no religion whatsoever, has not appreciably altered this state of affairs. In the Canadian religious context, therefore, two major cleavages are clearly apparent. The first separates a large, self-described Christian majority (over 80 percent) from a very small non-Christian and non-religious minority while the second divides a majority (approximately 80 percent) loyal to the three major denominations from a minority owing allegiance to other variants of Christianity (Statistics Canada, 1993; Maclean's, 1993).

MAINLINE RELIGION

The precise boundaries of "mainline" Canadian religiosity are inevitably unclear and cogent arguments may be advanced for inclusion of Presbyterian, Lutheran, Baptist and Eastern Orthodox organizations under this rubric (Nock, 1993:48). Whoever else is incorporated, however, Roman Catholics, Anglicans and the United Church of Canada are undoubtedly the dominant components.

Involved in the first explorations of this vast land in the sixteenth century and integral to the foundation of the colony of New France, Roman Catholicism has long constituted a commanding presence on the Canadian scene (Guindon, 1988:103–111; Beyer, 1993). Legally instated under the Crown by the Quebec Act of 1774 and the Constitutional Act of 1791, it has enjoyed something of a moral monopoly in Francophone Quebec until very recently. In unofficial concordat with local forces of reaction and expressing hostility to capitalism, industry, cities, liberalism, republicanism and other aspects of the Protestant–modernist axis, this conservative ultramontane church exercised an almost theocratic control over most aspects of Quebec's rural and urban life until the middle of the present century.

Beginning a century ago, progressive industrialization and urbanization culminated in the province's "Quiet Revolution" of the 1960s. Occurring alongside the reforms of the Second Vatican Council, the political modernization and social transformation of this period sounded the death knell of the old, omnipresent ecclesiastical order. The Quebec Church, accordingly, experienced an accelerating decline and a profound crisis which necessitated its virtual metamorphosis. During the last thirty-five years, the speed and intensity of Quebec secularization have been unmatched in any other province. The change in fortune of the triumphalist church whose power and grandeur have been undermined by this process has been so dramatic that it is not inappropriate to refer to its exile or abdication from the centre of Canadian Francophone life. Displaced institutionally by the state in its prime fields of activity (Zylberberg and Coté, 1993), beset by a perpetual vocational recruitment crisis and experiencing a drastic decline in the participation and commitment of its members, the Church has struggled to redefine its role in reduced circumstances. Confronted less by hostility than by widespread indifference, it now plays a truncated, marginal and diffuse part both in its members' lives and in society as a whole. Within this more restricted sphere of influence, however, its efforts have not gone entirely unrewarded. Whereas in the 1960s nearly 90 percent of Quebec Catholics claimed to attend church services regularly, attendance figures now fluctuate within the 25 to 30 percent range (Bibby, 1993:172; Beyer, 1993:153). Despite their clear reluctance to enter their churches, however, Quebecers adamantly refuse to resign their membership. Thus, approximately 86 percent, a vast majority of the provincial population, continues to identify itself, in some sense, as Roman Catholic while dissenting in significant numbers from official church teaching on such matters as birth control, legalized abortion and premarital sexual activity (*Maclean's*, 1993:49).

For its devoted and regular participants, the experience of membership has altered considerably over the last thirty years. The triumphal intolerance, aloofness, conservatism and rigidity of an organization confident of its power and influence have given way, in large measure, to liturgical flexibility, ecumenical dialogue and a compassionate concern for social justice which frequently demands that long-standing and extensive charitable activity be supplemented by radical political involvement. For the less committed and selectively obedient, it is the parochial school rather than the parish church which offers some institutional focus for an otherwise nebulous sense of Catholic identity. Though education is now under the secular control of the provincial government, the majority of Quebec schools remain under church administration. Thus, while they may rarely attend church themselves, most Quebec parents enrol their children in schools which provide explicit instruction in the Catholic faith. The paradox of empty pews and crowded classrooms provides an appropriate symbol of the new reality of Quebec Catholicism as an essentially cultural matter. Insisting that Catholicism *"représente toujours la référence religieuse normale de la très grande majorité de la population,"* Raymond Lemieux (1990) suggests that, in contemporary life, it has acquired a multi-faceted character. It has become a diffuse, churchless faith which simultaneously supports a vague, almost subliminal civil religion of reassuring familiarity and a privatized popular religiosity whose discrete spiritual quests evoke and involve "religious effervescence, emotional communion, affirmation of universal values (and) explosion of the imaginary." However, while such an amorphous religion clearly "transgresses the institution which gave birth to it," Lemieux pointedly refuses to pass the death sentence on the organized Church. In his view, this body still, "although grappling with its own quest for identity, remains the natural referent in the quest for meaning of the very great majority" (Lemieux, 1990:163–164) in a province, it might be added, whose motto is *"Je me souviens."*

Though Roman Catholicism ceased to be a Francophone monopoly in British North America at least a century and a half ago, the Quebec Church has long represented such a significant component of Canadian Catholicism that it might be termed, in the language of recent constitutional negotiations, a "distinct society" within a wider ecclesiastical community. In order to view this situation in proper perspective, attention must now be focused on the role of the church in English Canada and the place of Catholicism in the nation as a whole. While resting on foundations laid by a "first wave" of immigration emanating from France, the Canadian Catholic community is, in its entirety, the product of sources as diverse as might be expected in a body which lays claim to universality. From early in the nineteenth century, massive Irish immigration swelled the church's ranks creating internal ethnic and linguistic division as it simultaneously inflamed the animosities between Catholics and Protestants. As ultramontane and politically adept as their Francophone brethren, Irish clerics were to dominate an Anglophone minority church in an inhospitable Protestant environment for more than a century. Though their influence has not evaporated it has been heavily diluted since the Second World War as further surges of immigration, initially from south and central Europe and subsequently from Latin America and Asia, again radically altered the ethnic composition of Canadian Catholicism.

Numbering over twelve million and comprising 45 percent of the Canadian population, Roman Catholics are now the largest religious group in Canada. Moreover, a majority (52.5 percent) of Catholics now reside outside the province of Quebec, thus providing justification for regarding the Roman Catholic Church as Canada's leading denomination in a truly national sense (Statistics Canada, 1993). This rise in fortune has not been a matter of numbers alone, for a century of struggle has been rewarded with a high degree of economic advancement and status enhancement in all spheres of life. Even in the old Protestant heartland of Ontario, Catholicism is now eminently respectable. Nevertheless, for Canadian Catholics, their satisfaction in outnumbering Protestants and challenging their old social hegemony is somewhat guarded. It has come at a moment of profound internal crisis in an era when insubstantial cultural allegiance appears to be displacing active religious commitment in all major religious denominations. With regular attendance below 40 percent (*Maclean's,* 1993:48; Bibby, 1993:172), chronic shortages among clergy and widespread dissent from church teaching on contraception, clerical celibacy and the role of women, Canadian Catholicism is no longer the monolithic moral presence it once was. Such is the erosion of church authority that the recent papal encylical *Evangelium Vitae* is likely to be greeted, in many quarters, with even greater indifference than the ill-fated *Humanae Vitae* of a quarter-century ago.

In these circumstances, the church has been forced into sober and realistic assessment of priorities culminating in a strategy combining denominational détente with an emphasis on social justice (Cuneo, 1989:168–178; Hewitt, 1993:253–271). In adapting to the reality of religion's growing marginality, it has found itself bound in common cause with other major denominations at the same time as it has become (appropriately enough) increasingly aligned with the socially marginal and dispossessed. Struggling to maintain its role as a powerful participant within an ecumenical consensus grounded in a Christian version of progressive liberalism, the Canadian Roman Catholic hierarchy attempts to chart a course between traditionalist, revivalist and militant pro-life forces on its right and the liberation theologians, social justice vanguard and radical church reformers on its left. In trying to cope simultaneously with the secularized indifference of the many and the spiritual zealotry of the few, Canadian Catholicism provides a paradigm case of the dilemmas of the mainstream denomination in contemporary society. Perhaps more than any other religious group in Canada, the Anglican Church has confronted the difficulty of adaptation to reduced circumstances. In retreating from the religious and political centre of society, it has attempted to make a virtue out of necessity by embracing denominationalism, ecumenism and multiculturalism while renouncing establishmentarian elitism and privilege. An effective presence since the 1763 Treaty of Paris ceded most of the Franco-American empire to Britain, the Anglican Church (officially known as the Church of England in Canada until 1955) has decidedly establishment origins. Officially recognized as a legally established Church by the

Constitutional Act of 1791, the Anglican Church was viewed as a vital conservative bulwark against revolution, republicanism and representationalism in His Majesty's reduced and reorganized American possessions. Despite legal, social and economic advantages, Anglicanism never evolved into the naturally acknowledged Church of Canada envisioned by a British elite in the wake of U.S. independence. Encouraged by statutory guarantees of religious tolerance, a powerful Roman Catholic presence in Lower Canada and a rapidly expanding Methodist movement in the newly settled lands of Upper Canada rendered such monopolistic designs abortive. Thus, although Anglicanism retained a certain social status and elite influence, it acknowledged the denominational character of Canadian religious life long before its legal disestablishment by the Clergy Reserves Act of 1854. In contrast to its privileged position in the mother country, Canadian Anglicanism has long lived without legal leverage in the competition for souls. For more than a century, however, it retained considerable strength as the most culturally appropriate or "natural" religious affiliation for the many immigrant Britons who professed no other specific religious allegiance. More recently, the Anglican Church has faced the harsh reality of a perpetual membership crisis. Its continuous decline since the Second World War has accompanied significant reduction in British immigration apportionment as well as the weakening of Canadian political, economic and cultural ties with the United Kingdom.

Canada's approximately two million Anglicans now constitute only 8 percent of the nation's population, having declined steadily over the last fifty years from a figure representing nearby double that proportion. Though nearly half of all Anglicans are resident in Ontario, they are represented most strongly in Newfoundland (the nation's newest province) where they constitute over a quarter of the population. By contrast, only 1.5 percent of Quebec residents claim affiliation with the Anglican Church (Statistics Canada, 1993). Anglicanism is far from being alone in its decline and, indeed, its rate of descent is now significantly less than that of other major Protestant denominations. Nonetheless, such ceaseless and seemingly inexorable attrition is undoubtedly of concern, especially when it is observed that as few as 14 percent of those claiming affiliation may be regarded as active regular participants in church activities (Bibby, 1993:172). The Anglican Church faces a situation in which at least half, and possibly the vast majority of its declared adherents manifest mere cultural allegiance. Though resembling Quebec Catholicism (on a reduced scale) in this regard, it is far more restricted in its capacity to bring formal educational institutions to its rescue.

In seeking to avert a future fate as a purely ethnic body rooted in ancestry rather than activity, Anglicanism aspires to a more multicultural character through contact with immigrant communities at the same time as it defines the major emphasis of its ministry in terms of social concern. Tolerant, democratic and open to compromise, as it demonstrated in recent decisions involving Prayer Book reform, the Anglican community accommodates within its ranks a range of theological opinion from Anglo-Catholicism to evangelicalism. Its prevailing ideology, however, is a somewhat indistinct fusion of liberal theology and progressive politics which recalls an earlier Social Gospel and links it theoretically and practically with dominant trends in both the Roman Catholic and United churches. Charting a characteristically cautious via media in the realm of Christian social action, Anglicans increasingly identify themselves publicly with those inhabiting the margins of society and view the corridors of power from the remote vantage point of an ecumenical congeries of religious pressure groups.

Despite a certain aura of prestige which still surrounds Anglicanism, the leading Protestant denomination in a national context is undoubtedly the United Church of Canada whose more than three million members comprise 11.5 percent of the total Canadian population and 15 percent of those living outside the province of Quebec (Statistics Canada, 1993). More strongly represented than Anglicanism in all English-speaking provinces but Newfoundland, this church symbolizes both the Canadian art of compromise and the dilemma of denominationalism. Founded in 1925 as a result of a merger among Methodists, Congregationalists and a majority of Presbyterians, the United Church has, from its very beginning, faced the difficult task of forging a common religious identity from somewhat diverse theological, organizational and social traditions. With roots, like Anglicanism, among the pioneering elements of British settlement, it represents, in part, a product of denominational achievement in the socio-economic as well as pastoral aspects of two centuries of English-Canadian life. In recent decades, however, its efforts to cope with the damage inflicted by an increasingly secular environment have brought it close to the point of internal crisis.

Apart from a brief upsurge in the immediate post-war period, allegiance to the United Church has fallen steadily over the last half-century as a proportion of the Canadian population. In a pattern which resembles the Anglican experience, those professing affiliation with the United Church have declined from a figure of approximately 20 percent to a current standing in excess of 11 percent, the steepest fall in their representation having occurred in the most recent decade (Statistics Canada, 1993). Moreover, as in other denominations, affiliation by no means implies involvement. More than half of those claiming affiliation with the United Church may be classified as inactive while only 16 percent can be regarded as regular, active participants in its devotional life (Bibby, 1993:172). Of those reasonably active within its ranks, roughly two-thirds might be considered theological and political moderates while the remaining third are almost equally divided between conservatives and radicals. Overall, the United Church exhibits a moderate progressivism appropriate to its energetic role in ecumenical co-operation. In this context, it is typically positioned to the left of the Anglicans with a reputation for setting the agenda in matters of social justice. The broad consensus achieved by the United Church represents a triumph of practical Christianity. Originally envisioned in the era of the Social Gospel, its unity rests more on pastoral than doctrinal foundations, a circumstance which prompts frequent repetition of the sobriquet "the New Democratic party at prayer."

Suffering significant decline in numbers and commitment while struggling against the apparently inexorable advance of secularization, the United Church appears impaled on the horns of a classic denominational dilemma. Firstly, a fight to retain relevance in the modern world may entail adoption of an increasingly secular outlook which eventually spells its own redundancy. Second, an attempt to stand defiantly apart from the world on grounds of Christian principle may simply result in sectarian self-exile and irrelevance. In the United Church, a moderate majority stands between two minorities which battle for its soul. On the one hand, conservative fundamentalists preoccupied with matters of doctrine and sexual morality plead for a return to the beliefs and practices of the past as a necessary preparation for the world to come. On the other, radicals inspired by a prophetic vision of social justice, equity and inclusion demand a commitment to building the Kingdom of God through the transformation of the present world. Seven years ago, a bitter public debate on the propriety of ordaining professed homosexuals to the ministry became a symbolic focus for the clash between these two religious cultures and raised the possibility of defection and schism (O'Toole *et al.*, 1991). Though a major crisis was averted by compromise and procedural ambiguity, a high degree of tension between increasingly marginalized conservatives and organizationally influential radicals remains a crucial fact of life in the United Church. Few radical proposals are likely (in the future as in the past) to be widely accepted without significant modification. Yet, so dominant are the issues of human rights and social justice in United Church discourse, it appears certain that radicals rather than conservatives will set the church's future agenda.

Like Anglicanism, the United Church of Canada has attempted to shed its old British ethnic image by vigorous activity among immigrant communities, refugees, visible minorities and Native Canadians. Symbolized, in recent years, by the election of a Korean and an Aboriginal to its highest office, its policy of multicultural outreach is the most visible contemporary manifestation of its characteristic and long-standing social passion. Bloody but unbowed, this organization (like other mainline denominations) appears convinced that it can face the material and spiritual challenges of the future only if it is prepared to discard significant aspects of its past.

RELIGIOUS BRANCHLINES

Numbering nearly ten million, Protestants now constitute 36 percent of the Canadian population, a figure representing a decrease of 5 percent during the last decade (Statistics Canada, 1993). While much of this erosion has been experienced within the ranks of the Anglican and United churches (together accounting for more than half of Canada's Protestants), it has not been restricted to them. The three next largest Protestant denominations, each more than 600,000 strong, have also suffered significant decline in membership. Inclusion of the nation's nearly two million Presbyterians, Lutherans and Baptists within the ranks of mainline religion would not, therefore, improve its beleaguered condition, especially when low Presbyterian and Lutheran activity rates (18 percent and 20 percent respectively) are taken into account (Statistics Canada, 1993; Nock, 1993:48; Bibby, 1993:172).

Protestant prospects are not universally so gloomy, however. They appear brighter for the nearly two million Christians (7 percent of the Canadian population) who may be considered "conservatives" or "evangelicals" and whose churches are maintaining, or even increasing, their numerical strength (Statistics Canada, 1993). Evangelicals are, of course, by no means confined to membership in explicitly conservative organizations. As noted earlier, both the Anglican and United churches contain evangelical minorities while even Roman Catholicism incorporates traditionalist, charismatic and revivalist elements within its ranks. Associated primarily with sectarian forms of religiosity, Canadian evangelicalism is also identified with more familiar, larger organizations such as the Baptists and the Salvation Army. Immediately recognizable as major evangelical bodies are the Pentecostal Assemblies of Canada, the Christian and Missionary Alliance, the Christian Reformed Church and the Mennonites, together claiming a total of more than 750,000 members. Other evangelical organizations (with memberships roughly in the 5,000 to 25,000 range) include the Brethren in Christ, the Churches of Christ-Disciples, the Church of the Nazarene, the Church of God, the Apostolic Christians, the Evangelical Free Church, the Free Methodists, the Worldwide Church of God, the Canadian Reformed Church, the new Apostolic Church, the Missionary Church and the Wesleyans (Statistics Canada, 1993).

Popular accounts of the Canadian religious scene, undoubtedly inspired by perceptions of a conservative religious revival in the United States, portray a stark contrast between mainline church decline and evangelical growth and vitality. While such assessments possess considerable credibility, however, they also exhibit a tendency to caricature, especially in their sweeping depictions of evangelical success. The significant growth of many evangelical organizations is indisputable. Thus, between 1981 and 1991, the Pentecostal Assemblies acquired 100,000 additional members: a growth rate of 29 percent. During the same period, the much smaller Christian and Missionary Alliance sustained a 75 percent increase in its membership by welcoming 25,000 new adherents, while such groups as the Church of the Nazarene and the Churches of Christ-Disciples experienced modest but healthy growth of 12 percent and 14 percent respectively (Statistics Canada, 1993). The "old time" quality of the evangelical religious community undoubtedly exerts considerable appeal for certain sections of the Canadian population (either by virtue of their history or present circmstances) and its leaders have been astute and adept both in exploiting and, to some extent, creating this situation. Responding to a perceived demand for a religiosity which is authoritative, fundamentalist and emotionally expressive, evangelicals have creatively combined customary activities with modern communication techniques to transmit their message of rebirth and revival to a wide audience. While notable in itself, the growth of many evangelical churches is made more significant by their obvious success in securing and sustaining high rates of active participation (in the 43 to 57 percent range) and generous financial contributions within their congregations (Hexham, 1993:292–294; Bibby, 1993:108, 172).

While acknowledging such achievements, some sociologists have indicated the need for careful and critical assessment of the nature of evangelical growth. It may be noted, for example, that not all organizations usually labelled evangelical have grown in the last decade. Thus, Baptists, by far the largest group, declined by 5 percent while the long established and widely recognized Salvation Army experienced a 12 percent decrease in membership (Statistics Canada, 1993). Provoking controversy, Reginald Bibby (1987:27–31) has challenged the popular wisdom which regards evangelical growth as primarily fuelled by proselytization among and defections from mainline churches. In his opinion, close statistical scrutiny reveals that such expansion is a more prosaic product of higher birth rates and a circulation of members among the numerous organizations which espouse the evangelical cause. He suggests, accordingly, that as few as 10 percent of evangelicals are recruited from outside the broad evangelical community.

One corollary to the popular notion of spectacular evangelical development at the expense of secularism and mainline religious insipidity is the suggestion that Canadian evangelical sects may assume a decisive role in national politics paralleling that of the U.S. "Moral Majority," "Christian Right" or "Christian Coalition." As exciting as such a prospect might be to evangelicals, it can provoke only skepticism among sociologists familiar with the crucial differences between U.S. and Canadian religion. As noted earlier, sectarian Christianity of the kind associated with evangelicalism is a decidedly minority variant of Canadian religiosity. Whether growing or not, evangelicals comprise only 7 percent of the Canadian population compared with U.S. estimates of approximately three times that figure (Bibby, 1987:27; Nock, 1993:54). Furthermore, even a much larger evangelical population would find it impossible to sustain a national "politics of morality" on the U.S. model given the essentially dualistic and segmented character of Canadian society (Simpson, 1988:355–356; Simpson and MacLeod, 1985). In this regard, the hopes of some that the new federal Reform Party might become the political vehicle for their moral crusade have been disappointed. Evangelicalism is not, apparently, to become the Reform Party at prayer. If the significance of Canadian evangelicalism is religious rather than political, its particular strength is surely a matter of commitment rather than numbers. In this respect, mainline churches will continue to face stiff competition, especially in their struggle for the souls of the uprooted, the marginal and the disinherited.

Persistence of a minority sectarian element in Canadian religious life has not precluded the emergence of more contemporary alternatives to mainline religion especially in the form of new religious movements (NRMs). The Canadian public has, accordingly, not been spared predictable mass-media sensationalism concerning "cults" in their midst. Intermittently recharged by incidents such as the recent Quebec Solar Temple murders, popular discussion of NRMs proceeds along the familiar brainwashing-deprogramming axis with a prurient emphasis on the deviant, erotic and exotic. An appropriate foundation for more sober analysis of NRMs is provided by census documentation of membership in "para-religious groups." Incorporating such familiar NRM designations as Scientology, New Age, Paganism and even Satanism, this category is broad enough to include Theosophists, Rastafarians and practitioners of Native Indian and Inuit (Eskimo) religion. While their numbers have doubled in the last decade to a total of approximately 28,000 (0.1 percent of the Canadian population), para-religious adherents constitute a less than impressive presence in national religious life (Statistics Canada, 1993). Though Canada can boast some indigenous creations such as the Kabalarian and I AM organizations, most of its NRMs are branch plants of well-known international bodies such as the Moonies, Scientologists, Hare Krishnas, Rajneeshis and Wiccans (Kent, 1993; Ralston, 1988). While Canadian recruits typically resemble their U.S. or European counterparts and the attractions of NRM membership transcend national boundaries, a specifically Canadian variation on the familiar theme of NRM appeal to the marginal, confused and disoriented has been provided by Roland Chagnon (1985). Noting the erosion of Quebec Catholicism's moral authority and convinced that Quebec's Quiet Revolution has been succeeded by a mood of quiet disillusionment fuelled by political uncertainties, Chagnon suggests that Quebecers, both individually and collectively, are in search of a satisfying and coherent identity. The appeal of NRMs, especially for the young, thus lies in their presumed ability to deliver what mainline clerics, politicians, cultural elites, economists, planners and constitutional lawyers have been unable to provide. Apparently inspired by similar assumptions on a national scale, the Transcendental Meditation movement launched its own "Natural Law Party" to contest the 1992 federal election. Despite a climate of considerable uncertainty and disillusionment, however, its political message went unheeded.

The notion of NRMs filling the vacuum created by the disappearance of mainline churches has, of course, intrigued many sociologists. Most notably, Stark and Bainbridge (1985:471) have asserted that "cults abound where the churches are weak" and have ingeniously attempted to support this proposition with Canadian as well as U.S. evidence, particularly from the west coast. There seems little doubt, however, that these authors misjudge the potential of NRMs as alternatives to mainline or conventional Canadian religiosity. By overlooking the significance of the structural differences between U.S. and Canadian religion, they underestimate the capacity of inclusive denominationalism to accommodate religious dissent and overestimate Canadians' propensity to engage in religious innovation (Bibby, 1987:36–40). Since the 1970s, some sociologists have been prone to exaggerate the significance of NRMs, regarding them as harbingers of a new religious consciousness and a return of the sacred. This argument appears increasingly implausible in a Canadian context. Thus, while conventional religion is undoubtedly in decline, and may indeed be in crisis, there is no evidence to suggest that NRMs exert any notable attraction for its disillusioned adherents. Given that the number of Canadians professing no religious affiliation now exceeds three million (12.5 percentof the population), having nearly doubled in 1981 to 1991 as well as during the previous decade (Statistics Canada, 1993; Brinkerhoff and Mackie, 1993), it seems far more likely that those who abandon mainline churches will avoid all formal religious attachment than that they will assume the demanding obligations of NRM membership.

The "new religions" which are of growing significance are those "Eastern non-Christian" faiths (mainly Islam, Buddhism, Hinduism and Sikhism) which have expanded greatly during the last two decades as a result of the growth in non-Western immigration to Canada. Now totalling approximately750,000, the members of these religious groups comprise somewhat less than 3 percent of the national population (Statistics Canada, 1993). Though still of decidedly minority status in statistical terms, their concentration in major cities has lately given Canadian urban religious life an increasingly pluralistic or multicultural character. In this regard, some basic statistics and comparisons supply abundant and eloquent evidence of an intriguing recent development on the Canadian religious scene. Thus, Eastern non-Christian religions increased their numbers overall by 144 percent in the decade 1981–1991. More specifically, Islam grew by 158 percent, Hinduism by 126 percent, Sikhism by 118 percent and Buddhism by no less than 215 percent. A comparison with Judaism may put these figures in perspective for, in 1981, Jews and the adherents of Eastern non-Christian faiths both numbered approximately 300,000. Though by 1991 the number of Jews had grown by 7 percent, they were now less than half as numerous as Eastern non-Christian devotees. Similarly, though in 1981 Jews outnumbered Muslims by a ratio of three to one, in 1991 the Islamic population had reached 80 percent of the Jewish population and may be expected to achieve numerical parity within a few years. A final comparison is worthy of note: Eastern non-Christian religions in combination now outnumber each of the largest Christian churches outside the ecclesiastical triumvirate comprising Roman Catholicism, Anglicanism and the United Church. On average, Baptists, Presbyterians and Lutherans each fall short by approximately 100,000 members while Pentecostals (themselves experiencing notable growth) are exceeded by a figure in excess of 300,000 (Statistics Canada, 1993). The fact that the rapid growth of Eastern non-Christian religion has been generated by recent waves of immigration suggests, of course, that such affiliation may, in many cases, be of a purely formal or cultural character. Careful investigation of belief patterns, participation rates and varieties of commitment within Islamic, Buddhist, Hindu, Sikh and other communities is thus an essential enterprise for sociological research.

The contrast between U.S. and Canadian religious life is nowhere more apparent than in the realm of civil religion, for Canada has been singularly unsuccessful in forging an emotionally charged and binding national ideology (Lipset, 1990:1–2). Though the fathers of Canadian confederation supplied a scriptural charter for their new dominion (Psalms 72:8), the central precepts of their new political nationality were devotion to the Crown and respect for the British parliamentary tradition. Crown and Empire, however, were to prove inadequate foundations for an embryonic civil religion required to win the hearts, not merely of those of British origin, but of a large Francophone population and a growing immigrant minority utterly alien to British culture and institutions (Stahl, 1981). Not surprisingly, subsequent more tentative attempts to foster beliefs, rites and symbols as potential components of a post-colonial civil religion have proven equally abortive, inhibited mainly by bilingualism, biculturalism, regionalism and pervasive U.S. cultural influence (Kim, 1993). Nonetheless, the quest for a viable pan-Canadian civil religion has not been abandoned entirely; it survives amidst the nostalgia and utopianism of the perennial search for an elusive national identity (Blumstock, 1993).

CONCLUSIONS

What is the contemporary situation of Canadian religion? On the surface, it is much as it has been for the last century. Although growing numbers disclaim religious affiliation, Christianity still claims the allegiance of the overwhelming majority of Canadians and the major Christian churches still dominate the religious scene. Christian sectarianism also thrives, though it has been supplemented recently by more exotic minority faiths. At a deeper level, however, Canadian religion is dramatically different. Though secularization has not entailed its destruction or abandonment, it has "come adrift from its former points of anchorage" and has been transformed from a social institution into a cultural resource in a manner typical of advanced industrial societies (Beckford, 1992:170–171). In Canada as elsewhere, increasing autonomization of the individual has led to the radical disjunction of the customary link between believing and belonging (Luckmann, 1967; Davie, 1994). Canadians now choose to define the nature and content of their religiosity by drawing from that "reservoir of rites, practices and beliefs" with which they are most familiar "without responding to any institutional prerequisites or their consequences" (Voyé and Dobbelaere, 1993:95–96). In these circumstances, their religion has generally acquired the fragmentary, syncretic, consumerist character associated with the term *bricolage* (Bibby, 1987; Voyé and Dobbelaere, 1993:95–97). Widely disregarded as a source of authoritative meaning systems and an arena of total commitment, Canadian religion must now cater increasingly to the specific and highly selective needs of a capricious citizenry. Thus, on the eve of a new millennium, its condition may best be characterized as problematic, precarious and unpredictable.

REFERENCES

Beckford, J.A. 1992. *Religion and Advanced Industrial Society*. London: Routledge.

Beyer, P. 1993. "Roman Catholicism in Contemporary Quebec: The Ghosts of Religion Past?" In *The Sociology of Religion: A Canadian Focus*, ed. W.E. Hewitt, 133–156. Toronto: Butterworths.

———. 1994, "Religious Vitality in Canada: How Valuable Are Religious Market Theories?" Paper presented at Annual Meeting of the Religious Research Association, Albuquerque, New Mexico.

Bibby, R.W. 1987. *Fragmented Gods*. Toronto: Irwin.

———. 1993. *Unknown Gods*. Toronto: Stoddart.

Blumstock, R. 1993. "Canadian Civil Religion." In *The Sociology of Religion: A Canadian Focus*, ed. W.E. Hewitt, 173–194. Toronto: Butterworths.

Brinkerhoff, M., and M. Mackie. 1993. "Nonbelief in Canada: Characteristics and Origins of Religious Nones." In *The Sociology of Religion: A Canadian Focus*, ed. W.E. Hewitt, 109–132. Toronto, Butterworths.

Chagnon, R. 1985. *"Les nouvelles religions dans la dynamique socio-culturelle récent au Québec."* *Canadian Issues/Thèmes Canadiens* 7:118–151.

Cuneo, M.W. 1989. *Catholics against the Church*. Toronto: University of Toronto Press.

Davie, Grace. 1994. *Religion in Britain Since 1945: Believing Without Belonging*. Oxford: Blackwell.

Finke, R., and R. Stark. 1992. *The Churching of America, 1776–1990* . New Brunswick: Rutgers University Press.

Guindon, H. 1988. *Quebec Society: Tradition, Modernity, and Nationhood*. Toronto: University of Toronto Press.

Hewitt, W.E. 1993. "The Quest for the Just Society: Canadian Catholicism in Transition." In *The Sociology of Religion: A Canadian Focus*, ed. W.E. Hewitt, 253–271. Toronto: Butterworths.

Hexham, I. 1993. "Canadian Evangelicals: Facing the Critics." In *The Sociology of Religion: A Canadian Focus*, ed. W.E. Hewitt, 289–302. Toronto: Butterworths.

Kent, S. 1993, "New Religious Movements." In *The Sociology of Religion: A Canadian Focus*, ed. W.E. Hewitt, 83–106. Toronto: Butterworths.

Kim, A. 1993. "The Absence of Pan-Canadian Civil Religion: Plurality, Duality, and Conflict in Symbols of Canadian Culture." *Sociology of Religion* 54:257–275.

Lemieux, R. 1990. *"Le catholicisme québécois: une question de culture."* Sociologie et sociétés 22:145–164.

Lipset, S.M. 1990. *Continental Divide*. New York: Routledge.

Luckmann, T. 1967. *The Invisible Religion*. New York: Macmillan.

Maclean's Special Report. 1993. "God Is Alive" (Angus Reid Poll) 12 April 12:32–50.

McGowan, M.G. 1990. "Coming Out of the Cloister: Some Reflections on Developments in the Study of Religion in Canada, 1980–1990." *International Journal of Canadian Studies* 1:175–202.

Nock, D.A. 1993. "The Organization of Religious Life in Canada." In *The Sociology of Religion: A Canadian Focus*, ed. W.E. Hewitt, 41–63. Toronto: Butterworths.

O'Toole, R. 1982. "Some Good Purpose: Notes on Religion and Political Culture in Canada." *Annual Review of the Social Sciences of Religion* 6:177–217.

———, D.F. Campbell, J.A. Hannigan, P. Beyer, and J.H. Simpson. 1991. "The United Church in Crisis." *Studies in Religion/Sciences Religieuses* 20:151–163.

Ralston, H. 1988. "Strands of Research on Religious Movements in Canada." *Studies in Religion/Sciences Religieuses* 17:257–277.

Schwartz, H. 1990. *Century's End*. New York: Doubleday.

Simpson, J.H. 1988. "Religion and the Churches." In *Understanding Canadian Society,* eds. J. Curtis and L. Tepperman, 343–369. Toronto: McGraw-Hill Ryerson.

———, and H.G. MacLeod. 1985. "The Politics of Morality in Canada." In *Religious Movements: Genesis, Exodus and Numbers,* ed. R. Stark. New York: Paragon House.

Stahl, W.A. 1981. "Symbols of Canada: Civil Religion, Nationality, and the Search for Meaning." Ph.D. dissertation, Graduate Theological Union, Berkeley, California.

Stark, R., and W.S. Bainbridge. 1985. *The Future of Religion*. Berkeley: University of California Press.

Statistics Canada. 1993. *Religions in Canada*. Ottawa, Industry, Science and Technology Canada. (1991, Census of Canada, Catalogue number 93–319, Tables 1, 3 and 6.)

Voyé, L., and K. Dobbelaere. 1993. "Roman Catholicism: Universalism at Stake." In *Religions Sans Frontières?* ed. R. Cipriani, 83–113. Rome: Presidenza Del Consiglio Dei Ministri.

Warner, R.S. 1993. "Work in Progress toward a New Paradigm for the Sociological Study of Religion in the United States." *American Journal of Sociology* 98:1044–1093.

Zylberberg, J., and P. Coté. 1993. *"Les balises étatiques de la religion au Canada."* Social Compass 40:529–553.

CHAPTER 2

ON BOUNDARIES, GATES, AND CIRCULATING SAINTS:

A LONGITUDINAL LOOK AT LOYALTY AND LOSS

Reginald W. Bibby

Observers monitoring social trends in the United States and Canada have been maintaining that there has been a considerable decline in loyalty to institutions over the last half of this century. Americans such as Robert Bellah and his associates (1985:285) have written that accelerated individualism is severely threatening group life at all levels, while Allan Bloom (1987:320–321) has similarly claimed that the individualistic and relativistic legacies of the 1960s have been devastating for relationships and disastrous for institutions such as universities. In Canada, prominent journalist Peter Newman (1995) goes so far as to say that nothing short of a revolution took place between the mid-1980s and 1990s, characterized by Canadians moving from a mood of "deference to defiance" in virtually every area of life. The current author has similarly noted that individualism and relativism have functioned to severely fragment Canadian society, creating unity problems well beyond the threat of Quebec separation (Bibby, 1990).

In keeping with such commentaries on the decline in commitment to group life, it has been widely argued that there has been a sharp decline in the importance of religious denominations among North Americans. People are said to be abandoning loyalties to both mainline and conservative Protestant groups, as well as to other religious bodies such as the Roman Catholic Church (see, for example, Schaller 1987; Wuthnow, 1988; Mead, 1991; Posterski and Barker, 1993; Hoge, Johnson, and Luidens, 1994). As Loren Mead (1991:87) has succinctly put it, "The church of the future may not include our favorite liturgy or hymn, our central theological principle, or even our denomination!" Congregational experts tell us that, to the extent North Americans continue to want to participate in churches, they commonly are gravitating towards those congregations which are in touch with their needs, with little concern for denominational labels (see, for example, Barna, 1991; Anderson, 1992; Easum, 1993; Schaller, 1995; Woods, 1996; Bandy, 1997).

The issue of religious group identification is an extremely important one, since it has critical practical implications for how congregations carry out ministry—who, for example, they target for ministry, as well as what they should be doing to minister

effectively to the people with whom they are in contact. The status of religious identification in North America is consequently an issue that needs to be understood clearly.
In the face of sweeping generalizations about "denomination not mattering anymore,"
there is a need to examine carefully the empirical validity of the claim, as well as explore
possible denominational, regional, and national variations.

This paper attempts to contribute to improved clarity by looking at religious identification in Canada between 1975 and 1995 using both trend and panel data, and
reflecting on the implications of the findings for "the vanishing boundaries" thesis in
Canada and elsewhere.

WHAT WE KNOW TO DATE

The alleged demise of the importance of denomination presumably is showing up in
both actively involved North Americans and people who are not actively participating in churches.

Actives

A number of probes by the author and others into the importance of denomination
among active participants in North America, however, have found little support for
such an assertion. A 1985 examination of some 1,200 active Anglicans (Episcopalians)
in greater Toronto found that 86 percent viewed their "being Anglican" as important;
even more surprising was the finding that 77 percent of the 600 self-acknowledged
inactives placed the same level of importance on their Anglican tie as well (Bibby,
1986). An early 1990s study involving close to 500 of Canada's most actively involved
church members discovered that 82 percent regarded denomination as either a major
(52 percent) or moderate (30 percent) factor in their choosing a new congregational
home (Posterski and Barker, 1993:257). More recently, some 90 percent of active
Canadian laity in the United Church and 80 percent of their Conservative Protestant
counterparts indicated their respective denominations are "very important" or "somewhat important" to them. In the United States, the same sentiment was expressed in
1996 by about 90 percent of the active members of the Cumberland Presbyterian
Church—including some 80 percent of infrequent attenders. And in 1998, a comprehensive study that included leaders from 28 U.S. denominations found that 87
percent were placing a high or moderate amount of importance on their denominational ties (Bibby, 1994, 1995a, 1997, 1998). Quite clearly, *denomination continues to
be very important to many people in many denominational instances.*

Switchers

The tenuousness of denominational identity, if not reflected in active members as a
whole, allegedly can be seen in the presence of "switchers"—people who come from
other groups, drawn more by what the new congregation has to offer than by their
own denominational history. As Demerath and Yang (1997) have recently pointed out,

---

switching may be compatible with Peter Berger's (1967:143–144) thesis that old religious boundaries are no longer as important to many people as non-religious criteria in their choice of affiliations; it also may reflect the rational-choice school of thought, where people are involved in active search for an affiliation that is religiously optimal (see, for example, Finke and Stark, 1992; Warner, 1993; Iannaccone, 1995).

It can be argued, however, that basic learning theory in sociology would suggest that there is little reason to expect that large amounts of pronounced religious switching will take place. In view of the pervasive tendency of children to identify with the religion of their parents, switching amounts to a form of deviant behaviour, and is subsequently greeted with a wide range of social controls that function to prohibit it. The inclination to switch is also limited by the reality of cultural commonality: culturally, it's a substantial stretch to move from a Jewish to Baptist world—sometimes from just a United Methodist to a Disciples' world. As such, religious switching would be expected both to be limited and to follow fairly predictable lines of affinity.

In keeping with such expectations, in Canada, approximately 90 percent of Canadians who come from Roman Catholic homes continue to identify with Roman Catholicism, with the intergenerational retention levels for mainline Protestants and conservative Protestants about 80 percent and 65 percent respectively (Posterski and Barker, 1993:53–54; Bibby, 1995:19). In the United States, the retention level between generations appears to be about 70 percent for mainliners and an even higher 80 percent for conservatives (Roof and McKinney, 1987:167; Demerath and Yang, 1997:3), reflecting in part the presence of a much larger evangelical population in the United States than in Canada.

Even when switching does take place, it typically involves fairly short theological and cultural trips. As Hoge, Johnson, and Luidens (1994:120) have pointed out, the size of our *tolerance zones* for acceptable religious traditions appears to exceed our personal *comfort zones* with those traditions. In the case of Presbyterian baby boomers, for example, they note that tolerance zones have expanded over the years, whereas personal comfort zones "are surprisingly narrow and traditional," extending for the great majority "no farther than mainline Protestantism" and for "quite a few … the Episcopalian Church." Kirk Hadaway and Penny Marler (1993:97), analyzing National Opinion Research Centre (NORC) survey data for 1973 to 1990, have concluded that "when Americans do switch, they often remain within the same broad denominational family." It's not that North Americans never switch groups: at least 40 percent of people on both sides of the border have switched denominations at one time or another (Roof and McKinney, 1987:167; Posterski and Barker, 1993:51). As Hadaway and Marler (1993:102) have put it, "Americans switch more today than they did in the early 1970s, but when they switch they are more likely to remain in the same larger denominational family." The same pattern appears to hold in Canada.

Dropouts

It's common for researcher and practitioner alike to assume that identification without involvement simply doesn't count. If, for example, someone says that he or she is a "Presbyterian" or "Lutheran" or "Baptist" but seldom attends a service, such a self-designation is typically assumed to mean very little. Policy-wise, such individuals are typically viewed as "unchurched" and, as such, are seen as "up for grabs" in the competitive religious marketplace. Officially they are the prime targets of groups which are attempting to evangelize and serve.

There are a number of problems, however, with such assumptions about dropping out and receptivity to recruitment. To begin with, in contrast to declining attendance figures—especially in Canada and particularly among Roman Catholics in Quebec—religious identification in North America has slipped only slightly in the post-1960s. Just over 10 percent of Americans and Canadians currently see themselves as "religious nones" (Davis and Smith, 1996; Statistics Canada, 1993). Further, such a status appears to be short-lived for many of these individuals, who frequently re-adopt the religious group identification of their parents in the course of requesting and receiving religious rites of passage (Bibby, 1993:157–159). The vast majority of North Americans continue to have psychological, emotional, and cultural links to their parents' religious groups. These links appear to be sustained not so much by religious content as by family history and rites of passage.

As for receptivity to recruitment, what is perhaps rather remarkable is not that large numbers of North Americans *identify but are not involved*, but rather that they continue to *identify even though they are not involved*. They can be chastised, ignored, and removed from church lists—and they frequently are. But still, they don't really leave. Psychologically, emotionally, and culturally, they continue to identify with religious traditions (Hadaway, 1990; Bibby, 1995b:20).

As a result, there is little reason to believe that North Americans are particularly open to being recruited by other groups, especially those with whom they see themselves having limited theological and cultural commonality. Many North Americans attended services with some regularity when they were growing up. Most turn to their identification groups when they require rites of passage, want to attend a seasonal service, or feel the need to expose their children to religious activities. The religious cultures of their groups are seen as normative for many. They accordingly feel comfortable or uncomfortable in certain worship settings, with certain hymns and prayers, words and phrases, symbols and rituals.

In support of such generalizations, it's significant that for all the rhetoric about evangelism, outreach and seeker-sensitive ministries, Americans and Canadians who are not actively involved (a) are seldom recruited by those "outside" groups, and (b) if they do become involved, tend to do so with the groups with which they have been identifying (see, for example, Demerath and Yang, 1997:5; Bibby, 1993:32, 36–37).

Denominational identification may well be on the decline. But, to date, a clear case for such a decline has not been made. Large numbers of the involved and non-involved alike give evidence of continuing to place importance on their denominational ties.

In addressing the question of declining group loyalties, what is needed is trend data, permitting an examination of patterns over time. As Hadaway and Marler (1993:99) have noted, existing studies tend to be based on "single-year cross-sectional surveys and merged multi-year polls. To examine possible *changes* in denominational mobility, switching data

are needed for more than a few years." Also, where possible, it is important to take denominational, regional, and family characteristics into account—given the significant role they
have been found to play in individuals staying versus switching groups (see, for example, Stark and Glock, 1968; Roof and Hadaway, 1977; Greeley and Hout, 1988; Sherkat,
1991; Marler and Hadaway, 1993; Roof, 1993; Hoge, Johnson, and Luidens, 1995). To
the extent that denominational identification persists, it also is important to have a clearer
understanding of what that identification actually means to people, particularly in relationship to what it has been understood to have meant in the past.

METHODOLOGY AND PROCEDURES

The Project Canada Surveys

Some of these issues have been addressed in Canada through a series of ongoing
national surveys carried out by the author every five years from 1975 through 1995;
a sixth and final survey in the series is planned for the year 2000. Together, the *Project
Canada* surveys provide comprehensive data on Canadian life spanning the last quarter of the twentieth century.

   All five of the surveys have included samples of some 1,500 Canadian adults, selected
from communities across the country using stratified and random sampling techniques. Response rates have averaged about 60 percent; co-operation levels that pollsters obtain in national surveys conducted by telephone or in person are typically
around 65 percent. Discrepancies between sample and population characteristics have
been corrected by weighting for provincial and community size, along with gender
and age. With appropriate weighting—where the samples are reduced to about 1,200
cases to minimize the use of large weight factors—the samples are highly representative of the Canadian population and are accurate within about 3 percentage points
either way, 19 times in 20 (methodological details can be found in Bibby, 1993). In
the analysis that follows, the weighted samples are being used.

Cross-sectional and Longitudinal Data

In an effort to explore social change and stability, the surveys have been designed to
provide both cross-section and panel data. Each of the four survey samples since 1980
has consisted of (a) a core of people who participated in the previous survey, and (b)
new participants, who are used to create the full national samples. For example, while
the first 1975 survey was a typical cross-sectional survey with 1,917 participants, the
Project Canada sample of 1,713 people comprised 916 people who took part in at least
one of the previous surveys and 797 new cases. Of the 916, a total of 400 had participated in the first survey in 1975.

   This 1975–1995 panel of 400 Canadians comprised the ongoing core who have
participated in all the surveys (230) and a special panel supplement (170), which was
obtained through our adding as many of the original 1975 participants as we could
that we had lost between 1980 and 1995. Realizing that a total of 400 was possible,

we set that figure as our quota goal; hence the even number. The 400 cases have been weighted for gender. While no claim is being made that these participants are representative of all Canadians, The Project Canada Panel provides unique data on religious trends—including the importance being placed on identification with religious groups—that complement the cross-sectional, trend data.

The Analysis

Drawing on both cross-sectional and panel possibilities, we will begin by looking at Canadians' attitudes towards other religious groups in 1975 versus 1995. Next, we will look at the amount of intergenerational switching reported in 1975 compared to 1995, as well see to what extent the panel switched groups over the twenty-year period. We will then focus on a number of 1995 survey items that probe the meaning that religious group identification has for Canadians. We will conclude by taking a look at some possible correlates of identification and switching, including family background and current involvement and commitment.

FINDINGS

Intergroup Attitudes

In both the 1975 and 1995 national surveys, respondents were asked how comfortable they would be worshipping in the services of a wide-ranging number of other religious groups. The item, borrowed from Glock and Stark's Bay-area study in the 1960s, attempts to probe the affinity levels that individuals have with other religious groups.

An examination of the findings shows that, without exception, Canadians are considerably more likely in the 1990s than they were in the 1970s to express comfort in the worship services of other groups (see Table 2.1). At the same time, "the comfort rankings" remain virtually unchanged from twenty years ago. People show the highest levels of affinity with the mainline Protestant, United, and Anglican churches. Comfort with Baptists has risen considerably, now matching the comfort levels of the two mainline denominations; Catholics continue to know a moderate level of acceptance; reticence remains greatest for Unitarians, Jews, Mormons, and—especially—Jehovah's Witnesses. The 1995 survey, incidentally, also found worship comfort levels of 37 percent for Native spirituality, 25 percent for Hindus, and 20 percent for Islam and New Age settings.

As would be expected, considerable variation in comfort levels exists by one's identification group. *Catholics outside Quebec* express greatest affinity with mainline Protestants and to a lesser extent Baptists; *Quebec Catholics* express particular comfort with Anglicans, and frequently indicate they "don't know enough to say" in the case of many other groups. *United Church and Anglican* affiliates appear to have high rapport not only with each other but also with Catholics, Baptists, and Lutherans. While *Conservative Protestants* exhibit moderate levels of rapport with mainline Protestant groups, they are particularly comfortable with other evangelical bodies, such as Baptists and Pentecostals.

TABLE 2.1: WORSHIP COMFORT ZONES: 1975 AND 1995

% Indicating Would Feel "Very Comfortable" or "Comfortable" in the Worship Services of the Following Groups*

		United	Anglican	Baptist	Lutheran	RC	Pent	Unitar	Jewish	Mormon	JW
NATIONALLY	1975	57%	57	45	40	34	24	20	19	10	10
	1995	80	79	77	64	63	44	34	34	32	17
RCs Outside Quebec	1975	63	68	35	38	95	29	23	26	15	10
	1995	77	78	58	57	99	33	31	41	32	10
United Church	1975	95	81	62	54	22	28	24	14	10	7
	1995	97	83	76	68	70	39	40	27	34	9
Anglicans	1975	94	99	71	65	45	25	24	23	8	9
	1995	93	99	74	56	78	36	42	39	29	10
Conservative	1975	72	51	82**	44	22	54**	19	16	9	5
Protestants	1995	64	68	80**	69	48	68**	20	32	21	8

* The response options have been "very comfortable," "Fairly comfortable," "Not very comfortable," "Not at all comfortable," and "Don't know enough to say."

** Baptists and Pentecostals, respectively, excluded.

What is striking is the tendency for denominations to express comfort with groups that are part of their "religious families"—mainliners with mainliners, conservatives with conservatives. Affinity levels tend to be highest between mainline groups and Catholics, lower for Catholics-mainliners and conservatives, and lowest between Protestants-Catholics and people of other faiths.

The findings for the 1975–1995 Project Canada Panel are consistent with the cross-sectional trend data. Over the period, the panel tended to become more comfortable with the idea of worshipping, for example, in United Church, Baptist, Pentecostal, Roman Catholic, and Jewish settings (see Table 2.2). Such sentiments were uniform among mainline Protestants, conservative Protestants, and Roman Catholics.

However, the panel data show that worship comfort with other religious groups is not perfectly linear. Substantial numbers of people actually have been less comfortable with Pentecostals over the two decades, as have many conservative Protestants and even some mainline Protestants in the case of the United Church—a denomination that has experienced considerable division over its decision in the late 1980s to extend full membership to gays and lesbians.

In general, the trend and panel findings show that comfort levels with other religious groups have increased in Canada since 1975. But discomfort continues to exist, particularly as one moves further away from one's theological and cultural group home. For most Canadians, religious group consciousness has far from disappeared.

TABLE 2.2: WORSHIP COMFORT LEVELS, SELECT GROUPS: PANEL, 1975 AND 1995*

Respondent's Religion	United			Baptist			Pentecostal			Roman Catholic			Jewish		
	Same	More	Less	Same	More	Less	Same	More	Less	Same	More	Less	Same	More	Less
TOTAL (%)	50	42	8	41	55	4	42	39	19	39	53	8	31	64	5
Mainline Protestant	55	35	10	41	55	4	47	34	19	23	69	8	47	49	4
Conservative Protestant	44	38	18	42	52	6	44	40	16	30	62	8	36	64	0
Roman Catholic	36	61	3	37	62	1	37	52	11	59	34	7	13	82	5

* United respondents excluded in Mainline-United figures; Baptist and Pentecostals similarly excluded in Conservative Protestant and Baptist-Pentecostal analyses. "Same" refers to no change in comfort levels between 1975 and 1995, "More" to a higher level of comfort, "Less" to a lower level.

Intergroup Switching

Ongoing data on religious identification in Canada are provided by the national census that is carried out each decade by the federal government's fact-finding body, Statistics Canada. Since 1871, the populace has been asked, "What is your religion?" As of the latest, 1991 census, some 88 percent of Canadians indicate that they "have" a religion.

The *Project Canada* surveys show that, in the course of acquiring a religious identification, most people in the 1990s—like their counterparts in the 1970s—are "inheriting" the religion of their parents or guardians (see Table 2.3). Approximately 9 in 10 Roman Catholics and Protestants continue to come from Catholic and Protestant homes respec-

TABLE 2.3: INTERGENERATIONAL IDENTIFICATION BY GROUP: 1975 AND 1995

Respondent's Religion									
	RCOQ	RCQ	CProt	MLProt	UC	Ang	Luth	Pres	No Religion
Same as mother									
1975	87%	99	74	90	76	73	95	86	27
1995	93	98	71	90	85	82	88	86	32
Same as father									
1975	89	99	68	92	81	79	92	86	31
1995	86	99	54	91	80	83	89	81	38

tively. Such an intergenerational identification pattern is particularly pronounced within the Catholic and mainline Protestant religious families. Offspring from homes where their parents had claimed no religion have increased, but only slightly. Most "Religious Nones" are people who have "defected" from Protestant and Catholic groups.

Once again, the panel data corroborate the cross-sectional trend findings. Limited switching between religious families took place. Some 90 percent of mainline Protestants and Roman Catholics, along with close to 85 percent of conservative Protestants, had the same religious identification in 1995 as they did in 1975 (see Table 2.4). To the extent switching took place, it tended to follow Protestant-Catholic lines, versus a pathway to other religions or the no religion category.

While the panel sample sizes are small for the conservative Protestant, "other religions," and "no religion" groups, the tentative findings point to conservatives infrequently being drawn to either the Catholic or "no religion" camps, and people identifying with "other religions" and "no religion" gravitating over time to Christian groups.

TABLE 2.4: INTERGENERATIONAL IDENTIFICATION BY RELIGIOUS FAMILIES: PANEL, 1975 AND 1995

1975 Identification	N	Stayed	Switched to ML Prots	Switched to Cons Prots	Switched to Catholics	Switched to Others	Switched to No Religion
Mainline Protestants	196	88%	—	4	3	2	3
Conservative Prots	31	83	11	—	0	6	0
Roman Catholics	102	90	3	4	—	2	1
Others	15	63	5	22	5	—	5
Nones	19	39	33	0	28	0	—
TOTALS*	363	85	4	4	3	2	2

*Identification data for 1975 or 1995 missing for 37 respondents.

Beyond Unobtrusive Measures: The Inclination to Stay

To this point, the analysis has focused on indirect evidence that Canadians are not abandoning their denominational families and, in the case of Catholics, identification with the Roman Catholic Church, by looking at attitudes towards other groups, and the extent of switching.

The surveys, however, have also asked respondents directly about their inclination to stay versus switch, along with the meaning of religious identification. Beginning with the 1985 national survey, respondents "not attending religious services regularly" were asked "how well" the following observation describes them:

Some observers maintain that few people are actually abandoning their religious traditions. Rather, they draw selective beliefs and practices, even if they do not attend services frequently. They are not about to be recruited by other religious groups. Their identification with their religious tradition is fairly solidly fixed, and it is to these groups that they will turn when confronted with marriage, death, and, frequently, birth.

Through 1995, about 85 percent of Canadians *who identify but attend less than monthly* have said that the statement describes them either "very accurately" or "somewhat accurately" (see Table 2.5). Nationally, there has been little change since the mid-'80s in the tendency of inactive attenders to acknowledge the accuracy of the description. Decreases in identification with the statement in the case of Quebec Catholics and mainline Protestants to date have been modest.

TABLE 2.5: ACCURACY OF THE RELIGIOUS IDENTIFICATION STATEMENT: CANADIANS IDENTIFYING AND ATTENDING LESS THAN MONTHLY, 1985 AND 1995

% Indicating It Describes Them "Very Accurately" or "Somewhat Accurately"

	NAT	Roman Catholics outside Quebec	Roman Catholics Quebec	Mainline Protestants	Conservative Protestants
1985	86%	85	90	89	85
1995	85	84	86	82	91

The Meaning of Religious Identification

In an effort to clarify what religious identification actually means to Canadians, the 1995 survey included a contingency item that began with, "If Protestant, Catholic, or another faith" and continued on to ask for simple "yes" and "no" responses to six brief questions regarding the nature and meaning of their religious identification. The questions probed (1) the importance of the group with which they identify, (2) the level of their commitment, (3) whether or not they grew up in the tradition, (4) their familiarity with the tradition, and (5) the extent of their current involvement. The sixth question attempted to explore whether people who identify but are not actively participating in their identification groups have any interest in future involvement by asking, "Would you consider being more involved if you found it to be worthwhile for you or your family?"

Some 60 percent of affiliates indicated that the groups with which they identify are important to them, ranging from 80 percent for conservative Protestants through about 65 percent for Roman Catholics to around 50 percent for mainline Protestants (see Table 2.6). Underlying the disparity between identification and involvement, less than 30 percent of these affiliates reported that they currently are very involved in their groups; the same 1995 national survey had found that only about 25 percent of

Canadians are weekly service attenders. Nevertheless, despite their frequent lack of active involvement, almost 40 percent of the respondents who identify with religious groups claim to be "deeply committed," led by conservative Protestants and Roman Catholics in Quebec.

TABLE 2.6: THE MEANING OF RELIGIOUS IDENTIFICATION BY RELIGIOUS GROUP: 1995

	NAT	RCOQ	RCQ	CProt	MLProt	UC	Ang	Luth	Pres
The group I identify with is important to me	61%	67	66	80	50	52	45	59	42
I am "deeply committed"	36	32	51	70	21	25	14	27	19
I currently am very involved	27	30	24	59	20	22	15	35	8
I grew up in this tradition	80	82	95	63	77	80	74	76	68
I am familiar with my tradition	70	73	82	80	57	62	52	59	49
I would consider being more involved	63	78	43	81	64	64	60	74	64

The family source of their religious identification "choice" is readily acknowledged: some 80 percent say that they "grew up" in their traditions. Again consistent with earlier trend and panel findings, the pattern is somewhat less typical for conservative Protestants than mainliners and Roman Catholics. Despite the common lack of involvement among these "identifying" Canadians, no less than 70 percent maintain that they are familiar with their traditions, with the highest levels found among conservative Protestants, Quebec Catholics, and people identifying with other faiths.

Rather than acting either hostile or indifferent to their identification groups, significant numbers of people indicate that they are receptive to greater participation. Some 60 percent—about twice the number who indicate they currently are very involved—say that they would be open to greater involvement if they "found it to be worthwhile" for themselves or their families (see Table 2.7).

These people who say they consider being more involved include about 7 in 10 currently weekly *attenders*, but also some 65 percent of monthlys and yearlys and over 40 percent of those who never attend. Age-wise, young Catholic and Protestant adults express the greatest amount of openness to being more involved. Variations in receptivity by *gender* are slight, being somewhat higher for females among Catholics outside of Quebec. *Regionally*, levels of openness to greater involvement range from about 80 percent in the Atlantic region through 70 percent in Ontario and the Prairies, slipping to 60 percent in British Columbia, and reaching a low of about 45 percent in Quebec. Yet the receptivity level in Quebec—when seen against current attendance levels for younger adults of approximately 15 percent—is impressive. Generally speaking, outside Quebec, receptivity of Catholics tends to be somewhat higher than that of Protestants.

TABLE 2.7: RECEPTIVITY TO GREATER INVOLVEMENT BY SELECT VARIABLES

	NAT (875)	RCOQ (198)	RCQ (215)	PROT (387)
TOTALS	63%	77	43	67
Weekly	69	85	35	73
Monthly	66	65	59	77
Yearly	64	81	44	70
Never	42	59	22	36
18–34	72	89	56	78
35–54	62	72	41	64
55+	53	67	27	61
Female	64	82	43	68
Male	62	73	44	67
BC	62	78*	—	59
Prairies	71	75	—	69
Ontario	72	79	—	69
Quebec	44	—	—	44*
Atlantic	77	76	—	79

*Numbers insufficient to permit stable percentaging; included for heuristic purposes.

Some Correlates of Identification

An examination of some of the anticipated correlates of religious identification confirms that family variables—notably having the same group identification as one's mother and to a somewhat lesser extent one's father—is fairly strongly associated with the *inclination* of inactive participants *not to turn elsewhere*. Such an outlook is further

enforced by the feeling among these people that religion and spirituality are important, and by the fact that they have had baptisms or weddings performed by their
groups (see Table 2.8). The inclination to "stay put" is highly pervasive among inactive attenders, differing little by religious group, age or residential mobility.

The sense that *the group with which one identifies is important*, however, tends to be
particularly associated with active attendance and the valuing of one's faith, rather
than religious history. Inclination to stay and the importance of identification are, in
turn, only modestly related to each other, suggesting that tradition and habit may frequently override commitment in keeping affiliates from defecting to other groups.

In the case of the panel, the factors most strongly associated with people having stayed
with their groups between 1975 and 1995, versus having switched, are family variables—one's marriage partner, mother and father all having the same religious group
identification. Current mainline Protestants were less likely to have switched in from
other religious families than people who now view themselves as conservative Protestants.

TABLE 2.8: SELECT CORRELATES OF IDENTIFICATION

| | 1995 Respondents | | Panel |
	Not Inclined to Turn Elsewhere	ID Group Important	Stayed with Same Religious Family
Mother ID same	.38	.10	.27
Father ID same	.23	.11	.26
Child attendance	.28	.14	.13
Spouse ID same	.10	.24	.37
Current attendance	n/a	.51	.10
Religion important	.39	.52	.11
Spirituality important	.21	.37	−.02
Baptism carried out for	.23	.13	.02
Wedding carried out for	.19	.07	.03
Funeral carried out for	.11	.05	.01
Not inclined to turn elsewhere	—	.27	.18
ID group important	—	—	.18
Mainline Protestant	.17	−.17	.23
Conservative Protestant	.03	.12	−.21
Roman Catholic outside Quebec	.13	.07	−.02
Roman Catholic: Quebec	.14	.06	.09
Age	.16	.07	.13
Residential mobility	−.14	−.08	−.03

DISCUSSION

In the last half of this century, active participation in organized religion in Canada has dropped fairly dramatically. At the end of the Second World War, some 60 percent of Canadians—led by Roman Catholics in Quebec and elsewhere—were attending services on a weekly basis. Today that figure stands at about 25 percent. The present findings, however, suggest that the sharp decline in attendance has not been accompanied by a significant decline in the importance people place on religious identification.

It's true that there has been a general softening of attitudes towards other religious groups on the part of just about everyone. In part this illustrates an expansion of tolerance zones. Canadians, steeped in multicultural ideals since the early 1970s, are expected to exhibit an acceptance of other religious groups. To say that one would not be comfortable worshipping with other groups is to border on bigotry—especially if one identifies with a justice-conscious mainline denomination such as the United Church. Whether an individual would actually feel as comfortable in practice as he or she suggests, where tolerance zones coincide with comfort zones, remains to be seen. What's interesting to note, however, is that even with the official expansion of tolerance zones over the past two decades, Canadians continue to express varying levels of comfort with other groups, with apprehension generally increasing the further one moves from one's "religious family." Ongoing identification has been accompanied by a psychological and emotional attachment to groups that clearly has outlived active involvement.

The decline in active participation also has not been associated with a widespread tendency for Canadians to move to other religious families, or to the "no religion" category. The religious economy of Canada continues to be one that is characterized by a very tight market where the expansion of market shares through the recruitment of people from rival groups is difficult to accomplish. To the extent that switching does take place, it follows fairly predictable lines of affinity, frequently associated with the breaking down of family-related "social controls." The panel findings suggest that current mainliners are somewhat more likely than others to have "stayed in," while current conservative Protestants are more likely than others to have "switched in." But overall, the market is not particularly open; intergroup movement is very limited.

At the same time, the examination of identification attitudes and correlates reveals that while parental and marriage partner factors contribute significantly to ongoing identification and the inclination to stay, they are not strongly associated with placing a high level of importance on one's religious identification. Here, the additional features of attendance and commitment are required. Family tradition and religious habit may foster loyalty and keep affiliates at home. But, by themselves, they are not sufficient to instill a sense that one's identification group has a high level of personal salience. Such a realization in the British situation, for example, has led Rosalind Fane (1999) to conclude that "it may prove helpful to conceptualize self-assigned religious affiliation as a component of social identity, rather than as an inadequate indicator of religious commitment."

This takes us to the dilemma that faces organized religion in Canada. The vast majority of people continue to identify with the religious traditions of their parents and are not going anywhere. However, they typically are not highly involved in their groups and do not see them as particularly salient when it comes to everyday life. Peter Beyer (1997:286) has recently summed up the Canadian situation this way: "The prevailing pattern seems to be one of occasional participation, which nonetheless proceeds largely along denominational lines." Most religious consumers, he says, "consume eclectically, with perhaps a fair degree of 'brand-loyalty,'" but without extensive involvement and intensive commitment.

Nevertheless, the 1995 survey findings do point to hope for the country's religious groups. High proportions of people who identify but are not actively involved indicate that they are open to greater involvement if they find that it is worthwhile for themselves or their families. If groups can get in touch with such people, explore their interests and needs, and respond with integrity to what they are hearing, there is good reason to believe that the participation levels of at least some of their affiliates will increase.

CONCLUSION

To return to where I began, the speculation about the decreasing importance of religious group identification has led many observers to assume that significant numbers of people who want to participate in organized religion are gravitating towards congregations that are responsive to their needs, with little regard for denominational labels. The policy implications of such a position are extremely important.

If North American churches see the religious market as essentially wide open, Americans and Canadians will be viewed as "religious free agents" who can be recruited through effective ministry and evangelism. The problem with such a "vanishing boundaries" outlook is that, in light of the kind of data presented in this paper, it may well result in congregations wasting much of their conscious recruitment resources.

In contrast, if Canadian and U.S. churches would concentrate not so much on "the switcher exception" but rather "the ongoing identification rule"—recognizing with Hadaway and Marler (1993:111) that most people "are stayers" who "do not switch from one denominational family to another"—they would be in a position to target the very people they have the best chance of ministering to women and men who are identifying with them. Identification represents a measure of affinity; it consequently is the logical place to start in connecting with people who need ministry.

Given the pervasiveness of ongoing religious identification, congregations would be wise to follow Hadaway's lead (1990:46) in seeing their members and others who identify with their denomination as a series of concentric rings, ranging from active members at the centre through less active individuals to an outer ring of inactive people. Working with such a model, churches need to develop creative strategies for ministering to the large number of Americans and Canadians who are not actively involved, yet have never really left home, and have no intention of doing so.

As the twentieth century comes to an end, themes such as freedom, inclusiveness, and the dismantling of boundaries are widespread. The saints are said to be circulating freely. Yet, in the midst of it all, the saints and the less-than-saints are circulating primarily among "the religious families" of their parents. Their ongoing presence calls for both recognition and response.

REFERENCES

Anderson, Leith. 1992. *Church for the 21st Century*. Minneapolis: Bethany House.

Bandy, Thomas G. 1997. *Kicking Habits: Welcome Relief for Addicted Churches*. Nashville: Abingdon.

Barna, George. 1991. *User Friendly Churches*. Ventura: Regal Books.

Bellah, Robert, Richard Madsen, William Sullivan, Ann Swidler, and Steven Tipton. 1985. *Habits of the Heart*. New York: Harper and Row.

Berger, Peter L. 1967. *The Sacred Canopy*. Garden City: Doubleday Anchor.

———. 1997. "Religious Vitality in Canada." *Journal for the Scientific Study of Religion* 2:272–288.

Bibby, Reginald W. 1986. *Anglitrends*. Toronto: Anglican Diocese of Toronto.

———. 1990. *Mosaic Madness. Pluralism without a Cause*. Toronto: Stoddart.

———. 1993. *Unknown Gods: The Ongoing Story of Religion in Canada*. Toronto: Stoddart.

———. 1994. *Unitrends*. Toronto: Department of Stewardship, United Church of Canada.

———. 1995a. *EvangelTrends*. Markham, ON: Evangelical Fellowship of Canada.

———. 1995b. *There's Got to Be More!* Winfield, BC: Wood Lake Books.

———. 1997. *FutureTrends*. Memphis: Cumberland Presbyterian Church.

———. 1998. *The PCPA Congregational Resource Study Report*. St. Peters: PCPA.

Bloom, Allan. 1987. *The Closing of the American Mind*. New York: Simon and Schuster.

Davis, James Allan, and Tom W. Smith. 1996. *General Social Survey, 1996*. Chicago: National Opinion Research Center. Distributed by The Roper Center for Public Opinion Research, Storrs, CT.

Demerath, N.J. III, and Yonghe Yang. 1997. "Religious Change and Changing Religions: Who's Switching Where and Why?" Paper presented at the annual meeting of the SSSR, San Diego, November.

Easum, Bill. 1993. *Dancing with Dinosaurs*. Nashville: Abingdon.

Fane, Rosalind S. 1999. "Is Self-Assigned Religious Affiliation Socially Significant?" In *Theology and Sociology*, ed. Leslie J. Francis, 113–124. London: Cassell.

Finke, Roger, and Rodney Stark. 1991. *The Churching of America, 1776–1990*. New Brunswick: Rutgers University Press.

Greeley, Andrew, and Michael Hout. 1988. "Musical Chairs: Patterns of Denominational Change." *Sociology and Social Research* 72:75–86.

Hadaway, C. Kirk. 1990. *What Can We Do about Church Dropouts?* Nashville: Abingdon.

———, and Penny Long Marker. 1993. "All in the Family: Religious Mobility in America." *Review of Religious Research* 35:97–116.

Hoge, Dean R., Benton Johnson, and Donald A. Luidens. 1994. *Vanishing Boundaries*. Louisville: Westminster/John Knox Press.

———. 1995. "Types of Denominational Switching among Young Protestant Adults." *Journal for the Scientific Study of Religion* 34:253–258.

Iannaccone, Laurence R. 1995. "Voodoo Economics? Reviewing the Rational Choice Approach to Religion." *Journal for the Scientific Study of Religion* 34:76–89.

Marler, Penny Long, and C. Kirk Hadaway. 1993. "Toward a Typology of Marginal Members." *Review of Religious Research* 35:34–51.

Mead, Loren B. 1991. *The Once and Future Church*. Washington: The Alban Institute.

Newman, Peter C. 1995. *The Canadian Revolution: From Deference to Defiance*. Toronto: Viking.

Posterski, Donald C., and Irwin Barker. 1993. *Where's a Good Church?* Winfield: Wood Lake Books.

Roof, Wade Clark. 1993. *A Generation of Seekers*. San Francisco: Harper.

———, and C. Kirk Hadaway. 1977. "Shifts in Religious Preference in the Mid-Seventies." *Journal for the Scientific Study of Religion* 16:409–412.

———, and William McKinney. 1987. *American Mainline Religion*. New Brunswick: Rutgers University Press.

Schaller, Lyle. 1987. *It's a Different World: The Challenge for Today's Pastor*. Nashville: Abingdon.

———. 1995. *The New Reformation*. Nashville: Abingdon.

Sherkat, Darren B. 1991. "Leaving the Faith." *Social Science Research* 20:171–187.

Stark, Rodney, and Charles Y. Glock. 1968. *American Piety*. Berkeley: University of California Press.

Statistics Canada. *1991 Census of Canada*. Catalogue no. 93-319.

———. 1993. *Religions in Canada*. Ottawa: Industry, Science and Technology Canada.

Warner, Stephen R. 1993. "A Work in Progress toward a New Paradigm for the Sociological Study of Religion in the United States." *American Journal of Sociology* 98:1044–1093.

Woods, C. Jeff. 1996. *Congregational Megatrends*. Bethesda: The Alban Institute.

Wuthnow, Robert. 1988. *The Restructuring of American Religion*. Princeton: Princeton University Press.

CHAPTER 3

RESISTING THE "NO MAN'S LAND" OF PRIVATE RELIGION: THE CATHOLIC CHURCH AND PUBLIC POLITICS IN QUEBEC

David Seljak

In his book *Public Religions in the Modern World* (1994), José Casanova argues that, contrary to the models *described* by dominant modernization theories and programs *prescribed* by liberal political theories, there are new forms of participation in public debates by religious communities which do not represent a regression to pre-modern religious practices or a rejection of modern values. *Modern* public religions do not violate the consciences of individuals, the autonomy of political society and the state, or the democratic norms of pluralism and liberty. Instead, they protect those very values when they participate as actors in important ethical debates at the level of civil society. They do not reject modernity but offer a moral critique of "specific forms of institutionalization of modernity" (p. 221). Casanova labels these new forms of public activity the "deprivatization of religion," since they resist the "privatized role to which they were being relegated by secularist modernization theories and by liberal political theories" (p. 221).

Following David Martin's theory of secularization, Casanova argues that the decline of religious mentalities and the privatization of religion predicted by dominant theories of secularization have not occurred. Only secularization as a function of differentiation has been proven to be a "structural trend" in modernizing societies. This process encourages agents and institutions to operate in their own specialized spheres according to the logic of their own rational operations, free from barriers imposed by "irrational" religion, custom and tradition (Casanova 1994:40). Public religions challenge the claims of the enormous rational bureaucracies created by the modern state and market to operate solely according to the inherent logic of their distinct spheres. In doing so they challenge the dominant cultural division of society into neat realms of "public" and "private," where the public sphere is dominated by so-called universal reason and the private by ethnic and religious particularisms. While affirming the separation of church and state and of religion and politics, proponents of modern public religions argue that moral and cultural values, spirituality and ethics must not be relegated to the "private" realm of individual experience, family, ethnic community and parish. By introducing ethical criticism into questions of public policy, which technocratic elites claim must be solved only in rational or instrumental terms, Casanova argues, modern public religions serve to protect the integrity of "civil society," that public arena dominated by neither state nor church which serves as the heart of a modern democracy.

THE QUEBEC EXPERIENCE: FROM CIVIL RELIGION TO PUBLIC DENOMINATION

The participation of the Catholic Church in the 1980 and 1995 referenda on Quebec's sovereignty is an interesting illustration of Casanova's thesis. Examining the church's public reaction to this new nationalism is a particularly effective measure of its successful "deprivatization" as a *modern* public religion, because before 1960 the Catholic Church enjoyed a privileged position in Quebec society, what Casanova calls a position of "social establishment." While the state and political parties were officially secular, Catholicism provided the basic elements of French Quebecers' "civil religion." The church controlled virtually all education, health care and social services for French Quebecers, who formed the majority of the population. In 1958, 99 percent of the French speakers (more than 85 percent of the entire population) were Catholic and more than 88 percent of all Quebec Catholics reported attending Sunday mass regularly (Bibby, 1993:6, Table 1.1).[1] Both Quebec society and the church were highly clerical; in 1961, more than 45,000 nuns, priests and brothers oversaw the church's massive bureaucracy (Hamelin, 1984:173, Table 13). Quebec culture and nationalism legitimated this semi-established status and public presence by uniting a conservative Catholicism with French-Canadian ethnic identity. As David Martin has shown elsewhere, this relationship was not unique.[2]

During the Quiet Revolution of the 1960s, the church rapidly lost control over Quebec's social bureaucracy to the new interventionist state. The rapidity with which secularization overtook Quebec society and political culture was staggering. One illustration will serve to make the point: before 1960 every important nationalist movement or party had also been Catholic. Twelve years later not a single significant movement or party was openly so. The political modernization of Quebec, according to sociologist Marcel Rioux (1976), meant an explosion of the rational, critical spirit in a culture dominated by custom, religion and traditional authority. In the early 1960s, both substantive and instrumental issues were subject to critical reason. Within the Liberal party and its offshoot, the Parti Québécois, groups raised ethical questions about the very structure, values and goals of Quebec society. However, according to Paul-Marcel Lemaire (1993:17–18), by the end of the 1960s *"uncertain pragmatisme d'allure typiquement nord-américaine"* took over, relegating deeper ethical debates to the margins. In the 1970s, it was the agents of the interventionist state bureaucracy, capitalist institutions and the militantly secular intelligentsia who claimed to represent the forces of reason and progress.[3] Public Catholicism was identified with the discredited Duplessis regime even though privately French Quebecers remained faithful to their heritage. In mainstream culture, Catholicism became almost wholly privatized as a religion of rites of passage and a cultural touchstone (Milot, 1991).[4]

In the 1980s, with the rise of neo-conservatism (called more accurately *néolibéral-isme* in French), the non-interventionist state and market institutions claimed that they now represented the forces of reason. Neo-conservatives saw in the laws of the market *natural* laws which, like the laws discovered by physics and chemistry, are immutable and beyond human control. They argued that any intervention in this "nat-ural" process is an inevitably self-defeating violation which could only lead to injus-tice and harm for the very people the intervention sought to help (for example, generous social programs harmed the poor by discouraging economic growth and personal responsibility). Finally, neo-conservatives argued that the market was the only neces-sary basis for social organization; they believed that other large-scale institutions which operated according to a logic other than the rational laws of the market harmed soci-ety, hence their mistrust of the state (Sharp, 1995:232). This belief in the market's abil-ity to create spontaneously the most just social order meant that neo-conservatives mistrusted "ideological" or "political" solutions (that is, all alternative models) and offered no other social project than adaptation to the reality of market laws. They sus-pected anyone who disagreed with their rational analysis and program of having a "political agenda" or representing a "special interest group." Consequently, they rele-gated social projects inspired by particular values, ethics, or ethnic or religious tradi-tions to the private sphere. According to Charles Taylor (1991:109–110), this obsession with the maximization of market efficiency closed down all ethical debates. People's attention was turned to instrumental questions of how to produce more, rather than substantive questions about the common good. Societies organized around a "single principle" (either on the left or right) precluded ethical debates and consequently sti-fled freedom. All debates were flattened out and reduced to a calculus of individual or collective material self-interest.

In Quebec, neo-conservatism had become an increasingly important guide for gov-ernment policy during the second administration of René Lévesque's Parti Québécois (PQ) from 1981 to 1985, the tenure of Robert Bourassa's Parti Libérale du Québec (PLQ) from 1985 to 1994, and Jacques Parizeau's PQ government from 1994 to the referen-dum in 1995. This shift led to the privatization of Crown corporations, reduction of gov-ernment spending on social programs, and the creation of a pro-business environment by encouraging investment and limiting the powers of labour unions (*ibid.*:341–423). In all of these initiatives, the governments of Lévesque, Bourassa, and Parizeau limited or rolled back the involvement of the state in the capitalist economy (McRoberts, 1988:358–423). This represented a major shift in the political culture of Quebec, which, since the Quiet Revolution, was dominated by the idea that government intervention in the economy was the most important strategy of national and social development.[5]

While the church reacted to the secularization of Quebec society with relative seren-ity,[6] at each stage of this two-step process it protested the privatization or "folkloriza-tion" of Catholicism. This reaction, as Gregory Baum argues elsewhere in this volume, must be understood in the context of the Second Vatican Council, which redefined the position of the church to modern society, accepting the autonomy of political society and the state, affirming the rights of individual consciences in political matters, and call-ing Roman Catholics to participate in the important political and social debates of their societies (Casanova, 1994:71–73). In Quebec, the decisions of the council rendered unworkable the conservative nationalism of traditionalist Catholic groups, allowed liberals and radicals to be critical of the old church and the old Quebec while remaining Catholic, and inspired Catholics to redefine the public role of the church (Seljak, 1996). The Catholic hierarchy established a Royal Commission-style public inquiry into the church's relationship to the new society in 1968. In 1971, the Dumont Commission published a multi-volume report which closed the door on the old-style semi-established religion but also rejected the privatization of Catholicism, which it labelled a religious "no man's land" (*Commission d'étude,* 1971:83). The church had a public role in the new society, the commission concluded, even if this role would be radically different from its earlier one (pp. 129–37).[7] In the 1970s, the church's new public role was most visibly defined by its social teaching on a wide variety of justice issues, ranging from the rights of Aboriginal peoples, immigrants, welfare recipients and women to economic inequality, workers' rights and the environment (Rochais, 1984).

THE 1980 REFERENDUM AND CATHOLIC SOCIAL TEACHING

Elected in 1976, less than eight years after its formation, the PQ scheduled a referendum for 20 May 1980 to give the government of Quebec a mandate to negotiate with the federal government to establish a new relationship of "sovereignty-association," that is, some form of political sovereignty with strong economic ties to Canada (McRoberts, 1988:301–310). While most Quebecers defined the issues in the 1980 referendum in political and economic terms, groups within the Catholic Church also defined the whole debate as a spiritual and ethical decision, touching upon Catholic values such as the common good, solidarity among citizens and social justice. As such, they felt, the church had to participate in the debate as a public actor. The bishops, Catholic journals and social action groups had learned to become effective public pressure groups, and they applied the techniques learned in the 1960s and 1970s to the new situation.

The decision to participate in a public and highly politicized debate put the Catholic Church in an awkward position. While the "Yes" and "No" committees were officially non-partisan, it was clear that the PQ government and official opposition Liberals were closely identified with each respectively. For the episcopacy or church leadership to come out in favour of one side or the other was clearly unacceptable since this would have resurrected the spectre of the *grande noirceur* of the 1950s. During the referendum campaign, the bishops took pains to ensure that the church was not identified with either side. Members of the clergy were allowed to take sides, but they could not present their own opinions as church teaching (Martel, 1980; Béliveau, 1980b).[8] As the *Assemblée des évêques du Québec* (AÉQ) argued in its first pastoral letter on the 1980 referendum, the gospels could inspire certain values, attitudes and concerns, but neither sovereignty-association nor federalism could be defended as directly dictated by Christianity.[9] Individuals, however, were allowed to make their own decisions (*Assemblée des évêques,* 1984b:144). Neither the bishops nor Catholic leaders assumed that they spoke for all Quebecers or that they could tell Catholics how to vote. The pastoral letters and other gestures were offered as ethical reflections on a pressing political question from members of an important institution with historical ties to Quebec society. While Catholic groups, journals and public figures did publicize their choices in both referenda, they consistently distanced their political options from direct identification with the Gospel message.

CATHOLIC VALUES AND QUEBEC POLITICAL CULTURE

However, the bishops did take firm positions on more fundamental ethical matters. The first was their defence of the right of Quebecers to determine their own future through a democratic process. The bishops defined "the people of Quebec" as members of the Francophone majority, the Anglophone community, the ethnic communities, and the Aboriginal peoples. Together, these citizens of the territory of Quebec had the right to negotiate the terms of their political alliance with the rest of Canada (*Commission d'étude*, 1971:140–141).[10] Nationalism, so far as it promoted the rights of people to self-determination as defined in the 1966 Covenant of the United Nations and the 1971 World Synod of Bishops' document *Justice in the World*, was ethically acceptable.[11] The right of Quebecers to self-determination was given its most articulate defence in the pages of *Relations*, the journal of a group of Montreal-based Jesuits engaged in social questions. There, Père Irénée Desrochers (1978c; 1979c) defended the right of Quebecers to decide their fate as a moral principle which preceded the whole referendum debate. Most engaged Catholics did not defend Quebecers' right to self-determination; they simply assumed it. This position was shared by both of the major political parties and even by the leaders of the "No" campaign. Quebecers were understood as a people and not as an ethnic minority (Desrochers, 1979a).

Because, in the church's social teaching, every right is balanced by a responsibility, Catholics did not understand this right to a national identity as absolute. In their second letter on the 1980 referendum, the Quebec bishops argued that the right to national self-determination was circumscribed by the duty to promote the common good, solidarity among nations and social justice (*Assemblée des évêques*, 1984a:146–148). Nationalism could not be defined in narrow ethnic terms, nor could it fixate on preserving the past. The bishops outlined their vision of a just society without supporting any specific political parties or policies. To make specific recommendations would again identify the church too closely with either the social democracy of the PQ or the liberalism of the Liberal party. The bishops' vision of a just society was based on five "*grandes orientations*" defined by Catholic social thought in the 1970s: (1) the responsibility of citizens to participate in public policy decisions; (2) the balancing of rights and duties of persons in light of the common good; (3) an equitable distribution of goods and responsibilities; (4) a serious concern for the spiritual and cultural elements of society; and (5) solidarity among peoples (*ibid.*:145–146).

Finally, the bishops argued that the democratic process of the referendum itself was an important step in the maturation of Quebec political culture. In their 1979 and 1980 pastoral letters on the referendum, the bishops warned that Christians were obliged to support the democratic process, respect their opponents, and continue to serve the community whatever its choice (*ibid.*:145–146; 1984b:139). Two weeks before the referendum, Monseigneur Grégoire issued a brief statement entitled *"Le référendum: avant et après"* in English and French. The letter, which was reprinted in *Le Devoir*, stated that the Christian faith demanded that people respect the truth, recognize the limits of their own positions, and refuse to demonize or maltreat their opponents in the debate. It also demanded that Christians become fully aware of the question and the stakes in the debate, make a rational and sincere decision, and then participate fully in the name of that decision. Catholicism did not allow indifference or apathy on important social questions (Grégoire, 1980). The argued that without these basic Christian values, the democratic process itself would collapse. These sentiments were seconded by the progressive Catholic press. Particularly important to the Catholic left was the consciousness-raising of ordinary Quebecers. In the May 1980 editorial of *Relations*, Albert Beaudry wrote that the referendum was a historical event, *"non seulement parce qu'il représente un exercice authentique de liberté démocratique, mais par la prise de conscience collective dont il devient l'instrument"* (Beaudry, 1980 :131).

SOVEREIGNTY AS A SOCIAL JUSTICE ISSUE

Some Catholics felt that the bishops did not go far enough in their analysis of the sovereignty issue as a question of social justice. In his 1979 book *Une foi ensouchée dans ce pays*, Jacques Grand'Maison (1979:26–30) blasted the bishops for their "stratospheric absenteeism" on injustices committed against the French-Canadian community in Quebec. In *Relations*, Desrochers complained that the bishops' first pastoral letter on the referendum implied that the constitutional status quo was morally acceptable. While Gospel values did not dictate a "Yes" vote in this referendum, he argued, the Gospel message of justice for all did preclude the continuation of the current situation (1979b:266–268). Confederation, according to these Catholics, had two purposes: to formalize the national oppression of French Canadians in Canadian federalism and to assure the oppression of all workers in oppressive capitalist structures. Still, they argued, one had to maintain a critical distance between the Gospel and any specific political project. The PQ project of sovereignty-association, they argued, was limited by the *petit bourgeois* nationalism of its artisans, its affirmation of the free market, and its bureaucratic orientation which centralized decision-making power in the new middle class of technocrats rather than in the workers. The demands of social justice required a much more radical restructuring of Quebec society, and independence was just the first step in this revolutionary project. This *"oui, maix ..."* (yes, but ...) position was also adopted by the *Réseau des chrétiens politisés,* the Quebec incarnation of Christians for Socialism and the editorial team of *Dossiers "Vie ouvrière,"* the journal of the *Centre de pastorale en milieu ouvrier* (CPMO), *Jeunesse ouvrière catholique,* and the *Mouvement de travailleurs chrétiens* (MTC). Some Catholics even helped to form an ecumenical coalition called the *Comité chrétien pour le oui* during the referendum debate to publicize this "yes, but ..." position (Seljak, 1995:472–502).[12]

The church's support of the right of Quebecers to self-determination, the democratic referendum process, and the values and virtues which sustain a democratic political culture were met with public approval. The entire texts of the bishops' letters were carried in all of the daily newspapers and editorialists generally welcomed their participation (*Montreal Gazette*, 1979; Lachance, 1980; de Lagrave, 1979). They did not see the participation of Catholics—*as* Catholics—in public debates as a demand for special privileges or a threat to pluralism or democracy. Of course, the more radical position taken by progressive independentists raised more objections. Claude Ryan, the leader of the Liberal party and head of the "No" committee, charged progressive Catholics with replacing a clericalism of the right with a clericalism of the left. He denounced the *Comité chrétiens pour le oui* as false priests and false brothers who were dragging the Gospel into a purely secular, political and rational debate (Bouchard, 1980; Béliveau, 1980a). Marcel Adam (1980), the editor of Quebec's largest daily newspaper *La Presse*, sharply criticized the committee's introduction of Christianity into the referendum debate as a throwback to *duplessisme*, that unholy ideological alliance between Catholicism and French-Canadian nationalism. But members of the Catholic left defended their participation in public debates. Members of the *Comité chrétien pour le oui* replied to Ryan's attacks claiming that it was he who manipulated latent Catholic conservatism and its identification with the political status quo (Bouchard, 1980; Béliveau, 1980a). Indeed, polls showed that churchgoing Catholics tended to reject independentism more readily than other French Quebecers (Nevitte, 1978). Still, most Quebecers seemed to accept the public participation of the church in the referendum debate.

NEO-LIBERALISM AND THE 1995 REFERENDUM

Having established its new public role through its social teaching in the 1970s and its participation in the 1980 debate, the Catholic Church had a tradition—however short—on which to draw in the 1995 referendum. Indeed, the church did not alter the nature of its public performance; the only difference in the church's position was the context now defined by the shift to neo-conservatism. Groups who wanted to carve out a public Catholicism tended to define the 1995 referendum debate as a battle against neo-conservatism, which they saw as the dominant ideology in Canada and the world. They argued that this new orientation was reflected in the proposed bill on Quebec's sovereignty, which was the subject of the referendum. The bill, composed of a preamble and seventeen articles, did not mention any socio-economic rights or project for a more just society. Catholic critics of the bill—even those who supported sovereignty—argued that this absence of a social project stemmed from the government's neo-conservative assumption that the marketplace would define the social reality of an independent Quebec (Baum, 1995:13–14).

It was not surprising that Catholic groups in Quebec would find this approach unsatisfactory on two counts. First, the referendum debate, they argued, was structured to preclude ethical issues. Both sides argued that their option offered Quebecers the most advantageous position in the new global economy. Second, the most vocal groups had consistently opposed even Keynesian liberalism in the 1970s, and neo-conservatism was even less interested in addressing issues of inequality and exploitation. Inspired by the criticism of world capitalism expressed in papal and ecclesiastical documents such as Paul VI's *Populorum progressio* and *Octogesima adveniens*, the 1971 World Synod of Bishops' *Justice in the World*, and John Paul II's *Laborem exercens*, a number of important Catholic groups, including the *Assemblée des évêques du Québec*, adopted a radical critique of liberal democracy and the capitalist economy. Despite a general collapse of the left in Quebec after 1981, the bishops and some important Catholic groups had remained committed to their criticism of liberal capitalism and promoted models of development based on social democracy or a more decentralized participatory democracy.[13] For example, in 1994 a group of bishops, along with economists, labour leaders and businesspeople, created a document entitled *"Sortons le Québec de l'appauvrissement,"* which criticized the neo-conservative philosophy of the Liberal government and suggested alternative economic strategies based on co-operatives, job-sharing, worker management and local initiatives (*Sortons le Québec*, 1994). Along with other Catholic groups the bishops have supported the province-wide anti-poverty movement *Solidarité populaire Québec* (SPQ), a coalition of popular movements, small co-operatives, labour unions and other community groups formed to fight the dominant neo-conservative orthodoxy (Baum, 1995:13). Consequently, it was not surprising that Catholic groups would be uncomfortable with a project for Quebec sovereignty which did not address their demands for a blueprint for a more participatory, egalitarian and solidarity-oriented society. Jean-Marc Biron and Dominique Boisvert published an open letter in *Le Devoir*, arguing that because the referendum question did not address a social project, it could only divide Quebecers along ethnic lines (Baum, 1995:14).

THE CATHOLIC CRITIQUE OF NEO-CONSERVATISM DURING THE REFERENDUM

Eight months before the 1995 referendum, the executive committee of the *Assemblée des évêques du Québec* released a pastoral letter entitled *"Le référendum sur l'avenir du Québec."* In it, the bishops affirmed the position which they had adopted during the 1980 referendum concerning the right of Quebecers to self-determination, the liberty of individual consciences and the autonomy of political society, the legitimacy of the democratic process, and the Christian values of honesty, openness, co-operation and tolerance. The letter ended on an optimistic note, observing that Quebecers have not abandoned all of their ethical and cultural values to the demands of the market. According to the bishops, Quebecers insisted that their politicians solve the problem of the deficit and reform social programs without blaming the poor or placing the burden squarely on their shoulders (*Comité exécutif de l'Assemblée des évêques*, 1995:104–105).

Despite this implicit criticism of neo-conservatism, the 1995 pastoral letter was much more restrained than the bishops' 1990 submission to the Bélanger-Campeau Commission, established in the wake of the failed Meech Lake Accord by Bourassa's Liberal government. In their earlier report entitled *"Les chemins de l'avenir,"* the bishops argued that neo-conservatism promoted the material welfare of certain individuals over the solidarity of the entire community and justice for the poorest members of society. Moreover, they complained that neo-conservatism tended to reduce all human relations to market relations. Consequently, so-called rational economic values auto-matically excluded cultural, ethical and religious values in all questions of public policy. Such an approach, the bishops argued, promoted an economic fatalism, a resignation to the allegedly natural laws of the market. In opposition to this fatalism, the bishops insisted that Quebecers seek out an ethical project which would reform society. They underlined the need for constitutional reform not only as a question of national integrity but also as a way to ensure social justice for the more than one million poor people in Quebec and the impoverished regions of the province. They affirmed the distinct-society position outlined in the Meech Lake debate, the priority of French as the public language, the greatest autonomy possible for the First Nations, respect for the rights of minorities, the decentralization of powers towards the regions, the responsibility of Quebecers for the welfare of Francophones outside of Quebec, and the creation of a participatory democracy founded on values of equality and mutual responsibility (*Assemblée des évêques*, 1991). In their February 1995 letter, the final position was much more restrained (Biron, 1995). Perhaps the relatively vague nature of the letter may be explained by the episcopacy's policy of maintaining a posture of political non-partisanship. Again the bishops were very careful to avoid having the church identi-fied with any one political party by openly criticizing the PQ law on sovereignty.

Two days after the referendum, the executive committee of AÉQ released a second pastoral letter entitled "*Le référendum et l'évolution de la société québécoise*" calling for calm, tolerance and a renewed commitment to the development of a more just soci-ety. The referendum vote, they argued, did not settle the constitutional issue nor did it move Quebec society towards a consensus on a *projet de société*. Because the after-math of the referendum was marked by division and disorientation, responsible citi-zens were called to adopt "the Gospel-inspired attitudes of respect and dialogue, rigorous quest for truth and justice, acceptance of our diffferences [sic] and attention to the weakest members of our society" (*Assemblée des évêques*, 1995:1).[14] The solu-tion required a commitment to the collective good and an openness to others. The bishops lamented the fact that the proposed sovereignty bill and the debate led by the major players did not address important social issues. Still, the tone of their letter was optimistic; they warned against cynicism. The referendum was not a "useless exercise" but an expression of political maturity and of a democratic culture. It encouraged people to reflect on every aspect of their political, economic, cultural and social lives instead of short-term issues of economic self-interest (p. 2). This in itself was a protest against the economic fatalism which dominated Quebec political culture in the 1990s.

For the writers of *Relations* as well, the nationalist movement and referendum process were exciting expressions of democratic participation. Joseph Giguère applauded the fact that community-based groups had succeeded in transforming the regional and national commissions on Quebec's sovereignty into opportunities of civic participa-tion and direct democracy. In contrast to the discourse of the PQ, the participants tied Quebec national identity to "*La démocratisation de la société civile, la justice sociale, l'en-racinement territorial et la consolidation du caractère communautaire de la société québé-coise*" (Giguère, 1995a:100). Similarly, Jacques Boucher (1995a:99–100) felt that participation by grassroots groups in the commissions had succeeded in widening the debate, moving it past the narrow confines of its original *économisme* and putting forth models of development based on social democratic ideals.[15]

FEDERALISM AND NEO-CONSERVATISM

While the bishops criticized neo-conservative values without taking a position on the 1995 referendum question, certain Catholic groups argued that the church's concern for social justice demanded a "Yes" vote.[16] Most prominent among these groups were the *Regroupement des religieuses et religieux pour le oui* and the editorial team of *Relations*. They agreed that popular participation in the referendum debate itself was the first step in overcoming the fatalism engendered by the dominant *économisme* of Quebec political culture. But, beyond affirming the referendum process and the introduction of ethical debate into the public sphere of Quebec politics, they argued that sovereignty was a first, necessary, but not sufficient, step in opposing the neo-conservative agenda of the federal government.

Le Regroupement des religieuses et religieux pour le oui brought together some 400 nuns, brothers and priests involved in social work to sign a strongly worded letter supporting a "Yes" vote.[17] The letter stated that, while the Gospel did not dictate either political option, their own commitment to the poor led them to support a "Yes" vote. The alternative to sovereignty, they argued, was an acceptance of the dominant neo-conservative discourse which contributed to the desperate social conditions they faced in their daily work. Since the government of Jean Chrétien had abandoned its commitment to the welfare state, Quebecers were better off on their own. The *Regroupement* presented their open letter to the press at a brunch and press conference attended by approximately 120 of the signatories in a working-class area of Montreal. The event was attended by two PQ ministers, the local MLA and MP (Baillargeon, 1995) and was covered by *Le Devoir*, *Journal de Montréal*, *Radio Canada*, television news outlets, and the regional press.[18]

In its letter, the *Regroupement* lamented the fact that the referendum debate had been dominated by a pro-business agenda that focused solely on the economic risks associated with sovereignty. Totally absent from this discourse was any concern for social solidarity, any worry about the growing division between the wealthy and the poor, and any reference to the fight against exclusion and poverty (*Regroupement des religieuses et religieux pour le oui*, 1995). Its analysis of the federal government and Canadian society was even more pessimistic. Pointing to the weakening of unemployment insurance protection, the abolition of federal transfer payments for welfare programs, the abandonment of social housing programs, and cuts to the budgets of the Canadian International Development Agency (CIDA), they argued that Chrétien's government had committed itself to dismantling the social safety net. The position of the *Regroupement* was not just a short-term defence of social programs but rather a stance against what they saw as the ideological foundation of a new Canada. They interpreted a "Yes" vote as a rejection of the economic fatalism of the neo-conservatism promoted by the federal government that would allow the progressive forces in Quebec *"un nouvel espace de liberté et de responsabilité"* in which to express their solidarity and compassion in new and creative social structures. For the *Regroupement,* a "Yes" vote was the best way to build *"une société plus solidaire, sans violence, sans sexisme, sans discrimination."*

Another group which saw a "Yes" vote as a step towards building a more just and participatory society was the editorial committee of the Jesuit journal *Relations.* The editorial committee also supported a "Yes" vote for roughly the same reasons they did in 1980, but now their support for sovereignty was tied directly to their opposition to neo-conservatism. In an editorial published just before the 1995 referendum, the writers of *Relations* argued that the Chrétien government had a double agenda: to create a more centralized Canadian state and to submit the whole country to the imperatives of economic liberalism. Well aware that the PQ government of Parizeau had also adopted a neo-conservative agenda, they still supported sovereignty as a first step towards creating a more egalitarian, compassionate and just society. They argued that the very structure of Confederation made Quebecers' fight against neo-conservatism impossible since so many of the powers the people of Quebec needed to define their *projet de société* were monopolized by the federal government (Paiement, 1995:227). As well, federalism combined with neo-conservatism promoted feelings of power-lessness and apathy (Paiement, 1995:228). While sovereignty was no guarantee of a more democratic and just Quebec, federalism, recast in a neo-conservative model, vir-tually prohibited the development of such a society. Jacques Boucher (1995b:164) noted that it was significant that the staunchest defenders of federalism in Quebec— such as the *Conseil du patronat* and the PLQ headed by Daniel Johnson—were at the same time the most enthusiastic promoters of the neo-conservative model of devel-opment.[19] Because of this connection, sovereignty became much more urgent.

CONCLUSION: PUBLIC CATHOLICISM AND QUEBEC SOVEREIGNTY

In both the 1980 and 1995 referenda, Catholic groups attempted to redefine a public role for the church in Quebec society. In doing so, they have rejected both the old-style public Catholicism of the Duplessis era as well as the privatization of religion prescribed by liberalism. Such Catholics are a minority but, because they have the support of the bishops and several important religious communities and organizations, they are a sig-nificant one. Their attempts at the "deprivatization" of religion take the form of resist-ance to the dominant political culture, which would relegate both religion and alternative ethical perspectives to the "private" realm of subjective values and experiences. Informed by social scientists, such as Jacques Grand'Maison at the l'Université de Montréal and Fernand Dumont at l'Université Laval to name two, church leaders have conscientiously adopted a modern posture: affirming the autonomy of political society, the liberty of individual consciences, *and* the Enlightenment agenda of the application of critical reason to the perfection of society. Moving beyond a simple instrumentalist definition of critical reason, Catholic leaders have sought to define a rational, ethical critique of the new secular nationalism, a critique which was, at the same time, identifiably Catholic.

The definition of this modern, public Catholicism was made possible only by the fact that the Catholic Church had come to redefine its relationship with Quebec society at a time when international Catholicism had come to accept the modern values of democracy, the rights of peoples to self-determination, and social justice. The Second Vatican Council and the emergence of a faith and justice movement within the church allowed Catholics in Quebec to engage in the important debates of their societies *as Catholics*, without resorting to the pre-modern modes of public religion (see Baum, 1991; Seljak, 1995, 1996). It is an excellent example of a much broader phenomenon described so well by Casanova—an example which should lead us to rethink the categories of public and private, universal and particular, rational and ethical, which permeate our political culture and social-scientific models of secularization.

NOTES

1 A parallel system of education, health care and social services for English-speaking Quebecers was provided by the Protestant churches and by voluntary associations, but was funded largely by the state.

2 Martin shows that in those cases where a national enclave in a wider federation is united by religion (for example, Croatia, Slovakia, Brittany, the Basque country), national identity and claims-making is often mediated by Catholicism. In cases of conquered people living in empires marked by a majority of a different ethnicity and religion (such as Poland and Ireland) the identification between religion and nationalism has often been complete. Such societies are marked by a high degree of clericalism, low tolerance of dissent and pluralism, and extraordinarily high levels of practice and Sunday observance (Martin, 1978:42–45). Baum (1991:15–47) applies Martin's analysis to Quebec fruitfully.

3 Lemaire argues that the rise of instrumental reason over substantive reason expressed itself in the intellectual world as a *néoscientisme technocratique*, an American-style positivistic approach to the study of society and the person defined against the humanities as "value-free." Continuing symptoms of the victory of technocratic reason in Quebec intellectual life include the abandonment of literary, philosophical and historical studies; positivism in science; the ubiquitous faith in the cybernetic model under a veneer of cognitive science; and a runaway "*économisme*," the dominance of economic determinism over political choice in public debates (Lemaire, 1993:18).

4 Gregory Baum discusses the importance of "cultural Catholicism" in Quebec in his chapter of this volume.

5 Louis Balthazar (1986:132–139) has argued that the idea that the Quebec state was the national state of all Quebecers was the foundational idea behind the Quiet Revolution. Consequently, a shift away from the idea that the Quebec state should be the primary agent of the political, economic and social development of Quebecers represents a rejection of some of the founding principles of the Quiet Revolution.

6 Relying on the framework provided by David Martin, Gregory Baum (1991:15–47) argues that this parallels the experience of the Catholic Church in Belgium.

7 For the limited but significant impact of the Dumont Commission's report, see Baum (1991:49–65), and J. Harvey (1990). Gregory Baum deals with the significance of the commission in the context of the secularization of Quebec society in his chapter of this volume.

8 The press noted the efforts of the bishops to assure that neither sovereigntists nor federalists tied their political options directly to Christian values. See Martel (1980) and Béliveau (1980b).

9 Quebec Catholics frequently complained that English-Canadian Christians were not so careful. They tended to identify federalism directly with the Christian virtues of unity, peace and security. Even some Catholic bishops and parishes prayed for political unity as if it were God's will. In 1978, other Christians offered prayers for Canadian unity during the Week of Prayer for Unity among Christians announced by Pope Paul VI (see Desrochers, 1978a, 1978b). For a fascinating report on how English-speaking Christians in Canada continued to spontaneously and uncritically identify God's will for unity with Canadian federalism

during the 1995 referendum, see Harry Hiller's chapter in this volume.

[10] The Quebec bishops were following a position outlined by the Canadian Catholic Conference in a 1972 letter entitled, "On Pastoral Implications of Political Choices," in which the Canadian bishops wrote that when Quebecers considered their political future—including independence—"all options which respect the human person and the human community are a matter of free choice on the individual as well as the community level" (Canadian Catholic Conference, 1987:230). The Canadian bishops, in turn, were inspired by the 1971 document *Justice in the World* (produced by the World Synod of Bishops), which sought to guarantee peoples the right to self-determination and freedom to develop according to their particular genius.

[11] The World Synod of Bishops wrote that people had the right to development, that is, modernization, according to their own particular identity. Thus, the right to development was tied to the right to self-determination. See *Justice in the World* (nos. 13–19) in Gremillion (1976:516–518).

[12] The Catholic left's critical acceptance of the new nationalism is discussed at length in Chapter 6 of my doctoral dissertation (Seljak, 1995:367–513).

[13] For a discussion of Catholic groups which have adopted these positions, see Vaillancourt (1984), and Baum (1992).

[14] The French version reads: *"Les attitude évangéliques de respect et de dialogue, de recherche rigoureuse de la vérité et de la justice, d'accueil de nos différences, d'attention aux plus faibles de notre société."*

[15] In fact, Giguère (1995b:35) argued that Quebecers' distinct identity was founded on their communitarian and democratic heritage and orientation. This heritage was expressed in Quebec's voluntary associations, popular movements, co-operatives, labour unions, chambers of commerce and credit unions, as well as in its affirmation of local and regional identities, affirmation of popular education and mobilization, and promotion of a communitarian culture.

[16] It is important to remember that such Catholics were in a strict minority. Polls since 1976 have consistently shown that churchgoing Catholics have been the least likely among all Francophone Quebecers to support independence, sovereignty association or the PQ as a political party. See Nevitte and Gingras (1984), Grenville and Reid (1996), and Grenville, Reid, and Lewis (n.d).

[17] One of the instigators of the letter, Sister Thérèse Soucy, stated that those most likely to sign the letter were people most directly involved in providing services to workers and those on social assistance (Venne, 1995). While its members came from some thirty different religious communities, and were very active in a number of Catholic and secular social justice groups, they signed the letter as individuals and not on behalf of any community or group.

[18] The press conference included a modest brunch. The cost of the brunch and setting up the conference was covered by *le Comité chrétien pour le oui*, since all expenditures for the debate had to come under the umbrella of the official government-approved campaigns.

[19] In a speech after the referendum, Ed Broadbent (1996) tied popular support for sovereignty to Bouchard's defence of the welfare state. While the federal government and the provincial governments of Ontario and Alberta all adopted the rhetoric of neo-conservatism, Bouchard has consistently rejected it in favour of a "conservative" Keynesian liberalism. In an interview with this author on 23 May 1996, the editor of *Relations*, Carolyn Sharp, mentioned that she was not entirely comfortable with the tendency among progressive Francophones in Quebec to identify federalism with "neo-conservatism." She worried that they often ignored progressive federalists who lamented the dismantling of the welfare state.

REFERENCES

Adam, Marcel. 1980. *"Dieu, le Christ et le pape sollicités en faveur du oui?"* Editorial. *La Presse*, 12 April, A6.

Assemblée des évêques du Québec (AÉC). 1984a. Construire ensemble une société meilleure: Deuxieme message de l'Assemblée des évêques du Québec sur l'evolution politique de la société québécoise, le 9 janvier 1980. In *La justice sociale comme bonne nouvelle: Messages sociaux, économiques et politiques des évêques du Québec 1972–1983*, ed. Gérard Rochais. Montreal: Ballarmin.

———. 1984b. Le peuple québécois et son avenir politique: Message de l'Assemblée des évêques du Québec, sur l'evolution de la société québécoise, le 15 août 1979. In *La justice sociale comme bonne nouvelle: Messages sociaux, économiques et politiques des évêques du Québec 1972–1983*, ed. Gérard Rochais. Montreal: Ballarmin.

———. 1991. "Les chemins de l'avenir. Mémoire à la Commission Bélanger-Campeau." *L'Église Canadienne* 24, 1 (3 January):7–10.

———. 1995. *Le référendum et l'evolution de la société québécois. Message du Comité exécutif de l'Assemblée des évêques du Québec à l'occasion du vote référendaire sur l'avenir du Québec, le premier November 1995.* Montreal.

Baillargeon, S.. 1995. "Les religieuses répondent à l'appel du OUI." *Le Devoir*, 23 October, A3.

Balthazar, Louis. 1986. *Bilan du nationalisme au Québec.* Montreal: L'Hexagone.

Baum, Gregory. 1991. *The Church in Quebec.* Montreal: Novalis.

———. 1992. "The Catholic Left in Quebec." In *Culture and Social Change: Social Movements in Quebec and Ontario*, ed. Colin Lays and Margueritte Mendell, 140–154. Montreal: Black Rose.

———. 1995. Christian Social Justice Statements on the Upcoming Referendum. *Socialist Studies Bulletin* 40:11–21.

Beaudry, Albert. 1980. *"Le référendum: Un pas dans la bonne direction." Relations* 40 (459):131–133.

Béliveau, J. 1980a. *"Le chrétiens pour le OUI demandent à Ryan de retirer ses paroles." La Presse*, 23 April, A15.

———. 1980b. "Mgr Grégoire est satisfait de la discrétion des prêtres." *La Presse*, 9 May, A12.

Bibby, Reginald W. 1993. *Unknown Gods: The Ongoing Study of Religion in Canada.* Toronto: Stoddart.

Biron, Jean-Marc. 1995. "Les évêques et le référendum." *Relations* 611:132–133.

Bouchard, P. 1980. "Notre choix est légitime." *Le Devoir*, 23 April, 13, 14.

Boucher, Jacques. 1995a. "Les commissions et l'avenir de la démocratie." *Relations* 610:99–100.

———. 1995b. *"La question nationale." Relations* 612:163–164.

Broadbent, Ed. 1996. "Broadbent's Lament for a Nation." *Catholic New Times*, 18 February.

Canadian Catholic Conference. 1987. "Or Pastoral Implications of Political Choices," 21 April 1972. In *Do Justice! The Social Teaching of the Canadian Catholic Bishops, 1945–1986*, ed. E.F. Sheridan, SJ. Sherbrooke. Toronto: Editions Paulines and Jesuit Centre for Social Faith and Justice.

Casanova, José. 1994. *Public Religions in the Modern World.* Chicago: University of Chicago Press.

Comité exécutive de l'Assemblée des évêques du Québec. 1995. *Le référendum sur l'avenir du Québec. L'Église canadienne* 28 (4):103–105.

Commission d'étude sur les laics et L'Église. 1971. *L'Église du Québec: Un héritage, un projet.* Montreal: Éditions Fides.

de Lagrave, J.-P. 1979. "Un message de liberté." Editorial. *Le Devoir*, 28 August, 4.

Desroches, Irénée. 1978a. "La politique et les croyants au Canada: I. L'Église catholiques et l'unité canadienne." *Relations* 38 (436):116–121.

———. 1978b. "La politique et les croyants au Canada: II. L'oecuménisme et l'unité canadienne." *Relations* 38 (437):131–5.

———. 1978c. *"Québec-Canada: Self-reliance et solidarité des peuples."Relations* 38 (440):225, 238–240.

———. 1979a. "Le droit du Québec et les tactiques de M. Clark." *Relations* 39 (449):167–172.

———. 1979b. Les évêques du Québec et l'avenir du peuple en vue du référendum. *Relations* 39, 452: 264–268.

———. 1979c. *"Jean-Paul II et le peuples qui siegent pas encore a l'ONU." Relations* 39 (454):326–328, 349.

Giguère, Joseph. 1995b. "Souverains et communautaires." *Relations* 608:35–36.

Grand'Maison, Jacques. 1979. *Une foi ensouchée dans ce pay.* Montréal: Éditions Leméac.

Grégoire, P. 1980. "Le référendum, avant et après." *L'Élgise de Montréal* 98 (19):291–293.

Gremillion, Joseph. 1976. *The Gospel of Peace and Justice: Catholic Social Teaching since Pope John.* Maryknoll, NY: Orbis.

Grenville, Andrew S., and Angus E. Reid. 1996. "Catholicism and Voting No." *Ottawa Citizen,* 2 January, A9.

———, Angus E. Reid, and D.C. Lewis. n.d. "Quebec Nationalism and Catholic Communitarianism: An Analysis of the Catholic Vote in the 1995 Quebec Referendum." Unpublished paper.

Hamelin, Jean. 1984. *Histoire du catholicisme québécois.* Le XXe siècle, vol. 2, De 1940 a nos jours, ed. Nive Voisine. Montreal: Boréal Express.

Harvey, David. 1990. *The Condition of Postmodernity.* Oxford: Blackwell.

Lachance, P. 1980. *"L'Église au secours de la société."* Editorial. *Le Soleil,* 17 January, A6.

Lemaire, Paul-Marcel. 1993. *Nous Québécois.* Ottawa: Leméac.

Martel, J. 1980. *"L'Église se fera discrète."* Editorial. *Le Soleil,* 26 April, B2.

Martin, David. 1978. *A General Theory of Secularization.* Oxford: Basil Blackwell.

McRoberts, Kenneth. 1988. *Quebec: Social Change and Political Crisis.* 3rd ed. Toronto: McClelland & Stewart.

Milot, Micheline. 1991. "Le catholicisme au creuset de la culture." *Studies in Religion/Sciences religieuses* 20 (1):51–64.

Montreal Gazette. 1979. *"Le ton modéré des évêques." Le Soleil,* 27 August, A4.

Nevitte, Neil. 1978. "Religion and the 'New Nationalisms': The Case of Quebec." PhD dissertation, Duke University.

———, and Françoise-Pierre Gingras. 1984. "An Empirical Analysis of Secular-Religious Bases of Quebec Nationalism." *Social Compass* 31 (4):339–350.

Paiement, Guy. 1995. "Projet de société et souveraineté." *Relations* 614:227–278.

Regroupement des Religieuses et Religieux pour le 'Oui.' 1995. "Regroupement des religieuses et religieux pour le 'Oui.'" Open letter. Montreal.

Rioux, Marcel. 1976. *La question du Québec.* Montreal: Parti Pris.

Rochais, Gerard, ed. 1984. *La justice sociale comme bonne nouvelle: Messages sociaux, economoques et politiques des évêques du Québec 1972–1983.* Montreal: Bellarmin.

Seljak, David. 1995. "The Catholic Church's Reaction to the Secularization of Nationalism in Quebec, 1960–1980." PhD dissertation, McGill University.

———. 1996. "Why the Quiet Revolution Was 'Quiet': The Catholic Church's Reaction to the Secularization of Nationalism in Quebec after 1960." Canadian Catholic Historical Association, *Historical Studies* 62:109–124.

Sharp, Carolyn. 1995. *"Le mensonge néo-libéral: L'idolâtrie continue du nous appauvrir." Relations* 614:232.

Sortons le Quebec de l'appauvrissement. 1994. Montreal: Secrétariate de l'Assemblée des évêques du Québec.

Taylor, Charles. 1991. *The Malaise of Modernity.* Concord, ON: Anansi.

Vaillancourt, Jean-Guy. 1984. *"Les groupes sociopolitiques progressistes dans le catholicisme québécoise contemporain."* In *Les movements religieux aujourd'hui: Théories et practiques,* eds. Jean-Paul Rouleau and Jacques Zylberberg. Montreal: Bellarmin.

Venne, M. 1995. *"Jé suis aurait-il voté OUI?" Le Devoir,* 14 October, A12.

CHAPTER 4

A LOOK AT CULTURAL EFFECTS ON RELIGIOSITY:
A COMPARISON BETWEEN THE UNITED STATES AND CANADA

Samuel H. Reimer

INTRODUCTION

The vitality of religion in the United States puts it well ahead of other Western countries in most measures of religiosity. An oft-used example of this is the church attendance rate, which has long been a classic measure of religious participation, and often of religiosity as a whole (Greeley, 1989:42). United States church attendance rates have been remarkably stable over the last five decades, while other industrialized countries show marked declines (Gallup, 1990). Not only is the United States unique in the stability of its church attendance, but its weekly attendance rate of roughly 40 percent (Gallup, 1990) is far above that of other industrialized countries (Hatch, 1989:210f). In comparison to their closest (both geographically and culturally) neighbours, the Canadians, Americans are still well ahead of Canadian levels of religiosity even though the Canadians outdo most European countries. Canadian polls show that about 27 percent attended church weekly in 1990 (Gallup 1991:444),[1] though that rate continues to decline (Bibby, 1979:115; 1993:3f). A look at orthodox beliefs, such as the belief in God, life after death, or private practices such as Bible reading and prayer, also consistently show that Americans have higher levels of religiosity than Canadians (Lipset, 1990:84f.; Michalos, 1982:143f.; Bibby, 1987:216f.). Although Canada and the United States share many cultural and historical tendencies, their differences in levels of beliefs and practices are stark. This paper explores this difference. I submit that the anomaly of high levels of religiosity in the United States has more to do with cultural supports for religiosity than with deeper religious conviction. That is to say, impressive levels of religiosity in the United States do not indicate that Americans have more inner religious convictions, but, rather, indicate a conformity to socially approved behaviour, a phenomenon that will be referred to as "conventional" religiosity. By contrast, religiosity in Canada may be prompted to a greater degree by personal religious devotion; it is more likely to be based on "conviction."[2] In this study, measures of religiosity are limited to orthodox belief, practice, experience and salience. A look at the pervasiveness of belief and practice among the unchurched and the strength of the linkages between religious belief and practice demonstrates support for this thesis.

RELIGIOUS DIFFERENCES BETWEEN THE UNITED STATES AND CANADA

To say that the United States has cultural elements that promote religiosity is nothing new; it has been observed by Tocqueville (1959), Herberg (1955), Lipset (1963), Bellah (1975) and others. Although the United States and Canada share many historical events, cultural influences and religious groups, previous research into American–Canadian religious differences has pointed to a variety of historical and structural distinctions that affect cultural differences, which in turn have ramifications for the religious environments in the two countries. Religious differences stem from ideological and cultural differences, including individualism, civil religion, ecumenism, voluntarism, populism and liberalism (to name only some), which have been influenced by major or minor historical differences in religious disestablishmentarianism, frontierism, denominationalism, congregational polity, Puritan influence, national population and geographic size, immigration patterns, revolution, the 1960s counterculture, and other factors (Lipset, 1990; Westhues, 1976; O'Toole, 1982; Bellah, 1975; Hiller, 1978; Mead, 1975; Grant, 1976; Roof and McKinney, 1987).[3] Although it is beyond the scope of this paper to trace the structural and historical sources of cultural differences, some of these differences should be noted that distinguish the religious climate in the two countries.

First, the strength of what might be called "culture-religion" has had a long history in the United States, but not in Canada. In *Protestant–Catholic–Jew*, Will Herberg observed the meshing of culture and religion in the United States. He argued that religious affiliation was a main source of "self-identification" and "social location" for Americans, and that church attendance and certain orthodox Judeo-Christian beliefs (that is, belief in God) were imbedded in culture (1955:35, 63f.). Seymour Martin Lipset also ties U.S. religion and culture together when he states that

> the persistent traits in American religion resemble the constant traits in the American character. They have continued to distinguish America from other countries, precisely because they have stemmed from the basic American values that have remained relatively stable. (1963:169)

Thus, Lipset connects the persistence of religiosity in the United States to the "American character" or "basic American values." For Lipset, U.S. religion has had a unique all-pervasive quality throughout its history (Lipset, 1963:140f.; see also Tocqueville, 1959: 141; Bellah, 1968:6f.).

Lipset also notes that U.S. religion demonstrates the unique blend of both "secularization and widespread adherence," indicating that religious behaviour often lacks conviction (1963:168). He observed that at the same time public religious practice was on the increase, religion was adjusting to secular society in a way that "does not reflect greater religiosity" (Lipset, 1963:141f.; see also Herberg, 1955:13–14). How does one account for this paradox? Herberg says that it occurs because religion has become intertwined with culture, or the "American way of life," which defines religion as desirable. As a result of this cultural precedent, Americans believe the right things and act in religious ways in order to conform, but it is "frequently a religious-ness without serious commitment" (1955:88, 276).

Related to culture-religion is the notion of "civil religion," popularized by Robert Bellah (1968, 1975). Unlike the United States, Canada lacks a pervasive civil religion (O'Toole, 1982; Westhues, 1976; Lipset, 1990; Blumstock,1993; Kim, 1993), if by "civil religion" we mean the tendency to interpret "historical experience in light of transcendent reality" (Bellah, 1975:3). Lipset claims there is no clear historical expres-sion of "national truth" or a sense of a national mission in Canada (1990:79). Westhues finds "no significant evidence for a common interdenominational and national reli-gious creed in Canada, as there is in the United States" (1976:217).

The connection between culture and religion in Canada has been diminished by its failure to establish a clear national identity (Lipset, 1990:42*f.*), largely because Canada maintains two official languages and diverse cultural groups (Curtis and Tepperman, 1990). If Canadians can salvage any kind of national identity, it would likely be the notion of a "mosaic"—a racially and culturally heterogeneous society where ethnic and linguistic diversity are not only tolerated, but celebrated. In a soci-ety that promotes differences, it is difficult to see how a cultural pressure towards con-formity can exist. By contrast, Lipset argues that the United States established its identity on "ideology." Unlike any other nationality, being American involves the appro-priation of "American values," and is not a matter of shared history or birth (1990:19). This difference clearly points to a pressure towards ideological conformity in America (a "melting pot"), which does not exist in Canada.

In sum, then, conventional religiosity is less prevalent in Canada because the soci-ety lacks a strong civil religion, has not intertwined culture and religion to the same degree as the United States, and displays little pressure towards ideological conform-ity. Despite modern cultural changes in both countries, data suggest religious and cul-tural distinctions remain (Lipset, 1990:38*f.*, 212*f.*). Evidence suggests that the United States continues to be influenced by the conventional religiosity noted by Herberg.

HYPOTHESES

If culture-religion in the United States is widespread, as Lipset and Herberg suggest, its effect will not appear except in contrast with another nation; hence, it is necessary to perform a cross-national comparison. In addition, one cannot simply compare levels of religious commitment, for individuals can act and believe religiously because of either social convention or personal conviction. Although private religious practice may at first glance seem a more valid indicator of inner religious conviction (since pre-sumably social pressure would have less effect on private behaviour), it is only meas-urable when reported, a public act that exposes it to societal influences (DeMaio, 1984). Thus, even private religious practices may be subject to overreporting in a socially desirable direction. This means that culture-religion could promote either the overreporting of religious practice, or could produce beliefs and behaviours that match reported levels but are influenced by social convention. As a result, the influence of cultural pressure on religious practice and belief is difficult to identify. To do so, we need to attend to relations among various dimensions of religiosity rather than to the level of any one indicator. That is to say, the effect of cultural aspects that support religiosity cannot be directly measured; instead, they must be measured indirectly. Here, I do not attempt to measure culture-religion directly, but to offer circumstantial evidence that suggests that the normative pressure to believe and act religiously observed by Herberg still exists today. I submit that by examining the levels of orthodox belief among those who rarely attend church and by studying correlations among different measures of religious commitment, it will be possible to uncover evidence for the proposed thesis. The data allow me to test the following three hypotheses.

Hypothesis 1: Levels of orthodox belief and practice will be higher among non-attenders in the United States than in Canada.

By *orthodox belief* I refer to adherence to such traditional Judeo-Christian tenets as belief in God and life after death. Beliefs that are acceptable to the "official" religions—Protestantism, Catholicism and Judaism—are those that are supported by "the American Way of Life," according to Herberg (1955:901). Secondly, orthodoxy refers to a rejection of beliefs that would be considered unconventional compared to traditional Judeo-Christian tenets. These beliefs include an acceptance of extrasensory perception (ESP), precognition, and the belief that it is possible to communicate with the dead. *Orthodox practices* include reading the Bible, saying grace and saying prayers. *Non-attenders* are those who attend religious services several times a year or less.

The justification for this hypothesis comes from the argument of Lipset (1963) and Herberg (1955) that U.S. culture-religion is pervasive. It seems reasonable to predict that aspects of culture-religion would be held by those who rarely attend church as well as those who attend regularly. If the conventionality of church attendance or of orthodoxy stems from cultural roots, non-attending Americans should be affected as well, which should lead to a measurable difference in the prevalence of these beliefs and practices among the unchurched in the two countries. It is important to look at non-attenders here because we are trying to control for levels of religious participation so that we can attribute differences in levels of belief and practice to cultural differences.[4]

Hypothesis 2: There will be a greater difference in levels of orthodox belief and practice between non-attenders and attenders in Canada than in the United States.

If religious belief and practice are culturally supported among those who rarely attend church in the United States, then non-attenders and attenders should be more closely matched on measures of religious beliefs and practice than they are in Canada. If a smaller spread is found in the United States, then differences cannot be attributed to differential levels of religious participation, once church attendance has been controlled. This points to a source of religiosity that is external to religious participation, which, I argue, is culture-religion in the United States.

Hypothesis 3: Indicators of religious commitment will be more highly correlated in Canada than in the United States.

The concept of religious "commitment"—developed and refined by Stark and Glock (1968)—encompasses five dimensions: belief, practice, experience, knowledge and consequences (1968:14). This study makes use of three of Stark and Glock's dimensions—belief, practice and experience—to explore U.S./Canadian differences.[5] In addition, a measure of religious salience (importance of God to the individual) is used (Kellstedt, Green, Guth, and Smidt, 1993; Guth and Green, 1993). Arguably, if these dimensions are found to be more closely linked, or more tightly coupled in one country than the other, this would suggest that individuals are motivated to believe or behave religiously more out of conviction than social convention.

Correlations between the beliefs, practices, experience and salience should indicate how closely linked different measures of religious commitment really are. If religious beliefs stem from social or cultural pressures to conform, one is less likely to interconnect belief with other aspects of commitment. Similarly, if it is socially desirable to report that God is important to one's life, one may state that God is important while showing low commitment on other measures.[6]

METHODS

Three data sets were used to test these hypotheses. The World Values Survey of 1981–1983 (WV) is dated, but provides a perfect match of variables in Canada and the United States. The data set is derived from interviews given to a representative sample of adults eighteen years or older in twenty-two countries (Inglehart et al., 1990; Campbell and Curtis, 1994).

The 1988 General Social Survey (GSS) and the 1990 Project Can90 survey (Can90) were also used because these surveys are recent and have additional matching items. The GSS is drawn from a sample of American, English-speaking, non-institutionalized adults, eighteen years old or older (Davis and Smith, 1991:1). The Canadian Can90 sample is stratified by province and community size, and respondents were drawn from telephone directory listings. It consists of adults, eighteen years or older, from both French- and English-speaking populations. This sample is weighted to ensure a close match to population characteristics, and had a return rate of 61 percent (Bibby, 1993: 315f.). Partly because the Can90 data were collected from a mail survey and the GSS data were collected by face-to-face interviews, not all items used are perfectly matched. Thus, some differences reported from these data sets could be related to methodology.[7] Despite methodological disparity, the results are included because they provide additional comparisons and more current results than those of the World Value Survey.

As I noted previously, the analysis uses Stark and Glock's (1968) measures of commitment, including beliefs, practices (devotional and ritual), and experience. In the GSS/Can90 surveys, "belief" is measured by the items "belief in God," "life after death" and the rejection of beliefs like "ESP," "precognition," and "communication with the dead."[8] Each item was recoded as a dummy variable. The "practice" dimension includes the measures "Bible reading" and "saying grace."[9] To measure "devotionalism," a scale was created from the "Bible reading," "prayer," and "saying grace" items in the GSS/Can90 poll. Items were recoded similar to the belief items above, forming a scale from zero to three (alpha: U.S. = .5486, Canada = .7600). Church attendance is used to tap the "ritual" aspect of practice. In the GSS/Can90 data, church attendance is measured by a nine-point scale, ranging from those who never attend to those who attend "several times a week or more." To measure "experience" an item asks the following:

United States — How close do you feel to God most of the time?
Canada — Do you believe that you have experienced God's presence?

Because these questions are not good matches, they can only suggest differences in religious experience between the countries.

In the World Values survey, "belief" measures include "belief in God," "life after death," "the soul," "the Devil," "Hell," "Heaven," "sin," and rejection of the belief in "reincarnation." The only measure of devotionalism from the World Values survey asked: "Do you take some moments of prayer, meditation or contemplation or something like that?" Thus, only this "prayer" item was used. "Ritual" is measured by a similar church attendance item as the GSS/CAN90 measure, except it uses a seven-point scale. "Salience" is measured by the "importance of God" item, which asks respondents to answer the question "How important is God in your life," coded on a ten-point scale.

RESULTS

Tables 4.1 and 4.2 strongly support hypotheses 1 and 2. As previously stated, orthodox belief and practice are expected to be higher in the United States among those who rarely attend, because these beliefs are part of the wider culture-religion held by attenders and non-attenders alike. In columns A and D in both tables, percentages are given for those who attend church only several times a year or less. Columns B and E show the percentages for those who attend "nearly every week" or more (Table 4.1) and "weekly" or more (Table 4.2). Columns C and F give the differences between weekly attenders and non-attenders. As predicted in hypothesis 2, the Canadian differences are larger than the U.S. differences, which suggests that U.S. levels of religiosity may be influenced by culture-religion.[10]

In Table 4.1, a comparison between columns A and D reveals that U.S. non-attenders are more orthodox in belief and claim higher levels of religious practice than Canadian non-attenders. With a difference of proportions test of significance for independent samples (Harnett, 1982:401), the percentages in column D were significantly greater (at the .01 level) than those reported in column A, except for the "ESP" item (n.s.), and the "communicate with the dead" item, on which Canadians are significantly more orthodox. All remaining differences support hypothesis 1. Figures in column C are significantly greater (at the .01 level) than those in column F except for the "say grace" item (n.s.). The significantly greater differences in column C provide

TABLE 4.1: FREQUENCIES OF MEASURES OF RELIGIOSITY FOR NON-ATTENDERS AND WEEKLY ATTENDERS IN CANADA AND THE UNITED STATES: PROJECT CAN90 AND GSS 1988

	Canadian Respondents (N = 1249)				United States Respondents (N = 1481)		
	A Rarely attend (N = 815)	B Attend weekly (N = 288)	C Difference		D Rarely attend (N = 724)	E Attend weekly (N = 495)	F Difference
Percent Who:				Percent Who:			
believe in God	74.1	96.5	22.4	believe in God	90.6	99.2	8.6
believe in life after death	59.3	84.3	25	believe in life after death	71.4	88.4	17
believe they have experienced God's presence	30.3	74.7	44.4	feel at least somewhat close to God	71.7	97.6	25.9
do not believe in ESP	34.8	57.4	22.7	have never felt in touch with someone far away	35.1	36.9	1.8
do not believe that it is possible to communicate with the dead	75.5	81.8	6.3	have never felt in touch with someone who has died	59.8	62.3	2.5
do not believe that they have experienced an event before it happened	49.2	65.5	16.3	have never seen events at a great distance while they were happening	70	77.9	7.9
read the Bible weekly or more	3.5	64.5	61	read the Bible weekly or more	15.1	57.8	42.7
say grace	13.7	65.4	51.7	say grace	29.8	76.6	46.8

Note: Figures in column D are significantly higher (at the .01 level) than figures in column A, except for the "ESP" (n.s.) and "communicate with dead" items. Figures in column C are significantly greater (at the .01 level) than those in column F exceptt for the "say grace" item (n.s.).

strong support for hypothesis 2, which predicts a greater divergence between Canadian attenders and non-attenders on items of orthodox belief and practice.

For the World Values Survey data in Table 4.2, all the percentages in column D are significantly higher (at the .01 level) than those in column A except the "reincarnation" item (n.s.), further supporting hypothesis 1. The differences listed in column C are significantly greater (at the .01 level) than those in column F except for the "reincarnation" (n.s.), "pray" (.05 significance level), and "soul" (.05 significance level) items, supporting hypothesis 2. Overall, the evidence points to the continued effect of culture-religion on levels of belief and practice in the United States.

Supporting evidence has been found by the Princeton Religious Research Center. In *The Unchurched American* studies, Gallup and associates found that levels of ortho-

TABLE 4.2: FREQUENCIES OF MEASURES OF RELIGIOSITY FOR NON-ATTENDERS AND WEEKLY ATTENDERS IN CANADA AND THE UNITED STATES WORLD VALUES SURVEY: 1981–1983

	Canadian Respondents (N = 1254)				United States Respondents (N = 2325)		
	A Rarely attend (N = 698)	B Attend weekly (N = 386)	C Difference		D Rarely attend (N = 906)	E Attend weekly (N = 991)	F Difference
Percent Who:				Percent Who:			
believe in God	88.1	99.5	11.4	believe in God	94.7	99.9	5.2
believe in life after death	59.5	85.8	26.3	believe in life after death	70.1	87.6	17.5
believe in the soul	78.5	96.5	18.0	believe in the soul	84.7	97.9	13.2
believe in the Devil	31.4	63.8	32.4	believe in the Devil	57.4	81.3	23.9
believe in Hell	27.4	66.9	39.5	believe in Hell	57.6	85.6	28.0
believe in Heaven	61.9	94.8	32.9	believe in Heaven	77.8	97.8	20.0
believe in sin	66.3	89.8	23.5	believe in sin	84.0	95.7	11.7
do not believe in reincarnation	62.2	72.6	10.4	do not believe believe in reincarnation	66.5	77.5	11.0
take time to pray, meditate, or contemplate	62.1	91.5	29.4	take time to pray, meditate, or contemplate	72.1	97.0	24.9

Note: Percentages in column D are significantly higher (at the .01 level) than those in column A except for the "reincarnation" item (n.s.). Differences are significantly larger in column C than in column F (at the .01 level) except for the "reincarnation" (n.s.), "pray" (.05 level) and "soul" items (.05 level).

dox beliefs have increased between 1978 and 1988, even among those considered "unchurched" (1978, 1988).[11] When other measures of commitment either hold steady (e.g., church attendance) or decrease (prayer, Bible reading and Biblical knowledge), increases in orthodox beliefs would seem to indicate that beliefs are influenced by a source other than by religious participation.

Tables 4.3 and 4.4 present correlation coefficients representing relationships between measures of commitment in Canada and in the United States. these coefficients allow us to determine whether the dimensions of commitment are more closely linked in Canada than in the United States, as suggested by hypothesis 3.[12] The differences reported in the bottom section of the tables were obtained by subtracting each correlation from the U.S. sample from the corresponding correlation in the Canadian sample. A positive difference indicates that the dimensions are more closely linked in Canada. The significance of the differences was computed by Fisher and Yates's (1963) test for

TABLE 4.3: DIFFERENCES BETWEEN CANADIAN AND U.S. RESPONDENTS IN THE MAGNITUDE OF CORRELATIONS FOR SELECTED MEASURES OF COMMITMENT: PROJECT CAN90 AND GSS 1988

	Belief in God	Life after death	Devotionalism	Attend church	Experience God
Canadian Correlations (N = 1249)					
Belief in God	1.0				
Life after death	.469	1.0			
Devotionalism	.367	.346	1.0		
Attend church	.357	.272	.669	1.0	
Experience God	.384	.352	.493	.457	1.0
U.S. Correlations (N = 1481)					
Belief in God	1.0				
Life after death	.337	1.0			
Devotionalism	.229	.265	1.0		
Attend church	.219	.220	.492	1.0	
Feel near God	.320	.267	.359	.358	1.0
Differences					
Belief in God		0			
Life after death	.131**		0		
Devotionalism	.137**	.081*	0		
Attend church	.139**	.053	.177**	0	
Experience/feel near God	.064*	.086*	.134**	.099**	0

Significance: ** = .01; * = .05 for one-tailed test.

Note: In the top two sections of the table, all Canadian and U.S. correlations are significant at the .01 level. In the bottom section, a positive difference means that the correlation was greater in Canada.

comparisons between independent correlations (see Cohen and Cohen, 1975:50*f*.).

Tables 4.3 and 4.4 offer strong support for hypothesis 3. All significant correlations are higher in Canada, indicating that Canadians interconnect each aspect of commitment more closely than their U.S. counterparts.

DISCUSSION

In Western societies, religious and secular forces compete for dominance in a culture, each having its advocates. But what happens in a society where religious ideology is supported by culture? In such a situation, the distinction between the secular and

TABLE 4.4: DIFFERENCES BETWEEN CANADIAN AND U.S. RESPONDENTS IN THE MAGNITUDE OF CORRELATIONS FOR SELECTED MEASURES OF COMMITMENT: WORLD VALUES SURVEY 1981–1983

	Belief in God	Life after death	Pray, meditate, contemplate	Attend church	Importance of God
Canadian Correlations (N = 1254)					
Belief in God	1.0				
Life after death	.288	1.0			
Pray, meditate, contemplate	.264	.244	1.0		
Attend church	.292	.262	.350	1.0	
Importance of God	.526	.366	.514	.519	1.0
U.S. Correlations (N = 2325)					
Belief in God	1.0				
Life after death	.233	1.0			
Pray, meditate, contemplate	.189	.288	1.0		
Attend church	.226	.200	.328	1.0	
Importance of God	.382	.282	.455	.412	1.0
Differences					
Belief in God	0				
Life after death	.055*	0			
Pray, meditate, contemplate	.075*	–.043	0		
Attend church	.067*	.062*	.022*	0	
Importance of God	.144**	.084**	.060*	.107**	0

Significance: ** = .01; * = .05 for one-tailed test.

Note: In the top two sections of the table, all Canadian and American correlations are significant at the .01 level. In the bottom section, a positive difference means that the correlation was greater in Canada.

sacred is clouded, and each can be espoused without rejecting the other. Individuals can accept aspects of both the sacred and the secular, intertwining beliefs and behaviours from both sides even though the assumptions on which they are based conflict in ways that are not always clear.[13] Such a society may contain "a paradox—pervasive secularism among mounting religiosity," or a "religiousness" and "secularism" that "derive from very much the same sources" (Herberg, 1955:14–15). I argue that high levels of religiosity exist in the United States partly because of cultural elements that bring the secular and religious together in such a way that they seem complementary instead of conflicting. U.S. culture-religion prompts religiosity through social convention. Other studies support this conclusion.

In 1990, Gallup came to a similar conclusion that Herberg made in the 1950s: namely, that Americans demonstrate high religiosity but low conviction. Gallup gave evidence that religiosity in America is "broad, but not deep" (1990:7). "When we use measurement to probe the depth of religious conviction, we become less impressed with the sincerity of our faith," Gallup stated. He concluded that the "highly committed segment of the populace ... account for a very small percentage of the population" (1990:6–7). Gallup's findings support the thesis I present here.

In related studies, Hadaway, Marler and Chaves (1993) and Chaves and Cavendish (1994) have found that self-reported attendance rates in surveys are nearly twice as high as actual in-church counts. They suggest that this may partially stem from the "social desirability" attached to church attendance, a clear indication of cultural supports for religion. If a measurable public practice like church attendance is over-reported in the United States, it could easily be that private practices, which are much harder to substantiate, are also overreported. While Motz has found overreporting of church attendance in Canada as well, it is difficult to determine from his research the degree to which polling overstates attendance rates (1990:17–18). If my thesis is correct, one would expect less overreporting in Canada than in the United States.

The argument presented here needs to be qualified in several ways. First, I am not suggesting that Canadians are more religious than Americans. As previously noted, Canadians have consistently shown lower levels of private and public religious practice and orthodox religious belief. However, I argue that one cannot detect the effect of a culture-religion by looking at levels of religiosity per se. Thus, it is only through comparisons of the pervasiveness and interconnectedness of these dimensions, contrasted with a country that does not have a strong culture-religion, that the cultural factor becomes evident.

Second, although cultural differences are emphasized in this paper, this does not mean that structural differences are inconsequential.[14] As suggested above, structural distinctions can be the mechanisms through which many cultural differences are realized, and structure and culture can jointly influence religious outcomes (Wuthnow, 1989:17).[15]

Third, there are several possible ways to interpret the gap between U.S. and Canadian levels of religiosity found in this data. First, the gap could indicate a fairly ubiquitous culture-religion or civil religion.[16] Second, observed national level distinctions may be explained better by regional or subcultural influences than by a national culture that characterizes most or all Americans. That is, the observed national-level differences do not necessitate national-level explanations. The observed differences may be better explained as the sum of regional religious or ethnic subcultural differences. For example, the combining of cultural and religious elements may be characteristic only of predominantly white, or middle-class, or older, or less educated, or conservative Protestant

Americans. In Canada, the quasi-establishment of Catholicism in Quebec may mean that some cultural supports for religion have endured in French Canada (Lemieux, 1992). Within-country comparisons would be necessary to flesh out these possibilities.

Finally, evidence shows that, since the 1950s, the cultural supports for religion in America have been weakened by divisive factions and events that challenged its plausibility (Roof and McKinney, 1987:13; Wuthnow, 1988:266). Yet these results suggest that cultural supports for religion may be weakened but nonetheless still remain. The extent to which it remains and how it has changed since the 1960s are beyond the scope of this research.

CONCLUSION

This paper suggests that religion in the United States has conventional elements. To fully establish this proposition, more comprehensive measures will be needed. Nonetheless, these results identify one possible reason for the unusually high levels of religiosity in the United States: the intertwining of cultural and religious elements, which increases levels of religiosity beyond what would be expected from individual religious conviction.

In his classic comparison, *Continental Divide*, Lipset states that "knowledge of Canada or the United States is the best way to gain insight into the other North American country" (1990:xiii). Explanations for the United States' religious vitality have been limited because religious research often stays within U.S. borders. This is particularly limiting because much that has been said about the American "exceptionalism" becomes evident only through cross-national comparison (Lipset, 1963; Shafer, 1991; Tuveson, 1968). The explanation suggested here has been largely ignored, I submit, because cross-national religious data are relatively sparse. If students of religion in the United States look beyond their national boundaries, they may discover a great deal that reflects back on them.

NOTES

1 Pollster Reginald Bibby says the Canadian attendance rate is 23 percent, based on those who say they attend "nearly every week or more" in his 1990 survey (1993:10). A comparable figure in the United States, which comes from the 1988 General Social Survey, is 33 percent. These polls are the ones used in this study.

2 In this paper, the term *conviction* deals with motivations behind religious beliefs and practices. It is used instead of Stark and Glock's term *commitment* (1968) because the conviction/convention distinction is not clearly separated in their measures of commitment. It is also recognized that the terms *convention* and *conviction* carry positive and negative connotations that are not intended here.

3 The connections between culture and religiosity given here do not indicate that there exists in the United States an ideological consensus, or that the combining of religion and culture characterizes all aspects of American religious life. Rather, some cultural and religious elements are combined in the United States, and this culture-religion is more prevalent in the United States than in Canada. I define culture after Geertz: "an historically transmitted pattern of meanings embodied in symbols, a system of inherited conceptions expressed in

symbolic forms by means of which men communicate, perpetuate, and develop their knowledge about and attitudes toward life" (cited in Lipset, 1990:8).

4 I recognize that this hypothesized relationship could also reflect a more religious upbringing, as measured by frequency of church attendance as a child or by attendance at private or parochial schools. Unfortunately, there are no items in the World Values Survey to measure religious upbringing, and there are no responses to the item in the 1988 GSS that measures church attendance in the respondents' childhood years. Canadians are much more likely to have attended parochial schools, whether they are presently non-attenders (25.2 percent) or frequent attenders (38.6 percent), than are Americans (16.6 percent and 23.1 percent respectively). Note also that church attendance levels were higher in Canada than the United States prior to the 1960s (Michalos, 1982:152). In Canada, a more active religious upbringing would presumably have an opposite effect to the hypothesized one, because a more religious upbringing would produce higher orthodoxy.

5 Because there were no matching measures of Stark and Glock's *knowledge* dimension in the data sets used in this study, it could not be included. The *consequence* dimension is not clearly operationalized by Stark and Glock. Because consequences (that is, moral attitudes) are not overtly religious, they are left out of this study, which makes claims only about religiosity.

6 Gallup found that roughly three-fourths of Americans say that religion is very important to them but commonly list other values as more important (1990:7). By comparison, Bibby found that only 26 percent of Canadians say that religion is very important to them (1993:83).

7 It could be argued that interviewing, rather than mail surveys, increases pressure to respond in a socially desirable manner, so that methodology is partly responsible for the inflated religious responses in America. However, a comparison of the Can90 data (obtained by a mailed survey) with the Rawlyk/Angus Reid national Canadian study (obtained by phone interviews) reveals that the interviewing did not increase levels of religiosity on similarly coded items. The polls give equal percentages for weekly church attendance and belief in God, and the Can90 poll gives a slightly higher

percentage for belief in the divinity of Christ. No evidence from the percentages reported from these polls supports the contention that methodology alone would explain away the difference between countries (*Maclean's*, 1993; Swift, 1993).

8 The "belief in God" measures in the two surveys are not good matches. The PC90 survey uses a response scale ranging from strongly agree, agree, disagree, strongly disagree for the statement "God exists." The GSS gives six options: "I don't believe in God," "I don't know whether there is a God and I don't believe there is any way to find out," "I don't believe in a personal God, but I do believe in a Higher Power of some kind," "I find myself believing in God some of the time, but not at others," "While I have doubts, I feel that I do believe in God," and "I know God really exists and I have no doubts about it." For this paper, I have considered the first and second U.S. options negative responses. If the divisions between negative and positive responses in both countries are equidistant from matching Gallup percentages, the third U.S. response would be coded negative as well. The International Gallup Poll puts belief in God at around 95 percent in the United States, and around 87 percent in Canada (1991), both about 8 percentage points below those who chose the last three options in the United States (87 percent) and the first two in Canada (79 percent). For other differences in wording between GSS/Can90 "belief" items, see Table 4.1.

9 The wordings for the "Bible reading" and "say grace" items are as follows:

> GSS — Have you read any part of the Bible at home in the last year? If yes, how often have you read the Bible in the last year?
>
> Can90 — Approximately how often do you read the Bible?
>
> GSS — At your family meals at home, does anyone say grace or give thanks to God aloud before meals?
>
> Can90 — Approximately how often do you say table grace?

Note that in both cases the more restrictive items are from the U.S. survey, which should work against the thesis of this paper.

10 It is feasible that the difference in levels of beliefs for non-attenders could stem from different levels of confidence in organized religion. That is, people with orthodox beliefs may not attend because they

have lost confidence in churches but continue to be religious. The argument is not supported, however, since confidence in organized religion is not higher in Canada (7.8 percent have a "great deal" and 22.9 percent have "little or no" confidence) than in the United States (20.6 percent have a "great deal" and 31.9 percent have "hardly any" confidence).

[11] The "unchurched" are those who are not members or have not attended church in the past six months (Princeton Religious Research Center, 1988:2).

[12] Although there are only five matching measures of commitment in the GSS/Can90 data sets, the World Values Survey has a total of 15. To simplify the tables, only five are reported which matched the GSS/Can90 items. Of the nearly one hundred correlations that could be reported, roughly 80 percent supported the pattern of tighter linkages between variables in Canada.

[13] Berger's notion of "cognitive contamination" is instructive here (1992:38f.). The existence of pluralism, relativism and other forces in a heterogeneous and urbanized society call into question traditional explanations of the world, reducing the taken-for-granted status of these explanations to possibilities. Some will seek "cognitive retrenchment" and reject or even try to re-conquer secularized domains. Others may engage in "cognitive bargaining" or "cognitive surrender" (1992:41). This appears to be the current situation in the United States, where the progressives and the conservatives represent different reactions to secularizing forces, producing the well-documented "Culture Wars" (Hunter, 1991).

[14] Social structure is seen as the context that constrains, legitimates and provides resources for the creation of cultural objects (Berger, 1991; Burns, 1992). I maintain an analytical distinction between structure and culture while recognizing that the plausibility of this distinction is debated by some.

[15] One possible example of culture and structure jointly effecting religious outcomes is in the notion of religious "competition." Although proponents of the New Paradigm (Stark and Bainbridge, 1985; Greeley, 1989; Iannaccone, 1991; Finks and Stark, 1992; Warner, 1993) offer a largely structural (that is, denominational pluralism) explanation for the United States' religious vitality, competitiveness is also more culturally viable in the United States, where an ideology for "utopian moralism," "individualism," and the "pursuit of truth" sponsor it, but not in Canada, where a culture of "tolerance," "ecumenism," and "deference to authority" leaves religious groups to "coexist for servicing" (Lipset, 1990:27, 76f; Bibby, 1987:217; see especially Beyer, 1994).

[16] Christenson and Wimberly have argued from their research that there exists a "fairly uniform level of support for tenets of civil religion" (1978:77) and that "practically all respondents hold civil religious beliefs irrespective of their Christian religious identities" (Wimberly and Christenson 1981:42), which indicates the widespread acceptance of civil religious tenets at that time.

ACKNOWLEDGMENTS

An earlier draft of this paper was presented at the Annual Meeting of the Religious Research Association, Albuquerque, New Mexico, 4–6 November 1994. Thanks to Reginald Bibby for access to his Project Can90 data. I also thank Michael Welch, three anonymous reviewers, the Religion Colloquium at Notre Dame, and especially Mark Chaves for their helpful comments.

REFERENCES

Bellah, Robert. 1968. "Civil Religion in America."
In *Religion in America*, eds. Robert McLoughlin
and Robert Bellah, 3–23. Breton: Houghton
Muffin.

_____. 1975. *The Broken Covenant*. Chicago:
University of Chicago Press.

Berger, Bennett M. 1991. "Structure and Choice in
the Sociology of Culture." *Theory and Society*
20:1–19.

Berger, Peter L. 1992. *A Far Glory: The Quest for
Faith in an Age of Credulity*. New York: Free
Press.

Beyer, Peter. 1994. "Religious Vitality in Canada:
How Valuable Are Religious Market Theories?"
Paper presented at the Annual Meeting of the
Religious Research Association, Albuquerque,
New Mexico, 4–6 November 1994.

Bibby, Reginald. 1979. "The State of Collective
Religiosity in Canada: An Empirical Analysis."
Canadian Review of Sociology and Anthropology
16:105–116.

_____. 1987. *Fragmented Gods: The Poverty and
Potential of Religion in Canada*. Toronto: Irwin
Publishing.

_____. 1993. *Unknown Gods: The Ongoing Story of
Religion in Canada*. Toronto: Stoddart.

Blumstock, Robert. 1993. "Canadian Civil
Religion." In *The Sociology of Religion: A
Canadian Focus*, ed. W. E. Hewitt, 173–194.
Toronto: Butterworths.

Burns, Gene. 1992. "Materialism, Ideology and
Political Change." In *Vocabularies of Public Life:
Empirical Essays in Symbolic Structure*, ed.
Robert Wuthnow. London: Routledge.

Campbell, Robert A., and James E. Curtis. 1994.
"Religious Involvement across Societies:
Analyses for Alternative Measures in National
Surveys." *Journal for the Scientific Study of
Religion* 33:215–229.

Chaves, Mark, and James Cavendish. 1994. "More
Evidence on U.S. Catholic Church

Attendance." *Journal for the Scientific Study of
Religion* 33:376–381.

Christenson, James A., and Ronald C. Wimberly.
1978. "Who Is Civil Religious?" *Sociological
Analysis* 39:77–83.

Cohen, Jacob, and Patricia Cohen. 1975. *Applied
Multiple Regression/Correlation Analysis for the
Behavioral Sciences*. Hillsdale, NJ: Lawrence
Erlbaum Associates.

Curtis, James, and Lorne Tepperman, eds. 1990.
Images of Canada: The Sociological Tradition.
Scarborough: Prentice-Hall Canada.

Davis, James A., and Tom W. Smith. 1991. *General
Social Surveys, 1972–1991: Cumulative
Codebook*. Chicago: National Opinion Research
Center.

DeMaio, Teresa. 1984. "Social Desirability and
Survey Measurement: A Review." In *Surveying
Subjective Phenomena*, eds. Charles Turner and
Elizabeth Martin, 257–282. New York: Russell
Sage Foundation.

Finks, Roger, and Rodney Stark. 1992. *The
Churching of America, 1776–1990*. New
Brunswick, NJ: Rutgers University Press.

Fisher, R.A., and F. Yates. 1963. *Statistical Tables
for Biological, Agricultural and Medical Research*.
6th ed. New York: Hafner.

Gallup, George Jr. 1990. *Religion in America*.
Princeton: Princeton Religious Research
Center.

_____. 1991. *International Gallup Poll*. Princeton:
Princeton Religious Research Center.

Grant, John Webster. 1976. "A Decade of Ferment:
Canadian Churches in the 1960's." In *Religion
in Canadian Society*, eds. Stewart Crysdale and
Les Wheatcroft, 207–218. Toronto: Macmillan
of Canada.

Greeley, Andrew. 1989. *Religious Change in America*.
Cambridge MA: Harvard University Press.

Guth, James, and John Green. 1993. "Salience:
The Core Concept?" In *Rediscovering the*

Religious Factor in American Politics, eds. David Leege and Lyman Kellstedt, 157–176. Armonk, NY: M.E. Sharpe.

Hadaway, C. Kirk, Penny Long Marler, and Mark Chaves. 1993. "What the Polls Don't Show: A Closer Look at U.S. Church Attendance." *American Sociological Review* 58:741–752.

Harnett, Donald L. 1982. *Statistical Methods*. 3rd ed. Reading, MA: Addison-Wesley.

Hatch, Nathan O. 1989. *The Democratization of American Christianity*. New Haven: Yale University Press.

Herberg, Will. 1955. *Protestant–Catholic–Jew*. Garden City, NY: Doubleday.

Hiller, Harry H. 1978. "Continentalism and the Third Force in Religion." *Canadian Journal of Sociology* 3:189–204.

Hunter, James Davison. 1991. *Culture Wars*. New York: Basic Books.

Iannaccone, Laurence R. 1991. "The Consequences of Religious Market Structure." *Rationality and Society* 3:156–177.

Inglehart, Ronald, *et al.* 1990. *World Values Survey 1981–1983 Computer File and Codebook*. 2nd ed. Ann Arbor: Inter-University Consortium for Political and Social Research.

Jacquet, Constant, ed. 1990. *Yearbook of American and Canadian Churches*. Nashville: Abingdon Press. Office of Research, National Council of the Churches of Christ in the U.S.A.

Kellstedt, Lyman, John C. Green, James L. Guth, and Corwin E. Smidt. 1993. "Religious Traditions and Religious Commitments in the U.S.A." Paper presented at the 22nd International Conference of the International Society for the Sociology of Religion, Budapest, Hungary, 9–12 July 1993.

Kim, Andrew E. 1993. "The Absence of Pan-Canadian Civil Religion: Plurality, Duality, and Conflict in Symbols of Canadian Culture." *Sociology of Religion* 54:257–276.

Lemieux, Raymond. 1992. *"La Catholicisme Quebecois: Une question de culture."Sociologie et societes* 22:145–164.

Lipset, Seymour Martin. 1963. *The First New Nation*. New York: Basic Books.

_____. 1990. *Continental Divide*. New York: Routledge.

Maclean's. 1993. "Maclean's Special Report: God Is Alive." 12 April:32–50.

Mead, Sidney. E. 1975. *The Nation with the Soul of a Church*. New York: Harper and Row.

Michalos, Alex C. 1982. *North American Report*, vol. 5. Dordrecht, Holland: D. Reidel.

Motz, Arnell. 1990. "The Condition of the Canadian Church." In *Reclaiming a Nation: The Challenge of Re-evangelizing Canada by the Year 2000*, edited by Arnell Motz, 13–34. Richmond: Outreach Canada Ministries.

O'Toole, Roger. 1982. "Some Good Purpose: Notes on Religion and Political Culture in Canada." *Annual Review of the Social Sciences of Religion* 6:177–217.

Princeton Religious Research Center. 1978. *The Unchurched American*. Princeton: Princeton Religious Research Center.

_____. 1988. *The Unchurched American—Ten Years Later*. Princeton: Princeton Religious Research Center.

Roof, Wade Clark, and William McKinney. 1987. *American Mainline Religion*. New Brunswick, NJ: Rutgers University Press.

Shafer, Byron E. 1991. *Is America Different?* Oxford: Clarendon Press.

Stark, Rodney, and Charles Y. Glock. 1968. *American Piety*. Berkeley: University of California Press.

Stark, Rodney, and William Sims Bainbridge. 1985. *The Future of Religion*. Berkeley: University of California Press.

Swift, Allan. 1993. A Nation of Private Christians? *Faith Today* July/August:21–28.

Tocqueville, Alexis de. 1959. *Journey to America*. New Haven: Yale University Press.

Tuveson, Ernest Lee. 1968. *Redeemer Nation*. Chicago: University of Chicago Press.

Warner, R. Stephen. 1993. "Work in Progress Towards New Paradigm for the Sociological

Study of Religion in the United States."
American Journal of Sociology 98:1044–1093.

Westhues, Kenneth. 1976. "Religious Organization in Canada and the United States." *International Journal of Comparative Sociology* 8:206–223.

Wimberly, Ronald C., and James A. Christenson. 1981. "Civil Religion and Other Religious Identities." *Sociological Analysis* 42:91–100.

Wuthnow, Robert. 1988. *The Restructuring of American Religion.* Princeton: Princeton University Press.

_____. 1989. *Communities of Discourse: Ideology and Social Structure in the Reformation, the Enlightenment and European Socialism.* Cambridge, MA: Harvard University Press.

CHAPTER 5

RELIGIOUS VITALITY IN CANADA:
THE COMPLEMENTARITY OF RELIGIOUS MARKET AND SECULARIZATION PERSPECTIVES

Peter Beyer

INTRODUCTION:
THE CANADIAN CASE AS MEDIATOR

In recent years, rational choice/religious market theories of religion have achieved sufficient prominence especially in U.S. sociology of religion that some commentators have even begun talking about a Kuhnian "paradigm shift" in the field (*cf.* Warner, 1993). Hadden (1987), for instance, argues that the "old" paradigm, manifest in secularization theories such as those of Peter Berger and Bryan Wilson, is inadequate: empirically because religion has in fact not declined as a vital force in modern times; and theoretically because secularization is less a theory than it is an ideological position that laments the decline of certain forms of religion, not religion as such (*cf.* Stark and Iannaccone, 1994). Most intriguing for my purposes here, the contrast between secularization and rational choice/religious market, between old and new paradigm, is also explicitly one between religion in Europe and religion in the United States. A central assumption running through current rational choice/religious market theories is that, contrary to the claim of the old paradigm that the high religious vitality of the United States is an exception to the rule of secularization, just the opposite is the case: the currently low vitality of Europe is the exception for which the United States provides the more general rule.[1] More precisely, religious market theories claim that greater competition within the U.S. religious market has resulted in greater efficiency in the supply of religion and therefore greater religious vitality; whereas in Europe, regulated and even monopolistic religious markets have resulted in inefficiency and hence much lower religious vitality (Finke, 1990; Iannaccone, 1991; Stark and Iannaccone, 1994). The key variable is the degree of competition among suppliers of religion, not the degree of secularization of the society.

Looking at the matter in terms of a contrast between Europe and the United States suggests, however, that what we have here may be a case of name-calling. If a central problem with secularization theory be that it falsely universalizes the European experience (at least to "Western" countries), then religious market theories run the same risk, except that their provincialism would be American. More pointedly, in terms of the theories, if religious market theories allow the reinterpretation of European "secularization" as the result of depressed religious competition, then the defenders of secularization theory might well argue that a "competitive religious market" is simply a synonym for the way secularization has played itself out in the United States (*cf.* Martin, 1978; Stark and Iannaccone, 1994:231; Wilson, 1982:148–153). The implication of this twin possibility is that a potentially better theory than either of the "paradigms" might result if we used the two to correct each other rather than viewing the matter as itself a competition in which one party must be declared the winner. In this paper I develop some possibilities for moving in this direction; and I do this by concentrating on another particular case, the Canadian.

The Canadian case is well suited to this purpose because in many ways it seems to present a hybrid form between Europe and the United States, or at least a third form. This is certainly the case as concerns religion. French-Canadian Roman Catholicism has in the past behaved much like Irish or Polish Catholicism and yet since the 1970s has seemed to conform more to the continental pattern of low practice with continued vague identification (*cf.* Hervieu-Léger, 1993; Lemieux, 1990). In English-speaking Canada, that same denomination has had a history more parallel with the U.S. experience. On the Protestant side, the Church of England was at one time the legally established church in Canada; and Canadian Methodism and Presbyterianism during the nineteenth century had strong British links. Yet all the Protestant denominations have since the middle of the nineteenth century switched to completely voluntaristic organization both in fact and in principle, much like their U.S. counterparts. And Canada has long exhibited the kind of religious pluralism typical of the United States. Most critical for my purposes here, however, is that Canada in the nineteenth century experienced a "churching" of its population in a way that was apparently similar to what happened in the United States at the same time (*cf.* Finke and Stark, 1992; Grant, 1988; Rawlyk, 1990; Westfall, 1989). And yet, since the end of the Second World War, religious practice in Canada seems to have undergone the sort of decline that reminds one more of the European situation. Canada is both similar to and different from the United States and Europe: it would seem to be a quite suitable empirical testing ground for the "duelling paradigms."

The examination of the Canadian case contained in this article reaches the following conclusions: Competition in a pluralistic religious "market" was indeed a factor in the nineteenth-century "churching" of Canada, but this in spite of significant market regulation, not because regulation had first been lifted. What the situation suggests is not simply a correlation of deregulation and religious vitality, but as importantly the rise to prominence of a particular organized form of religion that thrived precisely because it responded to an increasingly secularized socio-structural context: *secularized in the sense of the differentiation of religion and state*.[2] This form was denominational (and to a far lesser extent, sectarian), voluntaristic and evangelistic/devotional—that is, precisely competitive—with a high stress on belonging and regular participation. The domination of this form continued until after the Second World War. Thereafter, religious vitality, as measured by the standards of this hitherto dominant organizational form, declined even though the market was as deregulated as it was in the United States. Although the Canadian religious market has been and continues to be less pluralistic than the U.S., that situation prevailed from the 1870s and cannot be used to explain the post-war decline. The upshot is that the Canadian market is quite clearly "less competitive" and "less vital" than the U.S. one, but *not* due to insufficiency on the "supply side" of the Canadian market. Instead, one should look to shifts in the "demand" structure which have to do with the secularization of much that the religious denominations used to stand for, namely the social project of building Canadian society. Once the demand for religion was no longer supported by its implication in this social project, Canadians shifted in large number to a preference for nondenominational, occasional, and less organized religious consumption that usually affiliates and believes to an extent, but more often prefers not to belong or participate regularly. Thus the denominational form lost much of its "vitality" and with it, institutionalized religion in Canada has lost much of its previous social influence. Taken separately, both secularization and religious market perspectives fail to explain key aspects of this overall Canadian history. Together, they present a more satisfying picture.

THE CHURCHING OF CANADA: 1760–1900

For the sake of clarity, I divide the discussion of the nineteenth-century "churching" of Canada into three parts: a historical overview that sets the scene, a consideration of the statistical evidence, and finally, in a separate section, an interpretation of both the history and the data in terms of secularization and religious market perspectives.

In 1763, the former French possessions in North America passed to the British Crown. It is difficult to say whether Canada was "churched" at this time or not, for this depends on what standards one applies. The vast majority of the population was French-speaking and Roman Catholic. Their church had been the state church under the French regime; it had had the legal power to enforce such things as mass attendance and confession. In 1754, New France had 156 priests and around one hundred churches and chapels for a population of 55,000 (Census of Canada, 1871; Trudel, 1956–1957). Yet it is difficult to say just how high French-Canadian "attendance" was, and the concept of "membership" is meaningless in this case. The historical accounts vary (*cf.* Jaenen 1976:120–157), indicating something short of regular devotion but nowhere near massive indifference. In any case, the Roman church lost power, churches and priests as a result of the conquest: it had to rebuild before it could expand.

As concerned Protestants, it was only after the American Revolutionary War that significant numbers of them even began to arrive. The new colonial masters brought with them an established church in the form of the Church of England. Yet state efforts to enforce the official religious monopoly were half-hearted to non-existent. The Roman Catholic Church was tolerated largely for strategic reasons; and other Protestant groups thrived without much difficulty (*cf.* esp. Clark, 1948). At the beginning of the nineteenth century, the Canadian religious market was, as a result, regulated but nonetheless pluralistic.

The largest portion of the early Protestant settlers in Canada after 1760 came from the United States, especially after the Revolutionary War. Roughly from that war to 1812, Methodist, Baptist and other evangelical movements experienced great success among this segment of the population, launching what S.D. Clark (1948) has called the Great Revival in Canada. Essentially, this was the spread of U.S. evangelical revivalism into Canada. These movements were quite fluid, and therefore what few participation figures survive from this era are not particularly useful. George Rawlyk (1994:121–123) estimates that by 1812 as much as 50 percent of the Protestant population was involved. Even if we doubt the rigour and precision of this historian's conclusion, substantial growth did occur, and this in an atmosphere of official state regulation of religion: if the Methodists and Baptists were not overtly suppressed, the Church of England was certainly given a range of financial and legal privileges. Moreover, one notes that this revival was to a large degree a case of U.S. immigrants bringing their religion with them, and not just an indigenous development. Patterns of immigration and the wider global context have always had a significant effect on how the Canadian religious market has taken shape.

The War of 1812 changed the Canadian Protestant situation in two important ways: new immigrants henceforth came predominantly from Britain, not from the United States; and correspondingly, the style of Canadian evangelicalism shifted in a less radical, less overtly sectarian, and hence more orderly direction that in certain respects was expressly anti-American. Under the influence of the more settled and conservative British versions, most of the Methodists, the Presbyterians of the non-establishment variety, and to a lesser extent the Baptists, gradually moved in the direction of a greater identification with social order and the state. This did not immediately lessen rivalry among these groups, nor did it manifest a wish to join or become the state church. Rather, the now strengthened idea of loyalty to the Crown encouraged most of the religious organizations to see their evangelical project as part of a general effort to build a Christian Canadian society in co-operation with the state. Among the Anglicans and Church of Scotland Presbyterians, we see different but parallel developments. First, as the century wore on, the evangelical style gained ground, even among the Anglicans. Increasingly, evangelical Christianity and its personal, congregational and more emotional style became prominent in most of Canadian Protestantism, regardless of denomination. In conjunction, Anglicans and Presbyterians drifted more and more away from their previous commitment to the idea of church establishment. By the 1850s, the last significant planks of establishment were abolished without significant opposition (see Moir, 1967). The principle of voluntarism had triumphed (cf. Clark, 1948; Rawlyk, 1990; Grant, 1988; Westfall, 1989).

By the 1870s, and certainly by the end of the century, these transformations in Canadian Protestantism had two significant results for our purposes. One was that the different denominations, in spite and because of their competition in a common and peculiarly Canadian social and political context, moved towards one another in terms of the way they offered religion: the consequence of competition was not product specialization so much as product convergence (cf. Noll, 1992:262–284). One expression of this convergence was the move towards church unions which saw almost all the Presbyterians forming one church in 1875 and almost all the Methodists doing likewise in 1884. The second outcome was the successful "churching" of a very large portion of the Canadian nominally Protestant population by these same converging and unifying denominations and not by potential rivals. In an atmosphere where the churches that grew were the ones representing and building the Canadian social order, the sectarian groups by and large lost out (see Hiller, 1978; Westfall, 1989).

As concerns Canadian Catholicism of this period, between 1760 and 1840, the Roman Catholic Church of Canada was overwhelmingly French-speaking and located in what is now Quebec. It concentrated its resources on institutional survival and the setting up of basic structures. The 1840s, however, ushered in significant changes. Large numbers of Irish immigrants swelled the English-speaking Catholic population; the colonial regime lifted what remained of the restrictions on Catholic operations; and the spread to Canada of the nineteenth-century Catholic devotional revolution meant that this church also shifted its focus to consistent involvement of the mass of believers as the basis of institutional strength. What evangelicalism was for the Protestants, devotionalism was for the Roman Catholics.

In Montreal during 1840 and 1841 it began. Charismatic preachers, temperance campaigns, the introduction of new devotions and pious confraternities, the importing and founding of new orders, the control of Catholic education were all part of the new strategy. By the 1870s, ultramontane, devotional Roman Catholicism was solidly established in Quebec. In the 1850s, bishops in English Canada began seriously to take up the torch. Seeing the poverty, destitution and religious laxity among their new charges from Ireland, they mobilized to rescue them from irreligion and Protestantism— terms close enough to being synonymous for them just as the reverse was the case for many Protestants. Charitable efforts helped in this endeavour; but the religious key was again the building up of parishes and the introduction and spread of devotions and confraternities. By the 1890s, the Catholics of Canada—both English- and French-speaking—much like those of Ireland and the United States (*cf.* Finke and Stark, 1992:109*ff.*), had succeeded not only in rescuing nominal Catholics from Protestantism and the secular liberal world, but in positively turning the large majority of them into devoted and practising Catholics (see Murphy and Stortz, 1993). Catholics, therefore, conformed to the pattern of how Canada was "churched." They shared in the success and for some of the same reasons.

The statistical data for nineteenth-century Canadian religion, although not without problems, all point in the same direction as the qualitative material of historians: by the closing decades of the nineteenth century, the Canadian population was significantly "churched," quite possibly to the tune of over 50 percent of the population as regular participants.

The nominal affiliation figures available from various censuses, while not very useful for gauging the percentage of the population actually "churched," do give one good indication of the relative strength of the different denominations. Table 5.1 summarizes the available census data from 1842 to 1901. Catholic percentages diminish and then stabilize, but this is largely due to the greater growth through immigration in predominantly Protestant Ontario as compared with overwhelmingly Catholic Quebec. The most notable trends are the growth of Methodist and, to a lesser extent, Presbyterian and Baptist groups; and this even well before the end of establishment in the 1850s. Also important is the extent to which these five denominational groupings dominated

TABLE 5.1: RELIGIOUS AFFILIATION IN CANADA: 1842–1901

% of total population

Denomination	1842/1844[1]	1851[2]	1861[2]	1861	1881	1901
Roman Catholic	53.8	50.5	47.1	44.4	41.4	41.5
Anglicans	12.8	14.8	15.0	15.0	13.3	12.9
All Presbyterians	10.9	13.1	13.8	15.3	15.6	15.9
All Methodists	8.3	12.6	15.2	14.2	17.2	17.1
All Baptists	1.7	2.8	3.1	6.4	6.9	5.9
Total of above	87.5	93.8	94.2	95.3	94.4	93.3
No affiliation[3]	8.5	2.6	1.3	1.4	2.1	0.9

[1] = Ontario (Upper Canada) in 1842 + Quebec (Lower Canada) in 1844
[2] = Upper and Lower Canada only
[3] = No religion or not stated

Source: Canadian Censuses, 1842–1901.

the Canadian religious market from mid-century and before. With over 90 percent of affiliates, the examination of Canadian "churching" can effectively be restricted to them.

A more solid indicator of actual religious involvement can be found in the census figures for the number of church buildings possessed by each denomination. Table 5.2 shows a veritable boom in construction for all the major denominational groupings in Ontario and Quebec (with over 80 percent of the national population) especially from 1851 to 1871. That the boom was underway before this time is indicated by Quebec figures for the 1827–1851 period, which show church growth of 176 percent during a time when population grew by only 87 percent (Census of Canada, 1871). By 1901, Canada's churches had a seating capacity of 3,842,332 seats for a total population of 5,371,315 (Census of Canada, 1901). If one considers that the majority of these churches held more than one Sunday service, then it becomes apparent that Canada's churches had seating to accommodate more than the total population. As a small and partial indicator of how many of these seats were occupied on any given Sunday, two surveys carried out by newspapers in Toronto in 1882 and 1896 showed, respectively, 78 percent and 57 percent of seats occupied during any given service (*Globe*, 1882; *Evening Telegram*, 1896).[3]

Nineteenth-century Canadian church membership data is somewhat difficult to use, because it is often sparse, but more importantly because the category is difficult to apply to Roman Catholics and to a lesser extent Anglicans, denominations that together constituted well over half the population. In 1901, Canadian census officials made an unrepeated attempt to measure the total number of "communicants," without, however, trying to control what this term meant to the many church officials queried. These results show church "membership" in Canada at that time of about 48 percent if estimates are made to include children. Table 5.3 gives membership statistics for the three main Protestant denominations for the period 1881 to 1951. At least for the Methodists and Presbyterians, one notes growth from 1881 to 1901 both in terms of members and overall "market share." Thereafter, we see a slight weakening with respect to this last measure, but overall a fair amount of stability. The Anglicans, for whom reliable nineteenth-century figures are not available, show growth more or less throughout the first half of the twentieth century, notably benefitting from the massive immigration of the first two decades. The Roman Catholic affiliation percentages are given as the best available indicator of the comparative strength of this numerically dominant denomination. The 1901 Census shows Catholic "communicants," adjusting for children, as constituting about 28 percent of the total population, but this is the only even approximately reliable "membership" indicator we have for this denomination during this era.

In general, although the available statistical data from the era under scrutiny are wanting in certain aspects, they do support the notion that the mainline denominations experienced steady growth during the nineteenth century, and, roughly speaking, stasis during the first half of the twentieth century. In spite of slightly stronger or weaker performance for this or that denomination, this relative stasis will become especially clear when we compare this era to the declines after the Second World War.

TABLE 5.2: NUMBER OF CHURCHES PER DENOMINATIONAL GROUP IN ONTARIO AND QUEBEC: 1851–1901

Denomination	1851	1871	1901	% church increase	% affiliate increase
Roman Catholic	511	903	1398	173.6	99.0
Anglicans	344	687	1179	242.7	67.4
All Presbyterians	344	791	1268	268.6	125.3
All Methodists	592	2055	2441	313.7	209.6
All Baptists	140	411	490	250.0	150.1
All Groups	2134	5164	7569	254.7	105.1

Source: Canadian Censuses, 1851–1901.

DEREGULATION AND COMPETITIVE PLURALISM AS REFLECTION OF SECULARIZATION

Interpreting the nineteenth-century Canadian story in terms of religious market and secularization perspectives shows that both offer insights, but that neither can account in any complete way for what happened. On the religious market side, the rise of the various denominations did occur in a context of pluralistic competition among various religious groups; and in the second half of the century, this occurred in the absence of any official state regulation. One quasi-established church, the Church of Scotland, declined substantially in the deregulating atmosphere after 1840, losing out to Canadian and voluntaristic Presbyterian groups until union absorbed them all in 1874 (*cf.* Moir, 1987). As well, two groupings least associated with establishment, the Methodists and the voluntaristic Presbyterians, were the most successful in gaining "market share"; while the establishment Church of England lost some ground by this measure. Finally, the Roman Catholic Church seems to have experienced its best growth only after state restrictions on them were abandoned after 1840, although here the quantitative data are inconclusive.

TABLE 5.3: MEMBERSHIP IN LARGEST PROTESTANT DENOMINATIONS: 1881–1951

Number of Members (in 1000s), and as % of Total Population

		1881	1901	1921	1941	1961
Methodist/United[1]		170[2]	289	401	717[3]	834
	% Members/ population	3.9%	5.4%	4.7%	6.2%	6.0%
Presbyterian[1]		117	214	351	174[3]	177
	% Members/ population	2.7%	4.0%	4.0%	1.5%	1.3%
Anglican[4]		—[5]	368	690	836	1096
	% Members/ population		6.9%	7.9%	7.7%	7.8%
Roman Catholic						
	% Aff./population	41.4%	41.5%	38.6%	43.3%	43.3%

1. Membership figures do not include children.
2. 1884 figures.
3. Methodist and half Presbyterians became bulk of new United Church of Canada in 1925.
4. Inclusive membership category = "Total Souls on Parish Rolls"
5. Not available.

Source: Censuses of Canada 1881–1951: Yearbooks of the three Protestant denominations.

Not so favourable to religious market explanations is that much of this Canadian church growth did happen in an atmosphere of state regulation. Before the 1850s, tolerance, sometimes grudging, was there, but not the equal treatment of all religious providers. Yet voluntaristic and denominationally organized religion was gaining sway in spite of attempted regulation, not because of its absence. The causal chain predicted by current religious market theories was here somewhat reversed: competitive, pluralistic religion was part of a development that lead to deregulation, not the other way around. Moreover, although it lost somewhat in "market share," the previously established Anglican Church, far from collapsing under the weight of its own inflexibility and torpor, could and did become competitive in a pluralistic and more and more deregulated environment. On the other side, one notes the relative failure of the supposedly highly competitive Baptists to gain a large "market share." Quite clearly, in nineteenth-century Canada, more factors than state regulation and pluralism are at work in determining winners and losers.

Here cannot be the place for considering all the other possible factors (*cf.* Hiller, 1978; Murphy and Perin, 1996; Westfall, 1989). Instead, I look at the insights offered by secularization theory for understanding the situation. By secularization theory, I refer not to some simplistic notion of religious decline under conditions of modernity, but rather to a more elaborate and nuanced theoretical framework such as that of David Martin (1978). For Martin, as for most other main defenders of the "old paradigm," what is fundamentally at issue is the differentiation of religion from other spheres of social life: the secularization of non-religion, and not simply the decline of religious influence. What is to be examined in each region where such differentiation occurs are the religious changes that express the new context. To what extent and when the decline of religious influence sets in as a result depends to a large degree on the character of those changes.

In the case of nineteenth-century Canada, what secularization theory points to is in one sense the same as what the religious market perspective emphasizes, namely the separation of religion and state in conjunction with the rise of a competitive religious "market" characterized by pluralism and privatization (voluntarism). Secularization theory, however, does not require that one happen before the other. The Canadian push towards religious organizations independent of state tutelage paralleled the tendency of the state to put less and less stock in direct religious legitimation. More than anything else, that twin change expressed itself in the principle of voluntarism, which had become the norm by the 1850s. This voluntarism points to competition among religious groups, but where secularization theory goes beyond market explanations is by including the notion that differentiation presents a challenge for religion to maintain its broader social influence. Both Canadian Roman Catholics and Protestants of the nineteenth century provide good illustrations of what is at issue here.

For the broader Roman Catholic Church of the late eighteenth and nineteenth centuries, the "liberalization" and "rationalization" of Western societal structures represented the threat of societal apostasy and thus chaos. The "religious" competition or threat for the Roman Catholic leadership was therefore not just the Protestants, but more broadly what the Protestants represented: precisely the democratic, liberal and rationalist—that is, secular—ideals which seemed to be sweeping so many nations. In response, once the defence of the *ancien régime* alliance of throne and altar had failed, the Catholic Church switched to a triumphalist, pillarizing and competitive policy of reclaiming Catholics directly rather than via the old medium of the state. This was the direction pursued in most countries, including Canada. The Roman Catholic Church, in other words, was competing against the secularization of societal structures as much as it was against Protestants.

The scenario is well exemplified in the Roman Catholic nationalism that took hold in Quebec during the latter part of the nineteenth century. There the French-speaking nation was identified as necessarily Catholic; and in opposition to an English-speaking

Protestant nation, one of the hallmarks of which was deemed to be that core structure of liberal modernity: capitalism. The Catholic and national elite accordingly regarded the survival of the French-Canadian nation, the defence of Roman Catholic faith, the distrust of capitalism and the modern state, and the rejection of Protestantism as of a piece. To compete was essential for the sake of the nation, religion and social order; and that meant incorporating the French-Canadian masses into the church as participants and not just as subjects.

On the Protestant side, the Anglican divines of the earlier nineteenth century who opposed disestablishment again illustrate that the problem was modernity as much as it was other religious groups. In particular, they lamented the attraction that the evangelical forms of religion had for the mass of ordinary people. Central to their fears was that evangelical religion was but one aspect of a more general democratization of society which radically questioned the more hierarchical and authoritarian order that they represented. Their notion of religion was aristocratic in the sense that it saw the close relation between church and state as essential for upholding a proper social order. State support was necessary precisely because the power of religion should not be beholden to the masses for its upkeep and health. Vitality, in other words, was simply not defined in terms of voluntary membership and regular participation of the masses. This of course was desirable, but not at the cost of denaturing what they considered to be "true" religion. Quite clearly, the establishment leaders in the late eighteenth and early nineteenth centuries were not "market" oriented; the evangelicals were (*cf.* Clark. 1948; Grant, 1988; Noll, 1992; Rawlyk, 1990).

Like the Catholics both inside and outside Quebec, the Anglicans ended up joining the movement towards the denominationalizing of religion; or, what amounts to the same, towards the democratization of religion in the sense of a shift in emphasis to the participatory incorporation of all nominal affiliates. That shift was necessary for a religious market to arise in the first place. "Market deregulation" only makes sense if people start treating religion as something to be marketed.

If we now continue with the question of why such a market orientation took place, then secularization theory again offers a possible answer. The denominational form of religion is precisely an expression of the fact that religious authority was no longer or could no longer be enforced by or expressed through the state. More generally, as functionally differentiated societal systems with their own, increasingly independent values and rationalities strengthened in the eighteenth and nineteenth centuries, religion was, so to speak, thrown back more and more on its own particular resources. It became less and less possible in the Western world to define religious strength or vitality in terms of societal authority buttressed and enforced through the triple mechanisms of the state, the church and an aristocratically defined social order. If religion was to continue to thrive as an institutionalized form of human endeavour, it had to find alternative ways of defining and reproducing itself. In North America, at least, the very effective answer was to develop religion deliberately as a form quite separate from all others, whether political, economic or class-based. That form was voluntaristic, communal in the sense of congregational (including parochial), and organized.

On the negative side, where secularization theory apparently fails in nineteenth-century Canada is precisely in the absence of a meaningful decline of religious influence. Rather the opposite seems to be the case. A critical factor needs to be underlined, however. The Canadian churches in the nineteenth century were more than purely religious organizations. They were also social service agencies, social clubs, substantial providers of education at all levels, and health-care providers. They provided critical resources that were not controlled by the Canadian state, but that helped the state to develop Canadian society. These auxiliary functions supported and contributed to their growth, and not simply the efficient provision of purely religious goods. It is only in light of developments in later twentieth-century Canadian religion, however, that the nineteenth-century success reveals itself to have been a very effective, but ultimately temporary solution to the challenge presented to religion in secularizing social structures.

THE SECULARIZATION OF THE CANADIAN RELIGIOUS MARKET

Post-Second World War Developments to 1991

The possibility that the foregoing raises is that denominational competition, at least in Canada, may have been the expression of a transition of religion from a churchly and state-supported form to a privatized form. But does privatized religion necessarily mean the continued strength and vitality of the denominational form? Evidence from Canada of the post-Second World War period suggests that it may not.

We can summarize the story of Canadian religion between the end of the nineteenth century and the end of the Second World War very briefly with three observations. First, the movement towards church union continued such that in 1925 most of the Presbyterians, almost all the Methodists, and a smattering of smaller organizations united to form the United Church of Canada. As a result, the four largest religious organizations became three: the Roman Catholics, the Anglicans and the Uniteds. Second, the religious market continued to be dominated by these oligopolistic players. As Table 5.4 shows, the Canadian censuses of 1941 and 1951 indicate that the three of them could still claim around 78 percent of the population as affiliates. Presbyterians, Baptists and Lutherans accounted for a total of another 15 percent and 12.5 percent in the two years. Third, and perhaps most important for our purposes, at the end of this period, the Canadian population as a whole seemed to be at least as "churched" as it was at the beginning, perhaps even more so. In 1946, the Gallup organization conducted a poll which showed an attendance rate of 67 percent for a seven-day period; 83 percent of Catholics and 60 percent of Protestants claimed attendance (see Table 5.6). The statistics on membership are also quite impressive. Table 5.5 shows membership numbers and "market share" for the six largest Protestant denominations as well as an estimate of the total "churched" population, which adds Catholics according to the rough proportion who attended at around the same time. This measure lacks somewhat in precision because of difficulties in judging membership figures for some denominations (see Mentzer, 1993) and because it uses a proxy for Catholic membership. If anything, however, it underestimates Canadian membership because it does not include from 7 percent to 13 percent of the religiously affiliated population. Conservatively, therefore, in 1951, at least 56 percent of the population was members of the seven groups, quite possibly a higher proportion than at the end of the nineteenth century.

TABLE 5.4: RELIGIOUS AFFILIATION IN CANADA: 1901–1991

Denomination	% of Total Population						
	1901	1921	1941	1951	1961	1981	1991
Roman Catholic[1]	41.5	38.6	43.3	44.7	46.7	47.3	45.7
Anglican	12.9	16.0	15.2	14.7	13.2	10.1	8.1
Methodist/United[2]	17.1	13.2	19.2	20.5	20.1	15.6	11.5
Presbyterian[2]	15.9	16.0	7.2	5.6	4.5	3.4	2.4
Baptist	5.9	4.8	4.2	3.7	3.3	2.9	2.5
Lutheran	1.7	3.3	3.5	3.2	3.6	2.9	2.4
Pentecostal	—	0.1	0.5	0.7	0.8	1.4	1.6
Total of above	95.0	92.0	93.1	93.1	92.2	83.6	74.2
No affiliation	0.9	0.5	0.3	—[3]	—	7.4	12.5

1. Includes Ukrainian Catholics in all years but 1901 and 1921.
2. See note 3, Table 5.3 above.
3. "No religion" or "not stated" were not options in 1951 and 1961.

Source: Statistics Canada 1949:155; 1980:162; 1993.

By these measures, then, Canada remained a country in which people participated regularly within the framework of their religious denominations of the nineteenth century. After a century and a half of competition among religious denominations, and approximately sixty years of a market in which three or four "firms" held over three-fourths of the "market share," Canada was and remained a religiously vital place in terms of typically denominational criteria.

Although the 1950s were, as in the United States, religiously optimistic times, Canada did not maintain this level of religious vitality in the subsequent post-war decades. The 1950s already show some indications of decline, but not sharp ones (see Tables 5.5 and 5.6; Bibby, 1987:14–17; 1993:6). Notably the membership proportion remains about the same, largely because of continued Catholic strength and the overall post-war "baby boom." Between 1960 and 1990, however, declines were sharp on all fronts except certain segments of the conservative Protestant sector that accounted for less than 4 percent of the population.

Let me begin with the Catholics. Although the affiliation rates have remained high (45.7 percent of the population in 1991; Statistics Canada, 1993) and attendance rates remain above the national average, the Quiet Revolution in Quebec and the Second Vatican

Council more generally ushered in a period of rapid decline especially in regular atten-dance (see Table 5.6). Quebecers went from 88 percent stated regular attendance in 1965 to about 29 percent in 1990 (Bibby, 1993:6; see also Baril and Mori, 1991:22). Outside Quebec the change was not as drastic, but the corresponding 1990 figure is down more than 40 points from the late 1950s to stand currently at 43 percent. Indeed, Catholics accounted for most of the Canadian attendance decline after the mid-1970s. If we com-bine this with the well-known failure of Canadian Catholics to pay much attention to the moral directives of their church (cf. Jenish, 1993), then we must conclude that Canadian Catholics are much less committed to their church than they used to be.

TABLE 5.5: MEMBERSHIP IN SIX LARGEST PROTESTANT DENOMINATIONS: 1951–1991

Number of Members (in 1000s), Including children, and Members as % of Total Population (Members exclusive of children in brackets)

Denomination		1951		1961		1981		1991	
United		1011	(834)	1273	(1037)	1018	(900)	888	(786)
	% Members/ population	7.2%		7.0%		4.2%		3.3%	
Presbyterian		205	(177)	237	(201)	182	(164)	174	(157)
	% Members/ population	1.5%		1.3%		0.8%		0.6%	
Anglican[1]		1096		1358		915		848	
	% Members/ population	7.8%		7.4%		3.8%		3.1%	
Baptist[2]		162	(135)	168	(138)	242	(212)	249	(220)
	% Members/ population	1.2%		0.9%		1.0%		0.9%	
Lutheran		142	(121)	208	(172)	242	(219)	229	(208)
	% Members/ population	1.0%		1.1%		1.0%		0.8%	
Pentecostal[2]		57	(45)	75	(60)	254	(213)	332	(282)
	% Members/ population	0.4%		0.4%		1.1%		1.2%	
Total of above	% Members/ population	19.1%		18.1%		11.8%		10.1%	
National Estimate (includes Roman Catholics)	% Members/ population	56.0%		57.0%		35.0%		27.0%	

1. Inclusive membership statistics, children included.

2. 1951 and 1961 are taken from Bibby, 1987:14. For Baptists, this includes only Convention Baptists. 1981 and 1991 are taken from *Yearbooks*.

Sources: Yearbooks of American and Canadian Churches, 1972–1994; Bibby, 1987:14; Statistics Canada 1948, 1980, 1993; Table 5.6 on the next page.

On the Protestant side, the story must be divided into liberal and conservative versions. The liberal churches, including the large Anglican and United churches, have been hit especially hard. Following Bibby's research, both the Anglicans and Uniteds are down to 15 percent weekly attendance; the Lutherans and Presbyterians even lower. Since the early 1960s, absolute official membership numbers for the Anglicans, Uniteds and Presbyterians have declined (see Table 5.5). In addition, the Census Canada decennial affiliation figures for Anglicans, Uniteds, Lutherans and Presbyterians have all declined since their 1971 highs, in the case of the United Church by almost 18 percent. Between 1981 and 1991, the Baptists and the Salvation Army also joined this group (see Table 5.4).

The story among at least some of the conservative Christian churches is different. Here, overall attendance rates remain high. Bibby reported 60 percent regular attendance in 1985; and a still significant 48 percent in 1990 (1987; 1993). The conservative churches probably account for the arrest in the decline of Protestant attendance figures after 1975 (see Table 5.6; Bibby, 1993:104). The Pentecostal churches are just about the only Christian group of any size growing in terms of both membership and affiliated percentage of the population. Many other smaller groups such as Evangelical Fellowship Baptists, the Christian and Missionary Alliance and the Mormons also show good growth. Even here, however, Pentecostal growth, as perhaps the leading indicator, has slowed noticeably in the past decade both in terms of membership and affiliation (Bibby, 1993:6; Statistics Canada, 1993).

TABLE 5.6: CHURCH ATTENDANCE IN CANADA: 1946–1996

% who claimed attendance during 7-day period									
	1946	1957	1965	1970	1975	1980	1985	1990	1996
Overall	67	60	55	44	41	35	32	27	30
Roman Catholic	83	87	83	65	61	50	43	37	37
Protestant	60	43	32	28	25	26	29	24	37

Sources: Gallup Reports 1946–1996; Bibby, 1987:16.

Beside the relative strength of certain churches in the conservative Protestant segment, the two areas of solid growth in the Canadian religious market are in the "no-religion" category and among non-Christian religions. Thus, for instance, the religious "nones" have grown from 7.4 percent of the population in 1981 to 12.5 percent in 1991; in absolute numbers this represents 90 percent growth. Among non-Christians, Muslims, Sikhs, Hindus and Buddhists in particular have grown markedly, especially over the last two decades. In 1981, these groups accounted for 1.2 percent of the Canadian population; by 1991, this figure had risen to 2.7 percent (compare Pentecostals at 1.6 percent and Baptists at 2.5 percent). This growth, however, far from revealing successfully competing religious groups, is almost entirely the result of recent patterns of immigration, a familiar factor in Canadian religious history.

Interpreting the Canadian Story

Given this overall picture, the task that remains, of course, is to interpret the data. Are we dealing with patterns that current versions of religious market theory can explain? Is this simply proof for the secularization theorists? Or, as I suggest, is this situation, like the one of nineteenth-century Canada, best seen as a combination of both?

One possibility that springs directly from religious market theory is that Canada is now suffering the effects of a too highly concentrated religious market. The argument might go something like this: because they had such a large market share by the end of the nineteenth century; and because they had become identified with social order, power and privilege, the large liberal Protestant denominations eventually became uncompetitive. Beginning with the rise of the Social Gospel, the Anglicans, Presbyterians, and especially Methodists/Uniteds allowed their "product line" to lose much of its supernatural character and thus its identifiable religiousness. As long as this liberalization could be styled as the attempted "Christianization" of Canadian society in the face of industrialization, urbanization and massive immigration—the idea of building "His Dominion" (cf. Clifford, 1977)—liberal Protestants kept up their membership and regular participation. The failure of this effort, which gradually became manifest in the post-war era, left these denominations with little effective product to offer their affiliates: hence the decline, especially among the most socially oriented of the churches, the United Church.

On the Catholic side, the story has a different sequence. This church remained competitive both in French and English Canada, for the same reasons as in the nineteenth century: the perceived threat from an "a-religious," modernizing world identified with Protestantism. The result was a continuation of the buffering, pillarizing policy, with or without a nationalist overlay. In the early 1960s, however, the Second Vatican Council abandoned precisely this policy, permitting Catholics to be like everyone else: the religious product no longer maintained a requisite tension with surrounding society and thereby lost much of its value (cf. Stark and Finke, 1992:257ff.). In Quebec, the Quiet Revolution added to this development by effecting the transfer of the nationalist project to the Quebec state, thus depriving the Roman Catholic Church of a further large portion of its role in French-Canadian society. Predictably then, in English Canada the Catholic decline was significant, but not as sharp as it was in French Canada.

A final plank in this argument would be that Canadians, because of the religious capital they had invested in these dominant firms, are presently only gradually becoming available again for genuinely competitive religion, such as that offered by the conservative Protestants (cf. Hiller, 1978:204f.), integrist Catholics or perhaps non-Christian groups such as the Muslims. Accordingly, the turnaround in the Canadian situation awaits the next two or three decades.

Although this argument is certainly plausible in its broad outlines, two important problems arise as soon as one looks at the situation more closely. These have to do with the relative failure of other, particularly sectarian and conservative evangelical groups to make significant headway in churching mainline losses; and with the historical timing of the mainline decline. I deal with the second point first.

If the Canadian mainline Protestant churches declined because of their internal secularization, which in turn was due to their possession of what amounted to a religious cartel, then one would expect the effects of this to appear earlier than one hundred years after the secularization process had begun (cf. Clark, 1948, in particular for the Methodists) and the cartel had been established. Also, even though the decline began in some respects in the first decade after the Second World War, participation and membership (cf. Bibby, 1987:14–15; 1993:8) remained quite high until the 1960s. It therefore becomes entirely possible to see the post-1960 rapid decline—and now including the Roman Catholic Church—not as the result of what the churches, the suppliers, did wrong that they had done right before, but as the result of a change in the "market" in which the churches operated. This change will have had its antecedents well back in the nineteenth century along with corresponding changes in the churches, such as is evidenced by the rise of the Social Gospel movement in Canada. It was only in the post–Second World war era that there occurred the more critical denouement of these market changes which had the more critical effect on the churches.

Among those who have examined the situation, Jacques Zylberberg and Pauline Côté (Zylberberg, 1990; Zylberberg and Côté, 1993) offer a useful interpretation that proceeds along such lines. Their position, reminiscent of market theory, is that the decline in the churches had to do with the growth of the (Canadian) state and its interference in what was at one time the domain of the churches. One can divide their argument into two parts, corresponding to the pre- and post-war eras. Thus, from the late nineteenth century, the Canadian state, while not regulating religion in any direct fashion, co-opted the major churches in a nation-building project that favoured the progressive extension of state power at all levels without a parallel benefit to the churches: these were no more than resources and partners-of-convenience until the state structures could take over (cf. Westfall, 1989). In slightly different words, the Canadian state used the institutional power and influence that the churches—both French and English, both Protestant and Roman Catholic—had built up in the nineteenth and early twentieth century to further its own aggrandizement in terms of power and resources. The post-war era then witnessed the extension of this development to the point where the state no longer needed the churches as partners and took over completely their erstwhile functions in such areas as education, social welfare and the like. The churches, thus deprived of resources and their previous partnership in building the country, declined as a result.

While one could argue with some specifics of this viewpoint, especially its rather Machiavellian and anarchistic overtones, the intriguing aspect for our purposes here is that it points to a convergence of market and secularization explanations of Canadian religious history. For what we have here is the extension of state regulation to all areas of social life in such a way as to make the churches irrelevant to the largest portion of what happens in Canadian society. This, of course, is entirely in line with secularization theory, which sees the root of the process in the desacralization and expansion of those spheres of society not expressly and differentiatedly religious. Yet it also corresponds with religious market theory to the extent that it shows how state regulation makes those religious firms most identified with it—culturally if not administratively and legally—uncompetitive. It shows how indirect state regulation might both be conceived and work concretely.

This said, Zylberberg and Côté's interpretation of religious decline in Canada also contradicts religious market theory. From their perspective, lack of competitiveness applies to all religious groups, not just those previously co-operating with the state, precisely because they are all thrown back on purely religious activity alone. Left simply with a supernatural product, they would seem to imply, the churches cannot compete in the successful way they did before. Indeed, following this line of argument, the conservative churches should be able to compete better in this new market than the liberal ones, and the Roman Catholics better than the liberal Protestants, because they concentrate more on the purely religious. That is the upside. But the market is now much smaller since it consists only of those potential adherents who want large amounts of such a supernatural product: the rest will become occasional consumers, people who, as Bibby says, don't so much drop out as drop in when the mood or exceptional need strikes them (1987).

This line of argument also addresses the comparative failure or at least lack of success of other religious groups, notably the conservative-evangelical wing of Protestantism, in Canada. If the reason that the Canadian churches of the nineteenth century succeeded so well was that they fulfilled functions that the state and other secular institutions, once developed, could also fulfill, then one would not expect alternative religious groups uninvolved and unconcerned with the project to be particularly strong. Correspondingly, other religious groups would not fill the breech left by the post-war decline of the mainline churches because the market conditions have changed. Put in terms of supply and demand, the demand for religion before the 1960s was high because it was bolstered by the demand for, strictly speaking, non-religious goods. This is what the mainline churches offered. After the 1960s the demand went down because those "secular" attachments declined. In such an environment, as Bibby says (1993:6), groups such as the Pentecostals do well just to hold onto their "market share," let alone increase it.

Finally, the interpretation thus presented allows a reconsideration of the impact of the Second Vatican Council. Was the Second Vatican a symptom or a cause? Did it give Catholics fewer reasons for attending church or did it simply give them permission for what they would have done anyway, if more gradually? Here, the simultaneity of the sharpest Protestant decline and the Catholic one only after the mid-1960s is striking. The statist argument of Zylberberg and Côté would account for this, even though the greater decline in Quebec than in the rest of Canada would still point to an independent effect of the Second Vatican. Yet here we may be dealing with an immediate as opposed to an underlying cause. Put somewhat metaphorically, it may be that treating the Second Vatican as cause rather than symptom is a little like blaming the collapse of the Soviet Union on Gorbachev's policies of *glasnost* and *perestroika*. In each case, the events in question are certainly the immediate antecedents, but their striking "effect" is probably better seen as a case of taking the cap off an overheated radiator, than as the cause of the overheating.

CONCLUSIONS

Regardless of how one interprets the causal character of the Second Vatican, the main consequence of the foregoing interpretation of Canadian religious history is to suggest that denominationalism may well have been a temporarily dominant form of providing religion in a Canada undergoing structural secularization. This argument would apply especially to the large denominations. Detached from their former secular social roles, they must rely more on attracting involved members through religion alone. This does not spell complete disaster because, judging by most surveys, Canadians, much like the inhabitants of other Western countries, still show a high level of identification, belief and interest in matters religious (Rawlyk, 1996; Campbell and Curtis, 1994; Bibby, 1987, 1993). The people therefore want what the churches have to offer. Yet the operative question is, do they want it in denominational and evangelical/devotional style, where church membership and very regular participation are deemed to be required aspects of considering oneself religious? Judging by present trends and those of the past two decades, the answer for Canada would seem to be yes, many will; but no, even more won't. The prevailing pattern seems to be one of occasional participation, which nonetheless proceeds largely along denominational lines. Formally organized religion in this scenario still has a place and can under certain circumstances yield large and powerful religious organizations: there is still a substantial "market" for which they can compete and we can probably expect certain religious organizations to keep growing. But most religious consumers, with a relatively modest demand for purely religious product, will consume eclectically, with perhaps a fair degree of "brand" loyalty, but more often than not without membership and the sort of commitment that produced regular participation and communal incorporation in an organized body.

Whether we call this secularization or not, the result is the same, and it is certainly one that secularization theory can accommodate: religious organizations in Canada are presently operating in a market of not only inelastic but also depressed "demand," meaning all those factors not covered by "supply" and "regulation." This market suffers from no direct regulation and has not done so for well over a century (*cf.* Doyle, 1984a, 1984b). If Canadians are to return to denominational religion in the numbers that they did in the past, then the religious "suppliers" will have to offer more than good and pure religious product lines. They will have to find a replacement for the social projects of the past, for re-entry into the secularized structures of power and influence; and they will have to wrest control and resources from some very powerful secular institutions, only one of which is the state.

If we accept this conclusion, then Canada can be seen to offer a critical corrective to the debate between religious market theorists and those deemed to represent the old paradigm. Canada differs from the United States in many ways, but it is also similar enough in history, culture and social structure to disallow its allocation to the group of allegedly monopolistic European examples. At the very least, the Canadian story addresses a challenge for rational choice/religious market theories to expand the range of their central concepts; and to reconsider the extent to which their contributions are in fact not the stuff of a new paradigm, but most definitely a potentially valuable corrective to the old one. For secularization theory, religious market theories offer a different but also important corrective: that the secularization of the most powerful social institutions does not mean the necessary and inevitable decline of religious influence, although it will do so in many, perhaps the majority of, cases.

NOTES

1 Warner states this contrast explicitly: "The newer paradigm stems not from the old one, which was developed to account for the European experience, but from an entirely independent vision inspired by American history" (1993:1045). To be fair, Warner explicitly defends the new paradigm only for understanding religion in the United States. Nonetheless, those whom he calls the "most outspoken exponents of the new paradigm" (1993:1055), Finke and Stark, do present it as a universally applicable theory.

2 I emphasize this last statement because, in consonance with the major representatives of the secularization paradigm such as Wilson and Berger, I am using a multi-dimensional conception of secularization along the lines suggested by Dobbelaere (1981) and Simpson (1988). Accordingly, secularization refers to the effects of institutional differentiation at the level of social systems, that is, to the secularization of non-religious institutional spheres; to secularization at the organizational level; or to secularization at the level of the individual. The arguments I present in this article depend on such a multi-dimensional view, and especially on the inclusion of the social-system dimension.

3 The two surveys found attendance rates of around 45 percent and 41 percent, respectively, a rate based on actual physical counts.

REFERENCES

Baril, Alain, and George A. Mori. 1991. "Leaving the Fold: Declining Church Attendance." *Canadian Social Trends* Autumn:21–24.

Bibby, Reginald W. 1987. *Fragmented Gods: The Poverty and Potential of Religion in Canada*. Toronto: Irwin.

———. 1993. *Unknown Gods: The Ongoing Story of Religion in Canada*. Toronto: Stoddard.

Campbell, Robert A., and James E. Curtis. 1994. "Religious Involvement across Societies: Analyses for Alternative Measures in National Surveys." *Journal for the Scientific Study of Religion* 33:217–229.

Census of Canada. 1881–1901. Ottawa: Dominion Bureau of Statistics.

Clark, S.D. 1948. *Church and Sect in Canada*. Toronto: University of Toronto.

Clifford, N.K. 1977. "'His Dominion': A Vision in Crisis." In *Religion and Culture in Canada*, ed. Peter Slater, 23–42. Waterloo: Wilfrid Laurier Press.

Dobbelaere, Karel. 1981. "Secularization: A Multi-dimension Model." *Current Sociology* 29(2):1–216.

Doyle, Denise J. 1984a. "Religious Freedom and Canadian Church Privileges." *Journal of Church and State* 26:293–311.

———. 1984b. "Religious Freedom in Canada." *Journal of Church and State* 26:413–435.

Evening Telegram. 1896. "One Day in City Churches." Toronto. Monday, 4 May.

Finke, Roger. 1990. "Religious Deregulation: Origins and Consequences." *Journal of Church and State* 32:609–626.

Finke, Roger, and Rodney Stark. 1992. *The Churching of America, 1776–1990: Winners and Losers in Our Religious Economy*. New Brunswick, NJ: Rutgers University Press.

Globe, The. 1882. "A Religious Census." Toronto. Tuesday, 7 February.

Grant, John W. 1988. *A Profusion of Spires: Religion in Nineteenth-Century Ontario*. Toronto: University of Toronto Press.

Hadden, Jeffrey K. 1987. "Toward Desacralizing Secularization Theory." *Social Forces* 65:587–611.

Hervieu-Léger, Danièle. 1993. *La religion pour mémoire*. Paris: Cerf.

Hiller, Harry H. 1978. "Continentalism and the Third Force in Religion." *Canadian Journal of Sociology* 3:183–207.

Iannaccone, Laurence R. 1991. "The Consequences of Religious Market Structure." *Rationality and Society* 3:156–177.

Jaenen, Cornelius J. 1976. *The Role of the Church in New France*. Toronto: McGraw-Hill Ryerson.

Jenish, D'Arcy. 1993. "Empty Pews, Angry Members: Churches Confront the Decline." *Maclean's*, 12 April:48–50.

Lemieux, Raymond. 1990. *"La catholicisme québécois: Une question de culture." Sociologie et sociétés* 22(2):145–164.

Maclean's. 1993. "Special Report: The Religion Poll." 12 April:32–50.

Martin, David. 1978. *A General Theory of Secularization*. Oxford: Basil Blackwell.

Moir, John S. 1987. *Enduring Witness: A History of the Presbyterian Church in Canada*. Toronto: Presbyterian Church in Canada.

Moir, John S., ed. 1967. *Church and State in Canada 1627–1867: Basic Documents*. Toronto: McClelland & Stewart.

Murphy, Terrence, and Gerald Stortz, eds. 1993. *Creed and Culture: The Place of English-Speaking Catholics in Canadian Society, 1750–1930*. Montreal and Kingston: McGill-Queen's.

Noll, Mark A. 1992. *A History of Christianity in the United States and Canada*. Grand Rapids, MI: Eerdmans.

Rawlyk, George A., ed. 1990. *The Canadian Protestant Experience, 1760–1990*. Burlington, ON: Welch.

Rawlyk, George A. 1994. *The Canada Fire: Radical Evangelicalism in British North America, 1775–1812*. Montreal and Kingston: McGill-Queen's.

———. 1996. *Is Jesus Your Personal Saviour? In Search of Canadian Evangelicalism in the 1990s*. Montreal and Kingston: McGill-Queen's.

Roberts, Keith A. 1990. *Religion in Sociological perspective*. 2nd ed. Belmont, CA: Wadsworth.

Simpson, John H. 1988. "Religion and the Churches." In *Understanding Canadian Society*, eds. James Curtis and Lame Tepperman. Toronto: McGraw-Hill Ryerson.

Stark, Rodney, and Laurence R. Iannaccone. 1994. "A Supply-Side Reinterpretation of the 'Secularization' of Europe." *Journal for the Scientific Study of Religion* 33:230–252.

Statistics Canada. 1949. *Canada Year Book 1948*. Ottawa: Statistics Canada.

———. 1980. *Canada Year Book 1978–79*. Ottawa: Statistics Canada.

———. 1993. *Religious in Canada: The Nation*. Ottawa: Statistics Canada.

Trudel, Marcel. 1956–1957. *L'Église canadienne sous le régime militaire, 1759–1764*. 2 vols. Quebec: Presses de l'Université Laval.

Warner, Stephen. 1993. "Work in Progress toward a New Paradigm for the Sociological Study of Religion in the United States." *American Journal of Sociology* 98:1044–1093.

Westfall, William. 1989. *Two Worlds: The Protestant Culture of Nineteenth-Century Ontario*. Kingston and Montreal: McGill-Queen's University Press.

Wilson, Bryan. 1982. *Religion in Sociological Perspective*. Oxford: Oxford University Press.

Zylberberg, Jacques. 1990. *La régulation étatique da la religion: Monisme at pluralisme*. Social Compass 37:97–116.

Zylberberg, Jacques, and Pauline Côté. 1993. *Les balises étatiques de la religion au Canada*. Social Compass 40:529–553.

CRITICAL THINKING QUESTIONS

1. Thinking about your community, what evidence do you see of secularization?
2. Using any resources you can think of, map the religious life of your community.
3. Keep a media journal on religion for a week. What are the types of stories you hear/read?
4. Talk to someone a generation behind you and ask about her or his religious life history.
5. How can Canada as a nation preserve religious diversity?
6. Is there a difference between religion and spirituality? Does this split create methodological challenges for those studying religious life?

FURTHER READINGS

Beckford, J. 2003. *Social Theory and Religion.* Cambridge: Cambridge University Press. This book is sure to become a classic in the sociology of religion. Beckford takes a social constructionist approach to the study of religion and examines key issues such as religious pluralism, globalization and the relationship between the self, religion and society. Beckford says: "What counts as religion are constructed, negotiated and contested" (7).

Brinkerhoff, M., E. Grandin, I. Hexham, and C. Pue. 1991. "The Perception of Mormons by Rural Canadian Youth." *Journal for the Scientific Study of Religion* 30(4):479–486. This paper is an applied example of exchange theory, a variation on the rational choice theory. Simply put, the researchers found that the more cosmopolitan a person's world view, the more accepting they are of alternative belief systems.

Casanova, J. 1994. *Public Religions in the Modern World.* Chicago and London: University of Chicago Press. Casanova's study is an important contribution to understanding secularization in a theoretically sophisticated manner.

His work examines the meaning of secularization and its links to modernity. He explores the public–private divide and asks important questions about its usefulness in thinking about the place of religion in contemporary societies.

Lyon, D. 2000. *Jesus in Disneyland: Religion in Postmodern Times.* Cambridge: Polity Press. Lyon tackles the intersection of religion and postmodernity, examining a number of fronts on which religion and spirituality are thriving, including places we might not expect—hence the Disneyland metaphor. Rather than focusing on secularization, Lyon turns his attention to new ways of religious expression.

Mol, H. 1974. "Marginality and Commitment as Hidden Variables in the Jellinck/Weber/Merton theses on the Calvinistic Ethic." *Current Sociology* 22:279–297. This article brings together some key sociological concepts to think about religion. In particular, Mol draws on the concepts of marginality and commitment, asking to what extent "universal traditional" religions have contributed to social cohesion.

PART II: TRANSITIONS

The chapters in this part move from the historical context and current debates explored in the last part to explore some transitions in sociology of religion. These transitions are multi-faceted, and include the redirection of traditional religion to address social problems; the interplay of science and religion; the reworking of a particular religious identity category in the day-to-day lives of believers; the multiple identities and transitions between them assumed by the researcher in the process of exploring religious life; and the conceptual transitions between religion and spirituality and the need for a transition from narrow definitions of religion and religiosity.

Does religion cause transitions, shifts in political structure or people's beliefs? We are not so much concerned with mapping causality as we are in exploring the ways in which religion weaves through everyday life. Whether prescriptive (I should do …) or explanatory (it happened because …) religion is both socially constructed and socially constructs. Causal explanations tend towards the simplistic, leaving out the texture and richness of the varieties of ways people believe and practise their religions.

Transitions can be both subtle and dramatic, and take place at the individual, community, national, and global levels. Often interrelated, they may take unanticipated directions. Religious ideology can provide the impetus for transitions, again, in unexpected ways. An evangelical woman may be prompted to work for change in her local congregation if she recognizes, for example, that the doctrine of submission is sometimes seen by abused Christian women as an injunction from the church to stay in an abusive relationship. She might talk to her pastor, invite speakers from the local transition house to the church women's group, or develop other strategies to deal with violence against women.

Religion can be both constraining and empowering, and a sense of religious community can offer a place from which activism may begin. Thus, transitional directions can shift within religion, which can provide the seeds for or means for both oppression and liberation. A well-documented example of the liberating possibilities is the liberation theology of the Roman Catholic Church, which developed as a way to address poverty in South and Central American countries. Liberation theology arose as a way to challenge the status quo in Latin America, using religion to question and address the injustices of poverty.

By the same token, we can see the oppressive aspects of the same Church: it refuses to ordain women, bans abortion, and is fundamentally hierarchical in its organizational structure. To be clear, all religions seem to possess these emancipatory and oppressive tendencies, often simultaneously. It is how these tendencies are worked out in local contexts that is as important to attend to as stated or written ideology. Rather than framing this as a belief/practice distinction, it is perhaps more useful to focus on the ways in which human actors work through their beliefs in the complex situatedness of everyday life and their own identities.

A growing awareness of the multiple possibilities of identity construction and its shifting nature has sparked a possible shift in the ways in which religion and social life are studied. Methodologically, life histories can help us to appreciate the ebb and flow of religion in an individual's life, and to gain insight into the intersection of life events and religion. Moreover, some researchers have looked past formal religious affiliation to the multiple ways individuals create religious life. Most famously, Robert Bellah identified "Sheilaism," after a woman he interviewed who wove together bits and pieces of beliefs and practices to "create" her own religion.[1] Another variation on this way of thinking about religion are "seekers," who seek spiritual fulfillment from a variety of sources. Although some researchers are disparaging of this way of creating religious identity, others, like William Closson James (whose work appears in this volume), celebrate it.

Transitions also involve compromise, resistance, and boundary negotiation and fortification. Some religious groups may seem to make no changes over time, but there are often subtle transitions that enable the group to maintain its identity while at the same time being flexible enough so that their boundaries do not burst under pressure. The works included in this part are intended to illuminate a broad range of transitions on a number of levels.

Nancy Nason-Clark captures the empowering and oppressive aspects of religion in her chapter, which focuses on the response of organized religion to violence against women. Nason-Clark's methodology is action-oriented; in other words, she and her research team use their results to effect transitions both within organized religion and in the relationship between religious groups and "secular" community organizations. Nason-Clark argues that it is important to pay attention to the multiple layers of faith and race, class, and gender. These layers preclude a "one solution fits all" approach to violence against women and the role of religion. Nason-Clark's chapter raises the important question of the researcher's role in data collection and dissemination. What responsibility do we have to the communities with which we conduct research? Is the goal of social scientific research to facilitate transitions?

In interesting contrast to Nason-Clark's story of sociological engagement is William A. Stahl's chapter describing the relative absence of sociologists from the "Science Wars." Stahl's chapter explicitly considers the notion of boundaries and power relations. He asks who has the right to speak and whose knowledge counts, noting the dominance of science or rationality in modernity. The science–religion debate is an important case study of the effects of discursive separation and forces the question: can we separate science and religion? As Stahl points out, both involve practice and by implication human actors. Stahl adds another important dimension to our exploration of religion through his discussion of implicit religion. The notion of implicit religion presses us to consider religion outside of its conventional venues and forms. The possibility of implicit religion takes us back to the recurring question (and some might argue nightmare) of how, exactly, we define religion and what counts as religion. William Closson James takes these questions up in some detail.

William Closson James's work is suggestive of the need for a transition in the way we think about religion. James is interdisciplinary in his approach, and drawing on religious studies, literary critique, theology, and social scientific approaches (broadly defined), he argues "the locations of the sacred are found to be everywhere and nowhere, multiple rather than single, fluid rather than fixed, ephemeral rather than permanent, or at the margins rather than the centre." James's work can (and should) be taken as a critique of an approach that locates religion and the sacred in a static manner that misses the diverse ways that religion is lived and constructed, or "cobbled together," to use James's phrase. The transition called for by James opens up exciting possibilities for the sociology of religion, and it also raises some interesting questions: Is there a difference between religion and spirituality? How can our theories and methods capture religion conceptualized in this way? What does the study of organized religion tell us?

In this volume, the work of William Shaffir illuminates the complexity of the boundary maintenance process. Shaffir contributes a beautifully done "privileged insider" ethnography of an Hassidic Jewish community, the Tasher Hassidim, illustrating the subtle process of boundary negotiation and transition. Like many other orthodox or fundamentalist groups, the Hassidim seek, as much as possible, to isolate themselves from secular society. But complete isolation is impossible, and so there is selective interaction with the "outside world," whether in terms of the use of outside professionals or the use of computer technology. However, as Shaffir notes, "the degree of the Tasher's openness to the outside world is carefully limited through a series of meticulously engineered social boundaries." Nonetheless, subtle transitions, like a shifting in the dress code, are occurring. Shaffir's piece also reflects on methodological issues, focusing especially on the desirability of returning to a community for multiple site visits. He concludes that such an approach permits a richer analysis than might otherwise be possible. Shaffir's work raises important issues, including a consideration of the degree to which compromise is possible before a group significantly alters its identity.

Sîân Reid describes the care with which the researcher must consider her identity and her position as researcher. In her decision to distance herself from her own faith community, Reid gave up an important part of her identity, at least for a time, in order to carry out her research. This transition from participant to researcher-sociologist was not, by Reid's account, easy. Her forthright discussion gives us an inside look at the ways in which researchers must think about the impact of their research on their communities and on themselves. Moreover, her discussion reveals the dynamic nature of the Wiccan community, which is itself in transition in many respects. Wiccans are not a monolithic group, and we can see from Reid's work that they are by no means monolithic, ranging from sole practitioners to highly organized Wiccan "churches." We also gain a sense of the transitions that take place over an individual's life history in the context of Wicca and its fluid set of beliefs and practices.

NOTE

1 Robert N. Bellah, *Habits of the Heart: Individualism and Commitment in American Life*, Berkeley: University of California Press, 1985.

CHAPTER 6

WHEN TERROR STRIKES AT HOME:
THE INTERFACE BETWEEN RELIGION AND DOMESTIC VIOLENCE

Nancy Nason-Clark

In this short essay, I raise two particular questions concerning the interface between religion and domestic violence: the first focuses on religious victims, the second on religious perpetrators. For almost fifteen years, I have been intrigued by the story of what happens when religious people look to their faith communities for help in the aftermath of violence in the family context. For many religious victims, their faith sustains them through long periods of domestic crisis: it empowers them to ultimately flee their abuser and to seek refuge and safety where they begin a new life free of abuse (Nason-Clark and Kroeger, 2004). There are others who are not so fortunate: they are consumed by the "sacred silence" on the issue, never finding spiritual or practical support that would enable them to leave the fear or the reality of violence behind (Nason-Clark, 1997). As a result, there are many layers we need to unravel as we seek to understand the complex relationship between faith, violence, and family ties. I begin with a brief look at the prevalence of violence against women in families of faith and conclude my essay with several theoretical questions requiring further analysis.

VIOLENCE AGAINST WOMEN IN FAMILIES OF FAITH

Domestic violence knows no boundaries of class, colour or religious persuasion (Stirling *et al.*, 2004; Timmins, 1995). Despite the fact that religious rhetoric is replete with references to happy families (Edgell, 2003), many religious women are victimized by husbands who promised before God to love and cherish them for life (Nason-Clark, 1997). Although religious families may be considered sacred, they are sometimes unsafe. In 1989, the Christian Reformed Church in North America conducted a survey among a small random sample of adult church members: 28 percent had experienced at least one form of abuse (Annis and Rice, 2001), a figure close to those of national U.S. samples not specifically targeting church-going families. Whether particular religious theologies exacerbate violence in the family is something on which there has been some speculation but very little data. Bartkowski and Anderson (1996), using

U.S. data from the National Survey of Families and Households, argue that they found no clear evidence that men or women affiliated with conservative churches were especially prone towards violence. Similarly, Brinkerhoff, Grandin, and Lupri (1992) reported that conservative Christian men in Canada were not significantly more violent than those of other persuasions. Although many religious groups have been slow to acknowledge the prevalence of violence in their midst (Horton and Williamson, 1988), psychologist Andrew Weaver (1993) claims that "domestic violence is probably the number one pastoral mental health emergency."

There are specific religious contours both to the abuse that is suffered and to the healing journey. As a result, many in the secular therapeutic community do not like to work with clients who are particularly religious (Whipple, 1987). Without spiritual credentials, these workers find it difficult to challenge the religious ideation that is believed by the victim or perpetrator to give licence to abuse. Sometimes, secular shelter workers and others believe that it is in fact the religious ideology that gives rise to the violence and undergirds victims' reluctance to seek refuge or assistance in its aftermath. Consequently, they encourage the victim to leave behind both the abuse and their community of faith. In a similar vein, there are religious professionals who are slow to refer their parishioners who have been abused to outside sources of help, believing that a secular shelter is an unsafe place to claim faith. There can be suspicion on both sides and sometimes the voices of the caregivers drown out the voices of the victims (Timmin, 1995). For collaborative ventures between the steeple and the shelter to be successful, personnel operating from a secular or sacred paradigm must be willing to see that the condemnation of domestic violence requires both the language of contemporary culture and the language of the spirit (Nason-Clark, 2001). A cultural language that is devoid of religious symbols, meanings and legitimacy is relatively powerless to alter a religious victim's resolve to stay in the marriage no matter what the cost. Correspondingly, the language of the spirit, if devoid of the practical resources of contemporary culture, compromises a victim's need for safety, security and financial resources to care for herself and her children.

IN WHAT WAYS DO NOTIONS OF RECONCILIATION AND FORGIVENESS—CONCEPTS AT THE HEART OF A JUDAEO-CHRISTIAN WORLD VIEW—PLACE WOMEN VICTIMS AT GREATER RISK OF TERROR AT HOME?

In families of strong faith, many of the patterns that are observed within mainstream culture are intensified: the fear, the vulnerability, the isolation, the promise before God to stay together until *death do us part*. Although there is no compelling evidence that violence is more frequent or more severe in families of faith, religious women are more vulnerable *when abused*. They are less likely to leave, are more likely to believe the abuser's promise to change his violent ways, frequently espouse reservations about seeking community-based resources or shelters for battered women, and commonly express guilt—that they have failed their families and God in not being able to make the marriage work. To be sure, most women victims are reluctant to see their marriage end, experience financial vulnerability, and fear for their own lives (and the abuser's reprisal). Some cling to a fantasy of change and others harbour notions of working harder to ensure the marriage lasts. However, for religious women, these beliefs are commonly and strongly reinforced by a religious ideology that sees women's roles as wife and homemaker as pivotal to her sense of self-worth, believes that happy families build strong nations, and condemns divorce. Moreover, there are explicit religious notions that make it especially difficult for religious victims to see the full extent of their suffering or to sound out the call for help. Paramount among these are Christian notions of forgiveness and women's with Jesus the sacrificial lamb. Could battering be a religious woman's *cross to bear?* Are religious batterers' abilities to manipulate their victims dependent on specific features of their religious belief system?

Any discussion of the healing journey of victims of abuse eventually comes to the issue of forgiveness. Writing about forgiveness from a religious standpoint, Hudson argues that the cry of Jesus from the cross, "Father, forgive them; for they do not know what they are doing"[1] is often touted as the model by which victims ought to approach their aggressors. Yet, forgiveness does not erase the pain of the past, nor does it deny its implications. Rather, when forgiveness is placed within a broader context of the journey from victim to survivor, it is achieved when the pain of the past no longer controls the future and the victim is no longer entrapped in a complicated web of anger and despair (Nason-Clark and Kroeger, 2004). But the line is a fine one. Marie Fortune claims that forgiveness is the last step on the healing journey, the last rung on the ladder of a woman's struggle to overcome the brokenness of her past. As such, it cannot come before justice or the offender's accountability. In this way, premature forgiveness actually damages the possibility of healing and growth for both perpetrator and victim. Religious pressure on the victim to quickly "forgive and forget" prevents the abuser from being fully accountable for his actions and can be life threatening for the victim. Forgiveness might be the most charitable and compassionate gift religious groups can offer victims in their fold (Fortune, 1988), but it cannot be time-tabled by someone other than the victim and should never be regarded as a guarantee for safety or protection. Religious language must not pretend that everything is now okay and life for the family should return to normal, as if the abuse never happened.

HOW AND WHY WOULD MANDATED INTERVENTION FOR BATTERERS BECOME MORE EFFECTIVE IF THE COURTS RECOGNIZED THE POTENTIAL AND POWER OF RELIGION?

Justice, accountability and change are all central ingredients in the intervention services offered to men who have abused their wives. Although some come voluntarily, other men are mandated by the courts or referred by their wives, therapists or clergy to participate in an intervention program for abusers. Although abused *religious* women want the battery to stop, they may not wish to terminate their relationship with the abuser, either temporarily or forever. Consequently, the resources these women seek in the aftermath of violence in part differentiate them from their more secular counterparts. As a result, religious women in particular place a lot of trust in programs that purport to help men to stop the abuse and to alter their ways of coping with anger and frustration. Simply put, the stakes to keep the marriage together (and perhaps to accept the battery) are much higher for religious women (Horton and Williamson, 1988; Kroeger and Nason-Clark, 2001).

Woven through the narratives of abusive men who are travelling towards justice and accountability are the roles of religious congregations and their leaders in supporting the men as they seek help. A pastor or priest is a key player in ensuring accountability in the life of a religious man who is, or has been, abusive. Consequently, houses of worship and religious leaders are unique resources in any community-based efforts to create safe and peaceful homes.

However, there is little agreement about the efficacy of batterer intervention groups (Daly and Pelowski, 2000; Hanson and Wallace-Capretta, 2002; Scott and Wolfe, 2000). Although completion and recidivism rates vary amongst programs (Dalton, 2001; Gondolf, 2002), it is clear that intervention must be integrated into the overall social context of these men's lives (deHart et al., 1999). Researchers have recognized the critical role played by the courts and other parts of the judicial system, but none has acknowledged any role for religious organizations. Yet, for many abusive men, a key component of their social context is their religious belief system (Dobash and Dobash, 1979; Ptacek, 1988; DeKeseredy and MacLeod, 1998).

In one faith-based batterer intervention program, a case file analysis of over 1000 closed files of abusive men revealed that men in such a program differ on many personal and family characteristics from men who enter secular programs for batterers (Nason-Clark et al., in press). The men in the faith-based program are more likely to be older, married and white; to have attained post-secondary education or a university or graduate degree; to be employed and in a white-collar occupation; and to have witnessed or experienced violence in their childhood home. On the other hand, men in this program had similar rates of alcohol abuse and criminal history as men in secular programs. Another finding to emerge from this data is the role of clergy and other religious leaders in encouraging or "mandating" men who seek their spiritual help to attend a faith-based intervention program. In fact, men who were clergy-referred were more likely to complete (and graduate from) the program than those whose attendance was mandated by a judge. When the clergy and the courts both referred such men, their rates of program completion were very high indeed.

Attempting to understand exactly why this might be so is important. Past research has shown that religious men and women stay longer in a relationship, even an unhealthy one (Horton and Williamson, 1988). Clergy, then, may be especially prone to assist abused women and their partners who are still married and to use the language of reconciliation as motivation for the men to seek help in a faith-based agency (Nason-Clark, 1999). Since the men themselves have more life-stability factors (currently married, employed, higher education, et cetera), this may reinforce their willingness to complete the program and to alter their abusive ways. Sharing a religious world view with the other men in the program may actually provide a *safe place* for these abusive men to challenge themselves and each other and look towards a day when their abusive past will no longer control their present reality.

Nonetheless, too often forgotten in the growing research literature on batterers is the role of religion in either supporting or challenging men's abusive ways. Achieving accountability is paramount to successful intervention. On this issue, there may be a difference between the sheep and the goats: for religious men having their violence condemned not only by the language of contemporary culture but also by the language of the spirit may be central. It may well be that accountability factors are more easily set in place in the life of a religious man. A key player in ensuring such accountability is the man's pastor, priest or other religious leader. But powerful, too, is a religious community—that is, the congregation—when perceived by the abuser or the family as supportive of his journey towards change and wholeness. For violence to be overcome, the personal struggle will need to acquire public dimensions. In families of faith, the religious community becomes that important ingredient, with the capacity to either augment or thwart the process of recovery. The question then becomes: How can a person's religious ideology be employed by sacred and secular intervention services in a way that will nurture, monitor and reinforce a violent-free future?

SUGGESTIONS FOR EXPANDING THE RESEARCH AGENDA

Outlined below are several questions that I consider essential in our efforts to unravel the nuanced relationship between religious faith and violence within families. Each of these queries could be addressed at an individual or community level. Each has political or social action implications that permeate beyond the boundaries of any specific groups. However, from my vantage point, it is inconceivable to separate theoretical gains from the direct impact on the lives of hurting people.

1. What are some of the central features of various religious traditions that negate community-wide efforts to raise awareness about violence against women and to suggest strategies that would empower women to reduce the risk of endangering their physical or emotional health in the aftermath of abuse?

I wish to highlight two "central features" of various religious traditions that work against raising awareness about domestic violence and empowering victims: discourse on the salience of *family* for women's lives and thus the undesirability of family dissolution, and the tendency by religious ideologies and leaders to "spiritualize" social problems. A third feature, gender segregation both within and beyond the religious group, contributes to the way the issue of abuse may be marginalized within the discourse of a specific group, but these same single-sex social contexts also offer the practical and emotional support on which many women victims depend. Notions about family values including, but not limited to, an anti-divorce sentiment reinforce a victimized woman's sense of failure and vulnerability. Moreover, when the abuse is conceptualized as a spiritual issue, this exacerbates her dependence on the religious group for guidance concerning the decisions she needs to make to ensure safety.

For fundamentalists of varied world religions, divorce is regarded as a dangerous trend (Hawley, 1994), evidence of narcissism at a personal level, and a conduit to later problems for affected children and adolescents. Some conservative Christian traditions argue that divorce is the result of female economic independence augmented by married women's introduction into the paid labour force (Bartkowski, 2001). Clearly, any religious tradition that regards women's primary raison d'être to be child-bearing and homemaking resists societal advances to ensure female participation in all sectors of society (Balmer, 1994). Sacred texts and their religious-elite interpreters play a critical role in how the issue of abuse is framed. When it is highlighted in the weekly routine of church life—through sermons or informational material available to congregants—victims feel safe to come forward; when it is absent from religious discourse, victims keep silent, seeing the issue as their own personal struggle. Working out one's salvation has never been easy, but it has almost always been gendered. Thus, family failure is interpreted by many religious women as a sign that they have failed God. When women's abuse is at the hands of their religious leaders, their vulnerability is especially high (Jacobs, 1989); sometimes, they suffer as secondary victims when priests or other religious leaders of congregations are convicted of sexual misconduct (Nason-Clark, 1998).

2. What are the intersections of race and class in any discussion concerning the abuse of women in the family context, especially women of faith?

Social theorists such as Patricia Hill-Collins (1997) remind researcher and activist alike of the "constructs of multiplicity" through which inequalities of race, gender and class are reproduced. The problems, as well as the solutions, have multiple layers. In the Caribbean, a Pentecostal woman may ask her prayer group to beseech God that the violence would stop, even as she takes his shirt to the shaman.[2] There is ample evidence that religious women support each other, both when things are going well and at times of great personal trial; often this occurs under the umbrella of women's ministry within congregational life.

Cheryl Townsend Gilkes (2000) recently asked us to consider what would have happened to African-American religious organizations and communities if it weren't for the women. Emilie Townes (1997) provides rich examples of womanist perspectives on evil and suffering. Milagros Peña has considered this issue from the perspective of Anglos and Latinas working together on both sides of the Mexican–U.S. border and it may be that the same degree of collaboration might be evident when violence erupts at home (Peña and Frehill, 1998). Ebaugh and Chafetz (2000) briefly mention congregational support for women in crisis within immigrant congregations; Timmins (1995) notes assistance within Aboriginal communities. The degree to which sisterly support for abuse victims is enhanced by social factors of heightened marginalization—through race, class or ethnicity—has yet to be examined in full.

3. To what degree do faith-based initiatives have an added advantage in working with clients for whom a religious world view is a salient feature of their lives?

Recent years have witnessed growing scholarly debates concerning faith-based initiatives to meet a variety of the social and practical needs of the U.S. population, but little attention has been drawn to the role of faith-based services for perpetrators of domestic violence. Yet as mentioned above, there is evidence that clients in a faith-based batterer intervention program may be more likely to complete the requirements of that program than men enrolled in secular equivalents, and that abusive men in the faith-based program who were encouraged by their priests or pastors to attend had higher completion rates than those whose attendance was mandated by the courts. Although faith-based initiatives cross the spectrum from no religious content in their programming to a high visibility of religious language and ritual, it is clear that there is an important interplay among the religious beliefs of workers, religious beliefs of clients, program content and the nature of the problems for which the program has been established. Teasing apart these interconnections is as interesting as it is timely.

4. As we consider the prevalence and severity of violence in families around the globe, what are some of the features of the interface among faith, fear and pressures to keep the family intact in various regions of the world?

Violence against women occurs in every corner of the world, taking a variety of different forms and affecting women's lives differently depending on the social context in which it occurs. A man in Bangladesh may throw acid on a woman's face, a Kenyan man may hit his wife with her own market stool, or an American may use his gun, but the result is the same: women learn to fear the men who claim to love them. Whether we consult data compiled by the United Nations Secretariat, the World Health Organization, or the departments of censuses and surveys of individual countries, the prevalence rates are startling: at least one in five women around the globe have been victims (see Kroeger and Nason-Clark, 2001).

Recent fieldwork experiences in the Caribbean[3] and eastern Europe[4] offer some interesting clues in the relationship between faith and families in crisis in different parts of the world. In the Jamaican capital of Kingston, a city known for its high rates of violence and prevalence of Christian churches, there is evidence of strong resignation about both the incidence and severity of abuse within the general culture and within families. In this context, individuals and institutions alike develop a strategy that refuses to ignore the problem (rather, it is widely acknowledged) but remain reluctant to conceptualize abuse in such a way as to demand a social-action response from either secular or sacred sources of help. Although there is little resistance to the principle of churches and community agencies collaborating, without framing the problem in ways that might lead to solutions, the result is impotence to act.

In post-communist Croatia, on the other hand, clergy and other religious leaders are slow to see the pervasive violence in church families and reveal great hesitation in accepting social-scientific explanations for why abuse is prevalent in families of faith.

Perceiving the problem to be primarily of spiritual origins, faith leaders are resistant to making referral suggestions to community-based resources. Social service delivery personnel and other victim advocates, on the other hand, are more likely to recognize the influence of post-traumatic stress disorder in this wartorn region of the world and to see religious ideology as silencing women who are suffering. Despite the high levels of violence experienced in both of these cultural contexts, the reaction to abuse in the family and collaborative ventures between the state and the church differ. In Jamaica, the absent father is considered a fact of life; fatherless families in Croatia are perceived in very negative terms. Religious professionals are regarded in Jamaica as instrumental in any effort for social change and clergy themselves reveal no resistance to working with others in community-based agencies; in Croatia, community-based activists and clergy alike appear very cynical about collaboration.

There are many more questions. What is the interface between religion and violence in same-sex relationships? What are the longer-term implications for children in devoutly religious homes who witness violence against their mother or are victims of parental rage themselves? What are the contours of the healing journey when it is an adult man who has been victimized by his religious partner? How is violence towards the elderly conceptualized in faith-based nursing homes?

Violence knows no religious boundaries: it is a global issue and it is gendered. The journey towards healing and wholeness for religious victims is replete with both secular and sacred overtones—as are its causes and the factors that reinforce it. Breaking the cycle of violence in the family requires both the language of secular culture and the language of the spirit. Researchers and activists alike must unravel the many layers involved in the interface of faith, family and fear for victimized women and their children.

NOTES

1. Biblical reference is Luke 23:34.
2. Field notes, Jamaican focus group, September 2003.
3. With the assistance of Lanette Ruff, a graduate student at the University of New Brunswick, I conducted personal interviews and focus groups in Kingston, Jamaica, in the fall of 2003, and offered training and violence sensitivity workshops to a wide range of religious and secular professionals as well as to students.
4. Together with colleagues at the University of Zagreb (Sinisa Zrinscak and Marina Ajdukovic), the Evangelical Theological Seminary in Osijek (Ela Balog), and within the social-science delivery sector (Suzanna and Zoran Vargovic), I have been considering religion and family violence in a post-communist context. After three fieldwork visits, we have collected both quantitative and qualitative indicators of the resistance and openness to discussion of family violence connected with churches in Croatia; here, too, I have been involved in training workshops.

REFERENCES

Annis, A.W., and R.R. Rice. 2001. "A Survey of Abuse Prevalence in the Christian Reformed Church." *Journal of Religion and Abuse* 3 (314):7–40.

Balmer, R. 1994. "American Fundamentalism: The Ideal of Femininity." In *Fundamentalism and Gender*, ed. J.S. Hawley, 47–62. New York: Oxford University Press.

Bartkowski, J.P. 2001. *Remaking the Godly Marriage: Gender Negotiation in Evangelical Families.* New Brunswick, NJ: Rutgers University Press.

Bartkowski, J.P., and K.L. Anderson. 1996. "Are There Religious Variations in Spousal Violence?" Paper presented at the Annual Meeting of the Association for the Sociology of Religion, New York.

Brinkerhoff, M., E. Grandin, and E. Lupri. 1992. "Religious Involvement and Spousal Violence: The Canadian Case." *Journal for the Scientific Study of Religion* 31:12–31.

Collins, P.H. 1997. "Comment on Hekman's 'Truth and Method: Feminist Standpoint Theory Revisited': Where's the Power?" *Signs* 22:375–381.

Dalton, B. 2001. "Batterer Characteristics and Treatment Completion." *Journal of Interpersonal Violence* 16 (l):971–991.

Daly, J., and S. Pelowski. 2000. "Predictors of Dropout among Men Who Batter: A Review of Studies with Implications for Research and Practice." *Violence and Victims* 15 (2):137–160.

deHart, D., R. Kennerly, L. Burke, and D. Follingstad. 1999. "Predictors of Attrition in a Treatment Program for Battering Men." *Journal of Family Violence* 14 (1):19–34.

Dekeseredy, W., and L. MacLeod. 1997. *Woman Abuse: A Sociological Story.* Toronto: Harcourt Brace.

Dobash, R.P., and R.E. Dobash. 1979. *Violence against Wives: A Case against the Patriarchy.* New York: Free Press.

Ebaugh, H.R., and J. Chafetz. 2000. *Religion and the New Immigrants: Continuities and Adaptations in Immigrant Congregations.* Walnut Creek, CA: AltaMira Press.

Edgell, P. 2003. "In Rhetoric and Practice: Defining 'the Good Family' in Local Congregations." In *Handbook of the Sociology of Religion*, ed. M. Dillon, 164–178. Cambridge: Cambridge University Press.

Fortune, M. 1988. "Forgiveness the Last Step." In *Abuse and Religion: When Praying Isn't Enough*, ed. A. Horton and J. Williamson, 215–220. Lexington, MA: Lexington.

Gilkes, C.T. 2000. *If It Wasn't for the Women … Black Women's Experience and Womanist Culture in Church and Community.* Maryknoll, NY: Orbis Books.

Gondolf, E.W. 2002. *Batterer Intervention Systems: Issues, Outcomes and Recommendations.* Thousand Oaks, CA: Sage Publications.

Hanson, R.K., and S. Wallace-Capretta. 2002. *Predicting Recidivism among Male Batterers 2000–06.* Ottawa: Public Works and Government Services Canada.

Hawley, J., ed. 1994. *Fundamentalism and Gender.* New York: Oxford.

Horton, A., and J. Williamson, eds. 1988. *Abuse and Religion: When Praying Isn't Enough.* New York: D.C. Heath and Company.

Jacobs, J.L. 1989. *Divine Disenchantment: Deconverting from New Religious Movements.* Bloomington, IN: Indiana University Press.

Kroeger, C.C., and N. Nason-Clark. 2001. *No Place for Abuse: Biblical and Practical Resources to Counteract Domestic Violence.* Downers Grove, IL: InterVarsity Press.

Nason-Clark, N. 1997. *The Battered Wife: How Christians Confront Family Violence.* Louisville, KY: Westminster/John Knox Press.

———. 1998. "Abuses of Clergy Trust: Exploring the Impact on Female Congregants' Faith and

Practice." In *Wolves among the Fold*, ed. A. Shupe, 85–100. New York: Rutgers University Press.

———. 1999. "Shattered Silence or Holy Hush: Emerging Definitions of Violence Against Women." *Journal of Family Ministry* 13 (1):39–56.

———. 2001. "Woman Abuse and Faith Communities: Religion, Violence and Provision of Social Welfare." In *Religion and Social Policy*, ed. P. Nesbitt, 128–145. Walnut Creek, CA: AltaMira Press.

Nason-Clark, N., and C.C. Kroeger. 2004. *Refuge from Abuse: Hope and Healing for Abused Christian Women*. Downers Grove, IL: InterVarsity Press.

Nason-Clark, N., N. Murphy, B. Fisher-Townsend, and L. Ruff. In press. "An Overview of the Characteristics of the Clients at a Faith-Based Batterers' Intervention Program." *Journal of Religion and Abuse* 5 (4).

Peña, M., and L.M. Frehill. 1998. "Latina Religious Practice: Analyzing Cultural Dimensions in Measures of Religiosity." *Journal for the Scientific Study of Religion* 37:620–635.

Ptacek, J. 1988. "How Men Who Batter Rationalize Their Behavior." In *Abuse and Religion: When Praying Isn't Enough*, ed. A. Horton and J. Williamson, 247–258. New York: D.C. Heath and Company.

Scott, K., and D. Wolfe. 2000. "Change among Batterers: Examining Men's Success Stories." *Journal of Interpersonal Violence* 15 (8):827–842.

Stirling, M.L., C.A. Cameron, N. Nason-Clark, and B. Miedema, eds. 2004. *Understanding Abuse: Partnering for Change*. Toronto: University of Toronto Press.

Timmins, L., ed. 1995. *Listening to the Thunder: Advocates Talk about the Battered Women's Movement*. Vancouver: Women's Research Centre.

Townes, E., ed. 1997. *Embracing the Spirit: Womanist Perspectives on Hope, Salvation and Transformation*. Maryknoll, NY: Orbis Books.

Weaver, A. 1993. "Psychological Trauma: What Clergy Need to Know." *Pastoral Psychology* 41:385–408.

Whipple, V. 1987. "Counselling Battered Women from Fundamentalist Churches." *Journal for Marital and Family Therapy* 13 (3):251–258.

CHAPTER 7

A CULTURAL CARTOGRAPHY OF SCIENCE, TECHNOLOGY, AND RELIGION

William A. Stahl

The last ten years have been lively times for the discussion of science and religion. In 1994 Paul Gross and Norman Levitt published *Higher Superstition*, attacking environmentalism, feminism, and every form of the social study of science and touching off a bitter—at times vicious—debate that came to be known as the Science Wars. Also in 1994 the Sir John Templeton Foundation began offering substantial monetary awards for offering new classes in science and religion. The Science and Religion Course Program transformed what had been a small-scale, fragmented discussion over the relationship of religion and the natural sciences into a large international debate, which became known as the science–religion dialogue. What was surprising about both debates was the absence of sociologists of religion.

Sociologists of religion went AWOL from the Science Wars. Sociologists of science were among the main combatants, but few of them showed much interest in religion. On the other side, Gross, Levitt and other "science warriors" took it as an article of faith that science debunked religion and that good scientists were atheists (e.g., Levitt, 1999).

The science–religion dialogue was entirely different in both form and content. While those engaged in the Science Wars tended to argue that science and religion were incompatible, the participants in the science–religion dialogue replied that conflict between science and religion was neither inevitable nor desirable. Two of the most prominent figures in the debate were Ian Barbour (1997, 2000) and John Pokinghorne (1996), both physicists who are cross-trained in theology (Pokinghorne is also an Anglican priest). Many biologists and philosophers defended evolution without dismissing religion (e.g., Gould, 1998; Miller, 1999; Ruse, 2001). Others talked about the spiritual dimension of science itself (e.g., Goodenough, 1998). Historians of science reinterpreted both archetypical conflicts—the trial of Galileo (e.g., Machamer, 1998; Wilson, 1999), the Scopes "Monkey Trial" of 1925 (Larson, 1997)—and the scientific revolution itself (e.g., Osler, 2000; Shapin, 1996). Others (e.g., Brooke, 1991) demonstrated the many complex ways science and religion have interrelated over the past four centuries. Unfortunately, this debate was also characterized by an almost complete absence of sociologists (see Stahl, Campbell, Petry, and Diver, 2002).

Both debates are now largely over. The Science Wars petered out by the end of the decade. The termination of the Science and Religion Course Program in 2002 signalled that much of the excitement of the dialogue was ending as its participants turned to institutionalizing their gains. Both discussions, however, raised important issues for the sociology of religion, even if they were not engaged at the time. This chapter will raise several questions crucial to the participation of sociology in debates over the natural sciences, technology, and religion. Using Thomas Gieryn's (1999) metaphor of "cultural cartography," we will examine some of the more important contributions that *were* made, and suggest several issues that might form an agenda for the sociological study of science and religion in the coming years.

CULTURAL MAPS AND AUTHORITY

Both the Science Wars and the science–religion dialogue were debates about boundaries. As such they were also debates about authority—who has the power to define the boundaries of science (and religion), who should be included within those boundaries, and who has the legitimate right to speak. Thomas Gieryn (1999) argues that a useful way to think about such disputes is as *cultural cartography*, that is, as debates over "maps" of culture. He contends that "As knowledge makers seek to present their claims or practices as legitimate (credible, trustworthy, reliable) by locating them within 'science,' they discursively construct for it an ever changing arrangement of boundaries and territories and landmarks, always contingent upon immediate circumstances" (1999:xi). Such conceptual maps delimit issues, establish agendas and designate who are the legitimate interlocutors in any debate.

The participants in such discourse engage in *credibility contests*, in which they try to gain *epistemic authority*, which Gieryn (1999:1) defines as "the legitimate power to define, describe, and explain bounded domains of reality." He sees three different kinds of credibility contests. The first, *expulsion* conflicts, occur when rival authorities each claim to be scientific. The fight over global warming is a good example. Each side claims that its own theories and models are exemplars of good science while their opponents propagate politically motivated junk science. (Of course there is a long history of this in religion as well, with the loser in theological debates becoming heretic.) In fact, there is a whole genre of literature that serves to police the borders of science, maintaining the authority of the cultural map by denouncing pretenders as pseudoscience and fraud (e.g., Carey, 1994; Park, 2000). Second are *expansion* conflicts, in which the contending parties try to extend the boundaries of their jurisdiction. For example, some science popularizers, such as Richard Dawkins (1996, 1998, 2003), have debunked religion for years. In the United States, Fundamentalists have waged a long, loud, and generally futile crusade against the theory of evolution (e.g., Morris, 1968, 1974). The Science Wars were largely this kind of conflict. The third form is *protection of autonomy*. Here contestants try to defend boundaries against attempts to redraw them. One of Gieryn's examples (1999:37–64) was British scientist John Tyndall, who in the nineteenth century drew cultural maps demarcating science from religion, on the one hand, and "pure" science from technology, on the other. Attempts to maintain university autonomy against encroachment by government or corporations would be a current example (e.g., Dalton, 2003). Trying to establish the authority of a new discipline or program would be another. Some of the science–religion dialogue would be an example of this last type.

Gieryn's cultural cartography provides a framework for tying together the disparate (and all too sparse) contributions sociologists have made to the study of science and religion. We will examine four maps. First, the cultural cartography of the science–religion dialogue has excluded social scientists from legitimate participation. We will consider why, and what alternatives sociologists might have. Second, we will discuss the secularization debate since this is the issue that is most likely to engage sociologists in the discussion of science. Third, implicit religion is seen by some to be almost the opposite of secularization. From this perspective we will review arguments that science is implicitly religious. Fourth, we will look at maps of religion and technology. We will conclude with a few reflections on reinterpreting maps.

CULTURAL CARTOGRAPHY IN THE SCIENCE–RELIGION DIALOGUE

One of the possible reasons that sociologists participated so rarely in the science–religion dialogue was that their involvement was not welcomed. The most influential maps of the relationship between science and religion, those of Ian Barbour and Stephen Jay Gould, left no room for sociology. Natural scientists, theologians, and philosophers all had a clearly visualized "place" in the debate while social scientists did not. If sociologists want to legitimately participate they will have to redraw the cultural map.

Ian Barbour was a pioneer in the science–religion dialogue. His map of the interaction between science and religion (Barbour, 1997, 2000) has clearly been dominant in the discussions over the past decade and has structured much of the debate that has taken place. It is widely copied in textbooks and was institutionalized in the John Templeton Foundation's approach to the dialogue. Other scholars have developed variations on Barbour (Haught, 1995; Southgate, et al., 1999). Barbour has probably done more than anyone else to establish the credibility and legitimacy of dialogue between science and religion.

Barbour's approach is typological, mapping out four possible types of relationship between science and religion. The first type is *Conflict*, which sees science and religion as mutually exclusive and inherently incompatible. Proponents of this approach create strong and thick boundaries between science and religion, some claiming that science has a monopoly on truth, others making the same claim for religion. Barbour discusses scientific materialists such as Richard Dawkins, Stephen Weinberg, or Jacques Monod, who believe science is the only valid form of knowledge and that it can explain all of reality. Religion is, therefore, false. On the other side of the argument, Biblical literalists argue that the first two chapters of Genesis give a full and accurate account of the formation of the universe. Scientific theories are therefore false.

The second type is *Independence*. Here science and religion are put in separate compartments that do not make claims upon each other. For theologians and philosophers such as Karl Barth, Rudolf Bultmann, George Lindbeck, and the early Langdon Gilkey (interestingly, Barbour does not mention any practising scientists), science and religion have contrasting methodologies, subject matter and languages that simply do not compete. This approach has been institutionalized in the "mainstream" churches and is probably the most common and widespread position among the public.

Dialogue sees that the spheres of science and religion are separate but do indeed impinge upon each other, requiring dialogue between them. There are a wide variety of positions here. Typical kinds of questions are: What are the presuppositions and limits of science? Are there methodological parallels between science and religion? And is there a nature-centred spirituality? Barbour mentions Wolfhardt Pannenberg, Karl Rahner, David Tracy, and Michael Polanyi as examples of people working from this position.

The final type is *Integration,* which is "A more systematic and extensive kind of partnership between science and religion [which] occurs among those who seek a closer integration of the two disciplines" (Barbour, 2000:3). This usually takes one of three forms, according to Barbour. Natural theology, as exemplified by the works of William Paley or Richard Swineborne, sees God's design revealed in scientific findings, or, as it is usually put, the Book of Nature reveals God as much as does the Book of Scripture. The theology of nature argues that specific scientific theories may affect the content of theology. This approach includes the works of Arthur Peacocke, Pierre Teilhard de Chardin, and Barbour himself. Finally, a systematic synthesis, as argued by process theologians such as John Cobb and Charles Hartshorne, tries to build an inclusive metaphysics uniting religion and science.

Barbour's map (together with its variants) has great value as a guide to the debate as it has occurred over the past decade. In Gieryn's (1999) terms, Barbour and his imitators were engaged in protecting the autonomy of the fledgling dialogue. But it was not the only map. Towards the end of the decade Stephen Jay Gould (1998, 1999) articulated a map of the science–religion dialogue that was deliberately at variance with Barbour's. Gould called his map NOMA, for Non-Overlapping Magisteria.

Gould defined a magisterium as: "a domain where one form of teaching holds the appropriate tools for meaningful discourse and resolution" (1999:3). Science and religion are each magisteria. Each holds sway over its own domain, science over the empirical realm of fact and theory, and religion over the domain of ultimate meaning and moral value. The two domains do not overlap, but their boundaries are not permanently fixed either. "A magisterium," he said, "is a site for dialogue and debate, not a set of eternal and invariable rules" (Gould, 1999:61). While the two domains are separate, he argued, "the contact between magisteria could not be more intimate and pressing" (1999:65). He explained: "The two magisteria bump right against each other, interdigitating in wondrously complex ways along their joint border. Many of our deepest questions call upon aspects of both magisteria for different parts of a full answer—the sorting of legitimate domains can become quite complex and difficult" (1998:274). This means dialogue is essential between the two, because: "Any interesting problem, at any scale … must call upon the separate contributions of both magisteria for any adequate illumination" (1999:65). On some questions theology has nothing to say, while others are beyond the scope of science. But for most of the important issues of the day—Gould uses the example of genetic engineering—debate is necessary to determine where the proper boundaries lie.

Gould consciously patterned his position after that of the nineteenth-century Darwinist Thomas Huxley, and for similar reasons, to protect the autonomy of evolutionary theory from outside attack. Gould savages Creationists for stepping over boundaries into the magisterium of science, and is just as harsh on those scientists who violate the domain of religion. The problem with Gould's map is that the philosophy behind it lies in the trifurcation of reason developed by Immanuel Kant during the Enlightenment. Science, for Gould as it was for Kant, is the domain of the cognitive-instrumental, religion that of the practical-moral. And while the aesthetic-expressive is not formally part of Gould's model, he recognizes its domain as well. Gould maintained that as magisteria, science and religion are different in their essence. However much they may need demarcation at the frontier, each is characterized at its core by unique, necessary and invariant qualities that distinguish them from one another. So Gould is not presenting anything radically new—his separation of fact from value, of science from ethics, is part of the mainstream of modern thought.

Neither of these maps leaves much space for the social sciences to participate. Barbour presents a dialogue between academic theology and a rather surprisingly narrow range of scientific theories rather than between a full spectrum of science and religion. He discusses what the content of science means for theology, instead of seeing both as processes or practices. His map is very abstract, intellectual and circumscribed, and sharply separates theory and practice. It is also static and ahistorical. Positions are categorized without explanation of how those categories arose or of the dynamics of the debate within or between positions. Each position is defined by its essence, rather than being seen as the result of boundary work. Consequently, there is little room for the social sciences. In his expanded Gifford Lectures, for instance, the sociology of science is dismissed in less than two pages, while the sociology of religion is ignored altogether (1997:144–146).

Gould's map is not any more hospitable to the social sciences. In following Kant's division of reason, Gould partitions knowledge into two essentially different ways of knowing about the world, separating fact from value. It is not clear where the social sciences might fit into his scheme. But while separate magisteria may be clear so long as one remains in the realm of pure theory, it becomes problematic as soon as one becomes practical. Inevitably, when one becomes practical the empirical and moral are intermixed. For instance, Gould's model cannot give an adequate account of technology. Because technology is instrumental, both questions of *how* and *should* are inherent in its practice. Technology crosses the boundaries between the realms of facts and values, and defies separation into distinct domains.

Fortunately for the social sciences, neither Barbour's map (including its variants) nor Gould's are the only ones available for the science–religion dialogue. Ronald Cole-Turner (1998) suggested a more encompassing map, which we developed further in *Webs of Reality* (Stahl, Campbell, Petry, and Diver, 2002). Instead of a theoretical debate between scientific theory and academic theology, Cole-Turner envisions a more broadly based dialogue. He posits four elements—science, religion, technology, and ethics—each of which interacts with all of the others (see Figure 7.1). He begins by insisting on the communal and experiential dimensions of all four elements in his model. Religion is not reduced to theology nor science to theory. Both are the practices of communities and, as such, each

FIGURE 7.1: RONALD COLE-TURNER'S MAP

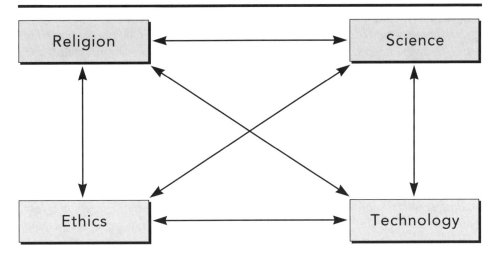

is an interweaving of experiences, norms, values, symbols, and rituals as well as beliefs. This is equally true of technology and ethics. Theory is important, but it is not given the privileged position it has on the other maps. Where the others are concerned with maintaining boundaries, Cole-Turner refuses to reify categories and recognizes that neat boundaries are rarely found in the lab or in the pew. Because they are concerned with practice, all four elements are inherently relationships or networks, which means that far from being autonomous, each is a form of social action. In doing this he counteracts the tendency of the others to produce essentialist definitions. With more encompassing boundaries of what is legitimate to discuss, it is much harder to limit the dialogue to a few interlocutors. Cole-Turner's map is fully transdisciplinary, not only giving the social sciences a place in the science–religion dialogue, but moving them into the very heart of the debate. What remains to be seen is whether or not sociologists will take advantage of his map.

SCIENCE AS SECULARIZATION

For most of the past two centuries, much of academic discourse has assumed that science and religion are incompatible. The more there is of the one, it is said, the less there will be of the other. This has been a central assumption in debates over secularization, the one place sociologists of religion regularly mention science.

After Newton, many Enlightenment thinkers believed that the only role for God was as Creator (Wertheim, 1995). The Enlightenment cultural map showed science and religion occupying the same territory. As science advanced its boundaries in the eighteenth and nineteenth centuries, the "space" for God kept retreating before continued scientific discoveries (often called the "God of the gaps" argument, in which theologians invoked the deity wherever science was unable to explain a phenomenon). The beginning of the social sciences in the nineteenth century opened a new, systematic attack on religion (Bellah, 1970). The founders of sociology were among the first to argue that science and religion were mutually exclusive.

In the 1830s August Comte posited the "Law of Three Stages." Early humans, he argued, did not know the origin of natural events and so attributed everything to the gods. Later, as knowledge grew, religion began to be supplanted by philosophy, which replaced divine intervention with philosophical concepts (for example, phlogiston). But now, Comte claimed, we have achieved the stage of science in which positive facts will replace religious and philosophical speculation. The other founders of social science, such as Marx, Durkheim, Freud, and Weber, also believed that traditional religion would disappear, although their various arguments were more sophisticated than Comte's. But while the Law of Three Stages is rarely heard today, the idea that religion is only an inadequate explanation of nature and will be replaced by science is still popular among scientific atheists (e.g., Dawkins, 1996, 1998, 2003; Levitt, 1999).

Surprisingly, while a good deal is assumed about science among sociologists discussing secularization today, science itself is not a central issue. Science is *invoked* philosophically or ideologically in the secularization debate, but rarely is its relation to religion actually studied sociologically. In other words, science is treated as an abstraction, not as a practice (e.g., Buckser, 1996; Rioux and Barresi, 1997; Voyé, 1999; Lambert, 1999). When it is mentioned, it is usually either as *differentiation*, the separation of scientific from religious thought and institutions (e.g., Dobbelaere, 1999), or as *rationalization*. Rationalization may be understood in either a Weberian sense as disenchantment of the world or in a more Comtean sense as a change from a religious to a scientific world view (Houtman and Mascini, 2002). In all these discussions, however, science is talked about as an abstract system of thought, but the theories and work of actual scientists are usually ignored.

When practising scientists are questioned about their religious beliefs, the results are not what secularization theory predicts, as Edward J. Larson and Larry Witham (1998, 1999) discovered in their surveys of natural scientists. In 1914 and again in 1933 psychologist James H. Leuba surveyed U.S. physical and biological scientists, asking them two questions: Did they believe in a God who could be influenced by worship, and in an afterlife? Larson and Witham replicated Leuba's study. In both his surveys, Leuba found that 40 percent of practising scientists answered affirmatively to his question about God and 50 percent believed in an afterlife. Even given the Evangelical slant to the question, Larson and Witham found that 40 percent of U.S. scientists today still believe in God as defined and 40 percent believe in an afterlife. Had they used a broader definition of God, they report, the number answering yes to the first question would have been higher. But Leuba also discovered that elite scientists were much more likely to reject both beliefs, with only 20 percent answering affirmatively. Larson and Witham found the same: "NAS [National Academy of Sciences] biologists are the most skeptical, with 95 percent of our respondents evincing atheism and agnosticism. Mathematicians in the NAS are more accepting: one in every six of them expressed belief in a personal God" (1999:90). Why is there such a discrepancy between rank-and-file scientists and the elite? Larson and Witham point out that the NAS is a self-perpetuating body, in which current members elect new members. It may very well be that an *epistemic culture* (Knorr Cetina, 1999) encourages an orthodoxy of unbelief.

Interestingly, only Rodney Stark (1999) has seen the significance of Larson and Witham's work for the debate about secularization. If science in fact displaces religion from the cultural map, as Comte theorized, scientists should all be atheists. Yet, throughout history great scientists, not least among them Galileo, Kepler, and Newton, were believers and significant numbers of practising scientists remain so today. Conflicts there may be, but there is nothing inherent in either science or religion to compel them. Sociologists who wish to argue for secularization cannot continue to do so from the authority of science.

SCIENCE AS IMPLICIT RELIGION

If secularization theory argues that religion will disappear off the cultural map, the study of implicit religion finds it re-emerging in all sorts of unlikely places. "Implicit religion" was coined by Edward Bailey (1998), but has a long pedigree in the sociology of religion. It can be defined as "those symbols and rituals directed to the numinous which are located outside formal religious organizations (e.g., churches) and which are often unrecognized, unacknowledged, or hidden" (Stahl, 1999:3). To speak of science as implicitly religious is a bit of intellectual judo that turns conventional cultural maps inside out.

Some of the most significant studies of science as implicit religion have come from outside social science. Mary Midgley (1992) looked at science as a modern myth. Frederick Ferré (1993) saw scientism as an (inadequate) form of ultimate belief. Margaret Wertheim (1995) analyzed "God talk" and gender in theoretical physics. Mikael Stenmark's (2001) thorough analysis of scientism saw sociobiology as usurping religion. Several sociologists have contributed to this line of thought.

Dorothy Nelkin (1995, 2000, 2004) was sharply critical of current language in genetics, evolutionary psychology, and sociobiology. People like Richard Dawkins and E.O. Wilson, for example, are among the fiercest critics of religion, yet their own work is itself implicitly religious. Nelkin (2000:20–27) explains: "Natural selection to evolutionary psychologists is a 'theory of everything,' an eternal principle that explains why we behave the way we do and what makes us what we are; it defines the very meaning of human existence." She continues: "Such beliefs are not theistic; they are not necessarily based on the existence of God or a spiritual entity. But they do follow a religious mind-set that sees the world in terms of cosmic principles, ultimate purpose and design." Their language is full of religious rhetoric and Biblical imagery, they propagate their ideas with missionary fervour, and for them evolution both is a guide to moral behaviour and mandates a political agenda. Nelkin concludes: "More than a scientific theory, evolutionary psychology is a quasi-religious narrative, providing a simple and compelling answer to complex and enduring questions concerning the cause of good and evil, the basis of moral responsibility and age-old questions about the nature of human nature." Nelkin believes the boundaries between science and religion are best kept clear. The right-wing, anti-feminist political program of most evolutionary psychologists leads her to question the agenda of the whole science–religion dialogue.

On Nelkin's cultural map, to see a science as implicitly religious is to deny it credibility. Steve Fuller (1997), Robert A. Campbell (2001), and the *Webs of Reality* team (Stahl *et al.*, 2002) draw the map somewhat differently. Following Fuller's lead, these studies turn the "scientific study of religion" upside down, examining science through Weber's five characteristics of religion: soteriology, saintliness, magic, theodicy, and mystery. In every category, these studies find aspects of science which display the attributes traditionally assigned to religion.

The underlying issue in all these studies is authority. Fuller (1997:43) says, "Faith in science marks a degree of deference to authority that is unprecedented in human history." Campbell (2001; Stahl *et al.*, 2002) finds the basis of this in the sacred myth of science. He begins by noting the frequency with which prominent scientists engage in metaphysical speculations. "Many of the assumptions behind the so-called scientific world view are implicitly religious," he argues. "As a sacred myth, science functions as soteriology, that is, it provides the salvation stories a religion provides for its adherents" (Stahl *et al.*, 2002:26–35). The heart of that myth is the idea of progress. He concludes that "As long as scientific exploration is predicated on the notion that given enough time and resources, all of the questions that we can ask will be answered, the scientific world view will remain a religion, blinded by faith in its own methods and accomplishments."

A map of science as implicitly religious is the reverse of seeing science as secularization. The clear boundaries of the latter disappear in the former. In both cases the central question is authority.

TECHNOLOGY AND RELIGION

If science and religion have often been wary of each other, that is not the case with technology and religion. The past decade has seen religious groups of every stripe enthusiastically embrace computer technology. The fantastic growth of the Internet has been accompanied by an enormous proliferation of religious databases and user groups. Nearly every church, sect, and cult has its own Web page. Computers have spread from the church office to the sanctuary, as projection technology was introduced to worship. There are even online churches.

Exuberant growth was accompanied by exuberant rhetoric. Both the media and the academy were full of talk of technology as a "brave new world." All of this was part and parcel of the hype surrounding the tech stock bubble of the nineties. The bursting of the bubble in 2000 saw the beginning of a return to some long-overdue realism. Sociologists are just beginning to sort out what real changes are being mediated by computer technology and the Internet from what was merely wishful thinking. However overheated, though, the debate did raise some serious issues.

One line of questions asks if technology is enabling new kinds of religious community. Certainly the Internet is an important new communications medium. To the extent that it changes the social context for all religious groups, it will have some effect on religion. But some have gone much further in claiming that the Internet is fostering a new kind of association—the virtual community—and that this will profoundly change religion in the future. (For the best summary and analysis of this debate, see

Dawson, 2000, 2001, 2002.) It is too early to answer this question one way or the other, but Lorne Dawson (2002:6) sets out some valuable criteria: "I would propose, in descending priority, that a group communication by computer warrants being considered a virtual community to the degree that it displays interactivity, stability of membership, stability of identity, and happens in a common public space, with a relatively large number of participants." Should a group display these characteristics, it might well have enough trust and shared experience to be considered a true community.

A second line of questions asks if technology itself is implicitly religious. Technological discourse is routinely utopian, but in the nineties rhetoric went beyond that to the magical and religious. While some saw an imminent apocalypse (e.g., Joy, 2000), others spoke of becoming like gods (e.g., Kurzweil, 1999). There were a number of analyses of technology as implicit religion (Noble, 1997; Stahl, 1995, 1999, 2002; Wertheim, 1999), which differed more in their evaluation of the phenomenon than in their analysis of its causes and development. Like Nelkin's dissection of science, David Noble's view (1997:208) saw the religion of technology as overstepping boundaries and he sought to delegitimate it: "The thousand-year convergence of technology and transcendence has thus outlived whatever historical usefulness it might once have had. Indeed, as our technological enterprise assumes ever more awesome proportions, it becomes all the more essential to decouple it from its religious foundation." By contrast, I (Stahl, 1999) argued that the only way to defeat a dangerous technological mysticism was to replace it with a redemptive technology.

As was the case with science, the debates over technology frequently resolved themselves into credibility contests between disputants trying to create or move boundaries in order to establish authority. So, for example, Kurzweil (1999) uses both his position as a leading computer scientist and "scientific" arguments based on technological determinism to give legitimacy to his fantastic visions. Wertheim (1999:271) draws a different map in which such visions are only the most recent in a long line of techno-spiritual dreams and, further, that in comparison to more traditional spirituality these visions are seriously deficient. "The cyber-soul," she says, "has no moral context." It is an expression of the Ego without either a vision of the good or a sense of obligation to others.

The significance of such visions, as Wertheim points out, is that they express spirituality where none was possible before. If the Enlightenment map displaced spirituality from the domain of science, cyberspace has recreated some room for the spiritual at the heart of science and technology. However mythological, fantastic or morally deficient any given vision might be, the fact that "respectable" scientists are getting them published is clear proof that cultural maps are changing.

CULTURAL MAP INTERPRETATION

An important branch of military science is called "map interpretation." It may be a useful metaphor for an agenda for the sociology of religion. The proliferation of cultural maps in recent years may very well make the ability to interpret such maps an important skill in the years ahead. What conclusions can we draw from the four sets of cultural maps we have uncovered?

First, we have to remember Gieryn's observation that maps are always the result of boundary work and the product of credibility contests. The fact that even this cursory overview found such a variety of maps is indicative that things are in a state of flux. While it is perhaps not surprising that we should have quickly changing cultural maps in a time of rapid social and technological change, nevertheless the magnitude of the changes we have witnessed is amazing.

It was not that long ago that the epistemic authority of science was virtually unquestioned in academia. Forty years ago, for those who bothered to study religion at all, the goal was to study it *scientifically* (see Gilbert, 1997). Even theologians were talking about the death of God and the secular city. Today, while that map is still strong in the academy—as witnessed by the secularization debate—it is no longer hegemonic. Some still believe that the "scientific world view" is incompatible with religion, albeit the most vocal now are in the natural, rather than the social, sciences. But for many more the unquestioned authority of science is a thing of the past. Indeed, the Science Wars may well have happened because not a few natural scientists felt their power and authority slipping away. The emergence of studies defining science and technology as implicit religions is perhaps more a symptom than a cause of this trend.

All of this is why the maps of the science–religion dialogue are important. Old maps and boundaries, some of which go back to the Enlightenment, are fading away. It is not yet clear what will take their place. While the Science Wars may have been purely a reaction to social change, the science–religion dialogue is more proactive, trying to fix new boundaries and chart new territory. Sociologists need to participate in that debate or risk having others fix the boundaries of the new cultural maps.

REFERENCES

Bailey, Edward. 1998. "Implicit Religion: What Might That Be?" *Implicit Religion*, vol. 1:9–22.

Barbour, Ian. 1997. *Religion and Science*. New York: HarperCollins.

———. 2000. *When Science Meets Religion*. New York: HarperCollins.

Bellah, Robert. 1970. *Beyond Belief: Essays on Religion in a Post-Traditional World*. New York: Harper & Row.

Brooke, John Hedley. 1991. *Science and Religion: Some Historical Perspectives*. Cambridge, UK: Cambridge University Press.

Buckser, Andrew. 1996. "Religion, Science, and Secularization Theory on a Danish Island." *Journal for the Scientific Study of Religion* 35 (4):432–441.

Campbell, Robert A. 2001. "The Truth Will Set You Free: Toward a Religious Study of Science." *Journal of Contemporary Religion* 16 (2001):29–43.

Carey, Stephen. 1994. *A Beginner's Guide to Scientific Method*, Belmont, CA: Wadsworth Publishing Company.

Cole-Turner, Ronald. 1998. "Theology's Future with Science." Address to the John Templeton Foundation Toronto Workshop on the Design of Academic Courses in Science and Religion, Victoria College, University of Toronto, 19 July.

Dalton, Rex. 2003. "Berkeley Accused of Biotech Bias as Ecologist Is Denied Tenure." *Nature* vol. 426, 11 December:591.

Dawkins, Richard. 1996. *Climbing Mount Improbable*. Original drawings by Lalla Ward. New York: Norton.

———. 1998. *Unweaving the Rainbow: Science, Delusion and the Appetite for Wonder*. Boston: Houghton Mifflin.

———. 2003. *Devil's Chaplin: Selected Essays*, ed. Latha Menon. London: Weidenfell & Nicolson.

Dawson, Lorne. 2000. "Researching Religion in Cyberspace: Issues and Strategies." In *Religion on the Internet* (Religion and the Social Order, Vol. 8), eds. Jeffrey Hadden and Douglas Cowan. New York: JAI Press.

———. 2001. "Doing Religion in Cyberspace: The Promise and the Perils." *The Council of Societies for the Study of Religion Bulletin* 30(1):3–9.

———. 2002. "Religion and the Quest for Virtual Community." Paper presented to a joint session of the ASR/ASA, Chicago, 16 August. To be published in: *Religion Online: Finding Faith on the Internet*, ed. Lorne Dawson and Douglas Cowan. London: Routledge, forthcoming.

Dobbelaere, Karl. 1999. "Towards an Integrated Perspective of the Processes Related to the Descriptive Concept of Secularization." *Sociology of Religion* 60(3):229–247.

Ferré, Frederick. 1993. *Hellfire and Lightning Rods*. Maryknoll, NY: Orbis Books.

Fuller, Steve. 1997. *Science*. Minneapolis: University of Minnesota Press.

Geiryn, Thomas. 1999. *Cultural Boundaries of Science*. Chicago: University of Chicago Press.

Gilbert, James. 1997. *Redeeming Culture: American Religion in an Age of Science*, Chicago: University of Chicago Press.

Goodenough, Ursula. 1998). *The Sacred Depths of Nature*. Oxford: Oxford University Press.

Gould, Stephen Jay. 1998. *Leonardo's Mountain of Clams and the Diet of Worms*. New York: Harmony Books.

———. 1999. *Rocks of Ages: Science and Religion in the Fullness of Life*. New York: Ballentine.

Gross, Paul R., and Norman Levitt. 1994. *Higher Superstition: The Academic Left and Its Quarrel with Science*. Baltimore, MD: Johns Hopkins University Press.

Haught, John F. 1995. *Science and Religion: From Conflict to Conversation*. New York: Paulist Press.

Houtman, Dick, and Peter Mascini. 2002. "Why Do Churches Become Empty, While New Age Religion Grows? Secularization and Religious Change in the Netherlands." *Journal for the Scientific Study of Religion* 41(3):455–473.

Joy, Bill. 1999. "Why the Future Doesn't Need Us." *Wired* April:238–262.

Knorr Cetina, Karen. 1999. *Epistemic Culture: How the Sciences Make Knowledge*. Cambridge, MA: Harvard University Press.

Kurzweil, Ray. 1999. *The Age of Spiritual Machines*. New York: Penguin Books.

Lambert, Yves. 1999. "Religion in Modernity as a New Axial Age: Secularization or New Religious Forms?" *Sociology of Religion* 60 (3):303–333.

Larson, Edward J. 1997. *Summer for the Gods*. New York: HarperCollins.

Larson, Edward J., and Larry Witham. 1998. "Leading Scientists Still Reject God." *Nature* 394(6691):313.

———, and Larry Witham. 1999. "Scientists and Religion in America." *Scientific American* 281 (3):88–93.

Levitt, Norman. 1999. *Prometheus Bedeviled*. New Brunswick, NJ: Rutgers University Press.

Machamer, Peter, ed. 1998. *The Cambridge Companion to Galileo*. Cambridge, UK: Cambridge University Press.

Midgley, Mary. 1992. *Science as Salvation: A Modern Myth and Its Meaning*. London: Routledge.

Miller, Kenneth R. 1999. *Finding Darwin's God: A Scientist's Search for a Common Ground between God and Evolution*. New York: HarperCollins.

Morris, Henry M. 1974. *Scientific Creationism*. San Diego, CA: Creation-Life Publishers.

————, ed. 1968. *A Symposium of Creation*. Grand Rapids, MI: Baker Book House.

Nelkin, Dorothy. 2000. "Less Selfish Than Sacred?: Genes and the Religious Impulse in Evolutionary Psychology." In *Alas, Poor Darwin: Arguments against Evolutionary Psychology*, eds. Hilary Rose and Steven Rose. New York: Harmony Books.

————. 2004. "God Talk: Confusion between Science and Religion." *Science, Technology & Human Values* 29(2):139–152.

Nelkin, Dorothy, and Susan M. Lindee. 1995. *The DNA Mystique: The Gene as Cultural Icon*. New York: W.H. Freeman.

Noble, David. 1997. *The Religion of Technology*. New York: Penguin Books.

Osler, Margaret, ed. 2000. *Rethinking the Scientific Revolution*, Cambridge, UK: Cambridge University Press.

Park, Robert. 2000. *Voodoo Science: The Road from Foolishness to Fraud*. Oxford: Oxford University Press.

Pokinghorne, John. 1996. *Beyond Science*. Cambridge, UK: Cambridge University Press.

Rioux, David, and John Barresi. 1997. "Experiencing Science and Religion Alone and in Conflict." *Journal for the Scientific Study of Religion* 36(3):411–428.

Ruse, Michael. 2001. *Can a Darwinian Be a Christian?* Cambridge, UK: Cambridge University Press.

Shapin, Steven. 1996. *The Scientific Revolution*. Chicago: University of Chicago Press.

Southgate, Christopher, Celia Deane-Drummond, Paul Murray, Michael Negus, Lawrence Osborn et al. 1999. *God, Humanity, and the Cosmos*. Edinburgh: T. and T. Clark.

Stahl, William. 1995. "Venerating the Black Box: Magic in Media Discourse on Technology." *Science Technology & Human Values* 20 (2):234–258.

————. 1999. *God and the Chip: Religion and the Culture of Technology*. Waterloo, ON: Wilfrid Laurier University Press.

————. 2002. "Technology and Myth: Implicit Religion in Technological Narratives." *Implicit Religion* 5(2):93–103.

————, Robert A. Campbell, Yvonne Petry, and Gary Diver. 2002. *Webs of Reality: Social Perspectives on Science and Religion*. New Brunswick, NJ: Rutgers University Press.

Stark, Rodney. 1999. "Secularization, R.I.P." *Sociology of Religion* 60(3):249–273.

Stenmark, Mikael. 2001. *Scientism: Science, Ethics and Religion*. Aldershot, UK: Ashgate.

Voyé, Liliane. 1999. "Secularization in a Context of Advanced Modernity." *Sociology of Religion* 60(3):275–288.

Wertheim, Margaret. 1995. *Pythagoras' Trousers: God, Physics and the Gender Wars*. New York: W.W. Norton and Company.

————. 1999. *The Pearly Gates of Cyberspace*. New York: W.W. Norton and Company.

Wilson, David. 1999. "Galileo's Religion *Versus* the Church's Science? Rethinking the History of Science and Religion." *Physics in Perspective* 1:65–84.

CHAPTER 8

DIMORPHS AND COBBLERS:
WAYS OF BEING RELIGIOUS IN CANADA

William Closson James

1. INTRODUCTION:
MONOTHEISM AND EXCLUSIVITY

First, a story picked up somewhere or other about a professor and student. The student is thanking the professor for his time at Oxford. When asked what he has learned, the young man answers, "Well, sir, I think I've learned to look at all sides of a question." The don replies: "I hope you've also learned how to choose one." Amidst exploration and investigation of options, the choice of a single path may be the counsel of the elders, tugging the young back from the brink of religious decadence. Is it just *fin de siècle* consumerism that sees more individuals following two or more different religious options? That used to be called syncretism, usually a pejorative term in popular religious discourse, and usually referring to a reconciliation or merger of two different religions into one. We need new terminology and more sophisticated analyses for consideration of the current and differing methods by which non-syncretistic combinations of religions with one another are taking place.

My brief "Conclusion" to *Locations of the Sacred* (James, 1998) offered a summary of the ten essays comprising the chapters of that book. Struck by the fact that there emerged no single paradigmatic way of being religious in contemporary Canada, I suggested that "the locations of the sacred are found to be everywhere and nowhere, multiple rather than single, fluid rather than fixed, ephemeral rather than permanent, or at the margins rather than the centre" (James, 1998:241). Early in Carol Shields's play *Thirteen Hands*, a Winnipeg housewife is asked by a pollster, "Do you think of yourself as marginal?" Her response is, "Well, that depends on where you think the centre is."[1]

Western monotheistic traditions assert their exclusive claims to centrality for the religious allegiance of individuals—one is not supposed to be a Christian or a Jew or a Muslim and at the same time be something else. Theism has stern warnings against idolatry, against putting other gods before or alongside the one supreme God. In the Hebrew Scriptures no other gods are to be worshipped than the God of Israel. The Book of Judges makes it clear that Yahwism is not to be supplemented with indigenous paganism during the settlement of Canaan. Yahweh is not only good at delivering slaves from

Egypt and establishing a covenant with them in the Sinai Desert, but Yahweh is supreme over nature and can look after Israel's agricultural needs.

In Tillichian language people are cautioned not to raise penultimate concerns to the level of ultimacy. One is supposed to make an unconditional commitment to a single and primary overarching source of meaning. Redwald of Kent was a seventh-century East Anglian king who received Christian baptism. When he returned home, so Bede says, Redwald succumbed to the advice of his wife and some other "perverse advisors" and tried to have it both ways. He "tried to serve both Christ and the ancient gods, and he had in the same temple an altar for the holy Sacrifice side by side with an altar on which victims were offered to devils" (Bede 1968:130). A classic instance of the apostate, and perhaps of uxoriousness too, Bede comments that Redwald's last state was worse than his first. Because of the demands of religious exclusivity we have not sufficiently noticed or analyzed some of the ways that monotheism is actually operating in practice today. Following two or more religious options at once may be less marginal and more central than we sometimes recognize.

Locations of the Sacred considered several illustrations of how the restrictive obligations of monotheism seemed to be compromised or violated in twentieth-century Canada. The first example was an Inuit group on Hudson Bay (see James, 1998:Ch. 5). The Belchers Islands Inuit, during a crisis cult in the early 1940s, drew upon the traditional Inuit religious practices of shamanism in combination with Christian theism in what appears to be a straightforward example of syncretism. Newspapers of the day portrayed the Inuit apocalyptic predictions, and especially the naming of two members of the community as "God" and "Jesus," as an example of "distorted theology" and the result of incomplete missionization. One sees how at a critical juncture in their history the Inuit reinterpreted their animistic view of a world populated by many spirits in terms of Christianity's ultimate metaphysical dualism of good versus evil (James, 1998:123).

This particular aggregation of Christianity with native traditions became a potent mix that resulted in the tragic deaths by murder or suicide of nine of the Inuit people. As John Webster Grant says of such crisis movements, they are not so much attempts to reject Christianity "as attempts to appropriate it on terms consonant with Native modes of thought and relevant to perceived needs" (Grant, 1984:263). The history of the interaction of native peoples in Canada with European immigrants exhibits different ways of conjoining ancestral religious practices with Christianity, a topic that will get more attention later on. Though this particular Inuit crisis cult may have been syncretistic in part, probably their more usual practice was to go back and forth in alternating fashion between Christianity and shamanism, selectively and situationally.

The second instance considered in *Locations of the Sacred* arose from an examination of the novel *Obasan*, Joy Kogawa's partly autobiographical rendering in fiction of the evacuation, internment and dispersal of Japanese Canadians during the Second World War and after (see James, 1998:Ch. 10). Several cases could be chosen to show how Christian and Buddhist practices sometimes oscillate or occur together throughout the novel. At one point during the internment in the former mining town of Slocan in the British Columbia interior, Naomi, the young narrator, recounts the funeral practices after the death of her grandmother. First, they hold a wake in the Odd Fellows Hall, with an Anglican funeral service following on the next day. But after the Christian funeral, because the grandmother's husband is Buddhist, a truck transports her coffin up the mountain for cremation that night. Subsequently her husband receives her ashes and bones for burial. Watching the cremation, the seven-year-old Naomi thinks of the furnace in their house back in Vancouver, remembering her aunt had told that "it's in the heat of fire where the angel is found" (Kogawa, 1983:131), a reference to the fiery furnace of the Book of Daniel from the Hebrew Scriptures. But Naomi's aunt had also said that "the best samurai swords are tempered over and over again in the hottest flames" (Kogawa, 1983:131), an explanation that draws upon a Japanese example. The fire of the cremation is thus interpreted by Naomi from two cultural vantage points.

Though in *Obasan* Naomi's grandmother is accorded death rituals from two different religions, Christian and Buddhist, the Christian funeral and Buddhist cremation are kept separate. They are brought together and reconciled only in the narrative mind of Naomi and in the convergence of the explanations. Japanese converts to Christianity sometimes yearn for Buddhism's death practices, especially the connection with their ancestors established there. An elderly Japanese professor of religions who had become a Christian and been ordained a minister after the Second World War told me before his death how he had arranged for a Buddhist burial. He saw the neglect of the ancestors as Christianity's largest failing from a Japanese perspective. Buddhist cremation removes death's impurities and transforms the corpse into purified ancestral spirit. At the end of *Obasan*, Naomi—so obviously a devout Christian in many ways—prays to her dead mother as a source of benediction and protection (see Earhart, 1984:60–61; James, 1998:234–235; Reader, 1991:77–106).

2. MOVING BACK AND FORTH

Examining some other examples from Japan and from Canadian Native peoples may help us see what is going on here. Anyone who has visited religious sites in Japan straightaway observes that frequently one finds a Shinto shrine and a Buddhist temple adjacent to each other. Sometimes the shrine and temple are found within the same precincts so that devotees can move quite readily from Shinto observances to Buddhist practices without any apparent sense of conflict or tension. At the Shinto shrine people purify themselves at the basin near the entrance, then ring a bell to wake the *kami* and clap their hands before offering prayers. Perhaps they stop to purchase a fortune. The same people then move on to the nearby Buddhist temple where they bow before images of deities, chant their sutras and throw coins in an offering box. Though conducted under the auspices of different religions, the observances fit together and complement one another.

Religious responsibilities in Japan, it is well known, are shared between these two major religions so that one is said to be "'born Shinto, and die Buddhist." Shinto looks after the rituals of fertility and birth while Buddhism attends to the practices relating to death. Today one might add that many Japanese also "marry Christian" and turn to new religions in a time of crisis or for spiritual healing. Though less visible and lacking incorporation into formal religious structures, the underlying influences of Taoism and Confucianism provide a long-standing part of the Japanese sense of order and of the family. As Ian Reader states it (1991:21–22), the religious world of the Japanese is not governed by cognitive belief, but by situational requirements. As one of Reader's students told him, "her parents sent her to a Christian school because of its good academic reputation, bought her Buddhist amulets and prayed at Shinto shrines before examinations, and celebrated New Year, *o-bon*, and Christmas" (Reader, 1991:51–52).

Byron Earhart suggests that seven major areas of Japanese religions—Shinto, Buddhism, Taoism, Confucianism, Christianity, folk religion and new religions—constitute "many traditions within one sacred way." The participation by Japanese people in most of these traditions "simultaneously or alternately" is "a way of life that is constructed and supported by most of the individual components" (Earhart, 1984:22). Ian Reader confirms this view and claims that they "work together rather than conflict with each other" (Reader, 1991:44). In a similar vein Winston Davis usefully differentiates the "genuine" pluralism of Western cultures, where choosing one alternative makes commitment to the others impossible, from what he terms Japanese syncretism in which "these alternatives coalesce, or dovetail, and, over the course of time, tend to become *layered, obligatory modes* of behavior and/or belief" (Davis, 1992:31). The term "syncretism," however, implies too unified (and perhaps too structural) a merger of opposing practices into one; it is preferable to find some other way of describing the notion of layering and dovetailing, thereby preserving the picture of separate things fitting together without loss of their distinctiveness. Davis makes a worthwhile clarification though when he states, "whereas in the west it was heresy (or pluralism, as it is called today) which seemed to threaten the unity of Christendom, in Japan, it was monopraxis (emphasis on a single religious practice) that posed the greatest spiritual menace to the traditional integration of society" (1992:33). In Judaism, Christianity and Islam the integrity of society required "belief in one God, one faith, and one religious practice" (1992:33) while Japanese integration depended on a multiplicity of gods and faiths.

Yoshinobu Miyake, a priest in the Shinto sect of Konkokyo, speaking to a group of students from North America visiting in Osaka, summarized his own background this way: "My personal history has some uniqueness because I studied Christian theology in Kyoto; I studied Buddhism in the United States; and then I became a Shinto minister. It is a typical postmodern way of life for the religious person" (lecture at the Konko Church of Izuo, 10 June 1995). His explanation is instructive and suggestive: what might appear to be "unique" from the standpoint of his Western guests he interpreted as "typical" of the fragmentation of postmodernity with its loss of hegemony. Perhaps the Japanese example of offering many traditions for practitioners to draw on may provide a pattern to explain certain features of contemporary North American religion.

The Cree people of northern Quebec exhibit a way of being religious similar to the Japanese people, though perhaps with greater separation among the different traditions. In the National Film Board production *Cree Hunters of Mistassini*, a film crew follows a group of Cree during a winter spent in their hunting camp in the early 1970s. In the course of the film several families are shown engaged in traditional religious rites related to hunting: they tie the bones of animals in a tree; they place some flesh from a pregnant cow moose into the mouths of the fetal calves to ensure continuation of life; after the kill of large game there is drumming at the feast and the men rub bear grease into their hair. Throughout the film there is no depiction whatsoever of any kind of Christian observance, but we know from other sources that when the Cree returned to the village of Mistassini during the summer months, they practised Christianity. It as if the new religion is for village life while ancestral practices related to hunting are for life on the land. As with the Japanese, situational needs determine which religion is being followed at a given time.

Adrian Tanner, writing about his life with the Cree of Mistassini in the early 1970s, says that everyone was Anglican. When they were in the settlement most people attended Sunday services, baptisms and weddings. During the summer in Mistassini, Tanner states, traditional Cree practices were limited to "two or three major feasts, gossip about suspected sorcery, and a rare 'shaking tent' performance" (Tanner, 1979:25). But in the winter "balance between European-based and Indian-based religious sources is reversed with the latter becoming most common" (Tanner, 1979:26). During the winter, Christianity was limited to the display or reading of religious books stored in a decorated bag or to observances of taboos on Sundays and Easter. Otherwise, traditional Cree religious practices, especially rites of hunting divination, were observed on a daily basis. Tanner claims that each religious tradition is connected with a specific mode of production: "traditional Cree religious sources predominate in the context of the hunting group, while Christian sources are most apparent among the Indians in the context of the cash economy and at the level of the village of Mistassini Post" (Tanner, 1979:109). He explains that "the two traditions are not in conflict, since each has its own social context, the settlement sector for Christianity, and the bush sector for Cree shamanistic religion" (Tanner, 1979:211). Because of the lack of conflict between the two religions, syncretic developments did not take place. As the occasion or the season required, the Cree people went back and forth between two religious traditions, but without bringing them together to forge some kind of synthesis. As with the case of Japanese religions, the practices are alternated rather than synthesized, according to situational demands.

3. RELIGIOUS DIMORPHISM

Cornelius Jaenen and John Webster Grant have both pointed out the discrepant understanding between what missionaries thought they were offering to Natives and what the Native peoples thought they were doing when they accepted Christianity. As Grant proposes in *Moon of Wintertime*, Indians found in Christianity an opportunity to supplement, not replace, their traditional ways (Grant, 1984:249). In a paper given at a conference at the University of Toronto in 1984, the year that John Webster Grant's magisterial book appeared, University of Ottawa historian Cornelius Jaenen proposed a model to explain how a First Nations person could adhere both to the new religion and to a traditional belief system. He called this compartmentalized dualism "religious dimorphism" (Jaenen, 1985:185).

Jaenen set forth a typology of four negative and four positive responses on the part of Amerindians to European missions in New France. They ranged from aggressive rejection of Christianity at one extreme to complete acceptance at the other. The response of the greatest number of so-called converts, Jaenen argued, was "religious dimorphism," that is, "simultaneous assent to both the old ways and the 'new religion,' each compartmentalized and called upon as circumstances and needs dictated" (Jaenen, 1985:192). This "internalized dualism" enabled Natives to draw upon both Christianity and their own inherited traditions selectively and situationally, and to cope within two different cultures. The key to the success of this dualistic operation is to maintain its compartmentalization, especially where the beliefs are mutually contradictory. In fact, the French missionaries recognized that the way to get rid of this dualism was to impose a Catholic society. The dualism of dimorphism differs from syncretism, another of Jaenen's eight typological responses to missions, in that the syncretic response fuses elements of both religions to form a new system different from either of its forerunners.

In general, dimorphism refers to the occurrence of two distinct forms within one type. The literal meaning of dimorphism is "having two forms." The *Oxford English Dictionary* gives various examples of dimorphism, most from the second half of the nineteenth century, in geology, zoology and philology. So, "aragonite and calcite are dimorphs"; "the worker bee is a dimorphic female"; and a foreign word may come into English in two different ways, for example, the Latin *ratio* as ration and reason. The term seems most used in zoology where dimorphism can be seasonal, sexual or functional (suggesting all kinds of rich metaphoric possibilities for religious studies scholars to borrow, mine, exploit or play with). Incidentally, Jaenen indicates that except in papers and addresses he himself has not further extended or developed the term since he first used it in 1984. He remarks, though, "I sometimes chide my colleagues of Presbyterian background that this model most closely fits the typical Calvinist businessman—a Christian on Sundays and a pagan during business hours!" He adds, "[O]f course I only make such comments when speaking to friends who know where I am coming from" (personal communication, 19 December 1997).

In botany, dimorphism may refer to two different forms of leaves or flowers developing on one plant, or within the same species on distinct plants. The *Random House Dictionary* gives an illustration of a single fanwort plant, rooted in the bottom of a pond and growing above the surface of the water. This solitary plant displays different leaves, depending on whether they are submerged beneath the water or floating above it. This example may provide an illuminating parallel for exploration into how a single human being can follow two different religions, each one related to a specific context or environment. Applied to communities rather than to individuals, these considerations might lead to the kind of ecology of religions that Åke Hultkrantz has suggested, stressing the formative interplay between religion and the natural environment.

To repeat: the exclusivity of Western religions means they do not mix well with other religions, either by amalgamation or by alternation. In general any kind of fusion or synthesis that involves monotheism combining with something else is frowned on—or simply not acknowledged. A clear example of such a view is found in John Stackhouse's (1993) article in *The Globe and Mail* entitled "Native Religion? It's Christianity." (Though the provocative title was probably not supplied by Stackhouse, it seems to represent his intentions.) Stackhouse argued, on the basis of the 1991 census figures, that "Canadian aboriginals ... overwhelmingly saw themselves as Christians." Further, he stated that journalists, academics and others "must stop exaggerating the influence of native spirituality among today's aboriginal people." Finally, in most cases "the *actual* religion of Canada's natives is not 'native religion,' but Christian faith." Responding by letter a few days later, Wayne Holst pointed out that the categorizations of the census did not capture the reality of how Native peoples affirm both their own traditional spiritual heritage and the Christian faith. Holst explained: "I have learned that native people do not tend to draw lines of demarcation between spiritualities." But while Holst suggests that authentic spiritualities for Natives all emanate from a single source, Stackhouse seems to prefer to distinguish the "primary religion" of Christianity from Native religions, presumed at best to be secondary.

Theresa Smith observes that the majority of the Ojibwe on Manitoulin Island in the late 1980s practised both Christianity and traditional Anishnaabe ways. Because they understood Kitche Manitou and the Christian God to be one and the same, she says, and, thereby seeming to be in agreement with Holst, they experienced no conflict between these two traditions. But Smith implies the presence of dimorphism when she claims that while Catholicism might be practised at a conscious level, ancestral beliefs were operating constantly at a subconscious level: "The traditional Anishnaabe ways are held at a somewhat deeper level than the Christian beliefs" (Smith, 1995:36). Here, some kind of separation between the two ways of being religious is suggested.

To return once more to the examples I considered in my book, the Belchers Inuit and the Japanese Canadians of Kogawa's novel confronted an insurmountable triple impossibility: they could not assimilate themselves completely to the majority culture's Christianity; they could not simply maintain their ancestral traditions of shamanism or Buddhism; and they could not, nor were they encouraged to, merge their traditional ways with the European religious ethos. But the way of religious dimorphism has to be distinguished both from a synthetic blending of two religious traditions and from a progressive passage through a number of religious options. In general, it is the compartmentalization of the two ways of being religious that keeps each separate from the other; it is having two or more traditions operate at different levels; or, it is drawing upon one religion or another selectively and situationally, depending on the needs or the circumstances. Perhaps religious dimorphism is most clearly illustrated—the clarity being enhanced by geographic distance—by a student of mine who says she is Roman Catholic when she is in Canada and Hindu when she is in India. But a friend who with his partner is in a Jewish-Christian marriage practises religious alternation locally. He attends both the Reformed Synagogue and the United Church. In fact, he was once Adult Education Co-ordinator for the synagogue while serving at the same time on the Outreach Committee of the church. A recent book by Sylvia Boorstein (1998) describes how to be both Jewish and Buddhist.

4. RELATING RELIGION TO CULTURE

To this point the examples being considered imply that religious dimorphism with its strategy of compartmentalization may be useful at an early stage of religious acculturation, perhaps becoming counter-acculturation or resistance at times of crisis. Another way of combining religions is syncretism, especially in attempts to bridge the old ways and the new. It could be argued that the examples of the student and the friend and the author, all just offered above, are exceptional rather than typical instances. An anonymous assessor for an earlier version of this article remarked: "The anecdotes are clearly about extraordinary people rather than average ones. The use of such a method carries the risk that the author may project the experiences of educated professionals like himself and his friends on the majority of the population." I want to suggest, however, that in actual practice religious dimorphism (or even polymorphism) may be the characteristic method by which most Canadians encounter and live out their experience of the sacred as it manifests itself in a myriad of forms and places. Perhaps in the context of pluralism, or amidst a decline in religious hegemonic culture, dimorphism becomes more apparent. As Cornelius Jaenen comments, "Probably all individuals hold beliefs which are mutually contradictory but these produce no behavioural crises so long as they remain compartmentalized" (1985:193).

Northrop Frye used to tell a story from Stephen Leacock about the Presbyterian minister who also taught ethics in a college. The simple strategy used to manage these different roles was, as teacher, giving the students three parts Hegel and two parts St. Paul, whereas on Sundays, as minister and for his parishioners, he reversed the dose and gave them three parts St. Paul and two parts Hegel (Frye, 1971:227). Frye says this story reflects a time when the major cultural force in Canada was religious; it was a time when no great degree of separation was required to manage roles that today we would think of as being rather different. When Frye related this joke at Queen's University in the early 1980s, he commented that it was typically Canadian, explaining that its account of the relation of religion to culture would only be intelligible within Canada.

Already we have slipped over into a different aspect of the subject under review here. We have moved from examination of a dimorphism of two different religions to an investigation of religion in relation to culture. In part, Jaenen's comment about everyone holding mutually contradictory beliefs opens this door. For the religion one holds may come into conflict not just with other religions but with other attitudes, world views and ideologies from various parts of culture. How are these conflicts to be reconciled? Perhaps monotheists do not see such a conflict as critical or fatal as long as the conflict lies between faith and culture and not between two ways of being religious.

More than twenty years ago Tom Faulkner was first considering the possibility of hockey having religious meaning for Canadians. Faulkner says that people have to find ways of moving among the different worlds represented, perhaps, by business, sports, church and the academy, "donning and abandoning new roles as required." He maintains that "the person does not have available to her one sacred cosmos which convincingly superordinates all reality." Instead, he argues, "she must cobble together her own religion, constructing it from material borrowed from her encounter as a sort of consumer with the different sacred cosmoses made available to her by the different competing *ecclesiae* of her society" (Sinclair-Faulkner, 1977:388).

From this quotation two terms warrant some more attention, deserving to be teased out a bit further. First, the verb *to cobble*. This "cobbling together" of one's own religion does not mean reconciling and harmonizing all of the disparate elements in some kind of grand constructive and synthesizing enterprise. Cobbling is a seat-of-your-pants, makeshift, provisional kind of endeavour. It is a way of making do and getting by with what you happen to have at hand. You use binder twine and fence wire or, today, duct tape; you straighten out a few nails taken from a six-quart basket. *To cobble* means "to mend or repair roughly or clumsily, to patch up" (*Oxford English Dictionary*). (By the way, the term is not, as one might have expected, derived from the Old French *coubler*, to join or couple.) Reconciling the incongruities and conflicts among all the disparate pieces seldom actually takes place, or if it does, then it may be a largely intellectual endeavour. For instance, a theologian might struggle to work out the contradictions between her feminism and her Christianity, or another very thoughtful Christian might try to think through an existential encounter with the sacred in the natural world in terms of what the biblical record says about divine revelation in history. These examples show the efforts necessary to achieve consistency when religion is understood as a cognitive endeavour. Usually, though, as Tom Faulkner says, people tend more often to don and abandon various roles as required and thereby to keep them separate and out of conflict with one another. This enterprise has more to do with behaviour than with belief. As such, it has more to do with the everyday realities of the "little tradition" than with the elevated practices of a religious cognoscenti.

The second thing from the description of how the sacred cosmos of hockey relates to other competing options is the notion of the consumer. The consumer frequently becomes the metaphoric exemplar for the activity of taking a little of this and a little bit of that to cobble together a religion. When I ask my students to propose various secular correlates of religion, that is, to suggest ordinary life activities in which people today might encounter the sacred, they frequently mention shopping as a possibility. They point out how shopping centres commonly have become the focus for communities, their architecture taking on the grandeur and being accorded the effort once bestowed on churches. They think too of how activities of consumption relate to power, transcendence, iconography and *arete*, and how advertising, business and marketing determine so much of how governments are run and decisions made within communities. Consumerism is frequently mentioned in discussions of the secularization process; accordingly, it is usually talked about in derogatory terms as something inimical to religion.

Sociologist Reginald Bibby developed his fragmentation theory of religion into a full-blown metaphor of the consumer and the marketplace in his often-wrongheaded though popular book of the late 1980s, *Fragmented Gods*. There Bibby contends that "the gods of old have been neither abandoned nor replaced" by Canadians. "Rather, they have been broken into pieces and offered to religious consumers in piecemeal form" (Bibby, 1987:85). Bibby's religious consumers draw on religion selectively, pushing their supermarket carts down an aisle labelled "Religion," choosing various items to place in their baskets and take home with them. Perhaps on one occasion they choose a baptism; maybe later the time has come for a confirmation or bar mitzvah; then, a wedding or a funeral. Religious ceremonies are selected particularly at crucial junctures in people's lives—passages, such as birth, maturation, marriage and death.

Reginald Bibby's own negative theology of culture tends to put a rather rigid division—indeed, an opposition—between religion and culture—whereas my own, mostly following Tillich, sees the one more as an aspect of the other. Bibby, for example, worries that "religion has become little more than a cultural product" (1987:2). Fragmentation occurs, he states, when religion is seen primarily as a human phenomenon. Religion becomes "worth listening to," Bibby asserts on the second-last page of his book, "when religion claims to be more than culture" (Bibby, 1987:270).

To cobble together various fragments, taking first a bit of this and then a bit of that, may be lamentable from the standpoint of an older religious hegemony with its intuition of a single superordinating sacred cosmos and a unified culture. The consumer's tendency to pick and choose what is placed in the shopping basket signals, in this understanding, the decline or fragmentation of organized religion in contemporary culture. But taking religious pluralism in its contemporary context seriously might mean, instead of putting religion in opposition to culture, recognition of viable and manifold locations of sacrality. Demands and expectations for exclusive devotion, fidelity and consistency (even on the part of Western scholars of religion) may inhibit our investigation of new modalities of religiousness.

Now all of this may be sounding a little bit more "old hat" and less new hat than at the outset. After all, H. Richard Niebuhr in *Christ and Culture* (1951) offered something comparable to dimorphism as one of the ways in which Christians had typically worked out the relation between God and the world. There Niebuhr termed it the "Christ and Culture in paradox" position. He also called it the "Dualist" position, and identified some of its proponents as Paul, Marcion, Augustine, Luther and Kierkegaard. But the great difference between religious dimorphism and Niebuhr's dualism is that he is talking about how Christians of a certain kind relate their Christian lives to their lives in culture. The issue with Niebuhr is more the kind of value attributed to culture by Christians than operating within a context of religious pluralism in which the religious consumer ceases to give a total and unconditional allegiance to a single source of meaning.

Canadians of European descent tend to take it for granted that their religion, usually Christianity, exists (whether actually or potentially) in some pure form, untrammelled with any kind of contamination from "culture." Perhaps they assume this most readily if they are born and grow up within Canada. Yet even they struggle (or perhaps they do not struggle, being unconscious of the issues) to reconcile the old with some form of the new. How are feminism, political beliefs or New Age spirituality, to cite a few examples, to be reconciled with monotheistic traditions? Within Western religions syncretism tends to be a bad word; and, religious pluralism sometimes tends in practice to mean, not the co-existence of different religions, but subsuming the other under Western monotheism and calling it "inclusiveness." For instance, to incorporate the Native practice of burning sweet grass into a Christian communion service is more takeover or cultural appropriation (if practised by non-Natives) than it is interreligious dialogue and reciprocity.

5. SYNCRETISM AND ECLECTICISM

Religious dimorphism (and that may not, after all, be the best phrase) needs to be differentiated from syncretism; perhaps it also needs to be distinguished from another term with negative connotations, *eclecticism*. Much of Wade Clark Roof's description of the religious journey of the baby-boomers in *A Generation of Seekers* carries this mood of disapproval of eclecticism as something casual, less than serious or unprincipled. Drawing on Martin Marty's work of the 1960s, Roof comments that whereas an older spiritual style depended on "homogeneity" (that is, "assent to the details of a grand theological or philosophical system"), today the range of options makes possible syncretism and eclecticism, or less elegantly, "mixings and matchings" or "a *pastiche*-style of spirituality" (Roof, 1993:245). Such examples as "macrobiotic kosher-observant Jews" or "Creation-Spirituality Catholics" border on the uncomplimentary or derisive. But Roof also speaks more positively of the "mixing of codes" as experiential concerns supplant inherited doctrinal norms. When Roof refers to the new contemporary forms of multiple associations as a "multilayered spirituality" (Roof, 1993:201), a more affirmative and constructive expression comes into view.

Scholars of contemporary religions need to find some way of getting at what is going on without resorting to older notions of an illegitimate syncretistic fusion of belief systems or to contemporary contemptuous references to a casual New-Age eclecticism. Even the discussion by Robert Bellah *et al.* in *Habits of the Heart* of "Sheilaism" has the nuance of something slighting about it. Sheila Larson was a nurse whose self-defined faith was named after herself. Her Sheilaism meant being kind and gentle with yourself, taking care of others, believing in God, but without going to church, and seeing Jesus in oneself. Yet for the authors of *Habits of the Heart* this individualistic "Sheilaism" continued the deist tradition in American religion, and represented the transformation of "external authority into internal meaning" (Bellah *et al.*, 1985:235). It might also, this "therapeutic privatization, the shift from casuistry to counseling" (Bellah *et al.*, 1985:224), be becoming the norm in contemporary religious life. Rather than regarding Sheilaism as an inferior or lazy form of religiousness, perhaps the amount of sheer effort behind such a mélange needs to be acknowledged. As Lorne Dawson has remarked, people who are trying to put together a multi-layered spirituality may be working a lot harder at finding an authentic way of being religious than did their parents, for whom being religious offered no conflicting choices or options (personal communication, 14 May 1998).

Finally, since so much of the authority of how we view contemporary religion in Canada derives from statistically based surveys, two approaches to surveying ways of being religious in Canada might be usefully contrasted. A recent Angus Reid poll begins with the premise that analyzing denominational identity has little value as organized religion loses its hold over people. Instead, the Angus Reid pollsters turned to a categorization based on levels of doctrinal orthodoxy and participation in personal religious devotions. One result of this survey is a table entitled "Six Schools of Thought on Faith," a cluster-based analysis of beliefs that puts forth a spectrum including atheists, agnostics, theists and so on. While the aim is, in part, to take private faith seriously, one still wonders about the value of reducing religion in Canada to some form of cognition in which people are measured according to the degree to which they subscribe to orthodox beliefs (Grenville, 1998). The approach is reminiscent of an earlier Angus Reid poll, the subject of a cover article in *Maclean's* magazine that proclaimed "God Is Alive" (1993). The *Maclean's* report argued, based on the degree to which people held Christian doctrines, that Canada could be said to be "an overwhelmingly Christian nation, not only in name, but in belief" (14 April 1993:32).

Another, contrasting approach is represented in a study done by Environics in 1993. Commissioned by Vision-TV, this study was entitled "A Survey Regarding the Spiritual Dimension in the Canadian Public." Here the surveyors examined religion that was based neither on denominational identification nor on theological or creedal formulations. In this study 59 percent of Canadians agreed with the statement "I'm not a religious person, but I am a spiritual person"; 46 percent did not believe in traditional religions, while 70 percent had constructed "their own personal religion." Among young people, 60 percent believed that "all religions are equally valid" (see *The Globe and Mail*, 7 December 1993).

6. CONCLUSION

As religion in Canada late in the twentieth century becomes more highly personal and individual, we should expect it to continue to be characterized more by an eclectic spirituality (or whatever better-sounding terminology we can muster) cobbled together from various sources rather than a monolithic and unitary superordinating system of beliefs. The means scholars use to get at how people are being religious will have to go beyond surveys examining denominational adherence, church attendance, traditional devotional exercises or profession of particular beliefs. Perhaps even more crucial, scholars of religions must guard against assuming as normative for their work the possibly blinding or confining exclusivity of monotheistic traditions. To find the sacred moved away from its customary centre and to the nooks and crannies of contemporary life, especially at the horizons of the ordinary, taken-for-granted world of every day, is what we should expect to be the future of religion in Canada into the next millennium. We have to be alert to the ways that people are combining two or more modes of religiosity without denigrating such an enterprise or assuming it to be an inferior or casual kind of religiousness.

NOTES

[1] Here the editor requests a reference. I saw the play performed at the Thousand Islands Playhouse in Gananoque, Ontario, 19 May 1998. The next day (it was my birthday, actually), my sister pointed out that these lines were quoted in the Preface to Gray (1997).

REFERENCES

Bede. 1968. *A History of the English Church and People*. Revised edition. Translated by Leo Sherley-Price. Baltimore: Penguin.

Bellah, Robert N., *et al*. 1985. *Habits of the Heart: Individualism and Commitment in American Life*. Berkeley: University of California Press.

Bibby, Reginald W. 1987. *Fragmented Gods: The Poverty and Potential of Religion in Canada*. Toronto: Irwin.

Boorstein, Sylvia. 1998. *That's Funny, You Don't Look Buddhist: On Being a Faithful Jew and a Passionate Buddhist*. San Francisco: HarperSanFrancisco.

Davis, Winston. 1992. *Japanese Religion and Society: Paradigms of Structure and Change*. Albany: State University of New York Press.

Earhart, H. Byron. 1984. *Religions of Japan: Many Traditions within One Sacred Way*. San Francisco: Harper.

Frye, Northrop. 1971. "Conclusion to a Literary History of Canada." In *The Bush Garden: Essays on the Canadian Imagination*. Toronto: Anansi.

"God is Alive." 1993. *Maclean's*, 12 April.

Grant, John Webster. 1984. *Moon of Wintertime: Missionaries and the Indians of Canada in Encounter Since 1534*. Toronto: University of Toronto Press.

Gray, Charlotte. 1997. *Mrs. King: The Life and Times of Isabel Mackenzie King*. Toronto: Viking.

Grenville, Andrew. 1998. "God and North American Society: Contrasting Attitudes and Affiliations." A paper presented at the conference Rethinking Church, State & Modernity: Canada between Europe and the USA. Queen's University, 16 May.

Jaenen, Cornelius J., 1985. "Amerindian Responses to French Missionary Intrusion, 1611–1760: A categorization." In *Religion/Culture: Comparative Canadian Studies / Études canadiennes comparées*, eds. William Westfall, Louis Rousseau, Fernand Harvey, and John Simpson, 182–197. *Canadian Issues, 7.* Ottawa: Association for Canadian Studies.

James, William Closson.1998. *Locations of the Sacred: Essays on Religion, Literature, and Canadian Culture*. Waterloo: Wilfrid Laurier University Press.

Kogawa, Joy. 1983. *Obasan*. Markham, ON: Penguin.

Niebuhr, H. Richard. 1951. *Christ and Culture*. New York: Harper & Row.

Reader, Ian. 1991. *Religion in Contemporary Japan*. Honolulu: University of Hawaii Press.

Roof, Wade Clark. 1993. *A Generation of Seekers: The Spiritual Journeys of the Baby Boom Generation*. New York: HarperCollins.

Sinclair-Faulkner, Tom. 1977. "A Puckish Reflection on Religion in Canada." In *Religion and Culture in Canada/Religion et culture au Canada*, ed. Peter Slater, 383–405. Waterloo: Wilfrid Laurier University Press for the Canadian Corporation for Studies in Religion.

Smith, Theresa S. 1995. *The Island of the Anishnaabeg: Thunderers and Water Monsters in the Traditional Ojibwe Life-World*. Moscow: University of Idaho Press.

Stackhouse, John. 1993. "Native Religion? It's Christianity." *The Globe and Mail*, 6 September: A15.

Tanner, Adrian. 1979. *Bringing Home Animals: Religious Ideology and Mode of Production of the Mistassini Cree Hunters*. St. John's: Institute of Social and Economic Research, Memorial University of Newfoundland.

CHAPTER 9

STILL SEPARATED FROM THE MAINSTREAM:
A HASSIDIC COMMUNITY REVISITED

William Shaffir

With some notable exceptions,[1] practitioners of fieldwork do not usually return to the research setting to examine whether it has changed or if their analysis has stood the test of time. Several explanations can be offered to account for this situation. For some investigators, the direction of new research endeavours is determined by theoretical interests; if the particular setting is secondary to the theoretical category within which it is situated, and the researcher is not interested in the setting *per se*, he will not be drawn to return to it. For others, the more disagreeable aspects of fieldwork are too demanding. For instance, they have to find a very great deal of time for the research and to renew contact with people who are increasingly different from them, so that after they leave a setting they later display little interest in ever returning. A third consideration focuses less on the investigator's interest than on the people studied. The latter, for a variety of reasons, have come to be unhappy about the intrusion of the researcher and discourage him or her from returning. They may have read what was written about them, or heard about the results of the study, and conclude that it would not be in their best interest to welcome another visit from the fieldworker.

In a perceptive discussion on the advantages of maintaining contact with subjects who have been stigmatized as deviants, Miller and Humphreys assert that little in the sociological literature argues "... for purposeful continuation of interaction with respondents after termination of the formal interview stage."[2] However, in their view, three such advantages are immediately apparent: first, triangulation, or the search for ancillary data to corroborate statements from interviews, is enhanced; second, a longitudinal dimension is added to the research, which in some cases is useful for research economy; and third, new or previously neglected areas of research could be discovered.[3] Shaffir and Stebbins have noted: "... field research projects tend to raise more questions than they answer, driving some investigators back to the original setting to do more work or simply to see what changes have taken place over the intervening years."[4]

Hassidic Jews are set apart by their distinctive dress and unique customs and traditions and they have voluntarily segregated themselves in order to maintain a chosen way of life, well away from the mainstream. They have organized bounded communities and have achieved high degrees of institutional completeness to accommodate their religious and socio-economic needs.[5] In contrast to ethnic communities which have gradually become assimilated into the mainstream, the Hassidim have kept at bay secularizing influences and, far from diminishing, are actually increasing in numbers and flourishing in communities along lines which were hardly anticipated a few decades ago.[6]

The hallmark of the Hassidim's social organization is their deliberate isolation from their secular surroundings—which has sometimes been interpreted by others as an assumption of superiority and has occasionally soured relations between them and their neighbours. However, it is probably because of their chosen lifestyle that Hassidim have attracted their share of publicity which—while perhaps temporarily unsettling— has not detracted from their ability to shield themselves from the surrounding society's assimilative influences. On the contrary: recognizing themselves to be the focus of attention, they have been drawn together and, in the process, have been strengthened in their commitment to their religious way of living.[7]

In this paper, I discuss several changes which characterize a Hassidic group about whom I first wrote in the June 1987 issue of this Journal: the Tasher.[8] They live in a community which they established in the 1960s in Boisbriand, Quebec, some 25 kilometres north of Montreal. I have maintained contact with them over the years and here I focus specifically on several demographic and institutional changes as well as on the Tasher's use of the media to enhance their own agenda. I conclude by speculating on future challenges that this community is likely to face in the years ahead.

DEMOGRAPHIC SHIFTS AND INSTITUTIONAL ADDITIONS

In a 1994 article[9] about the Tasher Hassidim in a popular magazine, the author states that they are "cloistered in their self-imposed ghetto in Boisbriand, lead a life of strict devotion totally dedicated to carrying out the will of *Ha-Shem* on Earth and to raising children to do the same." This is entirely consistent with the picture I drew of them in my 1987 article.[10] At first glance, the community's physical layout is not uncommon: bungalows, rows of attached duplexes, and a few buildings for the institutional needs of the residents. But also at first glance, the appearance of the inhabitants is striking: the men are bearded, have side-curls, and wear long black coats and occasionally fur-trimmed hats, while the women wear high-necked, loose-fitting dresses, with kerchiefs or traditional wigs covering their hair. Conspicuously, the dress of the youngsters, and even of the very young children, mirrors that of adults, and while one can see large numbers of children in the streets, there is a total absence of recreational or sports equipment such as skateboards, inline skates, hockey sticks or baseball gloves and bats. In fact, for reasons of modesty, the charismatic leader of the Tasher, their Rebbe, even outlawed bicycles, and scooters have served as a substitute. One is struck by the remarkable abundance of baby prams and strollers along the sidewalks and on front lawns. Pointing to the community's most populated street, a Tasher recently inquired of me: "Do you know of another street in all of Canada which has as many children as ours?" Another Hassid commented that the average household has six to seven children and that since the parents are young, many more children can be expected: some couples have a child every year.

The Tasher community is dedicated to living uncontaminated by contact with modern society, but a visitor returning after several years will note some changes. One of the most obvious is that although the actual acreage has hardly changed, there are now numbers of newly built bungalows and large multi-household houses. A new sign at the entrance to the Tasher enclave is printed in Yiddish, French and English and states: DRIVE CAREFULLY. CHILDREN AT PLAY. VIOLATORS WILL BE PROSECUTED. Several new structures have been erected since 1987 to cater to the population growth: from 115 households then, to 180 in 1996. A girls' school, Bays Tzirl,[11] which was under construction in 1987, has long been completed and it has a spacious auditorium which serves as a centre for wedding celebrations. The school's enrolment, drawn exclusively from the community's pupils, stands at close to 400, a significant increase from the 160 total in 1987. The classes extend from kindergarten until Grade 12, by which time the girls are expected to become engaged and married.

At the end of the main road extending through the enclave, opposite the yeshiva, stands a new imposing two-storey structure. It was completed in 1993 and named Talmud Torah Bays Yehuda D'Tash[12] and serves as the elementary school for boys. It has an enrolment of approximately 260 boys (up from 160 in 1987) and the boys range in age from three to thirteen years. A new school was under construction in 1996; it will be reserved for boys aged thirteen to sixteen years; there are about 140 pupils in that age group, seventy of them from Tash while the remainder have come from Hassidic homes in New York and reside in a dormitory attached to the yeshiva. In addition, approximately 200 males between the ages of sixteen and nineteen study in the yeshiva, the majority of whom are from Tash. Apart from a French-language specialist, all the teachers in the schools for boys and for girls are Tasher Hassidim. The names of the Talmud Torah's two main financial benefactors are displayed prominently in large letters on the face of the building.

Several other structures have been erected since 1987. The administrative offices, originally centred in the yeshiva and then for several years in a converted house, now have a new building which was completed in 1992. There are twelve offices, and the modern boardroom, for meetings with political and other dignitaries, has elegant mahogany furniture. The front entrance to this building leads to a counter behind which sits a male Hassid who deals with incoming telephone calls. During one of my recent visits to Tash, shortly after the assassination of the Israeli Prime Minister Yitzhak Rabin, a computer printout spelling "Shalom Chaver," in English letters, was displayed above the counter. These were the last words of President Clinton's eulogy to Rabin and I was surprised to see them in a community which opposes the establishment of the modern State of Israel. When I inquired about that sign, a Tasher employee replied with a twinkle in his eyes: "I don't know how it got there."

Two further buildings were added recently. One was completed in 1992; it is single-storeyed and serves as a home for the elderly, subdivided into twelve apartments. It is situated next to the administrative offices. The other building is a synagogue; it was completed in 1995 and includes four large rooms, three of which are used for daily prayers while the other is reserved exclusively for study.

The occupational breakdown for males has changed as the community has grown over the years. The majority of the men are still engaged in religious-oriented types of work (as teachers, ritual slaughterers and kashrut supervisors) and in religious study in the *kollel* (advanced Talmudic academy) for which they receive a financial subsidy. But there are now more small-scale, independent concerns, while some individuals have started businesses which they operate from their homes; these include stores selling hardware or sewing necessities, and a shop for altering clothes. Others sell supplies for photography, vitamins, toys, shoes, dry goods, books, jewellery, and computer hardware and software. According to a reliable source, about 10 percent of the men work outside the community: an electrician, a real estate agent and employees in two business concerns owned by Tasher Hassidim. As the community has grown, more men have been given administrative positions; there are several bookkeepers and other personnel who are paid salaries. An administrator explained to me that just as Canada derives income from the sale of its resources and the production of goods, so does Tash derive income from its unique speciality: the study of Torah for which it receives charitable private donations that help to provide salaries for the services of Tasher men.[13]

There have been no changes of any particular significance in the area of secular education; these Hassidim remain steadfastly committed to the view that secular education threatens their traditional values. I noted in 1987: "… secular classes are closely supervised to ensure that the pupils will not see any conflict with the contents of their religious studies."[14] Recent advances in computer technology have enabled them to assemble more readily specialized texts to suit their particular needs. A Tasher told me:

> We have a French department and an English department. We make our own books. So one of the girls is working on a computer and typing books…. Instead of buying books and putting black markers all over them [to censor some passages], we buy one original book and retype the story. Occasionally we change a name, we change the sex from a boy and a girl to two boys or vice versa.

He added that the result was very pleasing: the work occupies a girl while the children are given decent books to read, without torn or defaced pages. Another advantage is that a girl who has graduated from school is given employment, a subject to which I shall return in this paper.

The community's high degree of self-sufficiency has been maintained. The variety store is stocked with produce, canned goods and household articles, and recently expanded with more kasher products imported from New York. The Tasher's paramedic team, established some years ago, remains fully prepared for emergencies and in 1996 included some ten men who had acquired several levels of training. A new updated defibrillator is a very recent addition (the first one was purchased in 1968), and the ambulance, already present for several years, contains state-of-the-art medical equipment. The Tasher select with care, now as in the past, the medical and dental care provided outside the community. Where convenient, they use local services, such as garages and dry cleaners; they are aware that it is in their own interests to support the local economy, in order to foster good relations with the surrounding Francophone population.

If, as a collectivity, the Tasher have gained in political astuteness over the years— and they are indeed perceived by several in the mainstream Jewish community to have done so—they give the credit to one particular individual, a French-Canadian Catholic who has sharpened their awareness in the art of politics. He has developed a fascination for the Tasher and has committed much of his spare time to their benefit. Politics are his hobby and he has established contacts with politicians at various levels of government; he has not only lubricated relations between the Tasher and local politicians but has also helped them to gain access to senior provincial and federal figures. He extols the virtues of the Tasher Rebbe and values his blessings, declaring: "The Grand Rabbi is a very holy man. He has given blessings for me and my family."

Over the past decade, the citizens of Montreal and Quebec have become increasingly familiar with the Tasher through articles and reports in the French and English media. To a large extent, this exposure has been self-selected and based upon a calculation of the potential benefits to the community. For instance, when a teacher at a local school contacted the Tasher for permission to visit them with his students (who would engage in an exchange with their peers), the request was refused. Such an encounter could give rise to many problems: not only would the group have male and female pupils but, the Tasher reasoned, the two sides had too little in common. On the other hand, they have responded favourably in many cases to reporters who asked to write about the community.

The Tasher Rebbe continues to be at the very centre of the community. He was born in 1923 and appears to be in fine physical health. A conversation with any Tasher about the community, its growth and its future plans inevitably turns to accounts about the Rebbe's miraculous powers and incredible insights. His followers speak enthusiastically about the visitors who come from various parts of the world to consult him on various matters. One of them told me, "A guy sits down with the Rebbe with a list of twenty business decisions. Rebbe, should we open an office in this city? Should we close this shopping mall? Should I hire this guy? Yes? No? You wouldn't believe it!"

The Tasher pride themselves on the success with which they have preserved their distinctive lifestyle. To an outsider, the community is portrayed in idyllic terms as individuals and households who maintain a way of life steeped in Hassidic traditions. One Tasher pointed to the new buildings and asked, "What can be better than here?" He then added. "It's safe, it's not polluted, and most of all, the children are not exposed to bad things that you cannot help but see in the streets of the city." However, the community's rapid growth has presented serious challenges for the years ahead.

THE TASHER AND THE MEDIA:
THE BIKERS AND THE REFERENDUM

On 30 October 1995, the electorate in the province of Quebec voted in a referendum to determine the future status of Quebec. A vote in favour of sovereignty for Quebec would mandate the provincial government to begin negotiations with the federal government to lead to Quebec's independence; a "no" vote would maintain the province's status quo within Canada. Up to three months before the referendum, it appeared from public opinion polls that the "no" side would emerge victorious. Politicians and other public figures were increasingly concerned that dire economic consequences would follow the secession of Quebec from Canada.

As the Quebec government's campaign appeared to be almost stagnating, a dramatic change in momentum was achieved several weeks before the referendum, when Lucien Bouchard, the leader of the Bloc Québécois (a federalist party though confined within Quebec and deeply committed to Quebec sovereignty) replaced Jacques Parizeau, Quebec's premier, as the chairman of the sovereignty team. Bouchard was a passionate speaker and a charismatic figure; his public appeal transformed the fortunes of his party almost overnight.[15] Opinion polls now indicated that the gap between the sides was quickly narrowing and, only days before the referendum, that the outcome was too close to predict.[16]

During the course of the debate, politicians toured the province, appealing especially to those whose ethnic background was neither English nor French. For the Jews of Montreal, the anxiety of the previous months now turned to real alarm, since it appeared that the secessionists would score a narrow victory. They feared the expected economic and political uncertainty, coupled with the possibility of increased antisemitism under the guise of Quebec nationalism. It is within this context of heightened political, economic and social uncertainty that the Tasher Hassidim were catapulted on to centre stage in the unfolding political drama. By then, the inhabitants of Quebec had learned about the quaint community of ultra-observant Jews: several Tasher had rushed to the rescue of casualties of a bloody turf war between rival gangs. On 13 September 1995, a bomb had ripped through a biker's bar north of Montreal, injuring ten men and apparently signalling the resumption of a fierce war between rival motorcycle clubs.[17] The bomb was said by the police to have been placed under the outdoor terrace of a bar in suburban Boisbriand, not far from the Tasher enclave. Since the previous autumn, twenty-one persons had been killed in the conflict between the Hells Angels and Rock Machine gangs over control of drug sales in the streets of downtown Montreal. The blast destroyed the terrace and blew glass, furniture and bar equipment on to the streets, and rocked buildings for kilometres around. An Associated Press bulletin of that day, 13 September, stated: "Several members of a nearby orthodox Jewish community helped ambulance attendants tend to the burly, tattooed wounded men."[18]

On the following day, both the French and the English newspapers described the Hassidim's assistance more vividly. The daily *La Presse* commented that the Hassidic Jews from Boisbriand were probably the only Quebecers able to consider Hells Angels as sweet and gentle;[19] it reported that Tasher paramedics provided first aid to the nine bikers who had been injured in the explosion, which had occurred a few streets away from the Tasher community. One of the Hassidim was quoted as saying, "We were the first to arrive on the scene. We got there only four minutes after the alert was sounded."[20] *La Presse* gave some background data about the Tasher: they numbered about 1500 "with a birth rate of two babies a week" and they had organized their own paramedical system, including an ambulance; a Tasher administrator was quoted as saying that this was not the first time that such first-aid assistance had been given to outsiders: two weeks earlier, as the ambulance was returning from Montreal, it had stopped to help four persons injured in a car accident on Autoroute 15.[21]

The English-language daily, *The Gazette*, gave many of the details and added: "If one good thing came out of the bombing, it was that it drew the predominantly French-speaking, Roman Catholic community close to the four thousand Hassidic Jews who have settled there."[22] Moreover, *La Presse* noted the irony of Orthodox Jews, uncompromising in their faith, rushing to the assistance of persons involved in drug trafficking and murder.[23] That aspect had not entirely escaped the Tasher: one of them remarked, "At first, we didn't know that they were bikers. Even then, we were there as paramedics, not judge and police. The objective of our spirituality is to help others, all others...."[24] The man added an observation which reflected these Hassidim's enormous distance from the social world of bikers: "I am not naive, but I'd like to believe that our help in such dramatic circumstances might lead some of these men to see better ways to live their lives."[25]

The report in *La Presse* had some potential overtones relating to the sovereignty debate. It claimed that although the Tasher isolated themselves, they could be contrasted with other Hassidic groups by their openness to the modern world: "... these orthodox Jews are not afraid to take non-orthodox positions sometimes; during the commissions on the future of Quebec a few months ago, they took a position in favour of the sovereignty of Quebec."[26] That presumed "openness" was hardly evident when I told a Tasher that his community's heroics were featured on the front page of *Allo Police*, a French-language weekly tabloid.[27] Along a side-view of one of the Hassidic paramedics, there were three additional stories with accompanying photographs: one about a stripper, another about a triple-X-rated film on sex and a third about a prostitute. "What's *Allo Police*?" he asked, and when I added that the paramedic was featured along with a hooker on the front page, he inquired, "What's a hooker?"

The degree of the Tasher's openness to the outside world is carefully limited through a series of meticulously engineered social boundaries. However, a few months earlier, on 15 February 1995, a Tasher appeared before the provincial government's roving commission on sovereignty and, with the approval of his Rebbe, he unequivocally endorsed the sovereigntist cause.[28] At a time when ethnic minorities were for the most part steadfastly opposed to that cause, the Tasher's position was newsworthy. His remarks were punctuated by bursts of applause and attracted considerable attention. That set the stage later for a visit to the Tasher community by the premier of Quebec, some two weeks before the referendum date.

The Tasher argued that religious teachings, especially the Torah portion *Bekhukotei*, which admonishes Jews to follow Torah laws even at the risk of severe punishment, provided the basis for the decision to endorse sovereignty. He said that the last plague identified in the tractate is that the people will be exiled from their homeland and added:

> We see that the worst punishment that mankind can suffer is ... not having a homeland. A person who does not have his homeland is a person who suffers extremely ... and it prevents people from having freedom and true happiness.

These words clearly were welcome to the sovereigntists in the audience, who had already been pleased when the speaker had moments earlier apologized in his halting

French for having to speak in English, which he identified as "a foreign language" that Quebecers spoke not as a matter of policy, but of historical accident. He ordered his presentation around three central questions: 1) "Should we create a sovereign Quebec?"; 2) "Can we separate?"; and 3) "As a minority, how do we feel about a sovereign Quebec?" He said: "I think it is important ... to support a movement of a sovereign Quebec which would bring comfort and comfortableness [*sic*] in the lives of people that live in Quebec." The audience had been instructed not to applaud during the presentation, but some could not refrain from doing so when the Hassid added: "I believe that our neighbour nations should be the first ones instead of discouraging the idea of creating a sovereign Quebec, they should be the first ones to help us do so...." The use of this "us" was unmistakable evidence that the Tasher were in alliance with nationalist aspirations. The incongruity of this political stance must have been obvious both to the audience and to the public at large: a spokesman for the Tasher Hassidim— who were ultra-religious Jews isolated from the mainstream—was endorsing a position which was anathema to the overwhelming majority of Jews in Quebec.

When dealing with the second question, the Tasher representative focused on the economic implications of separation. He conceded that sovereignty would entail economic hardships and that "building an independent country will require hard work" but stressed the benefits of "freedom" and "happiness" which accompany independence and added, "[T]his surely is worthwhile the extra work that it requires."

The Tasher spokesman did not believe that minorities in the province had reason to fear that sovereignty would prejudice their position (as, indeed, the mainstream Jewish leaders in the province did fear) and stated that Quebecers, by virtue of their minority status within Canada, would necessarily be sensitive to the concerns of minorities. He mentioned that the Tasher Rebbe took such a stand in 1976, when the minorities were anxious after the Parti Québécois first assumed power and said: "At that time, our religious leaders, including the Grand Rabbi, instructed us that there's nothing wrong in living in Quebec and we started to reinvest and build up Quebec rather than move away." The Tasher would adopt the same position now: "It is now our responsibility ... to help develop a strong and prosperous Quebec for all." The Tasher relied upon the wisdom of their leaders in all important matters: "Our leaders told us not to run away but to invest in Quebec and we have a very fantastic relationship with the government and the people since then." He concluded with a message aimed at Anglophones: "I believe that everybody understands that most Quebecers feel at home and secure in their position and that they'll be a lot more tolerant and understanding of the needs of other languages and they should not get concerned over that." Applause followed once more and the Tasher spokesman later told me, "I walked out of there like a hero."

The Tasher's presentation greatly angered many in mainstream Jewry, but the Hassidim believed it was prudent to follow the will of the majority, and when I enquired "And what if the majority were opposed, would you also be opposed?" he replied, "Of course we would. We do what the majority wants." In the end, however, the Tasher did not vote uniformly. Sensitive to the wishes of federal politicians, whose goodwill was also to be cultivated, their vote was split. One Tasher told me, "So in other words, we did no harm, we did no good," but then he quickly added, "For the sake of the locals, we tried to give the perception that it's a 'Yes' vote."

On 12 October 1995, Quebec Premier Jacques Parizeau was greeted by the Tasher Hassidim when he attended a synagogue inauguration. The visit was important for its symbolic significance since the referendum was only some two weeks away; it was in the interest of the Parti Québécois to demonstrate that its position could be embraced by minorities and the Tasher could serve as an excellent vehicle to promote this objective. He addressed the Hassidim first in French, then in English:

> I'm very happy to have seen your community develop and prosper over the last few years.... You are showing that one can be attached to tradition, to religion and to a way of life, to a set of values and, at the same time, prosper, develop economically, financially, and that one objective is in no way a hindrance to the other. From that point of view, you are an example to a number of other communities.[29]

Referring to the referendum, he stated: "We shall decide all together ... no matter where we come from originally ... our future."[30] A Tasher administrator thanked the premier in French and summarized his remarks in Yiddish. A month earlier, in September 1995, the Quebec government had announced that it supported the initiative for a diamond centre to be located in Boisbriand.

On 2 April 1994, a brief news item in the *Financial Times*, a Canadian paper, was headlined "Diamonds Could Be Hasidim's Best Friends" and part of the text stated: "A tiny group of ultra-orthodox Hasidic Jews living in rural Quebec is hoping to turn their little community into a diamond-cutting centre."[31] Another report[32] stated that Boisbriand, the municipality surrounding Tash, was seeking a major diamond-cutting role. Quebec's vice-premier announced at a news conference on 5 September: "Boisbriand was chosen because that town's Grand Rabbi Forencz Lowy is a world-renowned religious leader ... and will contribute to Quebec's prestige";[33] he added that he expected Quebec to become the hub of the diamond industry in Canada, and that would also attract tourists. A Tasher administrator was quoted as saying: "It is a privilege for us to be in a position to contribute to the Quebec economy." By the time the premier arrived to visit the Tash in September 1995, the stage had been set: those Hassidim had endorsed the government's plans for independence and the government had committed financial support for the diamond centre.

PERSPECTIVES FOR THE FUTURE

Social scientists have been perplexed by the success which Hassidic communities have shown in resisting and countering the surrounding assimilative influences. Some have pointed to the strains and stresses which affected that lifestyle and threatened it. Kranzler, for instance, writing in 1961, believed that the external symbols of Hassidic traditions—including the men's long jackets, their fur-trimmed hats and side-curls—would not endure, adding: "Only a small minority will cling to the extreme pattern of their parents."[34] Poll commented in his 1962 study of the Williamsburg Hassidim: "As more members of the community move into a greater variety of occupations and as the types of occupations increase, there may be more extensive involvements in external systems of social relationships";[35] occupational mobility would enhance the possibilities for members to assimilate and lose their identity as Hassidic Jews. Rubin's 1972 study of the Satmar cited several strains affecting the community, including economic pressures and rapid natural increase of the population, which would pose a threat to forms of interpersonal relationships underlying this Hassidic group.[36] In the case of the Tasher, there is the challenge posed by a steadily increasing birth rate, coupled with the necessity to provide gainful employment for the residents. While the leaders of the Tasher are not obliged to secure such employment in any formal or legal sense, it is clearly in the community's best economic and social interests to ensure that its members are gainfully employed.

The institution of the *kollel* where married men receive a financial subsidy to pursue religious studies provides only a partial solution to this problem. However, this option does not suit all males, especially those who are not inclined to intensive and advanced religious learning. It is precisely for this reason that the proposed diamond centre is seen as a vital source of employment to meet long-term needs. The training for such work would be supervised by Hassidic Jews while the accompanying time constraints could be accommodated within the demands of their religious lifestyle, including Sabbath observance, religious holy days and daily prayer services.

Whereas males are expected to pursue religious studies for a prolonged period, a similar expectation does not obtain for females. A problem which the Tasher must eventually face will be how to occupy girls gainfully from the time they graduate from school until they marry and expect a child. So far, these young women have become teachers in the school for girls or worked as office employees in the Tash administrative offices. A Tasher told me, "Right now, we have 12 girls which isn't a problem to find jobs for them," but he added that within a few years 25 girls could be expected to graduate annually and that would pose a problem: "We won't have vacancies for 25, so we'll have a surplus of 12 or 13 which we're worrying about." The girls' school thus experiences a constant turnover of teachers who become employed following completion of Grade 12, at 17 or 18 years of age, but who later depart to raise a family—which, for the majority, occurs after the first year of marriage at age 18 or 19.

Population increase has not only required provision for employment opportunities but has presented the Tasher with a more critically immediate challenge: securing space for additional residential construction. Though settled on land which exceeds 130 acres, the community is situated in a predominantly rural area which is designated mainly for agricultural use. Therefore, plans for further housing construction must include a rezoning approval from the municipality. The Tasher have been granted such approval in the past and, in the process, have established a network of political contacts within the municipality. A new plot of land is currently under development which has already resulted in the addition of two streets. Further expansion plans will therefore necessitate friendly relations with the immediate neighbours of the Tasher. The pragmatics underlying this situation provide a context for a better appreciation of the Tasher's position on Quebec nationalism.

I stated in my 1987 article that the community's comparative isolation enables it to shield its members from exposure to undesirable temptations. This continues to be the case. There appear to be no greater tendencies towards an infusion of secularizing influences which are perceived as threatening to the traditional values of the Tasher. Radios are still banned in the home, but they are permissible in cars. The Tasher are aware of the difficulties of preserving their lifestyle. One of them told me, "We're not miracle men. And children with bad upbringing we can have as well. Thanks to God, we have so many years of knowledge of what's going on the streets that we have an advantage." Then he added sadly, "But we'll catch up"; he did not think that the Tasher would always be able to avoid the problems of dysfunctional families, but concluded: "At the moment, we're very advantaged that we're in a healthy environment." He then reflected that although flagrant violations would be comparatively easy to detect, there was the danger of the penetration of more subtle external influences; he gave as an example *tzeneeus* (modesty in dress), requiring a long hemline:

> The hemline of dresses is going up. The style used to be maxi and girls didn't have any problems with long dresses.… Now that the stores don't have, it's harder to find a long dress and mother is not a tailor. It's still long enough that we require but shorter than a year ago.… We're human.

CONCLUSION

This article has outlined some directions along which the Tasher community has expanded since I reported on it in 1987. I believe that, where possible and appropriate, it is in the interests of social scientists to return to research settings to evaluate how the community has changed, and whether the earlier analysis has withstood the test of time. In the conclusion of that 1987 article, I noted two features of the community's organization which would have long-range consequences: 1) its high birth rate would require additional housing and necessitate closer ties with government bodies and with mainstream Jewry for financial support and resources; and 2) the community's isolation would continue to shield it against the intrusions of external influences. I now believe that my predictions were close to the mark. The Tasher have been singularly successful in preserving their boundaries against external secular forces; and although ties with mainstream Jewry have not materialized, good relations with provincial government officials and local municipal politicians have intensified.

I was first introduced to the Tasher in 1969, when I served briefly as a secretary in their yeshiva. In evaluating my relationship with them over the years, I believe that I currently occupy the status of "privileged outsider."[37] I must quickly add, however, that this status reflects our mutual interests: the Tasher both require and demand distance between themselves and those who, like me, pursue a different lifestyle; but I have been unprepared to alter my lifestyle to resemble more closely their commitment to ultra-Orthodox Judaism and thereby, perhaps, gain a deeper acceptance. I have realized that in the final analysis it is the Tasher who will confer any significant change in my status. I have gained a little more sensitivity about the Hassidim's expectations for themselves and have become more familiar to numbers of Tasher who now appreciate that my knowledge of their community's lifestyle is more than perfunctory. We now move more speedily beyond perfunctory exchanges typically accorded to outsiders visiting for the first time. There were numerous occasions when I was taken into the community's confidence, which I attribute to my long-time standing among the Tasher.

I am now increasingly comfortable among the Tasher during my visits, but my access to the community is certainly not unlimited. There is one particular Hassid who serves as the chief gatekeeper and he usually supervises my introduction to people and places. Though I feel that I can discuss almost any topic with him, and though he usually allows me access to files and documents which I have requested to see, we both maintain our reserve during our encounters. I have come to realize that I cannot expect anything more. We have learned to enjoy one another's company and I respect that, above all, he must remain sensitive to the community's requirements when evaluating my requests for privileges. This occurred very recently when I asked to meet teachers from the girls' school to discuss the curriculum. I had assumed that this would be arranged easily and was somewhat taken aback when he told me that "… it would be against religious views, in general, to expose any woman to any man" and my request was therefore refused. On the other hand, he readily agreed to arrange for me to meet male teachers. We exchange greetings before religious festivals and on occasion he might even ask for my advice. The benefits from our relationship are reciprocal. While the barrier between us has thinned, it has not, nor will it, disappear completely. Whereas previously I would have seen this as a reflection of inadequate field-research skills, I am now inclined to believe that successful field research requires the respecting of boundaries between the researcher and the researched, which, while potentially limiting the scope of the fieldwork, need not detract from it and is, moreover, unavoidable.

When I asked a Tasher official in 1996 how the community might be organized in about fifteen years, he replied firmly, "Same as today except bigger"; major shifts in the present lifestyle were not expected and the Tasher would remain cloistered. A visitor to the community around the year 2010 would see these Hassidic Jews adhering tenaciously to their observance of Jewish laws and to their customs. But the Tasher would also embrace some of the benefits of technology which would help to maintain their chosen lifestyle. "We're going to have the best cellular telephones around," a Tasher told me with a smile, but he meant it seriously.

I continue to visit the Tasher for both personal interest and scholarship. Indeed, these two objectives have become almost seamlessly joined. Sometimes the community appears as a picturesque reminder of yesteryear caught in a time warp; but this is a gross misperception of the Tasher, who are, in several respects, very much part of the modern world. Finally, I have realized, at times grudgingly, that sound scholarship need not exclude personal interest and pleasure, and that the most satisfying research results when these are combined.

ACKNOWLEDGMENTS

The research for this study was supported by grants from the Social Sciences and Humanities Research Council of Canada and from McMaster University.

NOTES

1 Robert Stebbins has written about "concatenated research," which refers "… to a research process and the resulting set of field studies that are linked together, as it were in a chain leading to cumulative grounded, or inductively generated theory." See Robert Stebbins, "Concatenated Exploration: Notes on a Neglected Type of Longitudinal Research," *Quality and Quantity* xxvi (1992), 435–442. The topic of returning to the field is probably addressed more fully by anthropologists given the nature of their research in faraway places. However, it is a worthy topic for sociologists to consider.

2 See Brian Miller and Laud Humphreys, "Keeping in Touch: Maintaining Contact with Stigmatized Subjects," in *Fieldwork Experience*, 212–223. William B. Shaffir, Robert A. Stebbins, and Allan Turowetz, eds., New York, 180.

3 *Ibid.*

4 William B. Shaffir and Robert Stebbins, eds., *Experiencing Fieldwork: An Inside View of Qualitative Research* (Newbury Park, 1991), 146.

5 See Raymond Breton, "Institutional Completeness of Ethnic Communities and the Personal Relations of Immigrants," *American Journal of Sociology* LXX(2), September 1964, 193–205.

6 Though the numbers of Hassidim in the respective communities can only be estimated, there is a consensus that the general population of Hassidim is dramatically increasing. For an interesting discussion of numbers and size, see *New World Hassidim: Ethnographic Studies of Hasidic Jews in America*, ed. Janet S. Belcove-Shalin (Albany, 1995); Robert Eisenberg, *Boychiks in the Hood: Travels in the Hasidic Underground* (New York, 1995), 3–7; Sam Heilman, *Defenders of the Faith: Inside Ultra-Orthodox Jewry* (New York, 1992); and Jerome Mintz, *Hasidic People* (Cambridge, 1992).

7 The Hassidim have also been the subject of considerable controversy as not all portrayals of them and their lifestyle have been positive. Belcove-Shalin (*op. cit.* in note 6 above), itemizes some of the scandals which have involved the Hassidim.

However, such publicity and the ensuing controversy, while perhaps temporarily unsettling, have not detracted from the Hassidim's abilities to shield themselves from the assimilative influences of the larger society. On the contrary: recognizing themselves to be the focus of attention, they have been drawn together and, in the process, have been strengthened in their commitment to their religious culture. As social scientists have recognized, a social collectivity is bound together not only by basic values and ideas to which its members adhere, but also by the manner in which internal organization and outside forces impinge on one another. Along this line, see, for example, L.S. Coser, *The Functions of Social Conflict* (New York, 1956); Y. Glickman, "Anti-Semitism and Jewish Social Cohesion in Canada," R.M. Bienvenue and J. Goldstein, eds., *Ethnicity and Ethnic Relations in Canada: A Book of Readings* (Toronto, 1985), 263–284.

8 See "Separation from the Mainstream in Canada: The Hassidic Community of Tash'," *The Jewish Journal of Sociology* XXIX(1), June 1987, 19–35.

9 Gil Kezwer, "Shalom, Bonjour," *Canadian Geographic*, July–August 1994.

10 Shaffir, *op. cit.* in note 8 above.

11 Named after the Tasher Rebbe's mother.

12 Named after the father of the wife of the Tasher Rebbe.

13 Family income derived from employment is supplemented by a relatively generous family allowance program instituted by the government of Quebec several years ago, in an attempt to offset a declining birth rate. At the moment, the government offers a bonus of $500 for the first child, $1000 for the second, and $8000 for the third and subsequent children. The latter is paid over a period of five years in quarterly instalments of $400 each.

14 William Shaffir, *op. cit.* in note 8 above, p. 31.

15 A front-page article in *The Gazette* on 29 October was headlined "How Bouchard Shocked the

Experts," and included the following in bold print: "The Bloc Québécois leader shifted the referendum campaign from a numbers game to the emotional issue of francophone pride."

[16] In fact, opinion poll results indicated that the "Yes" side might be headed towards victory. Two days before the referendum sovereigntists continued to hold the lead but the outcome was impossible to predict because of a large "Undecided" vote. For example, according to a Leger and Leger opinion poll published on 28 October, the results were: 47 percent "Yes"; 41 percent "No"; and 12 percent "Undecided." Quebec newspapers regularly published the results of different opinion polls that were commissioned by newspapers and television networks, all of which showed that the "Yes" side was in the lead but that the final outcome would be determined by the significantly large "Undecided" or "Other" voter category. On 28 October, 100,000 people from across Canada rallied in downtown Montreal in support of Canadian unity. In the end, the referendum result was "No," 50.57 percent and "Yes," 49.43 percent.

[17] See, for example, *La Presse*, 13 September 1995, p. 3; *The Gazette*, 14 September 1995, front page; and *Le Journal de Montreal*, 13 September 1995, front page.

[18] "Ten Injured in Biker Bar Blast," *The Associated Press*, 13 September 1995.

[19] *La Presse, op. cit.* in note 7 above.

[20] *Ibid.*

[21] *Ibid.*

[22] *The Gazette, op. cit.* in note 17 above.

[23] *La Presse, op. cit.* in note 17 above.

[24] *Ibid.*

[25] *Ibid.*

[26] *Ibid.*

[27] *Allo Police*, 24 September 1995, front page.

[28] The sovereignty commission's hearings were public and were mandated officially to study and discuss the Quebec government's draft bill on sovereignty.

[29] From a taped recording of the premier's speech.

[30] *Ibid.*

[31] *Financial Times*, 2 April 1994, front page.

[32] *Nord Info*, 24 September 1995, front page.

[33] *The Gazette*, 5 September 1995, p. C7.

[34] George Kranzler, *Williamsburg: A Jewish Community in Transition* (New York, 1961), 240.

[35] Solomon Poll, *The Hasidic Community of Williamsburg* (New York, 1962), 253.

[36] Israel Rubin, *Satmar: An Island in the City* (Chicago, 1972).

[37] Personal experiences in the field, hearsay of others' experiences and an ever-growing literature on field research lead me to conclude that the researcher, by virtue of his or her research status, is always an outsider. See R. Wax, *Doing Fieldwork: Warnings and Advice* (Chicago, 1971), 43. Morris Freilich cautions against the common desire among anthropologists to go native: see his *Marginal Natives* (New York, 1970).

CHAPTER 10

TWO SOULS IN ONE BODY:
ETHICAL AND METHODOLOGICAL IMPLICATIONS OF STUDYING WHAT YOU KNOW

Síân Reid

I did not begin graduate school with the idea of becoming a sociologist. In fact, as a recent graduate with a degree in English Literature and no elective courses outside the Faculty of Arts, I am not sure I could have told you then what sociologists were, or what sorts of questions they were interested in. My foray into the world of graduate studies was motivated by my personal interest in neopagan witchcraft as the religion with which I self-identified. There had been very little academic material produced about neopaganism as a religious choice by the late 1980s, when I began my graduate career. Further, what there was didn't reflect the vision I had of myself as a practitioner, my perception of the practice, my own experience or the experience of other participants as it had been related to me anecdotally. It was this frustration with not seeing myself reflected in the literature that purported to discuss "people like me" that propelled me into graduate school in an attempt to give myself the tools to frame the presentation of neopaganism differently.

During my years spent in graduate school, many more works on neopaganism have come out of the academy, works in which I could see myself and others whom I know reflected more accurately. Luhrmann (1989), Berger (1999), Orion (1995) and Pike (2001) are all good examples of writing about neopaganism and neopagans in which their voices can be heard and in which their perspectives are presented without being negatively prejudged by the author. Each of these works is an ethnography and each contains an account of the process through which the author, who began as an outsider, came to acquire an understanding of the participants' world views, narratives and practices, the process which is at the heart of all good ethnography. In some, but not all of those cases, it also resulted in the authors adopting a neopagan religious identity, and redefining themselves as insiders.

BOX 10.1: WHAT IS "PAGAN"?

Pagan is an umbrella term that includes a variety of types of practices including reconstructionist paganisms (Asatru, Celtic and Egyptian reconstruction-
ists, et cetera), some high magical traditions and some practising Goddess
spirituality outside of a witchcraft framework. Most indicating "pagan" on the
census are probably practising in the witchcraft stream. Neopagan practitioners in North America tend to be younger, better educated and more likely than
other Canadians to be in school. Most are involved in the Craft by the time
they are thirty, and tend to live in urban and suburban environments. They have
strong labour force participation but a lower median family income than the
average in either Canada or the United States. They are also disproportionately female (Adler, 1986; Berger, 1999; Orion, 1995; Jorgensen and Russell,
1999; Kirkpatrick *et al.*,1986; Rabinovitch, 1992; Reid, 2001). Notably, the 2001
Census of Canada showed a dramatic increase in the number of people list-
ing some form of neopaganism as their religious affiliation.

REFERENCES

Adler, Margot. 1986. *Drawing Down the Moon.* Boston: Beacon Press.

Berger, Helen. 1999. *A Community of Witches.* Columbia, SC: University of South Carolina Press.

Jorgensen, Danny, and Scott Russell. 1999. "American Neopaganism: The Participants' Social
   Identities." *Journal for the Scientific Study of Religion* 38(3):325–338.

Kirkpatrick, R.G., *et al.* 1986. "An Empirical Study of Wiccan Religion in Postindustrial Society."
   Free Inquiry in Creative Sociology 14(1):33–38.

Orion, Loretta. 1995. *Never Again the Burning Times: Paganism Revived.* Prospect Heights, IL:
   Waveland Press.

Rabinovitch, Shelley. 1992. *"An' Ye Harm None, Do What Ye Will": Neo-pagans and Witches in
   Canada.* MA thesis, Department of Religion, Carleton University.

Reid, Sîân Lee. 2001. *"Disorganized Religion": An Exploration of the Neopagan Craft in Canada.*
   PhD dissertation, Department of Sociology and Anthropology, Carleton University.

Here, I discuss the ethical and methodological dilemmas that arose for me when I,
already an *insider*, decided to take neopaganism as my substantive area of study. For
orientation purposes, I will begin by presenting a brief overview of the values and
beliefs that inform this religious milieu.

What Is Witchcraft?

It is much easier to describe what modern witchcraft is not than to describe what it
is, as it is a decentralized movement with no sacred texts and little consistent dogma.
The label "witch" is descriptive rather than normative to most of those who use it as

a term of self-identification. Modern witches consider themselves to be members of a pagan religious movement or spiritual tradition that draws upon pre-Christian traditions, usually of Europe and the Middle East, but occasionally of other locales as well. They reject the concept of devil-worship as a Christian innovation. They worship a divine principle that is considered to be immanent and whose representations generally resolve themselves into a god and a goddess. These can be a god and goddess of any pantheon, in any aspect, depending on the season of the year and/or the nature of the working (celebratory, healing, divinatory, et cetera).

BOX 10.2: THE GROWTH OF PAGANISM AND NEOPAGANISM

For the first time in many pagan communities, there are children being raised in Craft families who will likely be themselves identified as "pagan" or "neo-pagan" on the next census. The increase in popular culture representations of witchcraft, and a witchcraft literature that is catering to ever younger readers suggest that witchcraft and neopaganism will continue to gather adherents at an increasing rate into the foreseeable future.

Some groups, especially those working out of a feminist consciousness, will place more emphasis on the goddess images and the ideas of female power contained therein, sometimes rejecting references to male gods altogether. Even in groups that are more balanced in their use of gendered references to the divine, the references to women and female aspects of divinity are both more positive and more prevalent than those found in the major Western religious traditions. In some traditions of witchcraft, the coven leader must be female, and in most others, it is just as likely to be a woman as a man. This gives women access to status and authority that is denied them in many other religions.

The major religious observances (sabbats) centre on the seasonal cycles, although there is neither a set mythology nor a set format connected with these observances. Individuals and groups are free to make their observances meaningful in any way that seems appropriate. The idea that the divine is immanent and the focus on the physical seasons as a framework for worship produces a sense among witches that the earth itself is sacred. This may, in some cases, lead to explicit environmental activism.

Witches believe that there is both a non-material and a material reality, and that the two are interconnected. They do not assert the superiority of one reality over the other. Most believe in "magic" although definitions of that word vary. Many assert that magic can be used for healing, in much the same way that Christian "faith healers" believe that the power of the Holy Spirit can heal. Witches subscribe to the general moral principle "An' harm ye none, do what ye will" and leave the specific application of it to the individual. This very contextual morality extends into the beliefs surrounding sexuality. Human sexuality is not stigmatized in any way; it is viewed as natural, and subject to the same sort of caveats that apply to any other natural ability. Witches also tend to believe in some variety of karma. This is often referred to as "the law of returns" and refers to a belief that everything one does will return on one, at least in equal measure, and some would say threefold. This can occur either in this life or in another life; most witches believe in reincarnation.

Where the notion of time is linear in historical religions such as Christianity, it is cyclical in witchcraft. Christianity begins with a historical event, and works through history on its way to another event, the final judgment. Similarly, Christians are born, work through their lives in a linear fashion, die and face a final judgment. There is no second chance. In witchcraft, this life is viewed as just one in a series of lives, just as this spring is one in a series of springs. After death, one may face some kind of judgment, but will eventually be reborn to build on the knowledge of past mistakes and to gather new learning. There are an infinite number of chances.

As a movement, witches publish but do not proselytize. As they tend to believe that all religions fulfill the same essential function, and that the differences between them are largely differences of "how" and not of "what," there is no ideological push to make converts. Among witches, there is a very high level of tolerance for religious differences, probably arising at least in part from the wide variety of practices within the decentralized movement itself, and partially from the consciousness of the cultural marginality of their beliefs.

There is a very explicit focus in witchcraft on self-knowledge and personal development. Many of the rituals, meditations, visualizations and other techniques, both those considered to be primarily "magical" and those considered primarily "spiritual" by those who care to make those distinctions, are directed at increasing the individual's level of self-knowledge and sense of personal direction and empowerment. In this sense, the movement has much in common with the new, spiritually oriented psychotherapies.

Many of the elements explicitly embodied in neopagan witchcraft are qualitatively different from those that neopagans perceive as being offered by more mainstream religions. Philosophical acceptance of gender equality, individual responsibility and the importance of the natural world, however, are not alien or marginal positions in our present culture. What makes neopagan witchcraft interesting is the way in which it explicitly integrates these contemporary concerns in a system that is both practical and spiritual, and the ways in which practitioners try to resist the negative stereotypes attached to their practice by outsiders.

TABLE 10.1: PAGANS IN CANADA			
Census Year	1981	1991	2001
Pagan	2,210	5,530	21,085
Source: Statistics Canada.			

Implications of Being an Insider

In order to prepare myself to undertake an examination of neopagan witchcraft, I began with a master's degree in religion. It soon became apparent to me that further work in a religious studies environment was not going to prepare me to examine the kinds of questions in which I was interested. Accordingly, I moved to the sociology department for my doctorate. There I realized that writing ethnographically about neopaganism was not going to be possible for me. As an insider, I had already been socialized into the norms of neopaganism. I had my own understanding of the world view and some of how it was expressed through people's forms of living.

Specifically, during the decade that intervened between when I began to define myself as pagan and when I needed to redefine myself as a sociologist, I engaged in many of the activities that are typical of Craft practitioners: I read books on the Craft and related subjects such as magic, mythology and herbology; I did meditation, visualization and self-knowledge exercises, keeping records of them, and of my reflections on them; I did spellwork and divination, also keeping detailed records; I wrote down dreams that seemed significant or were particularly clear; I participated in classes at my local occult shop and, as I became more experienced, I taught a few; I talked to people, mostly non-practitioners, about what it meant to me to be a witch and tried to dispel misconceptions where I could; I attended public rituals to celebrate and socialize; I went to the occasional festival; I wrote and performed sabbats and esbats, and recorded the feedback I got from others who participated in them; I contributed to a pagan newsletter; I took a first-degree initiation and then, three years later, a second degree; I ran a coven; I taught and initiated students. All of this was just part of the normal process of learning to be, and being part of, the priesthood in a neopagan context.

Further, I had seven lined physics notebooks of handwritten notes, feedback, correspondence and diary entries, and another two thick unlined notebooks full of hand-copied rituals and ritual elements that are the textual record of my own personal development inside the Craft context. These records extended from 1983 until 1992. I could not go back and re-experience my own socialization from a critical standpoint; it was already an accomplished fact. The research process for me would have to involve not how I was going to be accepted among neopagans as a peer, but how I was going to disengage from that identity and that way of thinking in order to create and establish myself as a researcher.

Epistemological Issues

Epistemologically, the chief issue was to problematize my own "taken for granted" world view. This is an issue addressed fairly extensively in the theoretical literature. Gadamer, for one, points out that no one approaches an object of study without preconceptions. The structure of knowledge and human knowing dictates that preconceptions, what he calls prejudices or fore-meanings, will arise simply out of one's ability to use a human language and one's position in a historical tradition (1975:191). He suggests addressing the problem of the inevitability of prejudice by problematizing one's relationship to one's own perspective. That does not mean to say that one can divest one's self of it, as the "objectivity" of the scientific method would seem to dictate, but merely that one is required, if one is to attain understanding, to treat an object as something foreign and in need of understanding even when it seems familiar. This has required the explicit and ongoing acknowledgment that my own perspective is not only simply one inter-pretation of the lived universe, but also only one of many possible perspectives that could have been derived from my own particular experiences.

Gadamer likens the process of understanding to the process of translation, whereby meaning that exists in one language must be conveyed in a different language. The trick to translation is to convey not only the literal meaning of the words, which often obscures the meaning, but the sense of the work as a whole. The context of a work cannot just be reproduced pristinely so that it can be experienced in exactly the same terms that the author or another reader experienced it. It must, in translation, acquire part of the context of the horizon into which it comes, if it is to be understood (1975:236–241). Gadamer asserts that the process of understanding is a conversation in which two parties come to an agreement about the object.

The danger inherent in the study of phenomena in which one is involved is the facile assumption that one already enjoys such an agreement. This assumption of an already shared meaning prevents one from grasping the meaning given to the object by the other. This formulation of meaning solely within one's own horizon makes understanding impossible. Because I shared a certain vocabulary with the subjects of my study, I could not therefore assume that I automatically knew what they were saying. I could not take my own usages and experiences as normative, although I recognized them as that which constructed, and continues to construct, my own fore-meanings. Language is an especially contested domain within the Craft, and the process of trying to understand my respondents required that I consciously bracket off my own assumptions in order to make the attempt to enter into their understandings and their world views. In short, I had to make a conscious effort to keep my pagan self out of the middle of conversations between my participants and my researcher self.

Ethical and Methodological Issues

In addition to discovering that ethnographic research was going to be very difficult for me due to my pre-existing status as a participant, I also discovered that partici-pant-observation techniques would be intensely problematic if I wished participants to have the level of confidence in my commitment to respecting their privacy that I wanted them to have. The choices about the sort of research methodology I would use were guided by my own experience of having been a research subject previously and knowing what it was like to feel exposed and betrayed by a piece of research. This led me to adopt a very conservative set of ethical parameters, consistent with my sense that I was entering a "spoiled" research site.

A "spoiled" site is one in which potential participants have been exposed to researchers before, with negative outcomes, and in which researchers are therefore viewed with suspicion. The immediate pagan community in which I lived had been the subject of an ethnography carried out by another researcher some years before. Like me, this individual was an "insider" to the community, and the "key informants" of the study were the most active individuals in the community at that time. The research was problematic because the events discussed in the study took place up to three years before the individual adopted the identity of a researcher. Thus, the researcher was privy to events and confidences as a member of the community, and not as a researcher.

When the study finally became available to members of the community, in all but one case after it had been submitted elsewhere, many of the individuals were unhappy with both what was represented and how those representations were made. Some believed that there were strategic omissions in the data so that they would better fit the interpretive paradigm, errors that only community members and not outsiders could catch; others felt that relationships they had believed to be personal had been exploited and betrayed. The manner in which the events were framed and discussed heightened the level of tension in an already tense community and damaged the researcher's reputation not only as a researcher, but as a trustworthy member of the community. It also served to make all researchers somewhat suspect.

Because of this experience, I felt compelled to take what might, under other circumstances, be considered extraordinary measures to minimize any possible ambiguity about my role as a researcher and my motivations for conducting the research. I detached myself from the activities of the community and gave participants clear indications of when our relationship was in the researcher–subject mode rather than that of co-participants. This determination to maintain that distinction in the minds of participants was the primary motivating factor both in my use of formalized settings for my interviews, including the deliberately obtrusive presence of a tape recorder, and my decision not to use participant observation as a data-gathering technique. I consistently presented myself, in all correspondence and conversations inviting participation in the research, as an active researcher on neopaganism, who was incidentally also Craft, so that it was almost impossible to mistake my intentions.

During the interview stage, I made a point of candidly answering questions about both my Craft background and training and my academic orientations and interests. I proactively divulged information about my current and former associations inside the Craft community, particularly with the large neopagan organizations, whenever the conversation turned in that direction. As some participants had very negative feelings about some of these organizations, I did not wish them to believe that they had been "tricked" into making negative comments, or to be uncomfortable subsequently, if they learned that I was acquainted with prominent members of those groups. While this may have affected some respondents' candour about those particular individuals, it was far preferable to me to lose that data than to potentially lose the respondent's willingness to participate in future iterations of the research.

In addition to these practical methodological steps, I altered my life outside of "research time" in the attempt to create myself as someone who was not perceived to be aligned with any of the numerous factions that exist inside the Craft. Although it is difficult, in some ways, for an outsider to gain access to the neopagan community, it is also difficult to do effective research as an insider if parts of the community will not speak to you because you are perceived to be a member of the wrong "camp." I began this disengagement process while still in the planning stages of the research. As early as three years before the survey and five years before the interviews were conducted, I withdrew from coven membership, ceased to take new students, ceased to have any publicly expressed opinion on happenings in both my own community and others I heard of, and ceased to attend most public gatherings. I maintained my existing friendships inside the community, but established myself as somewhat "outside" its religious and social life.

I did this to in order to gain access to the widest possible cross-section of respondents and to give my participants confidence about the extent to which they would be exposed by the research. I also did it to protect myself and my other identity as a trustworthy member of the neopagan community. Although I chose to be neither active nor visible as a practitioner in the broader community while my research was in progress, I still identify myself as neopagan and support the principles that guide interaction within the community. Despite my conspicuous absence for almost a decade, I wished to retain the option to return to a more visible practice at some future time with my reputation for integrity intact.

To the extent that these measures were intended to establish me as non-partisan, facilitate access to practitioners and prevent excessive bias in the reporting of my research results, I think that they were successful. Upon reflection, however, there were costs concealed in the choices I made that I did not anticipate when I began the research, and which, had I known about them at the time, might have dissuaded me from undertaking the project that I did. I could not have known, for example, that I would be delivering my survey to the printers on the way to the hospital to have my first child. I could not have known that my decision to remove myself from the community would mean that losing access to sources of pastoral support, comfort and social opportunities that otherwise would have been available to me at a time when, for a variety of reasons, I very much needed them. Having decided that coven membership was inadvisable, as was attendance at public rituals, and generally disliking solo work, I did not have the opportunity for celebration and reflection that ritual provides, or the companionship of others on the important holidays. It has also meant that my young daughter, although raised in a household where pagan values were entrenched, has not had the opportunity to become more thoroughly socialized in a context that is supported by the ritual celebrations that punctuate the pagan year.

But perhaps most of all, I had underestimated the extent to which doing a PhD in sociology would turn me into a sociologist. Having taught myself to ask different questions and look beyond and behind what I had taken for granted before, I am not sure to what extent I can ever return. I am not sure if, when I finally feel that it is "safe" for me to take up the mantle of "active practitioner" once again, it will even fit the person I have become in the meantime. I do not know if I will ever again be capable of taking a ritual simply as a descriptive statement about the universe in which I live, and not analyze in the back of my mind the way in which it narrates the transformative potential of modernity. I am not sure if I can attend a social gathering and not look for the subtle conversational markers that point to the articulation of broader tensions in the neopagan movement. I am not sure I can set aside the sociological lens and immerse myself fully in the lived presence of the divine. I have gained a way of seeing that has enriched me immeasurably on an intellectual level; it remains to be seen if that has cost me the way of seeing that organized my life, gave definition to my vision of myself and structured my spiritual landscape before I became a sociologist.

Had I known in the beginning the capacity the research process had to make me a stranger to myself, I would perhaps not have chosen to study something that was so close to the heart of my being, yet it was only the urge to study that particular thing that drew me to sociology in the first place. Perhaps the "old-fashioned" admonitions about being at an appropriate distance from your research interests are not meant to protect the research from bias and contamination, but to protect the researcher's sense of self. Doing responsible sociological research about a vital piece of my own identity has caused me to change the stories I tell about myself, the narratives through which I am constituted. My identity as a sociologist and researcher is too established in my mind and in the minds of others for me to be able to simply set it aside. At the end of the research process that culminated in my dissertation defence, I am faced with a different challenge: the task of reflexively constructing a narrative of myself capable of integrating elements that I am accustomed to bracketing off from each other. Otherwise, I will remain somewhat at odds with myself indefinitely, with two souls in one body.

REFERENCES

Berger, Helen. 1999. *A Community of Witches.* Columbia, SC: University of South Carolina Press.

Gadamer, Hans-Georg. 1975. *Truth and Method.* London: Sheed & Ward.

Luhrmann, Tanya. 1989. *Persuasions of the Witch's Craft.* Cambridge: Harvard University Press.

Orion, Loretta. 1995. *Never Again the Burning Times.* Westport, CT: Waveland Press.

Pike, Sarah. 2001. *Earthly Bodies, Magical Selves.* Berkeley: University of California Press.

GLOSSARY

Epistemology: The study of ways of knowing. Epistemology is an area of philosophy concerned with the limits, extent and basis of human knowledge.

Ethnography: The descriptive process through which living cultures are documented, often from the perspective of those for whom they are a way of life. Often produced by anthropologists who have immersed themselves in the subject culture for an extended period of time, and who have participated extensively in its day-to-day life.

Identity Narrative: A story through which we frame our understanding of ourselves and our presentation of

ourselves to others. Most people have more than one identity narrative.

Key Informant: A person within the community being studied who provides significant guidance and information to a researcher. Key informants must be selected carefully so that the research does not end up reflecting too strongly the interests of those informants.

Methodology: Consists in the practical decisions that are made about the appropriate research tools and approaches that will be used to gather and analyze data in a research project.

CRITICAL THINKING QUESTIONS

1. You are interviewing a fundamentalist Christian for your research project on Being Christian in a Secular World. Your participant asks you if you believe in God. How do you respond?
2. How has gender equality facilitated transitions in the religious traditions with which you are familiar?
3. How can religious groups accommodate the world around them without compromising themselves?
4. Why do you think there has been a tendency in sociology to define religion narrowly?
5. Is it possible for people to be privately religious without their beliefs influencing their public life?

FURTHER READINGS

Ammerman, N. 1987. *Bible Believers: Fundamentalists in the Modern World.* New Brunswick: Rutgers University Press. This classic in the sociology of religion is a study of fundamentalist Christians and how they make sense of the world. Ammerman is an expert interviewer and a key intellectual in the sociology of religion in the United States. This book is a model "how to" of sociological research in the area of religion.

Claussen, C., and L.L.Wong. 2004. "Bridging Unsettled Waters: Ethnic and Identity in the Calgary Jewish Community." *Canadian Ethnic Studies* 36(2):119–131. This piece examines the complexity of modern Jewish identity, noting that being Jewish is not just about religion, or about ethnic identification. Drawing on semi-structured interviews, this study explores the diversity of being Jewish.

Esau, A. 2004. *The Courts and the Colonies: The Litigation of Hutterite Church Disputes.* Vancouver: UBC Press. Primarily a legal and historical discussion of the Hutterite community in Canada, Esau's book is nonetheless an important contribution to the study of religious life in Canada. The book offers an insider glimpse into the ways in which beliefs can both unify and divide a religious community. It also raises broader questions about the degree to which a commitment to diversity should accommodate religious groups.

Irwin, L. 2000. *Native American Spirituality: A Critical Reader.* Lincoln: University of Nebraska Press. Following James's concern about how religion is defined, we encourage the student to turn to other understandings of religion that move outside of the Christian framework. This reader is an interdisciplinary collection of works that critically addresses methodological and theoretical concerns. It emphasizes the importance of dialogue in order to properly bridge gaps in understanding spirituality. Also examined are historical accounts of the politicization of Native American spirituality through activism and interactions with other religious traditions.

Poloma, M., and L.F. Hoelter. 1998. "The 'Toronto Blessing': A Holistic Model of Healing." *Journal for the Scientific Study of Religion* 37(2):257–273. Poloma and Hoelter look at the Toronto Airport Christian Fellowship, using over 900 surveys of people from a large number of countries who had visited the charismatic Christian church. The authors consider the issue of health and well-being in relation to spirituality.

Wilkinson, M. (2000). "The Globalization of Pentecostalism: The Rose of Asian Immigrant Pentecostals in Canada." *Asian Journal of Pentecostal Studies*, 3(2):219–226. This study reflects on the impact of globalization through the creation of transnational networks by immigrants between their home and host countries. The long-term impact of this on identity is as yet unknown, but Wilkinson raises it as an interesting area for future research.

PART III: INNOVATIONS

This part examines "innovations" in religion and society, and as with the previous parts we allow a broad interpretation. One of the most important innovations in the sociology of religion is a willingness to embrace a theoretical complexity that includes transcending disciplinary boundaries. To be sure, sociology has a unique contribution to make, but its strength is also in its ability to draw on other traditions to gain insight into the social world. This can be confusing for the student who is just beginning to enter the domain of specific disciplines. Yet, the ability to use different lenses to explore religion and society enhances our ability to appreciate the complexity of such an undertaking and to be wary of simplistic causal explanations.

Feminism has contributed a great deal to the ways in which we think about religion and society, and relations among and between women and men. It has engendered a number of responses to institutionalized patriarchy within organized religion and has contributed to the increased participation in women-centred religions such as Wicca. The wearing of the veil by Muslim women might be interpreted as an innovative strategy to bridge everyday life between tradition and feminism.

The topic of woman and religion—and women *in* religion—has been the subject of a number of books, and it is an important one, for women make up the majority of religious participants and are central to the running of organized religion and to the creation of new religious movements. Women have developed a variety of strategies to deal with patriarchal religion, including staying within its folds and attempting to improve it, separating themselves but remaining affiliated with a religious group, or abandoning organized religion altogether.

Innovative approaches to the sociology of religion may employ new theoretical insights, methodological stances, or a combination thereof. Such approaches may mean turning the sociological spotlight on new areas of study—the Internet, "baby" religions or the environment, and reopening discussion on the manner in which religion is defined. In this process we can use some old sociological tricks, like attempting to make the everyday strange or examining the taken-for-granted to inspect the power relations implicit in the construction of "what we all know." Who gets to name religion? Who defines it?

A specific version of this sort of question arises in relation to new religious movements. Both Palmer, and Dawson and Hennebry address this in their chapters in this part, but the issues bear repeating. The word *cult* has been used in a pejorative sense to invoke suspicion and fear. The use of the term *cult* to designate a religious group is used to signal that they are not a "real" religion, that its members are somehow brainwashed automatons who don't know what they are doing. Thus many social scientists use the term *new religious movement* (NRM) to move the discussion away from these negative preconceptions. The cult/new religious movement debate is heated, and there are good researchers on either side. It is critical for the student of religion to be aware of this debate, and of the knowledge construction involved in the use of either term. It is especially critical that we deconstruct media constructions of religion, asking critical questions about how religious groups are portrayed.

Dawson and Hennebry shift the focus to a more global theme, examining the Internet as a recruiting tool for new religious movements. This chapter touches on key issues in the study of new religious movements, including the notion that "cult" members are somehow "brainwashed." Dawson and Hennebry emphasize that conversion is a social process, drawing on a substantial body of social scientific research to substantiate this statement. Put another way, those who join new religious movements are active agents in the decision-making process. In short, their chapter concludes that the Internet as an innovation in information dissemination is not "luring" converts to new religious movements, and challenges the notion that those who join new religious movements undergo a process that is different from that which any person experiences in the process of joining a new group.

Susan Palmer's lighthearted piece is a window onto life as a new religious movements scholar. An important voice in the sociology of NRMs, Palmer has devoted her career to the exploration of "baby" religions, as she calls them. Her chapter raises some key issues of methodology and perspective. The notion of objectivity is nuanced with the idea of positionality; we as researchers are a part of the story that eventually gets told as "research results." Palmer gives us a view of the behind-the-scenes struggles that take place as a researcher attempts both distance and a close view of the groups she studies. Substantively, like Dawson and Hennebry, Palmer challenges the brainwashing thesis, presenting new religious movements as being like any religious group, but at a different stage of maturity. Palmer invites us to see NRMs as groups from which we can learn, rather than as dangerous cults to be feared. Their innovations on religious belief and practice are to be explored rather than dismissed.

Homa Hoodfar pushes past simplistic explanations for veiling and explores the complexity of meaning-making around the decision to wear a veil (or not). What becomes clear through the interviews she conducts is that the women she talks to are innovative in the ways in which they combine a religious world view and the pragmatics of day-to-day life. Their wearing of the veil is an exercise in boundary maintenance, but also in innovation, for they interpret the veil as a symbol of the freedom they are given from being bound by body images that they see as cloistering to Western women. Hoodfar teases out the religious and cultural strands of their meaning-making, juxtaposing Western stereotypes with the views of women who wear the veil. Hoodfar's chapter reminds us that lived religion is rich in texture, and that the ways in which people appropriate symbols are multi-faceted. We cannot, therefore, take for granted the symbolic references of religious practices. It is Hoodfar's carefully carried-out fieldwork that allows us a glimpse into the practice of veiling. She interviewed young women and parents and made some intriguing discoveries. In short, Hoodfar argues "against a one-dimensional treatment of veiling as an unchanging practice symbolizing oppressive patriarchy in Muslim societies." Hoodfar's chapter calls us to consider the notion of identity carefully; the ways in which people construct who they are in the world draws on a wide variety of possibilities and is not a static phenomenon. Rather, identity is dynamic and, in the course of a life's history, shifts. For those of us who study religion, this means that our theoretical toolboxes must be able to meet the challenge of making sense of shifting ground.

My piece on Aboriginal spirituality elaborates the notion of religious hegemony and points to the very real consequences as they play out when religion comes before law, using claims of religious freedom to maintain or expand boundaries. The very use of the term *Aboriginal spirituality* is problematic, for it is the descriptive phrase colonizers use to describe Aboriginal religion, and as such it is a concept that is highly contrived and does not begin to capture the spirit world of First Nations peoples. It is interesting that despite cultural differences, courts in both Canada and the United States seem to have a limited understanding of Aboriginal spirituality, and are intent on limiting it within the confines of the colonizers' view of religion and religious freedom. This piece takes us back to some basic questions that remain unresolved in the sociology of religion: How do we define religion? What is the impact of a religious hegemony on groups on the margins, or minority religious groups? Are there ways we can expand the definition of religion so as to protect diverse religious views? Are there limits we want to place on the idea that individuals and groups should have religious freedom? How does the law work to exclude certain groups from protection under constitutional guarantees of religious freedom? This chapter is perhaps a call for innovation rather than an examination of it, for courts need to move outside the boundaries of the traditional in thinking about the definition of religion and its protection.

As in the William Closson James chapter in the last part, sometimes it takes someone on the edge of disciplinary boundaries to help us make sense of religion and society. In this part Heather Eaton's work plays such a role: she moves through a wide-ranging discussion of the environment and religion by drawing on sociology, theology, feminist theory, and religious studies to examine ecofeminism. Her concern is to transform, and like Nason-Clark, she bridges the gap between theory and practice, or a "practical theory of liberation." Eaton's work calls us to re-examine some of the enduring questions of critical sociology, including the emancipatory potential of theory and research practice. She draws attention to power relations and patterns of domination. Without reifying Christian hegemony, she identifies a particular need for Christianity to be self-critical in its role in domination on many fronts. Eaton also recognizes both the oppressive and potentially liberating possibilities of religion. Drawing on the work of sociologist Dorothy Smith, Eaton calls for an approach that is grounded in the everyday. Eaton moves religion from the "private" squarely into the realm of the public and the political. Religion is an integral component of social processes. Eaton's work reminds us of the complexity of the everyday world, and pushes us to make disciplinary boundaries work to help us see those complexities more fully.

John Simpson is known for his wide-ranging discussion of religion and society, and has a unique ability to draw on diverse bodies of literature to bring fresh insights to the sociological study of religion. His chapter is perhaps even more salient now than when it was originally published. Using the body as a unit of analysis, Simpson draws on a comparative methodology to explore religion and politics, particularly on the issues of abortion and homosexuality. The intersection of religion and politics in acting upon the body is the central focus of this piece, and in the end Simpson concludes that there are some important differences between Canada and the United States. The body politics noted by Simpson have intensified in the past few years in the current political regime of the United States, and as we see same-sex marriage gradually legalized across Canada, the terrain is a bit more uneven south of the border. Similarly, the abortion situation in Canada seems to be relatively stable, but in the United States there is talk of overturning *Roe v. Wade,* the (simplistically characterized) pro-abortion decision of the U.S. Supreme Court. Simpson's textured analysis explores denominational difference as well as national difference, and includes a consideration of the distinctness of Quebec. His chapter raises the interesting problem of how to determine the influence of religion on politics. It also highlights the diversity between religions, and, in this case, their response to the "somatic" society.

CHAPTER 11

CAUGHT UP IN THE CULT WARS:
CONFESSIONS OF A CANADIAN RESEARCHER

Susan J. Palmer

> "It would seem, Dr. Palmer, that you have acquired a bit of a reputation for
> being 'soft on the cults.' Are you indeed ... a cultlover?"
>
> —High Solicitor

I was standing nervously in the carved oak witness box in the High Court, Lincoln's
Inn in London, when the High Solicitor asked this question. It was in 1994, when I
became embroiled in what the Children of God's lawyer described as "the longest and
second most expensive custody battle in the history of the British Empire." I protested
that I strove to be an objective, value-free social scientist when I studied new religions—but then admitted I also felt a sneaking aesthetic appreciation for "the cults."
This made the judge smile, but it made me wonder—are the two approaches really
incompatible?

As a mature researcher, somewhat scarred from my forays into that embattled terrain known as the cult wars, I am now ready to make a confession. I do see myself as
a *connoisseur*. For me, new religious movements (NRMs) are beautiful life forms, mys-
terious and pulsating with charisma. Each "cult" is a mini-culture, a protocivilization.
Prophets and heretics generate fantasy worlds that rival those of Philip K. Dick or L.
Frank Baum. When I venture into the thickets of wild home-grown spirituality, and
explore the rich undergrowth of what society rejects as its "weed" religions, I sometimes think of Dorothy's adventures in *The Emerald City of Oz*. Dorothy follows the
yellow brick road that leads her through Utensia, a city whose inhabitants are kitchen
utensils. Managing to escape King Kleaver (who threatens to chop her), she wanders
into Bunbury where houses are made of crackers with bread-stick porches and wafer-
shingles and are inhabited by living buns with currant eyes. She ventures on to meet
the evil headless Scoodles, then continues on down the yellow brick road.

New religions are no less phantasmagorical. Immersed in the *Oz* books as a malin-
gering schoolgirl, I wanted to "have adventures" when I grew up. My wish came true.
Today I find myself in the not-quite-respectable, morally problematic and impecunious
field of "cult" studies. Travelling the yellow brick road of social scientific research, I
encounter oddly coherent world views constructed higgledy-piggledy out of the most
incongruous elements: songs of Solomon, UFO lore, electric bulbs, biofeedback
machines, gnostic creation myths—all welded into one seamless syncretism. I drop in
on dreams of Utopia and discover quaint communes like Puritan villages, the brothers

and sisters marching to a tasteful percussion of Bible-thumping. I have felt trapped in nightmares—racist compounds, parodies of Paradise, Nietzchean dystopias.

Each new religion I encounter evokes in me a sense of awe not unlike what my art historian mother feels when she beholds Greek ruins, German cathedrals or Renaissance paintings. I see heretical religions as "totems" or testaments—not necessarily of Ultimate Truth, but rather of the creative power of the collective human imagination. Their prophets I approach cautiously, and with respect, as artists of the most radically experimental sort: unpredictable conceptual artists at best, semi-opaque con artists at worst.

This approach seems to aggravate almost everybody; they find it frivolous, irresponsible. One Sufi lady at the Abode of the Messenger stopped me mid-interview and said accusingly, "You're not *really* interested in the spiritual path. I get the impression you have more of a *literary* interest in what we're doing!"

Another time I was effervescing on the sheer fun of researching NRMs when a psychologist at a lunchtime lecture for the psychologists at the Montreal General Hospital interrupted: "So I suppose you think it's fun and OK for groups like the Solar Temple to go around killing each other!" I was irritated, since I had just spent ten minutes explaining that each "cult" is different, and statistics showed that only a tiny handful engaged in criminal acts, so I responded: "You must excuse me, I prepared this talk for the doctors; I didn't realize that the psychiatric *patients* would be invited here as well." I don't expect to be invited back.

When asked to define a cult, I explain that it is a baby religion. Personally, I find cults (and babies) attractive. Babies can be heartbreakingly adorable or intensely annoying, depending on the beholder's perspective—but also on the baby's mood and stage of development. So infant religions are not quite toilet-trained, like MOVE, a cult that annoyed neighbours by throwing garbage on the street; toddler NRMs, like the Rajneesh, run around naked in the park and knock over tea trays; and teenage missionary movements, like The Family, mooch off their parent society, refuse to get a job and flaunt their pimply sexuality.

I have heard mothers excuse their obstreperous infants by saying, "It's only a *phase* he's going through!" (teething, bed-wetting, screaming). NRMs also go through phases, shutting out the surrounding culture to form their own identity. NRM scholars may sound like overindulgent mommies making excuses for their spoiled brats when they protest that communal experiments, sexual innovations and apocalyptic expectations are merely developmental phases, and that society should grit its teeth and give these budding religions a chance to grow up.

Having confessed to singular tastes, perhaps I should explain how I got into "cult studies." My formal debut as a researcher of new religious movements commenced in the 1970s, when meditations—like 100-percent cotton wear or silk—were Oriental imports, and most of my cool friends had already left for India to seek the right guru. At that time we were, of course, wary of false gurus who sold useless *sadhanas* (spiritual guidelines), or leched after American blondes, but the notion of the charismatic cult leader as obligatory pederast, oppressor of women and designer of mass suicide had not yet been forged in the media. Professor Fred Bird was my MA adviser at Concordia University when the department received a grant to study new religious movements in Montreal. I was one of four students hired as research assistants, and was actually paid $60 a week to choose a cult, spy on it and write up field reports. When I look back on this period the word *halcyon* comes to mind; we researchers were lighthearted and naive, fancying ourselves spiritual PIs. We swopped bizarre anecdotes about our chosen groups and boasted of mild vicarious spiritual highs. As young, countercultural types we could easily pass as typical spiritual seekers, and, indeed, that's what we were in our own wishy-washy ways.

Like many of my fellow scholars, I have been called a closet cultist. Perhaps there *is* a grain of truth to this allegation, for although I have never joined a group I've researched, I did start out hanging around meditation centres as a spiritual seeker, and only ended up in the microsociology of NRMs by default—as a failed meditator. I tried many systems, but never got the hang of it. I realize, of course, that the whole point is not to try to be "good" at meditating … but I kept trying.

So I began *doing* sociology of religion inadvertently, simply because I was bored with trying to concentrate on my mantra or third eye. Sitting in lotus posture at 4:00 A.M. on a scratchy grey woollen blanket in Swami Vishnu Devananda's quonset hut in Morin Heights, Quebec, I would peek around at my fellow meditators chanting "AUM-MMMMM," and observe their subtle social interactions. Making beds and washing sheets, understood as karma yoga, I would question my fellow *chelas* regarding their conversions. At the visiting swamis' evening lectures, I paid more attention to the jocular rivalry between these shrewd old disciples of Swami Sivananda than I did to Hindu philosophy. Had I been able to make honest progress in my meditation practice, I would perhaps be living happily in the Himalayas—probably in Swami Shyam's Canadian enclave in Kulu—celibate, sattvic (pure), probably childless, my consciousness percolating up towards my seventh chakra.

Researching NRMs has its pleasures. I meet delightful people. I hear the intimate spiritual confessions of peaceful meditators, unselfish communalists and disciplined ascetics. But there are disadvantages to taking on the public role of "cult scholar." Courting me as an offbeat academic who represents the "other view," TV stations have offered me free travel and luxurious sojourns in Canadian Pacific Railway hotels, but then they edit my interview so I come across as a caricature of a misguided civil libertarian. In anti-cult circles I am dismissed as a naive dupe or a closet cultist. In France my name has been listed with the other "revisionists" who deny atrocities *dans les sectes*. As for my Mormon relatives, they urge me to return to the fold lest I end up in the "telestial sphere."

Many cults also look askance at me. Grossed out by the social-scientific method and sick of a sociologist's depressingly secular scrutiny, leaders have denounced me to their disciples as a hireling of a corrupt society. A Rajneesh therapist warned the other "super-moms" not to give me interviews because "she's coming from her head, not from her heart." E.J. Gold (the gnostic guru whose declared mission is "the education of the universe, one idiot at a time"), upon reading my MA thesis (about him), reportedly said, "This lady has the consciousness of a rubber duck!" When I asked a barefoot missionary from the Free Daist Communion for an interview, she explained she must first collect all my writings and send them to Fiji to be vetted. "Do you mean

Da Free John is going to read my articles?" I asked, thrilled. "Not exactly," she replied. "He *handles* them, and whatever wisdom they contain he absorbs through his fingertips." *Da Free John* never got back to me.

Excluded from Black Hebrew assemblies as a "leprous pale-eyed Amorite," shunned by the Asatru (racialist Druids) for looking "slightly Jewish," and dismissed by *les sectes Québécois* as a *carré tête* (square-head or Anglophone), I continue the struggle to present myself in such a way that my research attentions will be welcome. But what can be even more disconcerting is when I am besieged by groups *overly eager* to be studied, and subjected to that special kind of "love-bombing" that is a product of what sociologist Roland Robertson dubbed philomandarinism: "Susan, we just *love* you! You're so *beautiful*—and so *objective*!" Aside from that sticky feeling of entering a flytrap, I can foresee the day when they will all turn on me. In fifty years or so, after achieving the status of minority churches with the assistance of the dull ethnographics of academics like myself who function as alkaline neutralizers of the more acid anti-cult media reports, these once controversial cults will loose their church historians on me and my peers, and they will *condemn* our careful writings—all because we tried to include reasonable but unflinching explanations for their bad news, and neglected to indulge in what my Mormon relatives call "faith-promoting incidents."

COVERT RESEARCHER—OR CLOSET CONVERT?

One obvious solution is to resort to covert research. When I first began to "spy on cults" back in the 1970s, on Professor Fred Bird's research team, we four graduate students started out as strictly *covert*. We infiltrated our chosen groups, danced with sufis, hyperventilated with yogis, chanted with devotees. This created delicate dilemmas in etiquette later on. Once we got together and designed our questionnaires and interview schedules, the prospect of unmasking our real selves as ambitious academics in front of our fellow seekers on the path was daunting, and threatened an embarrassing loss of face. All four students had by now *joined* their chosen groups and some had "gone native." Steve was initiated into TM and refused to reveal his mantra to our team. Bill balked at handing out questionnaires to his fellow meditators in Integral Yoga, for he feared it would interfere with his spiritual path. Hugh had completely disappeared into a nine-week Arica training seminar; he was *incommunicado* and had mumbled something before he left about "how my energy has moved beyond academia."

We all got together after Hugh resurfaced in his new swashbuckling *persona* as an Arican space cowboy, and wrote up a manifesto justifying the "phenomenological" approach over the "quantitative" method, and confronted Professor Bird. He threatened to fire us all and replace us with more docile graduate students who were less spiritually squeamish. We backed down and crassly proceeded to hand out questionnaires, thereby compromising our hard-won spiritual credentials.

Today, covert research is generally considered *extremely* unethical and methodologically unsound. It is something investigative journalists did to the Moonies in the 1980s to expose their "brainwashing" methods. French reporters still do it to the Raelians, pointing hidden cameras at rows of chubby nudists, so their photos can appear (eyes blacked out), as they did in an article on *les sectes dangereuses* in *Echo Vedettes*. Scholars criticize covert research as psychologically unhealthy, morally compromising, potentially dangerous and methodologically inefficacious, and yet … I often find myself doing it still. There is always that ambiguous stage when I stumble across a new group and am trying to decide whether there is anything there worth studying. It is less bother to simply show up at the meetings, thereby placing oneself in the role of potential recruit, than to formally introduce oneself as a professor of religion (organized religion often gets a bad reaction), or a teacher of a course titled Cults and Controversy (which sets off the "we are not a cult" speech).

Now, when I decide to unmask my secular identity, I confront quite a different reaction than I did as a sociology student. Since I am now perceived as a professor who is open-minded and charitably inclined towards religious minorities, I am relentlessly hustled to perform dreary tasks: "Can you write us a letter of recommendation?"; "Can you phone the Hindu professor at McGill and tell her to invite us to her class?"; "CNN is making an unflattering documentary about us. They *promised* they would interview you if we gave them a list of our enemy ex-members. Can you phone up the television station and tell them how harmless and wonderful we are?"; "Can you find out for us at Dawson College how to organize free vegetarian cooking classes for the students?" My position also allows me deeper access to information in some ways. I was able to interview the elusive Eugene Elbert Spriggs, founder of the Twelve Tribes movement, at dawn in the Basin Valley farm. The ex-nun who channels sexy angels let me sit in on her group therapy session for free, and I didn't even have to do their silly exercises. When I researched the Children of God, I met "King Peter," the successor of the late David Berg, who is normally *selah* (hidden), and he played me a tape of the reclusive Queen Maria's scratchy Southern voice.

But in other ways my role as "cult scholar" impedes my research. The wide range of strange groups I have investigated appears in my books, and some straitlaced groups assume I must be immoral to hang out with the Rajneeshees, the Raelians, and The Family, whom they perceive as sinners and sex maniacs. Others feel a little queasy about my overly tolerant attitude towards atheistic or "heretical" groups who claim Jesus was a space alien, and wonder how I can bear to sit down and sup with a mystical pope or a vampire. I received a letter from a Krishna devotee complaining she felt "quite nauseous" that her interview appeared in the same book as one with a Moonie. Several core-group leaders have expressed jealousy and feelings of abandonment—that since I stopped researching their community I have flitted off to some silly UFO group that even I must realize does not possess the Truth.

When I meet young graduate students researching NRMs today, I envy them their freedom, their naive enthusiasm, their straightforward, unpoliticized curiosity. I recall how effortless it used to be to blend into a following. Even after declaring oneself a researcher, the response was often, "Oh well, you'll soon get over that!" I miss the intensity of real participant observation, the altered states the gruelling ordeals I was subjected to!

I recall how, in the late '70s, I was among a group of neo-gnostics who jumped out of a van at 8:15 A.M. in front of a suburban supermarket. We all wore skin-tight grey leotards, transparent plastic gloves, grey bathing caps, bare feet (painted grey)—and had shaved-off eyebrows! We formed a huddle around our core-group leader, who instructed us that we were all "hungry ghosts" and our mission was to enter the supermarket by following a customer through the revolving door—"Make sure you touch nothing. If any part of your body makes contact with anything or anybody, go back outside immediately and start over." Having fasted for three days we were hungry, but our exercise was to wander the aisles staring longingly at our favorite food, but to take nothing. After one hour we were meant to leave by shadowing a customer. We didn't last the hour, for one of the cashiers called the police. ("Who are all those weirdos?" we overheard the staff muttering. "They look like a biker gang … planning a robbery.") We leaped into the van and squealed off before the police arrived. We lay on the rusty floor, doubled up, holding onto each other as we lurched around corners, hysterical with laughter. The same group, a month before, had me crawling around a giant playpen wearing diapers, undershirt and bonnet for an entire day, gurgling incoherently, sucking huge bottles of warm milk and playing with building blocks with my fellow "babies." Anti-cultists might be on to something when they claim an important stage of mind control is to "humiliate the victim" by "reinforcing childish behaviour."

Today I am never invited to humiliate myself. I wear suits and shoulder pads and am taken on decorous tours, like visiting royalty. My eyebrows have grown in again, though they've never been quite the same!

Kai Erikson (1967:373) has argued that "it is unethical for a sociologist to deliberately misrepresent his identity for the purpose of entering a private domain to which he is not eligible; and second, that it is unethical for a sociologist to deliberately misrepresent the character of the research in which he is engaged." I find it difficult *not* to misrepresent my identity, since most of my informants ignore my staunch protests that I am merely a dreary academic, a boring social scientist doing my job. They insist that, deep down, I am a lost soul desperately struggling towards the light. It is often counterproductive to protest *too* vigorously, so I just let them think I am on the brink of a conversion—and, indeed, part of me secretly hopes I *am* still capable of what C.S. Lewis called being "surprised by joy."

TOO CLOSE TO THE CULTS?

I have been asked to justify my getting "too close to the cults." I have been criticized for staying in a commune for a week or two, for travelling on the road with a missionary team, for having private conferences with charismatic leaders, for participating in meditation retreats and so on. I felt a blast of criticism when I attended a meeting of the American Family Foundation in May 1997, attracted by the theme Cults and Children. The director of the Watchman Fellowship, a Christian counter-cult organization in Alabama, came up and introduced himself to me in the following disconcerting fashion: "Are you *the* Susan Palmer who wrote that *positive* chapter on The Family in *Sex, Slander and Salvation*? Why do you bother to go *into* these groups and talk to them. Don't you know they always lie?"

I was astonished. For a researcher to avoid the living community and to rely exclusively on data supplied by ex-members and the group's literature would be like an anthropologist claiming to be an expert on an Aboriginal tribe, but who only interviews Aborigines once they have migrated to the city; one who has never ventured into the outback let alone visited or lived with the tribe. Suppose Jane Goodall had never ventured into the Kenyan Masai Mara, but studied chimpanzees in zoos? It seems to me that any serious researcher who has the vocation to learn about new religions must seek them out in their purest form, and be present during their earliest, vital stages of development.

Anti-cultists have accused scholars of being *paid* by cults to say nice things about them, or accepting bribes to keep their mouths shut about the supposed atrocities ongoing in cultland. Any information centre on NRMs—CESNUR in Italy, INFORM in London, ISAR in Santa Barbara—that is not specifically set up to warn worried parents or concerned Christians about new religious horrors and heresies, is routinely accused by anti-cultists of receiving their funding from the cults. This very assumption—that NRMs are *capable* of networking with each other, or that they have heard and approve of the sociology of religion—reveals a profound ignorance of new religions in all their staggering diversity.

For certain large, international movements like the Unification Church, Scientology, International Society for Krishna Consciousness (ISKCON), and the Family, the word *sociologist* has an auspicious ring. For most groups, it denotes a boring, depressingly secular, time-wasting, spiritually contaminated nerd. When I told the *sannyasis* at my neighbourhood Rajneesh Meditation Centre in 1985 that I wished to do a sociological study of their commune, they rolled their eyes. "Talk about missing the point!" one remarked. One swami who had an MA in sociology commented, "It's a good way to avoid looking inside yourself and get your energy stuck."

As a Quebec scholar, I have had a great deal of difficulty explaining my academic intentions to the small anglophobic right-wing Catholic sectarian groups as well as to the magical-arcane lodges that make up a significant proportion of our French-Canadian groups. I tend to prefer virgin turf untouched by other researchers, and so I have had to start from square one trying to educate these adepts in the scientific study of religion. I have wasted much time trying in vain to convince them of the innocuous nature of my research plans and have often been ignominiously driven away.

THAT ELUSIVE THING CALLED OBJECTIVITY

Objectivity is not a fixed, eschatological state from whence unworthy and corrupt scholars plunge from grace. It is an ongoing balancing act, a kind of gradual sensitivity training. Any experienced scholar knows it is not easy to collect and analyze data on controversial movements, or to navigate the subtle terrain of real research situations. In the course of my own participant-observation studies I have experienced intense moments of aesthetic revulsion, emotional attraction or cultural bias. My initial impressions of a group have often been erroneous, and my hypotheses and hunches have frequently proven false upon further investigation. Rather than recoil sanctimoniously at external assaults upon one's objectivity, or castigate oneself for receptivity to unscholarly emotions or unwelcome mystical cognitions, the serious researcher will forge ahead knowing the adventure is just beginning.

Nevertheless, there is clearly a need for constructive suggestions concerning a new code of ethics, or at least some recognized guidelines, for the complex, nuanced situations field researchers encounter inside "world-rejecting" NRMs. In 1967, in response to the controversy over the infamous Milgram experiment, the American Psychological Association's Ad Hoc Committee on Ethical Standards in Psychological Research recommended that "members of the profession themselves should supply ethical problems as the raw material for discussion." They hoped that through this inductive approach ethical principles would emerge that were relevant to contemporary research (Palys, 1992:83). Until recently, the exchange of concrete examples and discussion of these dilemmas among NRM scholars has been largely informal and interpersonal. We need more open forums along the lines of Catherine Wessinger's sessions at the American Academy of Religion (AAR), where researchers exchange anecdotes that illustrate the unforeseen challenges met in the field.

There has been a mounting concern over the problem of *trusting* the published research of NRM scholars, whose work may be contaminated by making deals with the cult leaders, or by closet conversion experiences, not unlike the Patty Hearst "Stockholm syndrome," or—worst of all—through bribes or cult funding to "say nice things." Irving Horowitz (1983:180) first identified an academic weakness he called "slippage into unabashed support for groups and the quality of publications produced by academics who attended expenses paid Unificationist Church-sponsored conferences." Robert Balch and Stefan Langdon (1996:72) criticized the design of the AWARE group study of the then-controversial Church Universal and Triumphant (CUT), arguing that the scholars were willing victims of the group's "impression management" (Goffman, 1959). Balch's critique has been cited repeatedly by anti-cultists as evidence that *any* research undertaken on NRMs with the knowledge and co-operation of the cult leaders is by nature contaminated.[1] In my conversations with Rob Balch, he has expressed surprise that what he hoped was a constructive criticism to raise research standards within the academy was taken up and brandished by anti-cultists as evidence that any published research on NRMs that isn't of the explicitly cult-bashing sort is suspect, and that the researcher's objectivity has been corrupted!

Cult research poses its own peculiar set of problems. This was noted in the textbook I use for my course, *Research Methods in the Social Sciences*. The authors, Del Balso and Lewis (1997:222), claim that "certain social groups, such as religious cults or extremist political, groups, require covert observation." Other textbooks compare cults to motorcycle gangs and quasi-criminal, racist or anarchist groups that are so difficult and dangerous to study that covert research and snowballing techniques are recommended as the appropriate means to gather data.

Stephen A. Kent and Theresa Krebs (1998) also raise the issue of the ethics appropriate for researchers in NRMs, and proceed to outline the dangers that await scholars in the field, dangers that are seemingly insurmountable and so morally contaminating as to cast doubt upon the personal integrity and efficaciousness of field researchers. They relate a series of anecdotes of how cults gain legitimacy by using, manipulating or making deals with scholars, then sound the alarm for the future respectability and credibility of the discipline. There are several assumptions in their argument that I find disquieting: assumptions about the character of NRMs, about the brains of researchers and about research methodology in general.

First, they imply that a new religion's gradual acquisition of public acceptance is gained through *sneaky means*—that they somehow "got away with it," and that it is undeserved. I have heard this argument before, most recently from the director of an anti-cult organization who spoke to my class, warning them that cults resort to under-handed strategies to appear respectable or to gain legitimacy. They set up lectures at McGill University; their leaders are photographed shaking hands with politicians and respectable religious leaders. He was saying NRMs *don't deserve* social acceptance and tolerance because *we know* they are intrinsically evil, or at least socially dysfunctional. The underlying message was, "We *know* they are quasi- or proto-criminal organiza-tions, so their slimy efforts to suck up to us respectable people must be exposed!"

These authors (Kent and Krebs, 1998) actually imply that a religious minority's new-found freedom from stigma and cult stereotyping in the media or exoneration in court constitutes a kind of *litmus test* for the objectivity of the scholarly research cited in the affidavits and the news reports. I would agree heartily, as I assume my fellow researchers would, that academics should not be *partisans* in a religious movement's missionary efforts, charisma-building, millenarian preparations or eschatological aspirations. Whether a young religion's reputation thrives or dives *should be irrelevant* to the pur-suit of accurate knowledge and should not concern the scholar. But Kent and Krebs's emphasis seems to imply that *if* a researcher's findings *just so happen* to contribute to the NRM's struggle for social legitimacy, then the findings themselves are suspect.

History tells us that those new religions that managed to survive the death of their founder, weather persecution and schisms, and to socialize their second and third gen-erations, *inevitably* work out a more civil and mutually accommodating relationship with society. The Mormons, the Christian Scientists, the Lutherans and the Anabaptists all managed to do this without the assistance of "cult-sponsored scholars."

The third assumption—that researchers are naive and easily duped—could be made only by scholars who occupy a bleak and marginal outpost in this field. Kent and Krebs (1998) warn scholars that they are often the targets of public relations and "impression management" when they begin to study a community that is in dire need of outside support for their legal and media battles. These are realities of which active researchers are *already* (trust me!) acutely aware. Most NRMs have an outer vestibule where they can check out prospective initiates, where charming hosts or hostesses speak to the media and provide information to visiting scholars. Surely even an inex-perienced undergraduate student would not mistake this vestibule for the group's innermost sanctuary. Any discerning anthropologist expects to wade through open-ing courtesies and ceremonial PR before unearthing more interesting data. It is quite understandable that NRMs with a history of conflict with society and of stigmatiza-tion in the media are wary of admitting researchers and will try to feed them the "rel-evant" information, hide discrediting literature and reinterpret embarrassing events. Often these PR efforts are so poorly organized and transparent that they reveal more than they hide, drawing the inquisitive researcher's eye to the vulnerable points in the group's armour.

Kent and Krebs broaden the stigma surrounding cults to include the cult scholars who embark on first-hand research in the field. In the end they veer away from the thorny task of thrashing out ethical guidelines for researchers going into controversial groups. Instead of grasping the nettle by the thorns, they brandish it. Some might even mistake their message to be "Researchers beware! *Avoid* challenging research projects *entirely*, lest your objectivity suffer irremediable erosion!" Thus the scholar's overriding concern should be to preserve her or his *reputation* at all costs. This new "ethical" development in the field would be lamentable as research would come to a screeching halt in areas that badly need elucidation, such as racialist, survivalist and apocalyptic movements.

WEIRD ETHICAL DILEMMAS BEYOND YOUR WILDEST DREAMS

But the real ethical dilemmas and challenges to objectivity are encountered *after* the PR phase, once the researcher has won the trust of the leaders and received permission to engage in research. These *actual* threats to scholarly objectivity are beyond your wildest dreams! Tenured professors, experts in the microsociology of NRMs who read the latest cult scandal in the news, then knowingly quote Toqueville while gazing out at their lawn sprinklers, have no idea what fascinating adventures they are missing by avoiding the strenuous, time-consuming work of field research. Scholars who rely exclusively on ex-members or on secondhand research for their data understandably lack any sense of the complex political situations and serious ethical decisions that confront the more energetic, less squeamish scholars who are willing to go into controversial communities. Each group poses unforeseen challenges, and every researcher presumably has different chinks in his or her armour. Problematic situations might be encountered in the course of sleeping inside a commune, participating in rituals designed to induce altered states of consciousness, interviewing rival leaders who try to enlist the researcher in their struggle over the succession, or talking to rebellious teens who tell you stuff their parents really should know about…. These challenges can be complex and dramatic, requiring the researcher to improvise ethical guidelines as these situations come up.

I will now relate some of my adventures.

WHY I DON'T CONSIDER MYSELF A "KEPT SCHOLAR"

In 1992 I received two grants to study children in new religions. I approached two different sects in Quebec and was refused permission to interview their members (they suspected I was a spy sent by the Catholic school board to undermine their home schooling). Then two international NRMs heard about me and called me up, offering plane tickets to "come on out and study *our* kids!" I turned them down. The situation made me nervous for several reasons. First, I was concerned about preserving my "scholarly virginity." Second, I feared that if in the future I did not co-operate with their agenda, they might resort to blackmail (no doubt this is pure paranoia). Finally, I like to feel I am unhampered as a writer, free to poke fun at the group delicately if I feel like it, or mention stuff that is embarrassing. In short, I don't like being censored. I was aware that by choosing to study controversial child-rearing methods in NRMs, I would be vulnerable to criticism, but I didn't realize that I was stepping into the front line of a new battleground in the Cult Wars.

In April 1994 I was standing in the witness box at the High Court, Family Division, in Lincoln's Inn to testify during the *Turle* v. *Turle* custody battle over the grandson of a millionairess whose mother joined The Family. The same official solicitor who wanted to know if I was "soft on the cults" asked: "Who *paid* for your trip to San Diego to study The Family's home-school?" Fortunately I was able to respond: "I paid for it out of my SSSR grant"—and could have produced the receipts if necessary.

I have never accepted money from an NRM to study them, but I have had to make deals with leaders who have curtailed the areas I was allowed to go into. I have managed to preserve my scholarly virginity, but have engaged in mutual flattery and love-bombing, if not heavy petting (figuratively speaking), with charismatic leaders and their top aides. Personally, I don't know of any kept scholars in real life, but I am unsuited for the job since I prefer my NRMs wild and virgin. I seek out groups that are almost inaccessible and unself-conscious, groups that know *they* are not a cult, but I naively swallow what the newspapers say about other cults—groups that have never heard of the term *NRM*, groups that are suspicious of researchers and assume a sociologist is just a pretentious variety of journalist. Once they start sending out PR reps to conferences wearing suits, groomed hair and name tags, they're no fun anymore. Well, that's not true. They can still be interesting, but suddenly they seem tame, almost domesticated. Other scholars horn in and conduct schmaltzy interviews in the hotel breakfast nook and arrange visits.

If NRMs are baby religions, scholarly conferences provide the venues to set up *petting zoos*.

A CONDOMINIUM ON THE OUTSKIRTS OF HEAVEN

I have been offered bribes, so I keep all my receipts and correspondence to make it more convenient to sue anyone who suggests my research efforts or opinions can be bought. But I never turn down otherworldly rewards. Three different apocalyptic sects have awarded me a sort of last-minute squeezed-in salvation when the cosmic countdown comes. "We want you to know you will be *blessed* when Our Saviour returns," a bearded elder told me. Technically I deserve to be consigned to eternal oblivion or fall into the pit amidst other soulless beer-swilling sinners, but I have been promised a condominium on the outskirts of Heaven, according to "The Chosen People." I have been assured by another "biblically based" group that I will be beamed up before Armageddon gets too nasty. I was informed that Da Free John (currently known as Adidam) "meditated me" long before I appeared on their scene. An infamous "cult leader" prophesied I was "one of the three wise women sent by God to assist the Prophet in opening the seventh seal at the end of time." One Raelian guide suggested I might be eligible for cloning when the extraterrestrials arrive. And if linear time is indeed an illusion, I can look forward to a better rebirth, according to a member of Hare Krishna who suggested that I am a devotee of Swami Prahupada "in my heart."

Oddly enough, these assurances make me feel more secure on airplanes when I travel to conferences.

I also receive quite a lot of flattery. I am so accustomed to love-bombing that I have stopped blushing and now courteously return the blast: "I love you too! If I were even one-tenth as beautiful as you are, I would be so happy!" My own children have accused me of sycophantic behaviour in the presence of charisma: "That's my mom sucking up to Rael," I overheard my daughter say as she showed my photo album, Quebec Sect Tours, to a friend. I don't "suck up"! Prophets are fascinating people—although my excitement in their presence might more closely resemble that of a manic butterfly collector than a sincere spiritual seeker.

The Sociologist as Hired Gun

To agree to appear in court as a witness to help a NRM (or a member) win or defend their case is *not* the same as being a "cult-sponsored scholar." Charlotte Allen (1999) lumps kept scholars and court witnesses together, but since we live in a society where even religious minorities actually enjoy the right to a fair trial, expert witnesses are generally considered to be legitimate. Nevertheless, going to court raises a whole new spectrum of problems for the researcher who nurtures objectivity.

Personally, when I first accepted the gig of hired gun, I experienced it as a traumatic loss of innocence. Courts are scary. I felt dragged into an adversarial situation and the anti-cult newsletters were soon taking potshots at me. I felt uncomfortable when asked to name my fee. Then, later (when I found out what the *other* witnesses got), I was annoyed at myself for requesting so little.

Just asking about fees was an education in itself. I called one eminent British scholar who replied, "I would never agree to go to court, I would find it compromising to my scholarship." Another European scholar who had appeared in court on occasion said, "I never accept money as a witness. It looks and feels too much like a bribe." One French professor insisted, "In France an expert witness who accepts money is considered ineligible as a witness by the court." Then I phoned several U.S. scholars and noticed a very different view. "You must establish a substantial fee, or you will be perceived as a closet member of the cult, and your testimony won't be taken seriously," one scholar advised me. Another seasoned expert witness counselled, "Charge as much as you can—$150 an hour just for reading the affidavits—because lawyers talk to each other, and if it becomes known that you charge a low fee, your testimony won't be valued, and you won't get asked back."

The next time I was asked to appear in court by a different NRM, I told their lawyer I wouldn't charge anything because it would not require extra research, the group was not rich, and I could see the defendant had been unfairly treated. All I asked was that my expenses be covered. Initially I felt comfortable with that, but soon realized that my relationship with the group leaders had begun to take on a "covenantal" as opposed to a "contractual" character (Bromley and Busching, 1988). They were now firmly convinced I had been sent by God to aid them in their battle against the Prince of Darkness. That was OK, I told myself, I don't mind accommodating their world view, but the real problem was that they now expected me to be constantly on the alert and ready to jump into the fray. I flew out for the pretrial hearing, then they wanted me to fly out *again* for the last day of the trial, and now expect me to be on call for more upcoming cases. I am currently trying to figure out how I can gracefully bow out of their mythic landscape.

The Sociologist as Undercover Agent

Three months after the Solar Temple perpetrated their shocking mass suicide-homicide ritual "transit" to Sirius, I found myself in an office being grilled by two policemen from the Securité Québec concerning my belated and rather tentative research efforts into this controversial and criminal order. They wanted me to hand over a list of the Templars or ex-Templars I had met or interviewed. (It was impossible to tell the difference since none of them would admit to a current affiliation.) I refused, saying that to reveal the names of one's informants contravened ethics in the social sciences. "Excuse me, Madame," said one official, "What is that?" It was difficult to explain. Finally the "good cop" in the tweed suit joked, "Be very careful, Madame. But, if you find yourself on Sirius, send us a postcard."

The Sociologist as Soft Deprogrammer

I have noticed that the visit of a researcher is sometimes welcomed by NRM adherents as an opportunity for hedonism, a chance to gain access to luxuries and indulgences not normally available within the strict regimen of a commune or the workspace of even the more secularized religious institutions. This particular ethical problem has never been identified or discussed in anti-cult circles, because they view cultists as obedient robots incapable of rebelling. In my experience, the brainwashed are quite capable of sneakiness, of pursuing their own individualistic whims or vices.

The kind of situation I am talking about has occurred quite often, where the people assigned to host me and facilitate my research *very* often suggest we go outside to a local bar or restaurant and order a drink or a meal. Somehow, many NRMs seem to have gained the impression that most sociologists are borderline alcoholics. After one round of beers (paid for by the cult budget) they suggested we order another round. The first time this happened I unthinkingly and selfishly said, "No thanks," and then saw the anxious, disappointed looks on their faces. I realized this was perhaps their *only* opportunity to indulge in alcoholic beverages for the next few years, so I said, "OK, maybe I will," and paid for the second round. When I left half a glass, I noticed one of them swilled it down quickly as we got up to leave.

Since I privately feel many of the new religions I study are too strict and overly spartan, I am inclined to collude with my interviewees and encourage their secret rebellions—which places me in a morally dubious position, since I genuinely respect their religious principles and realize the rules are based on sound economics or communal ideals of humility and equality—or necessary measures to avoid assimilation. It puts sociologists like me rather in the position of being a "soft deprogrammer" by encouraging members to disobey leaders, break out of their conditioning, and place their own selfish desires before the group goals—perhaps the first tentative steps towards eventually leaving.

On one occasion I had arranged to spend a few days living with a rather puritanical, biblically based commune in order to interview members and study communal patterns. Two members in their forties, who had recently been given the exciting task of dealing with the public, picked me up in a car to drive me to the commune four hours away in the countryside. On the way they suggested we stop off at a beautiful hotel by a lake to get some refreshment and so that I could admire the prospect of the mountains. I agreed, still feeling jet-lagged. Upon our arrival at the hotel front desk it became clear they had booked rooms—one for the two women, and the other for the man. Then they turned to me and said, "Susan, you must be really tired with all your teaching and travelling. We thought it would be great for you if we all stayed here for three days. You could interview us, and catch up with your writing projects. We'll double up and give you the private room so you can work in peace." It became clear that their *real* agenda was to indulge a secret passion they had been harbouring for years. It turned out their love affair had started years ago, but had been squelched by the leaders, and they had been encouraged to marry more suitable partners. I was not unsympathetic to their romance, and I could appreciate their need for a little holiday away from the crowded commune.

In this situation we find the sociologist-as-chaperone. The two would no doubt later report to their leaders: "Dr. Palmer *insisted* on stopping at a hotel for three days en route," and they probably had been instructed to indulge a decadent sociologist. I had no problem personally with facilitating their affair, except that I really *did* want to conduct as many interviews as possible and realized if the situation became public this would not be good for my rep: I would very much look like a jet-setting, kept scholar using research trips to enjoy luxurious holidays. So I had to play the priggish spoilsport and say no, although I sat by the lake and reviewed my notes while they went to the room to "rest from the drive." Thus sociologists can have a corrupting effect upon the morals of members.

THE REAL ETHICAL QUESTION: WHO GETS HURT BY WHOM?

Ever since the Milgram experiment in 1963, the concern has been exclusively for the rights and dignity of the human subjects in experiments. And yet, all the recent discussion on research ethics in the microsociology of NRMs has focused on the potential harm to the discipline (due to sleazy researchers) and to the public who might mistake a cult for a respectable enterprise. I feel it is time we exhibited some concern for the informants in NRMs, who already have been stripped of dignity through being labelled brainwashed cultists.

Baker (1988:74) notes that "It has more often been the case that social researchers have studied those with lower status than themselves rather than higher. Indigent and poorly educated people do not have the resources or knowledge, the lawyers, or the 'I'm too busy' excuses to fend off social researchers." Many members of NRMs feel so outcast, so marginalized, that they exhibit a pathetic gratitude that here at last is someone who is willing to listen to their side of the story. In some instances they have been told by the leaders to co-operate with sociologists, since scholarly articles on their movements tend to be more balanced and accurate than news reports. Thus they are in a vulnerable position to be exploited and manipulated by the researcher.

Sometimes this happens in the process of writing. It is only too easy for sociologists to make their informants sound less educated and articulate than themselves. Obviously there is a difference in the way even PhDs express themselves verbally and on paper. What we find in many scholarly studies of new religions (including my own, I confess) are many indented passages in which the informant spills his or her guts in less than grammatical fashion. The informants' responses in interviews (often to touchy and impertinent questions concerning intimate conversion experiences, sensations while meditating, the group's controversial sexual mores, and their own deeply emotional first encounter with their God-in-flesh leader) are often liberally sprinkled with "like," "um," "kind of," "you know." On concluding the indented quote as a specimen of cultic thinking, the sociologist then lunges into an interpretation of the statement in the industrial Latin of American "sociologese," leaving the reader stunned by the disparities in the two prose styles.

Often it is quite evident to the reader that the "cultists" statements might be interpreted in several ways and are applicable to more than one hermeneutic context, but the impatient sociologist ignores these subtleties and proceeds to pounce upon the odd sentence that fits the theory presented in the article. References to Durkheim, Levi Strauss or Eliade unconsciously underscore the portrait of the modern urban "cultist" with the "Savage Mind"—as a sort of naive neo-primitive. In the end, the sociologist comes across as smarter than she or he might actually be, and the cultist as stupider, less self-aware than he or she probably would strike you in a real-life situation. By scrupulously including every "um" and "well, it's like …" the sociologist gets extra points for being a rigorous and accurate recorder of naturalistic data, while at the same time demonstrates intellectual superiority to—and distance from—the informant.

Scholars and researchers play an important role as educators in the global process of the proliferating new religious pluralism. Often they are the only go-betweens, the ones who have traversed that no-man's land between the "cult" and "normal society." In this situation it is tempting to fancy oneself as a "freedom fighter" or a *deus ex machina* who advises cult leaders on how to get out of trouble.

I find myself torn between the need to educate and the desire to entertain. By highlighting spiritual weirdnesses I grab my students' attention and please journalists, but I undermine the groups' struggle for respect. It is only too easy to forget that cult members are human beings too, and that many have found happiness, learned social graces, and received spiritual gifts participating in less-than-respectable religions.

Recently I invited a Knight of the Golden Lotus to speak to my class, after giving the students a rather unfeeling satirical sketch of the late leader's eccentricities. Our speaker appeared in the knights' orange and yellow garments, with mirrors fastened on his head-band. His companion wore amulets of swans, rainbows and mandalas pinned to her ample bosom. I stifled a smirk, and was feeling particularly frazzled—the VCR wasn't working and the audiovisual man refused to help and launched into a tirade on the college cutbacks that had robbed him of his assistant. My daughter had refused to brush her hair before leaving for school, and my students were now behaving badly, lurching in late and babbling at the back. My Knight of the Golden Lotus stepped forward: "Please be quiet! We have come to present to you our religion and would appreciate respect." The students immediately calmed down and he launched into a fascinating lecture.

Afterwards, walking down the hall beside him, I reflected that, in spite of his leader's execrable taste in architecture, here was an admirable human being. His swift social responses had shown considerable insight and intelligence. I suspected that on this particular day his mental health was superior to my own. In fact, he'd put me in a good mood—perhaps an altered state?

LEARNING HOW TO NAVIGATE THE CULT WARS

Over thirty-odd years, the controversial field of what Thomas Robbins (1988) dubbed the "microsociology of new religions" has blossomed, waxed in complexity and come to resemble a German late-Romantic string quartet in all its dark, foreboding dissonances. In the past five years, since Waco, we have witnessed a heightened awareness of religious liberty issues, the sudden demise of the Cult Awareness Network, and a softening of the boundaries separating NRM scholars from anti-cultists. Former deprogrammers present papers at the SSSR, and NRM researchers who have debunked the brainwashing theory are finally permitted to attend the American Family Foundation conferences. As the no-man's land that recently separated the anti-cultists from the "cult scholars" is tamed by footprints, and new, uneasy alliances are formed, each side shows signs of fissiparousness as various schools of thought—and backbiting—threaten the collegiality of cult scholars.

All the evidence at hand points to a future filled with a dizzying abundance of ever-proliferating new religions. This phenomenon begs to be studied and offers stimulating hands-on research opportunities for young scholars. And yet, inexperienced and ambitious aspiring academics are likely to be deterred by a kind of miasma hovering around the field, a miasma arising from rumours and stereotypes as well as occasional errors and poor judgment on the part of NRM researchers. Will the young field researcher who wishes to write about the vampire subculture and its rituals hesitate to embark on this project lest she later find herself *branded* as a morbid blood-drinker once she becomes a famous sociologist? Young scholars may feel reluctant to embark on the study of NRMs like the Church Universal and Triumphant, the Unification Church and The Family, groups that in the past have been known to exhibit "philomandarin" tendencies—to eagerly court, and even pay, scholars to study them. These groups continue to mature, mutate and institutionalize charisma in fascinating ways … but by associating with these groups, are young researchers compromising their most precious commodity: objectivity? Or, even more important, are they compromising their *reputations* as objective social scientists?

Paradoxically, there is pressure in the academy to steer clear of cults, but the news media exerts considerable pressure on scholars to comment on, and hence to study, the more controversial, outrageous or dangerous groups—and these are precisely the areas of unpredictable pitfalls. What NRM scholar does not feel trepidation upon hearing the following cautionary, but true tales? (1) A Japanese professor who wrote an encyclopedia entry on Aum Shinrikyo, and whose graduate student was recruited into the movement, was fired by the university—the rationale being, if he knew his stuff he should have been able to recognize danger signals and warn the proper authorities; and (2) an Oregon high-school teacher was fired after inviting two sannyasis from Rajneeshpuram to talk to his class.[2]

Like Dorothy on the yellow brick road, young researchers will occasionally lose their barking "Totos" of objectivity. They will rely on their Cowardly Lions (academic caution) and rusty Tin Woodmen (quantitative methods) as they wander off into the yet undreamt-of spiritual landscapes of the future. Perhaps in a few years it will be considered quite as respectable to receive research funding from NRMs as from the Vatican. Perhaps "religious minority" will have the same earnest ring to it as "sexual minority" or "women of colour." The best advice I can offer to my students who aspire to spiritual espionage is this: Be open about what you're doing, don't apologize for mistakes, grow a rhinoceros-hide, but cultivate an empathetic ear for spiritual confessions.

NOTES

[1] I heard Balch's "findings" cited four times at the American Family Foundation meeting in May 1997.

[2] From *The Oregonian*, a special issue on Rajneeshpuram, August 1985.

REFERENCES

Allen, Charlotte. 1999. "Brainwashed! Scholars of Cults Accuse Each Other of Bad Faith." *Lingua Franca* (January):26–37.

Baker, Theresa L. 1988. *Doing Social Research*. New York: McGraw Hill.

Balch, Robert, and Stephen Langdon. 1998. "How the Problem of Malfeasance Gets Overlooked in Studies of New Religions: An Examination of the AWARE Study of the Church Universal and Triumphant." In *Wolves within the Fold*, ed. Anson Shupe, 191–211. New Brunswick, NJ: Rutgers University Press.

Barker, Eileen. 1996. "The Scientific Study of Religion? You Must be Joking!" In *Cults in Context*, ed. Lorne L. Dawson, 5–27. Toronto: Canadian Scholars' Press.

Baum, L. Frank. 1910. *The Emerald City of Oz*. Chicago: Reilly and Lee.

Bromley, David, and Bruce Busching. 1988. "Understanding the Structure of Contractual and Covenantal Social Relations." *Sociological Analysis* 49:15–32.

Del Balso, Michael, and Alan D. Lewis. 1997. *First Steps: A Guide to Social Research*. Toronto: ITP Nelson.

Erikson, Kai T. 1967. "A Comment on Disguised Observation in Sociology." *Social Problems* 14 (14):367–373.

Goffman, Irving. 1961. *Asylums*. New York: Doubleday.

Horowitz, Irving. 1983. "Unusual Standards NOT Uniform Beliefs." *Sociological Analysis* 44:179–182.

Kent, Stephen, and Theresa Krebs. 1998. "Academic Compromise in the Social Scientific Study of Alternative Religions." *Nova Religio* 2:44–54.

Milgram, Stanley. 1965. "Some Conditions of Obedience and Disobedience to Authority," *Human Relations* 18:57–75.

Palmer, Susan J. 1994. *Moon Sisters, Krishna Mothers, Rajneesh Lovers: Women's Roles in New Religions*. Syracuse, NY: Syracuse University Press, 105–36.

———. 1995. "Women in the Raelian Movement." In *The Gods Have Landed: New Religions from Other Worlds*, ed. James R. Lewis. New York: SUNY.

Palys, Ted. 1992. *Research Decisions: Quantitative and Qualitative Perspectives*. Toronto: Harcourt Brace.

Robbins, Thomas. 1988. *Cults, Converts and Charisma*. Somerset, NJ: Transaction Press.

Singer, Margaret Thaler, with Janja Lalich. 1995. *Cults in Our Midst: The Hidden Menace in Our Everyday Lives*. San Francisco: Jossey-Bass.

CHAPTER 12

NEW RELIGIONS AND THE INTERNET:
RECRUITING IN A NEW PUBLIC SPACE[1]

Lorne L. Dawson and Jenna Hennebry

INTRODUCTION

The mass suicide of thirty-nine members of Heaven's Gate in March of 1997 led to public fears about the presence of "spiritual predators" on the World Wide Web. This chapter describes and examines the nature of these fears, as reported in the media. It then sets these fears against what we know about the use of the Internet by new religions, about who joins new religious movements and why, and the social profile of Internet users. It is argued that the emergence of the Internet has yet to significantly change the nature of religious recruitment in contemporary society. The Internet as a medium of communication, however, may be having other largely unanticipated effects on the form and functioning of religion, both old and new, in the future. In the following pages we review some of the potential perils of the Internet with reference to the impact of this new medium on questions of religious freedom, community, social pluralism and social control.

CONCERNS AFTER HEAVEN'S GATE

Twice in the last year (1998) the first author of this paper has been asked to speak to groups in our community about the presence of "cults"[2] on the Web, and the threat they might pose. These talks were prompted, undoubtedly, by the tragic death of the thirty-nine members of Heaven's Gate at Rancho Sante Fe, California, on 26 March 1997. To the surprise of many, it seems, the media reports of this strange and ceremonious mass suicide revealed a group with its own elaborate Web page (see Figure 12.1). What is more, this new religion designed sophisticated Web pages for other organizations. In fact, it received much of its income from a company called Higher Source, operated by its members. Heaven's Gate had been using the Internet to communicate with some of its followers and to spread its message for several years. This news generated a special measure of curiosity and fear from some elements of the public.[3] This reaction stemmed, we suspect, from the coincidental confluence of the misunderstanding and consequent mistrust of both the new technology and of cults.

FIGURE 12.1: HEAVEN'S GATE WEB PAGE

Despite the ballyhoo recently accorded the launch of the "information superhighway" (by the government, the computer industry, and the media), the Internet is still used, with any regularity, only by a relatively small percentage of the population.[4] In the absence of personal experience, the Web is popularly thought to be the creature of those believed to be its primary users: large corporations on the one hand (from Microsoft to Nike), and isolated "computer nerds" on the other. Most certainly, religious organizations are not commonly associated in the public perception with such leading-edge technologies (despite the omnipresence of televangelists on the U.S. airwaves). For most North Americans, in fact, the topic of religion calls to mind churches, and the churches are associated with traditionalism, if not with an element of hostility to the cultural influence of developments in science and technology. New religious movements (NRMs), in addition, are still rather crudely seen as havens for the socially marginal, and perhaps even for personally deficient individuals—those least likely or capable of mastering the social and technical demands of a new world order. The image, then, of cultists exploiting the Web seemed incongruous to many. Combined with the established suspicion of "cults" (e.g., Pfeifer, 1992; Bromley and Breschel, 1992) and the almost mystical power often attributed to the Internet itself, the example set by Heaven's Gate seemed ominous.

When compared with the familiar media used to distribute religious views, such as books, videos, tapes, radio and television programs, Internet sites are easily accessible and in many respects more economical to produce and operate. With the appropriate knowledge and minimal computer hardware and software, anyone can sample a wide array of alternative religious views, and, if they so choose, just as easily hide their exposure or consumption of such views from the prying eyes of others (for example, parents, partners, friends or employers). In fact, the Net opens surprising new opportunities to even start one's own religion (as will be discussed below).

Have cults found in the Internet, then, a new and more effective means to recruit members? If so, has the Web changed the playing field, so to speak, allowing quite small and unusual groups unprecedented access to a new and impressionable audience of potential converts and supporters?

Most scholars of new religious movements would be skeptical, we think, that the advent of the Web offered any reason for renewed concern about the presumed threat posed by "cults" to mainstream society. Within days of the Heaven's Gate deaths, however, several media stories appeared in prominent sources (for example, *The New York Times*, *Time* magazine, *Newsweek*, and CNN), each raising the prospect of "spiritual predators" on the Net. In the words of George Johnson in *The New York Times*:

> In the public mind—moulded by news reports on the old media, which are still more powerful and pervasive than anything on-line—the Internet is starting to seem like a scary place, a labyrinth of electronic tunnels as disturbing and seedy as anything Thomas Pynchon has dreamed up for the bizarre worlds in such works as *Gravity's Rainbow*, *V* and *Vineland*. The Heaven's Gate suicides can only amplify fears that, in some quarters, may be already bordering on hysteria. The Internet, it seems, might be used to lure children not only to shopping malls, where some "sicko" waits, but into joining UFO cults. [See the version of this article reprinted in Canada's national newspaper, *The Globe and Mail*, April 5, 1997: C27.]

CNN's online news magazine carried these suspicions further (http://cnn.com/TECH/9703/27/techno.pagans/index.html), citing comments from presumed experts on the Web, such as Erik Davis of *Wired* magazine, and "experts" on cults, such as Margaret T. Singer. A story, posted under the heading "The Internet as a God and Propaganda Tool for Cults," sought to create the impression that "computer nerds," and other compulsive denizens of the Net, might be particularly susceptible to cult recruitment (and hence eventually to abuse). In Davis's view, "identifying more and more of your life with what's happening on the other side of the [computer] screen ..." can have a "very dissociative effect," increasing the risk of cult conversion. What is more, Singer assures us, the cults are targeting these very people:

> What the cults want to recruit are average, normal, bright people and especially, in recent years, people with technical skills, like computer skills. And often, they haven't become street smart. And they're too gullible.

Wisely, the stories in *The New York Times* and *Time* magazine (5 April 1997) both seek to cast doubt on such scare mongering. They each seek to do so, however, by defending the integrity of the World Wide Web and not the cults. Their pointed concern is to disassociate the Net as a neutral means of communication from its use by religions (that is, don't confuse the medium with the message). No effort is made to even begin to address the realities of cult recruitment in general, let alone their actual use of the Net.

So what do we know about cult recruitment and the World Wide Web ? Do we have reason to believe that the Internet either has or someday could become a significant source of new converts? Is there something to worry about? A recent survey of adult Canadians reported that 12 percent claim they use the Internet for "religious purposes."[5]

This paper examines and compares what we know about the presence of new religious movements on the Internet and how people come to join these groups. The most reliable results of decades of research into religious conversions cast doubt on the special utility of the World Wide Web as a mechanism of recruitment. Face-to-face social interactions and networks of personal relationships play too large a role in the data about conversions collected by scholars. Further, previous studies suggest that such "disembodied appeals" as religious advertisements, radio shows and televangelism have little significant effect on rates of religious recruitment (Lofland, 1966; Shupe, 1976; Snow, Zurcher and Ekland-Olson, 1980; Rochford, 1982; Hoover, 1988). But these are broadcast media, and largely under the control of a relatively small elite. Might things be different within the interactive and more democratic, even anarchic, conditions of cyberspace? At present we cannot say, because there is little reliable information and because it is too soon. Discussions of the nature and impact of the new public space opened up by the Internet, however, suggest that the emergence of the World Wide Web may be changing the conditions of new religious life in our societies in significant ways. There are both promise and peril in the new technologies of cyberspace for the future of religion.

INTERNET SURVEYS

Our analysis of these matters is augmented with insights drawn from two surveys: our own survey of the "Web meisters" of several new religious movements, and an online profile of Internet users. Some interesting problems with the first survey will be discussed before proceeding with the analysis.

In the late spring of 1998, we surveyed the Web-page creators of thirty groups by e-mail (see Table 12.1). The brief survey asked twenty-three questions delving into such matters as the origins of their Web pages, whether professional help was used in their design or updating, whether the pages were official or unofficial in status, the primary purposes of the Web pages, their level of satisfaction with the Web pages and what measures of success they used, the mechanisms used for inviting feedback (if at all), the nature of the feedback received and the responses given, any knowledge of whether people had become affiliated with their groups as a result of contact with the Web page, and their views on whether and how the Web should be regulated.

The groups and individuals approached were selected according to three criteria: (1) they represented relatively well-known new religious movements; (2) they represented a fairly reasonable cross-section of the kinds of groups active in North America; (3) they were already known to be operating fairly sophisticated Web pages. In administering the survey by e-mail we had hoped to garner a higher rate of return from these

TABLE 12.1: SURVEY SAMPLE—NEW RELIGIOUS MOVEMENTS ON THE INTERNET

Group	Site name	URL site location
A.R.E.	A.R.E. Inc.	www.are-cayce.com/
Aumism	Aumism—Universal Religion	www.aumisme.org/gb
BOTA	BOTA Home page (Builders of the Atydum)	www.atanda.com/bota/default.html
Brahma Kumaris	Brahma Kumaris W.S.O	www.rajayoga.com/
	Brahma Kumaris W.S.O	www.bkwsu.com
Church Universal & Triumphant	Our Church (Church Universal and Triumphant)	www.tsl.org/intro/church.html
Churches of Christ	Boston Church of Christ	www.bostoncoc.org/
	International Churches of Christ	www.intlcc.com/
Covenant of the Goddess	Covenant of the Goddess	www.canjure.com
Eckankar	Eckankar	www.eckankar.org
Foundation for Inner Peace (ACIM)	A Course in Miracles—ACIM	www.acim.org/
	Miracles web site	www.miraclesmedia.org/
International Society for Krishna Consciousness	ISKON.NET A Hare Krishna Network	http://iskcon.net
Meher Baba Group	Meher Baba Group	http://davey;sunyerie.edu/mb/html
MSIA	MSIA—Movement of Spiritual Inner Awareness	www.msia.com/
Ordo Templi Orientis	Hodos Chamelionis Camp of the Ordo Templi Orientis	http://pw2.netcom.com/~bry-guy/hcc-oto.html
	Thelema	www.crl.com?~thelema.home.html
Osho	Meditation: The Science of the Inner	www.osho.org/homepage html
Raelians	International Radian Movement	www.rael.org/
Rosicrucian Order	Rosicrucian Order, (English) AMORC Home Page	www.rosicrucian.org/
	AMORC International	www.amorc.org
School of Wisdom	School of Wisdom Home Page	http://ddi.digital.net/~wisdom/school/welcome.html
Scientology	Scientology: SCIENTOLOGY HOME PAGE	www.scientology.org/
Shambhala	Welcome to Shambhala	www.shambhala.org/
Shirdi Sai Baba	Shirdi Sai Baba	www.saiml.com
Sikh Dharma (3H)	International Directory of Kundalini Yoga Centers (3HO)	www.sikhnet.com
Soka Gakkai	Soka Gakkal International Public Info Site	www.sgi.org
	Soka Gakkai International-USA (SCI-USA)	www.sgi-usa.org/
Subud	SUBUD: The World Subud Association Website	www.subud.org/english.menu.html
Quest for Utopia (Koufuku no kagaku)	Quest for Utopia	www.quest-utopia.com

TABLE 12.1: SURVEY SAMPLE—NEW RELIGIOUS MOVEMENTS ON THE INTERNET (continued)

Group	Site name	URL site location
	Institute Research Human Happiness (Koufuku no Kagaku)	www.quest-utopia.com/info/irh.html
Temple of Set	Temple of Set	www.xeper.org/pub/tos/noframe.htm
	Balanone: Temple of Set Information	www.geocities.com
The Family	The Family—An International Christian Fellowship	www.thefamily.org/
TM	Complete Guide to the Transcendental Meditation	www.TM.org/
Unification Church	Unification Church Home Page	http://www.unification.org/
Urantia	Urantia Foundation	www.urantia.org
Wicca	Wiccan Church of Canada Home Page	www.wcc.on.ca/
	Welcome to Daughters of the Moon (Dianic Wicca)	www.wco.com/~moonwmyn/index.html

"computer savvy" individuals and groups, thinking many might be able to respond almost immediately by return e-mail (as requested). To our surprise, however, the rate of return was very low: seven surveys or 23.3 percent.[6] Why the low rate of return? We are not sure, although we have some ideas. Using the Internet to do surveys would seem to be a subject in need of systematic investigation itself.[7]

All the same, some information from our seven respondents will be introduced here for strictly illustrative purposes, since this is the only empirical data currently available. Moreover, the seven respondents happen to represent several of the more prominent new religions and an interesting, if highly limited, cross-section of the kinds of new religions available (neopagan, Christian, Hindu, Buddhist and psychotherapeutic).[8]

The information derived from the other survey of Internet users, on which we are calling, is more straightforward and based on a large, if perhaps not completely reliable, sample (N = 9529) collected by the Inter Commerce Corporation and made available to all on the Net at www.survey.net (see Table 12.2).[9]

Better data on both counts would assist future investigations of the issues raised by this paper. But a timely, appropriate and significant response can be made with the data and theoretical insights at hand. Research into the nature, social and religious functions, and consequences of the Internet is only beginning and the issues raised in this discussion help to explain why we need to do more.

NEW RELIGIONS ON THE NET

To date we do not know much about how surfing the Web may have contributed to anyone joining a new religious movement. With the exception of the brief forays undertaken by Cottee, Yateman and Dawson (1996:459–468) and Bainbridge (1997:149–155),

TABLE 12.2: INTERNET USER STATISTICS (1997–1998) [www.wisdom.com/sv/sv-inetl.htm]

Age		Sex	
26–30 yrs. old	25.40%	Female	28.40%
22–25	16.50%	Male	71.50%
31–35	13.00%		
41–50	12.90%		
19–20	9.10%	Education	
36–40	9.00%	College	34.00%
51–60	4.60%	College Graduate	30.10%
13–16	4.00%	Master's Degree	18.20%
17–18	4.00%	Some High School	6.70%
61–70	0.90%	High School Graduate	6.60%
under 12	0.30%	PhD +	4.10%
over 71	0.20%	PhD Student	0.30%
Occupation		**Industry**	
Professional	59.20%	Education/Student	37.10%
Student	34.30%	Service	23.60%
Blue Collar	4.50%	Publishing	12.20%
Retired	1.90%	Other/Unemployed	7.10%
Sales	6.30%		
Occupation associated w/ computers	39.40%	Government	5.10%
		Manufacturing	5.10%
		Arts/Creative	3.40%
Primary Use of the Internet			
Research	44.50%		
Entertainment	24.50%		
Communication	15.90%		
Sales/Marketing	9.70%		
Education	5.30%		

Source: Inter Commerce Corporation, "SURVEY.NET."

we know of no specific studies, popular or academic, of this subject. The journalist Jeff Zaleski has written an interesting book about religion and the Internet called *The Soul of Cyberspace* (Zaleski, 1997). It contains some fascinating interviews with religious figures from many of the world's religions that have already heavily invested in the Internet as a tool of religious discourse (from the Chabad-Lubavitch Jews of New York, at www.chabad.org, to Zen Buddhists, at wwwl.mhv.net/~dharmacom/1htmlmro.htm). It also contains some equally intriguing conversations with a few of the founding or influential figures of cyberspace and virtual reality about the possible interface of religion and cyberspace. Zaleski's attention, however, is directed to discerning if anyone thinks that religious services can be performed authentically over the Web, and how. Can the spiritual essence of religion, the subtle energies of *prana*, as he calls it, be adequately conveyed by the media of cyberspace? Or will such hyper-real simulations always be inadequate to the task? The question of recruitment arises in his discussions, but it is never explored in any detail. On the contrary, in his comments on Heaven's Gate and the threat posed by "cults" on the Internet, Zaleski displays a level of prejudice and misunderstanding that is out of keeping with the rest of his book:

> Those most vulnerable to a cult's message—the lonely, the shy, misfits, outcasts—are often attracted to the Net, relishing its power to allow communion with others while maintaining anonymity. While the Net offers an unprecedented menu of choice, it also allows budding fanatics to focus on just one choice—to tune into the same Web site, the same newsgroup, again and again, for hours on end, shut off from all other stimuli—to isolate themselves from conflicting beliefs. Above all, the headiness of cyberspace, its divorce from the body and the body's incarnate wisdom, gives easy rise to fantasy, paranoia, delusions of grandeur. (Zaleski, 1997:249)

In echoing the comments of Davis and Singer, Zaleski is rather unreflexive about his own and others' fascination with religion on the Internet.

Reports on the Web say that Heaven's Gate did contact people by e-mail and through conversations tried to involve them in their activities, even encouraged them to leave home and join the main group in California. One particular conversation between a member of the group and an adolescent in Minnesota has been recorded (we are told), and it does not seem unreasonable to presume that there were more. How many? How successful were these contacts? Who knows. Reports in the news of the past lives of some of the thirty-nine people who died indicated that a few of the members first contacted the group through the Internet.[10] But we lack details of how and of what happened. Did these people know of the group before or not? Had they been involved in similar groups before? Did the Internet contact play a significant or a merely peripheral role in the decisions they made about joining Heaven's Gate? There are a lot of important questions that have yet to be answered.

Was the recruiting done over the Internet part of a fully sanctioned and prepared strategy of Heaven's Gate or something simply done by enthusiastic members—like an evangelist in any tradition, taking advantage of opportunities as they arise? At present we do not know. We briefly describe the presence of new religions on the Internet. Then we place our discussion in context by looking at the scholarly record about who joins new religious movements and how, to see how these data fit with the results of our survey of the creators of Web pages for the new religious movements and the survey of the users of the Net.

Heaven's Gate did have a relatively flashy Web site (for its time), making a lot of information available, although it was of variable quality. The site employed many colourful graphics, but in the main it consisted of programmatic statements of the group's beliefs, focused on the role played by aliens from space in the past, present and future life of humankind. Undergirding all was the warning that a great change was at hand: "The earth's present 'civilization' is about to be recycled—spaded under. Its inhabitants are refusing to evolve. The 'weeds' have taken over the garden and disturbed its usefulness beyond repair." In the days immediately preceding the mass suicide of the group, their Web page declared: "Red Alert. HALE-BOPP Brings Closure." It was time for the loyal followers of their leader Do to abandon their earthy "containers" in preparation for being carried off by a UFO, thought to be accompanying the comet Hale-Bopp, to a new home at "The Evolutionary Level Beyond Human" somewhere else in the galaxy. Few if any people, it now seems clear, were listening or chose to take their warnings seriously—an interesting indicator of the real limits on the vaunted power of the Web as a means of religious "broadcasting."

Apart from the imminent character of its apocalyptic vision, the Heaven's Gate Web site is fairly representative of the presence of new religious movements on the Internet. Most of the better known new religions (for example, Scientology, Krishna Consciousness, the Unification Church, Soka Gakkai, the Church Universal and Triumphant, Eckankar, Osho, and Sri Sai Baba) have had Web sites of some sophistication (in graphics, text and options) for several years (see Table 12.1 on page 184). The respondents to our survey said their sites were launched in 1995 or very early in 1996, when the World Wide Web was still more or less in its infancy. In addition, there are literally hundreds of other sites for more obscure religious or quasi-religious groups. Most of these sites are official in some sense, although some are privately run by devotees and others. Most of these sites simply replicate, in appearance and content, the kind of material available in other publications by these groups, and the Web materials are often meant to be downloaded as a ready substitute for more conventional publications. Most of these sites offer ways of establishing further contact to obtain more materials (for example, pamphlets, books, tapes and videos) and to access courses, lectures and other programs, either by e-mail, telephone numbers or mailing addresses. All of our respondents indicated that this was an important feature of their sites, most claiming that they respond to several messages every day, and one award-winning site claiming to receive "about 100 messages per day." Similar comments can be found in the conversations Zaleski had with other Web masters of religious sites. A few of the more elaborate sites (for example, Scientology, Eckankar) offer virtual tours of the interiors of some of their central facilities and temples. Many offer music and sound bites in real audio (for example, messages from their founders and other inspirational leaders). None of our respondents claimed that their Web sites had been professionally designed or altered. The individuals or groups had done the work themselves. Three of the respondents indicated, however, that they have since become engaged, to some extent, in the professional creation of Web pages for other groups within their own organization or tradition, as well as other clients altogether.

The primary use of the Web is clearly a way to advertise the groups and to deliver information about them cheaply. Most respondents stressed how ideal the medium was for the dissemination of their views (see also Zaleski, 1957:73, 75, 125). To this end, many of the new religions operate multiple pages with slightly different foci, all "hot-linked" to one another, to maximize the chances of a browser stumbling across one of the pages. Similarly, these pages are often launched with unusually long and diverse lists of "keyword" search terms, assuring that their address will appear when requests are made through search engines for all kinds of information that may be only tangentially related to the religious beliefs or mission of the group in question (see also Zaleski, 1997:105; see Table 12.3).[11] In these ways, the Web sites act as a new and relatively effective means of outreach to the larger community. They undoubtedly enhance the public profile of each of these religions and add to the revenues obtained by the sale of books, tapes and other paraphernalia. In fairness most of the literature available through the Web is offered free of charge to spread the word.[12]

THE INTERNET AND RECRUITMENT

The popular stereotypes of recruits to NRMs are that they are young, naive and duped, or that they are social losers and marginal types seeking a safe haven from the real world. In an inconsistent and opportunistic manner, some members of the anti-cult movement (e.g., Singer, 1995) have recently claimed that everyone is susceptible to being recruited. The comments of Erik Davis and Margaret Singer in the CNN story on cults and the Internet, and those of Zaleski in *The Soul of Cyberspace* manage to combine all three points of view. Heavy users of computers and hence often the World Wide Web are presumed to be "social nerds" and thus more vulnerable to the "loving" outreach of online cult recruiters. Is this the case? The evidence at hand shows that the situation is probably much more complex.

In the first place, the data acquired by sociologists over the past twenty or more years about who joins NRMs and how they join tends not to support the popular supposition (see the summaries and references provided in Dawson, 1996, 1998). It is true, as studies reveal, that "cult involvement seems to be strongly correlated with having fewer and weaker extra-cult social ties … [as well as] fewer and weaker ideological alignments." In the terms of reference of Rodney Stark and William Sims Bainbridge (1985), the "unchurched" are more likely to join (Dawson, 1996:149, or Dawson, 1998:70–71). If heavy users of the Net are indeed social isolates, then in at least one respect they may appear to be at greater risk of being persuaded to join an NRM.

But there are three other propositions about who joins NRMs and how, with significantly greater empirical substantiation, that offset this impression:

1. "[S]tudies of conversion and case studies of specific groups have found that recruitment to NRMs happens primarily through pre-existing social networks and interpersonal bonds. Friends recruit friends, family members each other, and neighbours recruit neighbours" (Dawson, 1996:147; Dawson, 1998:68);
2. "[I]n general, case studies of individuals who joined NRMs or of the groups themselves commonly reveal the crucial role of affective bonds with specific members in leading recruits into deeper involvements" (Dawson, 1996:148; Dawson, 1998:69–70);

TABLE 12.3: INVENTORY OF NEW RELIGIOUS MOVEMENTS ON THE INTERNET, DETAILED

Group	Site characteristics				Communications		
	Keywords	Design	Interactiveness	Special features	e-mail	Phone	Mail
A.R.E.	13	advanced	high	audio, links, books	X	X	X
Aumism	*93	average	med-high	petition	X	X	X
BOTA	*34	advanced	high (Java)	multi-language, regional, free brochure	X	X	X
Brahma Kumaris	7	advanced	med	books, regional links	X	X	X
Church Universal and Triumphant	*49	average	low	regional links, multi-language	X	X	X
Churches of Christ (Boston)	—	advanced	med	regional links, directory	X		X
Covenant of the Goddess	5	average	med-low	webring, regional links	X		
Eckankar	*20	advanced	med	free books		X	X
Foundation for Inner Peace (ACIM)	—	basic	low	catalogue, mailing list	X	X	X
International Society for Krishna Consciousness	49	advanced	high (Java)	audio, site host, search engine, international	X		X
Meher Baba Group	—	average	low	products, organization links	X		
Movement of Spiritual Inner Awareness	*19	advanced	med	multi-language	X		
Ordo Templi Orientis	—	basic	low	links to other Thelemic sites	X		
Osho	*14	advanced	high	audio talks, on-line shopping	X	X	X
Quest for Utopia (Koufuku no Kagaku)	—	average	high (Java)	audio, languages (Japanese)	X		
Raelians	—	advanced	low	multi-language, multi-geographical, counter	X		
Rosicrucian Order	—	basic	med-low	free booklet, counter	X	X	X
School of Wisdom	11	average	high (Java)	guestbook	X		
Scientology	*31	advanced	high (Java)	free info, film, search engine, multi-language	X		

TABLE 12.3: INVENTORY OF NEW RELIGIOUS MOVEMENTS ON THE INTERNET, DETAILED (*continued*)

| Group | Site characteristics | | | | Communications | | |
	Keywords	Design	Interactiveness	Special features	e-mail	Phone	Mail
Shambhala	*32	advanced	med	international server	X		
Sikh Dharma (3HO)	*39	advanced	high	chat room, search engine, international	X		X
Shirdi Sai Baba	—	advanced	high (Java)	multi-links	X	X	X
Soka Gakkai	—	advanced	med	international	X		
Subud	15	basic	med	international	X	X	X
Temple of Set	—	advanced	med	mailing list, language	X		
The Family	*26	advanced	med-high	audio, free info, music	X	X	
TM	*78	advanced	med-high	video, links, online books	X	X	
Unification Church		advanced	med-high	online bookstore, online newsletter, reading list	X	X	X
Urantia	4	advanced	med-high	international, online catalogue	X	X	X
Wiccan Church of Canada	—	average	low	regional links	X	X	X

*Keywords were not specific to organization.

Summary statistics.
47% used detailed keyword searches, with ten keywords or more; 30% high interactivity; 40% medium interactivity; 63% advanced Web sites; 97% provided e-mail addresses; 40% provided e-mail, telephone and mailing addresses.

3. "[E]qually strongly, from the same studies it is clear that the intensive interaction of recruits with the rest of the existing membership of the group is pivotal to the successful conversion and maintenance of new members" (Dawson, 1996:149; Dawson, 1998:70).

First and foremost, the process of converting to an NRM is a social process. If the denizens of cyberspace tend in fact to be socially isolated, then it is unlikely that they will be recruited through the Web or otherwise. What is more, there is little reason to think that the Internet, in itself, ever will be a very effective means of recruitment. As the televangelists learned some time ago (Hoover, 1988), the initial provision of information is unlikely to produce any specific commitments unless it is followed up by much more personal and complete forms of interaction, by phone and in person. Therefore, most of the successful televangelists run quite extensive "para-church" organizations to which they try to direct all their potential recruits. The religious Web masters, as Zaleski's interviews reveal (Zaleski, 1997:63, 73, 75, 125) do the same, pressing interested individuals to visit the nearest centre or temple. As the creator of one site, Christian Web, states:

> Internet ministries are never meant to be a replacement for the real church. It is impossible for anyone to develop a personal relationship with God without being around His people, His church. These Internet works are nothing more than something to draw in people who may otherwise not want to know anything about Jesus or not want to visit a church for fear of the unknown. For some reason, people find it less intimidating if they can sit at home in the privacy of their own room asking questions about the church and the Bible and God that they have always wanted to ask but never quite feel comfortable enough in the real church to do so. (Zaleski, 1997:125)

Approaching the same question from another angle, can we learn anything from a comparison of the social profiles that we have of Internet users and the members of NRMs (see Table 12.1 and Dawson, 1996:152–157 or 1998:74–79)? Both groups tend to be drawn disproportionately from the young adult population, to be educated better than the public, and they seem to be disproportionately from the middle to upper classes. In the case of the Internet users, the latter conclusion can only be inferred from their levels of education and occupations. But it is fair to say that the fit between this profile and the stereotypes of cult converts is ambiguous at best. By conventional social inferences, it would seem to be inappropriate to view these people as social losers or marginal. Nor clearly do they constitute "everybody." Are they more naive and prone to being duped or manipulated? That would be difficult to determine. But we do not have any reliable evidence to believe such is the case, certainly not for Internet users. On average, they are not as young as most converts to NRMs, are even better educated, and are overwhelmingly from professional occupations (or so they report). Given the extent of their probable involvement in computer technology, surfing the Web, and the real world of their professions, it is more plausible to speculate that they will be more skeptical, questioning and worldly-wise (in at least a cognitive sense) than other segments of the population.

But even if we were to somehow learn that this is not the case, there are other issues to be explored that raise doubts about the soundness of the popular fear of cult recruitment through the Net. The common complaint of educators, parents and spouses is that those drawn to the Web for hours on end are simply riding on the surface of things (surfing). They have substituted the vicarious life of the Web for real-life commitments. In this they call to mind certain individuals whom Eileen Barker (1984:194–198, 203; see also Dawson, 1998:108) noted in her comprehensive study of the Moonies. These are people who seem to fit the profile of potential recruits delineated by the anti-cult movement, yet in fact attend a few lectures with some enthusiasm, only to drop out in pursuit of some other novel interest on the horizon.

On the other hand, following the logic of the argument advanced by Stark and Bainbridge (1996:235–237) for the involvement of social elites in cults, we can speculate that there are special reasons why a certain percentage of heavy Internet users may be interested in cult activities and why NRMs may have a vested interest in recruiting these people. "In a cosmopolitan society which inflicts few if any punishments for experimentation with novel religious alternatives," Stark and Bainbridge propose, "cults may recruit with special success among the relatively advantaged members of society" (Stark and Bainbridge, 1996:235). Even within elites, they point out, there is an inequality in the division of rewards and room for individuals to be preoccupied with certain relative deprivations (Glock, 1964) not adequately compensated for by the power of the elite (for example, concerns about beauty, health, love, and coping with mortality). In fact, the very material security of this group may well encourage their preoccupation with these other less fundamental concerns. People moved by these relative deprivations are unlikely to be drawn to religious sects to alleviate their needs, because the sects are much more likely to be opposed in principle to "the exact rewards the elite possesses as a class" (Stark and Bainbridge, 1996:236). Alternatively, Stark and Bainbridge stipulate:

> ... [A]n innovative cult ... can offer a set of compensators outside the political antagonisms which divide the elite from other citizens, and focus instead on providing compensators for particular sets of citizens with a shared set of desires that wish to add something to the power of the elite while preserving it. (Stark and Bainbridge, 1996:236)

In addition, "in a cosmopolitan society ... in which the elite accepts and supports cultural pluralism and thus encourages cultural novelty," certain religious innovations may hold a special appeal because they are emblematic of "progress." Cults are often associated with the transmission of "new culture" and as such may have a certain appeal in terms of the cultural capital of the elite. More mundanely, of course, there is also the fact that the elite are the ones "with both the surplus resources to experiment with new explanations and, through such institutions as higher education, the power to obtain potentially valuable new explanations before others do" (Stark and Bainbridge, 1996:236–237).

From the perspective of the NRMs, members of an elite are particularly attractive candidates for recruitment, not just because of the resources they can donate to the cause, but because they are more likely to be involved in the kind of wide-ranging social networks essential for the dissemination of a new cultural phenomenon. "Since networks are composed of interlocking exchange relationships," Stark and Bainbridge reason, "a network will be more extensive, including more kinds of exchanges for more valued rewards, if its members possess the power to obtain the rewards" (Stark and Bainbridge, 1996:236). Recruitment from the elites of society can be instrumental in the success of a new religion.

Whether any of this is relevant in this context is a matter for empirical investigation. The survey of Internet users does suggest, however, that the Web provides a convenient point of access to a seemingly elite segment of our society. Access to computing technology and to the Internet, as well as sufficient time and knowledge to use these resources properly is still largely a luxury afforded the better-off segments of our society.

The conclusions we can draw about the threat posed by "cults" on the Internet are limited, yet important. First, while the Internet does make it cheaper for NRMs to disseminate their beliefs over a larger area and to a potentially much larger audience, it is unlikely that it has intrinsically changed the capacity of NRMs to recruit new members. In the first place, Web pages, at present at least, differ little in content or function from more traditional forms of religious publication and broadcasting. Second, we have no real evidence that Internet users are any more prone to convert to a new religion than other young and well-educated people in our society. All the same, there are other reasons for wondering if the World Wide Web is changing the environment in which NRMs operate in fundamental and perhaps even dangerous ways.

THE PERILS AND PROMISE OF THE NEW PUBLIC SPACE

We are starting to be inundated with discussions of the wonders and significance of cyberspace. Much of the dialogue is marked by hyperbole and utopian rhetoric that leaves scholars cold. A few key insights, however, warrant further investigation. Most fundamentally, it is important to realize that it may be best to think of the Internet as a new environment or context in which things happen, rather than just as another new tool or service. As David Holmes (1997) observes (citing Mark Poster, 1997):

> The virtual technologies and agencies ... cannot be viewed as instruments in the service of pre-given bodies and communities, rather they are themselves contexts which bring about new corporealities and new politics corresponding to space-worlds and time-worlds that have never before existed in human history. (Holmes, 1997:3)

When religion, like anything else, enters these new worlds, there are both anticipated and unanticipated consequences. The new religious "Web meisters" we questioned seemed to approach the Internet simply as a tool and showed little or no appreciation of the potential downside of their efforts. But in thinking about these matters, two disparate sociological observations by Anthony Giddens and James Beckford came to mind and we began to wonder about a connection.

With the advent of the technologies of modernity, Giddens argues (1990), time has become separated from space and space from place, giving rise to ever more "disembedded social systems." Social relations have been lifted out of local contexts of interaction and restructured across "indefinite spans of time-space" (Giddens, 1990:21). Writing, money, time-clocks, cars, freeways, television, computers, ATMs, walkmans, electronic treadmills for running, shopping malls, theme parks and so on, have all contributed to the transformation of the human habitat, incrementally creating "successive levels of 'new nature'" for humanity (Holmes, 1997:6). As sociologists since Marx (1846) have realized, new technologies bring about new forms of social interaction and integration that can change the taken-for-granted conditions of social life. This is especially true of communications technologies. Relative to our ancestors, we have become like gods in our powers of production, reconstruction and expression.

Yet the price may have been high. Even these pre-virtual technologies have changed our environments in ways that detrimentally standardize, routinize and instrumentalize our relations with our own bodies and with other people. As we have refashioned our world, we have in turn been remade in the image of techno-science (see e.g., McLuhan, 1964; Ellul, 1964; Marcuse, 1966; Baudrillard, 1970; Foucault, 1979; Postman, 1985). Does the advent of the Internet typify, or even magnify, these and other undesirable social trends? Some keen observers of the sociological implications of the Internet, like Holmes (1997), seem to think it does. If so, what unanticipated consequences might stem from the attempt of religions to take advantage of the disembedded freedom of cyberspace? A clue is provided in an observation by Beckford.

Beckford has intriguingly proposed that it might be better to conceptualize religion in the contemporary Western world as "a cultural resource … than as a social institution" (Beckford, 1992:23; see also Beckford, 1989:171). The social structural transformations wrought by the emergence of advanced industrial societies have undermined the communal, familial and organizational bases of religion. As a consequence, while "religious and spiritual forms of sentiment, belief and action have survived as relatively autonomous resources … retain[ing] the capacity to symbolize … ultimate meaning, infinite power, supreme indignation and sublime compassion," they have "come adrift from [their] former points of social anchorage." Now "they can be deployed in the service of virtually any interest-group or ideal: not just organizations with specifically religious objectives" (Beckford, 1992:22–23). Is this an apt description for what the Internet may be doing to religion? Like any "environment," the Web acts back upon its content, modifying the form of its users or inhabitants. Is the "disembedded" social reality of life in cyberspace contributing to the transformation of religion into a "cultural resource" in a postmodern society? If it is, what would be the consequences for the future form and function of religion? Perhaps developments in religion on the Web will provide some initial indications. After examining the pitfalls of life on the Web, we will briefly comment on one such development: the creation of truly "churchless religions."

With these conjectures in mind, we briefly itemize and counterpoise some of the noted benefits and liabilities of life on the Internet.[13] On the positive side, much has been made of the Net as an electronic meeting place, a new public space for fashioning new kinds of communities (Shields, 1996; Holmes, 1997; Zaleski, 1997). The defining features of these new communities are the various freedoms allowed by the technology. The Internet allows freedom from "the constraints of the flesh" (Holmes, 1997:7), from the limitations of interaction within Cartesian space and the natural cycles of time. It allows a greater measure of freedom from traditional forms of social control, both formal and informal. It allows for the "breakdown of hierarchies of race, class, and gender." It allows for "the construction of oppositional subjectivities hitherto excluded from the public sphere" (Holmes, 1997:13). It allows people, seemingly, to "bypass or displace institutional politics" (Holmes, 1997:19). The bottom line, we are told by the hard-core denizens and promoters of the net, is that the Internet constitutes a new and freer community of speech, transcending conventional institutional life.

All of these presumed freedoms, each as yet a worthy subject of empirical investigation (see, e.g., Shields, 1996; Holmes, 1997), rest upon the anonymity and fluidity of identity permitted and sometimes even mandated by life on the Internet. The technology of the Net allows, and the emergent culture of the Net fosters, the creative enactment of pluralism at the individual or psychological level as well as the social, cultural and collective level. This unique foundation of freedom, however, comes at a price that may vitiate the creation of any real communities, of faith or otherwise.

As noted, there is a marked tendency for life on the Net to be fashioned in the image of the current techno-science, with its new possibilities and clear limitations. This environmental influence on social relations is likely to spill out of the confines of the computer into the stream of everyday life—much like the virtual realities of television that influence the social ontologies of North America, Britain, Japan and much of Europe. Part of this new standardization, routinization and instrumentalization of life is the further commodification of human needs and relations. The pitch for the creation of new virtual communities bears the hallmarks of the emergence of "community" as a new commodity of advanced capitalism—a product which is marketed in ways that induce the felt need for a convenient substitute for an increasingly problematic reality.

But do "communities" shaped by the Internet represent real communities any more than do shopping malls? Are the possibilities of interaction and exchange sufficient in kind, number and quality to replicate and possibly even to replace the social relationships born of more immediate and spatially and temporally uniform kinds of communal involvement? There is good reason to be skeptical, for as Holmes notes:

> ... [T]echnologies of extension [like the Internet or freeways] ... characteristically attenuate presence by enabling only disembodied and abstract connections between persons, where the number of means of recognizing another person declines. In the "use" of these technologies ... the autonomy of the individual is enhanced at the point of use, but the socially "programmed" nature of the technology actually prohibits forming mutual relations of reciprocity outside the operating design of the technological environment. (Holmes, 1997:6–7)

Sharpening the critique, Holmes further cites the views of Michele Willson (1997:146):

> ... [T]he presence of the Other in simulated worlds is more and more being emptied out to produce a purely intellectual engagement, and possibilities of commitment to co-operative or collective projects become one-dimensional, or, at best, self-referential. "Community is then produced as an ideal, rather than as a reality, or else it is abandoned altogether." (Holmes, 1997:16)

In like manner, Willson points out (1997), the Internet seemingly allows us to celebrate and extend social pluralism. But appearances can be deceiving. In the first place, the largely ungrounded and potentially infinite multiplicity of the Net is often little more than "a play of masks," which serves more to desensitize us to the real and consequential differences between us. Secondly, the medium simultaneously and paradoxically tends to "compartmentalize populations" and physically isolate individuals, while also "homogenizing" them (Holmes, 1997:16–17). As in the rest of our consumer culture, the market of the Internet tends to favour standardization with marginal differentiation. Consequently, with Holmes we find that dialogues on the Net tend to be "quite transient and directionless, seldom acquiring a substantive enough history to constitute a political [or religious] movement" (Holmes, 1997:18).

To the extent that any of this is true, and speculation far outstrips sound empirical research at this point, it is clear that the side effects of involvement in the Net could be quite deleterious for religions, new and old. The lauded freedom of the Net merely compounds the difficulties, since the producers of content have little control over the dissemination and use of their material once launched. Things may be repeated out of context and applied to all manner of ends at odds with the intentions of the original producers. The Internet, as Zaleski says,

> is organized laterally rather than vertically or radially, with no central authority and no chain of command. (Individual webmasters have power over Web sites, as do ... system operators ... over bulletin board systems, and moderators over Usenet groups, but their influence is local and usually extremely responsive to the populations they serve.) (Zaleski, 1997:111)

There is little real regulation of the Internet and, to date, only a few organizations have been able to enforce some of their intellectual property rights (most notably, some software producers and the Church of Scientology—see Frankel, 1996; Grossman, 1998). The sheer speed and scope of the Internet and the complexity of possible connections can frustrate any attempts to control the flow of information. As several of the webmasters we surveyed stated, any attempt to regulate the Net would likely violate the freedom of speech and religion guaranteed by the United States constitution and in the process render the Net itself ineffective.

However, this state of affairs can have a number of other unanticipated consequences for religions venturing onto the Internet that our webmasters did not seem to realize:

> Because the medium influences the message, it's possible that in the long run the Internet will favour those religions and spiritual teachings that tend toward anarchy and that lack a complex hierarchy. Even now, those who log on to cyberspace may tend to gravitate to religious denominations that emphasize centrifugal rather than centripetal force, just as the medium that is carrying them does. Authority loses its trappings and force on the Net.... (Zaleski, 1997:111–112)

This reality of the world of the Internet might well pose serious problems for religions that have historically stressed the role of a strong central authority, such as the Roman Catholic Church or Scientology.

> As public information sources multiply through the Internet, it's likely that the number of sites claiming to belong to any particular religion but in fact disseminating

information that the central authority of that religion deems heretical also will multiply. (Zaleski, 1997:108)

When everyone can potentially circumvent the filters of an ecclesial bureaucracy and communicate directly and en masse with the leadership in Rome, Los Angeles or wherever, there will be a shift in power towards the grassroots (Zaleski, 1997:112). The Internet could have a democratizing effect on all religions and work against those religions that resist this consequence.

The elaborate theorizing of Stark and Bainbridge (1996) and their colleagues (e.g., Innaccone, 1995) suggests, however, another somewhat contrary unanticipated consequence of the emergence of the World Wide Web for new religions. As Stark points out in his discussion of the rise of Christianity (1996), the way had been cleared for the phenomenal triumph of Christianity in the Greco-Roman world by the *"excessive pluralism"* (Stark, 1996:197) of paganism. The massive influx of new cults into the Roman Empire in the first century created "what E.R. Dodds called 'a bewildering mass of alternatives. There were too many cults, too many mysteries, too many philosophies of life to choose from.'" (Stark, 1996:197) This abundance of choice had at least two consequences with parallel implications for the fate of new religions on the Internet.

In the first place, it assured that only a truly different religion, one that was favoured by other circumstances largely beyond its control, was likely to emerge from the crowd. For excessive pluralism, as Stark argues, "inhibits the ability of new religious firms to gain a market share" (Stark, 1996:195), since the pool of potential converts is simply spread too thin. The competition for this pool, moreover, is likely to drive the competing new religions into ever newer and more radical innovations to secure a market edge.

Second, as Stark and Bainbridge argue elsewhere (Stark and Bainbridge, 1985, 1996; see also Stark, 1996: Chapter 8), if many of the religious choices people have are "nonexclusive," as was the case in the Roman Empire and seems to be the case on the Internet—there is no way of demanding or assuring that people hold to only one religion at a time—then, given the inherent risks of religious commitment (that is, choosing the wrong salvific investment), people "will seek to diversify" (Stark, 1996:204). The most rational strategy in the face of such structurally induced uncertainty will be to maintain a limited involvement in many competitive religions simultaneously—quite possibly to the long-term detriment of all. Stark, Bainbridge and Innaccone suggest that true religious "movements" are much more likely to emerge from new religions that demand an exclusive commitment. As a medium, however, the Internet carries a reverse bias.[14]

This bias is reflected most clearly in some new religions to which the Internet itself has given birth—communities of belief that exist only, or at least primarily, on the Net. The ones people are most likely to know are intentional jokes, blatant parodies like the Church of the Mighty Gerbil (www.gerbilism.snpedro.com) or the First Presbyterian Church of Elvis the Divine (http://chelsea.ios.com/~hkarlinl/welcome.html). But there are other more problematic instances as well, one which we have begun to study: Thee Church Ov MOO (http://members.xoom.com/gecko23/moo). This new religion was invented, almost by accident, by a group of gifted students interacting on an Internet bulletin board in Ottawa, Canada, sometime in the early 1990s. Today many of these same people operate a sophisticated Web site with over 800 pages of fabricated religious documents covering a sweeping range of religious and pseudo-religious subjects. A visit to the Web site reveals an elaborate development of alternative sets of scriptures, commandments, chronicles, mythologies, rituals and ceremonies. Much of this material reads like a bizarre religious extension of *The Hitchhiker's Guide to the Galaxy*. It is irreverent and playful, alternately verging on the sophomoric and the sophisticated. Many of the texts of the Church ov MOO seem to have been devised with a keen awareness of religious history, comparative beliefs and practices, and some real knowledge of the philosophy, anthropology and sociology of religion. The site records a great many hits every day, we are told, and about 10,000 people have applied for membership.

Several of the key figures are currently pursuing training or careers in physics, mathematics, computer science and the other so-called hard sciences. With MOOism they are attempting to devise a self-consciously postmodern, socially constructed, relativist, and self-referential system of religious ideas, purposefully and paradoxically infused with humour, irony and farce, as well as a serious appreciation of the essentially religious or spiritual condition of humanity. In a typically postmodernist manner, the conventions we normally draw between academic reflection and religious thought are flaunted. An unsolicited essay we received from one of the church leaders on "MOOism, Social Constructionism, and thee Origins ov Religious Movements" begins characteristically, with the following note:

> Thee language ov this essay conforms to TOPY standards ov language discipline. Thee purpose ov this is twofold: first, to prevent thee reader from forgetting that E am not attempting to separate this sociological comment from religious text; second, to prevent thee writer from forgetting thee same thing. These ideas should be taken neither too lightly nor too seriously.

Similarly, the MOO home page declares:

> Among other things, MOOism has been called the Negativland of religion. Not only does it irreverently (and sometimes irrelevantly) sample innumerable other religious traditions, it uses recontextualization and paradoxical framing techniques to prevent minds from settling into orthodoxy. Paradox and radical self-contradiction are, in the postmodern context, the most reasonable way to approach the Absolute.

MOOism is certainly about having "fun" with religion. But the objective does seem to be to encourage and facilitate the rise of a new conceptual framework and language for religious experience suited to the changed environmental conditions of postmodern society. The "religion" seems to be influenced significantly by neopaganism and is representative of what is coming to be called Technopaganism. (But it is also influenced by such earlier and quite sophisticated joke religions as Discordianism and The Church of the SubGenius.) In line with many aspects of that movement it is seeking to provide an intellectual and social forum for fostering the kind of human imagination and creativity that empowers people to override the public demise of spiritual life or "realities" in our time (see Luhrmann, 1989). But unlike many other forms of neopaganism, this "religion" is well suited, in form and function, to life on the Net, perhaps because it is in many respects the witting and unwitting mirror reflection of the sensibilities of the Internet culture in which it developed. But, in truth, we do not know as yet whether MOOism is a "religious" movement or just a most elaborate hoax. The church solicited our attention and its Web page currently carries the disclaimer: "This page is in the progress of being altered to mislead *Lorne Dawson. It may therefore seem disjointed and confused.*" If it is all a joke, then one must marvel at the time and energy invested in its creation and perpetuation. In conversations, however, we have been led to believe that the originators of MOOism are beginning to have an ambiguous understanding of their creation and are seeking some assistance in thinking through the significance of MOOism as a social phenomenon. One thing is clear, without the Internet, this phenomenon is unlikely to have developed or exercised the influence it undoubtedly has on some people. But is it reflective of the future of religion in some regard? Joke or not, it may be similar to other current or future religious phenomena on the Net that are of a more serious intent. The Church ov MOO does appear to embody elements of both Beckford's conception of religion as a "cultural resource" and Stark and Bainbridge's speculations about the special appeal of cult innovations to *elites*.[15]

At present, most of the virtual communities of the Net are much less intriguing and problematic. Most new religions seem content to use the Net in quite limited and conventional ways. But the webmasters we surveyed are uniformly intent on constantly improving their Web pages using visual, auditory and interactive technology. So we must be careful not to underestimate what the future may hold. There is merit, we think, in the metaphorical conclusion of Zaleski:

> Virtual and physical reality exert a gravitational pull on one another. At present, virtuality is the moon to the real world, bound by its greater mass, but just as the moon influences tides, spiritual work in the virtual communities is influencing and will continue to influence that work in real-world communities. (Zaleski, 1997:254)

The new religious uses of the Internet are likely to exercise an increasingly determinant, if subtle, effect on the development of all religious life in the future (Lövheim and Linderman, 1998).

NOTES

[1] This paper was first presented to a special seminar on "New and Marginal Religions in the Public Space," held in Montreal on 25 July 1998, organized by Pauline Côté.

[2] The term *cults* is so strongly associated with negative images in the popular mind that academics have long preferred to use such terms as *new religions* or *new religious movements* (NRMs) (see, e.g., Richardson, 1993). The word will be used, nonetheless, at various points in this essay to call to mind the fears giving rise to this discussion in the first place.

[3] "Web of Death" was the double entendre used as the headline of a *Newsweek* cover story on the Heaven's Gate suicide.

4 In 1997, Statistics Canada reported that of all the homes in Canada with some type of facility to access the Internet, only 13 percent have made use of the opportunity. Reginald Bibby (1995) reported that 31 percent of Canadians had some contact with the Internet, ranging from daily to hardly ever. The rate of growth of the Net, however, is exponential and quite phenomenal. It is estimated that the World Wide Web is growing at a rate of close to 10 percent per month. Zaleski (1997:136) notes, for example: "In 1993, the year the Web browser Mosaic was released, the Web proliferated at a 341,634% annual growth rate of service traffic."

5 This finding, from a more general survey by the Barna Research Group in February 1997, is reported in *Maclean's* magazine (25 May 1998:12).

6 Five groups (potentially another 16.6 percent) informed us that our request had been passed along to higher authorities, but at the time this paper was submitted, a later reminder notice had merely earned us a reiteration of this reply. Another five groups or individuals declined to participate in our survey for a variety of reasons: several complained that they are simply not religions; one pointed out that they do not wish to be associated with the subject of cults in any way; and two said that they receive too many surveys and now refuse to respond to them. Some thirteen groups, or 43.3 percent of the sample, simply did not respond. (None of the messages were returned as undeliverable).

7 The questionnaire and accompanying information letter of our survey were reviewed by two other experienced survey researchers, as well as by the ethics review board for research with human subjects of our university. Nonetheless, some mistakes may have been made with regard to the sensitivity of these groups to outside investigations of any sort. Undoubtedly many new religions are wary about co-operating with any requests for information about their operations. Others are simply ignorant of the real nature of sociological research and mistrustful of the unknown in their own right. Further, it has been our experience that some of these groups are by no means as organized and professional in their activities as many exponents of the anti-cult movement would have us believe. It is likely that some of our surveys were simply overlooked or "trashed." Contrary to our expectations, in each regard, the immediacy and the anonymity of the Internet may actually have worked against us. Our colleague, Dr. John Goyder of the University of Waterloo Survey Research Institute, told us of two other e-mail surveys in which he participated that resulted in similarly disappointing rates of return (about 33 percent). These were, however, surveys of university faculty, which were dealing with relatively noncontroversial subjects. In one instance, when the first survey was followed by a mailed questionnaire to all non-respondents, the overall rate of return doubled. It is possible that the Internet is already a saturated medium and not well suited for survey research. However, research into these matters has just begun (see, e.g., Bedell, 1998).

8 Respondents to the survey were offered anonymity and most of the seven groups and individuals who did respond requested that they not be identified or quoted directly without permission. The groups will therefore not be named in this paper.

9 We wish to thank Jeff Miller for calling our attention to this data in his Senior Honours Essay (Sociology, University of Waterloo, 1998) on "Internet Subcultures."

10 As Zaleski reports (1997:249) and we recall from the news: "At least one of the suicides, 39-year-old Yvonne McCurdy-Hill of Cincinnati, a post-office employee and mother of five, initially encountered the cult in cyberspace and decided to join in response to its online message."

11 For example, the Web page for Osho actually employs a set of "keywords" for each page of its very large site and many of these search terms are very general: *meditation, Christianity, brainwashing, deprogramming, relaxation, self-esteem, sadness, depression, tensions* and so on.

12 Of course, the Web has offered new opportunities to the opponents of new religions as well. Entering the term *cults* in any search engine will produce a surfeit of sites dedicated to so-called watchdog organizations or the home pages of disgruntled ex-members (e.g., American Religion Information Center, www.fopc.org/ARIC_home.html; Watcher, www.marsweb.com/~watcher/cult.html; Operation Clambake—The Fight Against Scientology on the Net, www.xenu.net).

13 These reflections are strongly influenced by the ideas discussed by David Holmes in the introduction to his book on identity and community in cyberspace, *Virtual Politics* (1997).

¹⁴ Zaleski points out that the Web sites of the Holy See (www.vatican.va) and the Church of Jesus Christ of Latter Day Saints (www.lds.org) both characteristically commit what in cyberspace are two "cardinal sins." The sites offer no links to other sites, giving lie to the notion of Internet and World Wide Web, and they seek to misuse the Net as a broadcast medium since no e-mail or other facility is provided for interactivity.

¹⁵ This is not the only Net-created religion of which we are aware. A student is currently doing research on the Otherkin—a "religious movement" which, at least in some of its forms, largely exists only on the Net. The Otherkin believe they are reincarnated elves, dwarfs and other mythical and mystical creatures.

REFERENCES

Bainbridge, W. 1997. *The Sociology of Religious Movements.* New York: Routledge.

Barker, F. 1984. *The Making of a Moonie: Choice or Brainwashing.* Oxford: Basil Blackwell.

Baudrillard, J. 1998. *La société de consommation.* Paris: Editions Denoel, 1970. Translated and republished as *The Consumer Society.* London: Sage.

Beckford, J. 1989. *Religion in Advanced Industrial Society.* London: Unwin Hyman.

———. 1992. "Religion, Modernity and Postmodernity." In *Religion: Contemporary Issues,* ed. B. Wilson, 11–23. London: Bellew.

Bedell, K. 1998. "Religion and the Internet: Reflections on Research Strategies." Paper presented to the Society for the Scientific Study of Religion, Montreal.

Bibby, R.W. 1995. *The Bibby Report: Social Trends Canadian Style.* Toronto: Stoddart.

Bromley, D.G., and E. Breschel. 1992. "General Population and Institutional Elite Support for Social Control of New Religious Movements: Evidence from National Survey Data." *Behavioral Sciences and the Law* 10:39–52.

Cottee, T., N. Yateman, and L. Dawson. 1996. "NRMs, The ACM, and the WWW: A Guide for Beginners." In *Cults in Context: Readings in the Study of New Religious Movements,* ed. L. Dawson. Toronto: Canadian Scholars' Press (published in the United States by Transaction Pub.).

Dawson, L.L. 1996. "Who Joins New Religious Movements and Why: Twenty Years of Research and What Have We Learned?" *Studies in Religion* 25(2):193–213.

———. 1998. *Comprehending Cults: The Sociology of New Religious Movements.* Toronto and New York: Oxford University Press.

Ellul, J. 1964. *The Technological Society.* New York: Alfred A. Knopf.

Foucault, M. 1979. *Discipline and Punish.* New York: Vintage Books.

Frankel, A. 1990. "Making Law, Making Enemies." *American Lawyer* 3, March; http://www2.thecia.net/users/rnewman/scientology/media/amlawyer-3.36.html.

Giddens, A. 1990. *The Consequences of Modernity.* Cambridge: Polity.

Glock, C.Y. 1964. "The Role of Deprivation in the Origin and Evolution of Religious Groups." In *Religion and Social Conflict,* eds. R. Lee and M. Marty. New York: Oxford University Press.

Grossman, W.M. 1998. "alt.scientology.war." *Wired.*: www.wired.com/wired/3.12/features/alt.scientology.war.html.

Holmes, D. 1997. *Virtual Politics: Identity and Community in Cyberspace.* London: Sage.

Hoover, S. 1988. *Mass Media Religion.* Thousand Oaks, CA: Sage.

Innaccone, L.R. 1995. "Risk, Rationality, and Religious Portfolios." *Economic Inquiry* 33:285–295.

Lofland, J. 1966. *Doomsday Cult*. Englewood Cliffs, NJ: Prentice-Hall.

Lövheim, M., and A. Linderman. 1998. "Internet—A Site for Religious Identity Formation and Religious Communities?" Paper presented to the Society for the Scientific Study of Religion, Montreal.

Luhrmann, T.M. 1989. *Persuasions of the Witch's Craft: Ritual Magic in Contemporary England*. Cambridge, MA: Harvard University Press.

Marcuse, H. 1966. *One Dimensional Man*. Boston: Beacon Press.

Marx, K., and F. Engels. 1970 (originally published 1846). *The German Ideology*. New York: International Pub.

McLuhan, M. 1964. *Understanding Media*. New York: McGraw-Hill.

Miller, J. 1998. "Internet Subcultures." Senior Honours Essay, Department of Sociology, University of Waterloo, Ontario, Canada, April.

Pfeifer, J.E. 1992. "The Psychological Framing of Cults: Schematic Representations and Cult Evaluations." *Journal of Applied Social Psychology* 22(7):531–544.

Poster, M. 1997. "Cyberdemocracy: The Internet and the Public Sphere." In *Virtual Politics*, ed. D. Holmes, 212–228. London: Sage.

Postman, N. 1985. *Amusing Ourselves to Death*. New York: Penguin Books.

Richardson, J. 1993. "Definitions of Cult: From Sociological-Technical to Popular-Negative." *Review of Religious Research* 34 (4):348–356.

Rochford, E.B., Jr. 1982. "Recruitment Strategies, Ideology and Organization in the Hare Krishna Movement." *Social Problems* 29:399–410.

Shields, R., ed. 1996. *Cultures of the Internet: Virtual Spaces, Real Histories, Living Bodies*. London: Sage.

Shupe, A.D. 1979. "'Disembodied Access' and Technological Constraints on Organizational Development: A Study of Mail-Order Religions." *Journal for the Scientific Study of Religions* 15:177–185.

Singer, M.T. 1995. *Cults in Our Midst: The Hidden Menace in Our Everyday Lives*. San Francisco: Jossey-Bass.

Snow, D.A., L.A. Zurcher Jr. and S. Ekland-Olson. 1985. "Social Networks and Social Movements: A Microstructural Approach to Differential Recruitment." *American Sociological Review* 45(5):787–801.

Stark, R. 1996. *The Rise of Christianity: A Sociologist Reconsiders History*. Princeton, NJ: Princeton University Press.

———, and W.S. Bainbridge. 1985. *The Future of Religion: Secularization, Revival and Cult Formation*. Berkeley, CA: University of California Press.

———. 1996 (originally published 1987, by Peter Lang). *A Theory of Religion*. New Brunswick, NJ: Rutgers University Press.

Willson, M. 1997. "Community in the Abstract: A Political and Ethical Dilemma?" In *Virtual Politics*, ed. D. Holmes, 145–162. London: Sage.

Zaleski, J. 1997. *The Soul of Cyberspace: How New Technology Is Changing Our Spiritual Lives*. New York: HarperCollins.

CHAPTER 13

MORE THAN CLOTHING:
VEILING AS AN ADAPTIVE STRATEGY

Homa Hoodfar

INTRODUCTION: THE SOCIAL AND POLITICAL DIMENSIONS OF CLOTHING

While clothing fulfills a basic human need in most climates, what we wear also has significant social and political functions, serving as a non-verbal medium of ideological communication. However, until the recent surge of interest in popular culture (Barnes and Eicher, 1992; Hendrickson, 1996; Parkington, 1992), few social scientists paid serious attention to this important aspect of clothing. But despite such scholarly neglect, the public, as well as those in power, have always recognized the significance of clothing as a vehicle of communication. Since most people easily and readily understand its non-verbal message, clothing has historically been a potent political tool for both rulers and ruled. A review of the somewhat scanty literature on the history of dress codes, particularly in Europe and the Middle East since the fourteenth century, makes this quite clear (Brewer and Porter, 1993; Herald, 1981; Perrot, 1994; Sponsler, 1992; Webb, 1912).[1]

Clothing is probably the most silent of expressions used by human societies to demarcate social boundaries and to distinguish "self" from "other" at both the collective and individual levels (Barnes and Eicher, 1992; Hendrickson, 1996; Rugh, 1986). Clothing indicates that the wearer shares certain cultural values with others similarly attired, while minor details may distinguish an individual from others in his or her social group. Thus clothing is a means of visually creating community, while simultaneously delineating individual features of the wearer such as gender, geographical origin, religion, ethnicity, profession, class orientation and life cycle (Abu-Lughod, 1986; Rugh, 1986). Indicating social hierarchy, unity and collectivity, as well as individuality, clothing's multi-layered ability to communicate helps people at first glance to place those they meet within a context, be it class, religion, profession or even political rank, thus shaping subsequent communication.[2] It is this aspect of clothing as identity marker that has made it such a potent political tool for rulers since at least early Pharaonic times in Egypt (Brewer and Porter, 1993; Payne, 1965).

While a variety of dress codes emerged in Europe from the sixteenth to nineteenth centuries, both through state policy and in reaction to them in the form of popular resistance to such policy, it is perhaps the Ottoman Empire (1299–1922)—with its diverse religious and ethnic groups, and Islamic heritage—that provides the most compelling example of the social functions of clothing (Fandy, 1998; Quataert, 1997; Shahshahani, 1995). The turban in the Ottoman Empire (and in many parts of the Middle East) distinguished social groups in various ways. For instance, certain colours were reserved for members of the court and certain ones for urban Muslims, while others distinguished Armenians from Greeks, just as the particulars of a turban also indicated civilian versus military status; this highly regulated social marker served to reinforce visibly the ranking of society (Quataert, 1997:406). Later, with the weakening of the Empire and increasing breakaway tendencies—particularly among the less privileged ethnic groups—the Ottoman rulers began advocating a unified style of clothing and headgear in order to minimize social divisions and create an illusion of oneness, hoping thus to reinforce loyalty to a unified state (Berkes, 1964). Similarly Ataturk, despite considerable popular resistance, decreed European-style hats and clothing for all citizens in the name of Turkish nationalism and modernity, a project later emulated by other countries, notably Iran and Afghanistan (Baker, 1997; Fandy, 1998).

While early dress codes were mostly concerned with male attire, the most controversial aspects of modern dress codes in Turkey and the Middle East have been those pertaining to women, and the debates over women's attire are particularly pertinent to the central focus of this chapter, that is, the practice of veiling by Muslim women in North America and Europe. In this chapter, based on data collected during the period 1993 to 1996, I examine the social forces that encourage women outside Muslim societies to veil, and consider the implications of the "veiling movement" for Muslim communities, for the larger societies in which they are located and for gender relations among Muslims living in Canada and, by implication, in North America and Europe. By placing the debate over veiling into this broader context, I hope to avoid replicating methodological and epistemological problems present in many studies on veiling, which focus narrowly on the veil as a religious artifact but avoid analyzing it in its broader historical and social contexts. For this reason, I briefly review here the origins of the veil, and its emergence as an indisputable symbol of "Muslimness," before attempting to explore the meaning of the veil within the Canadian context.

THE VEIL AND COLONIAL DISCOURSE

In contrast to men's clothing, which was historically subject to legal rules in the Middle East, women's clothing was largely a concern of public mores. Historically, until the twentieth century there seems to have been little resistance to changes in women's dress or the adoption by women of diverse styles. One significant reason for this lack of concern with women's clothing may stem from the fact that, by the nineteenth century, women were largely excluded from formal political and public life. As well, even as women's clothing styles expanded, veiling became more encompassing. For instance, around the middle of the same century a thick black veil had come to replace the *yashmak*, the thin and filmy white veil worn by Turkish women. Similarly in Iran, the black *chador*, a long cloak that covers women from head to ankle, was becoming more widespread in most urban centres. The black veil/*chador* communicated to the public, particularly to men, that women's clothing was a private matter, not a public concern.[3]

With the expansion of European power and influence in Ottoman/Middle Eastern economies and politics, a huge body of "scholarly" and travel accounts of the people of the region emerged.[4] Considerable attention was paid by (mostly male) European writers to veiling practices (and, to a lesser degree, polygyny), and the alleged objectionable treatment of Muslim women by their male kin (Kabbani, 1986; Mabro, 1991). Implicitly or explicitly, the mission of these writings was to depict Muslim cultures as inferior or backward and in need of progress (Alloula, 1986). It is important to note that modesty—particularly expressed through clothing and through varying degrees of gender segregation—has historically been practised by a wide variety of communities, including most Mediterranean peoples, regardless of religion. Indeed, prior to the nineteenth century, the veil was never viewed as a symbol of Muslim culture; the practice of the veiling and seclusion of women is in fact pre-Islamic and originates in non-Arab Middle Eastern and Mediterranean societies (Keddie and Beck, 1978). The first reference to veiling dates to an Assyrian legal text of the thirteenth century BC, which restricted the practice to "respectable" women and forbade prostitutes from veiling (Keddie and Baron, 1991:3). Historically, veiling—especially when accompanied by seclusion—was a sign of status and was practised by the elite in the ancient Greco-Roman, pre-Islamic Iranian and Byzantine empires. Muslims subsequently adopted the veil and seclusion, and today it is widely recognized, by Muslims and non-Muslims, as an Islamic phenomenon, presumably sanctioned by the Qur'an.

However, despite belief to the contrary, veiling—particularly in the sense of covering one's hair—is nowhere specifically recommended or even discussed in the Qur'an (Hajjaji-Jarrah, in this volume; Hassan, 1994; Mernissi, 1991a). At the heart of the Qur'anic position on the question of the veil is the interpretation of two verses (*Su—rat al-Nu—r*, verses 30.31), which recommend that women cover their bosoms and adornments; this has been interpreted by some that women should cover themselves. Another verse recommends that the wives of the Prophet wrap their cloaks tightly around their bodies, so as to be recognized and not be bothered or molested in public (*Su—rah al-Ahza—b*, verse 59). Soraya Hajjaji-Jarrah, in another contribution to this volume, has traced the development of the ideology of veiling and seclusion in early Islamic history. By reviewing the works of several scholars of the early Islamic period, she demonstrates that the idea of veiling and seclusion developed later as a consequence of the widespread phenomenon of slave women in the wealthy, urban centres of the Islamic empire. Nonetheless, it was not until the time of the Ottoman Empire—which extended into most of the area that is today known as the Middle East and North Africa—and particularly until the reign of the Safavids (1501–1722) in Iran that the veil emerged as a widespread symbol of status among the Muslim ruling classes and urban elite. It is noteworthy that it is only since the nineteenth century, after the veil was promoted by the colonial occupiers as a prominent symbol of Muslim societies, especially in the travelogues and scholarly publications noted above, that Muslims have justified veiling as Islamic rather than as a cultural practice (Esposito, 1988).[5]

Broadly speaking, one can recognize two different reactions on the part of Middle Eastern Muslims to these representations, though neither decried them as inaccurate. The first group, recognizing their pejorative nature, responded by advocating that the veil be abandoned. This constituency also advocated education for women, in part to increase their public participation. The second, more conservative group claimed, on the other hand, that the veil was inherent to Muslim cultures and is a sign of their moral superiority. This group urged that veiling be preserved, insisting that any attempt to discard or modify veiling would push Muslim society towards immorality and decay. As well, they fundamentally opposed a higher public profile for women, and thus were hostile to girls' schools even when run and staffed exclusively by women, adopting—initially at least—a rigorous stance regarding veiling in Islamic educational institutions (Badran, 1995; Hoodfar, 2000; Paidar, 1995). Drawing on the popular perception of veiling as a religious practice, the conservatives galvanized some public opposition to unveiling and to the education of girls.[6] However, the issue of seclusion was difficult for the conservatives to justify or promote, in part because for all but the wealthiest segments of society, women's economic as well as reproductive labour was essential for the survival of their households. In reality, the majority of social classes, particularly in rural areas, practised segregation and sexual division of labour rather than seclusion. Thus, the goal of educating girls in all-girls schools was perfectly congruent with this practice.

Nonetheless, the veil, and to a lesser extent clothing in general, formed the symbolic battlefield on which the modernists and conservatives fought out their differences. After the First World War, both women's education and unveiling gained increasing support among the urban populations of the Middle East, making it easier for the modernists, whose political presence was expanding, to press for de-veiling. In Egypt, women had become a visible political and intellectual force, participating in anti-colonial and democratic struggles. They organized themselves both in small and in larger, more formal groups to debate issues relating to the status of women. These issues included veiling, which most politicized women at the time viewed as a corruption of Islamic ideals instituted by men in the name of Islam to prevent women's advancement. In 1928, Egyptian women activists publicly removed their veils amid public debate.

In other countries, such as Afghanistan, Iran and Turkey, the state played a direct role in discouraging the veil.[7] Although national rhetoric championed de-veiling as a strategy to liberate women and involve them in modern nation building, in reality women's interests and position were incidental—if they mattered at all. The "women's question" was simply the arena where the political struggle for power between the secular modernists and the religious authorities took place. The struggle pitted modernist governments, eager to loosen the hold of the religious authorities who had historically shared the state's power, against the clergy, who opposed the trend towards secularization because it would divorce them from political power and, in particular, deny them the monopoly over education they had enjoyed for centuries.

Thus, de-veiling laws were significant on at least two levels: they alienated religious leaders from the political structure and, through legislation, confirmed European culture as the model to emulate, hence the insistence on Western clothing for men and women as well as on de-veiling. It was on this ground that women's attempts to adapt to the new requirements, while retaining a sense of comfort by wearing head scarves and modest local dress, were rejected. Clearly, de-veiling was more than a simple clothing reform instituted to encourage women's participation in national economies and public affairs. As many argued, these goals were achievable without having to reproduce Western clothing styles—mobility and public participation for women was attainable through the modest attire that accommodated Muslim or local mores, as was the case in many Muslim cultures. It is, of course, very telling that in the drive towards modernization, the fledgling nations' goal of emulating European society engendered laws more concerned with clothing than with individual freedoms and the democratic rights of citizens, though the latter were viewed by these same democratic forces as the heart and soul of European civilization—and the very root of European dominance over the Middle East.

Given the continued absence of democratic participation and the omnipresence of censorship, it is not surprising that for the populace, clothing remained an important vehicle for political expression and for contesting state ideology. For instance, both the socialists and those who favoured a particular brand of Islamist ideology wore a distinctive style of clothing that silently proclaimed their political positions and opposition to government policy. It was in this context that the world witnessed the arrests, during the 1980s, of male students attempting to enter Egyptian universities in traditional Egyptian clothing. Few Egyptians were surprised that they were charged with the political crime of subverting the state. Similarly, the ban against Turkish women wearing head scarves when attending university, taking official exams or sitting in Parliament stemmed from the recognition that their presence represents a rejection of the state ideology. Thus it is not surprising that the presence of veiled women—women clothed in long, loose dresses and head coverings—has attracted so much attention nationally and internationally. In the absence of democracy in most Middle Eastern countries, Islamist political groups promote the veil as a symbol of their public presence and their political will, both to the public and to the state.

Similarly, the black-veiled women who participated en masse in the 1978 Iranian revolution became the most powerful symbol of the revolution and its rejection of the previous government's gender ideology and Westernization. Iran's new Islamic regime, well aware of the symbolic power of the veil after more than a century of political struggle between secularists and Islamists, initially encouraged the practice. Later, however, it went so far as to enforce veiling through legislation and even violence, so important had the veil become as a symbol of its political triumph over secular forces. The draconian nature of compulsory veiling laws, with beatings, fines and imprisonment for non-compliance, is in principle no different from the compulsory de-veiling that had taken place some forty years earlier. This clearly indicates that, once again, neither woman's rights nor democratic rights were concerns of the Islamic state. These interventions have invested clothing with ever more political meaning. Iranian women have responded to the unwelcome state interference in their choice of attire by pursuing several initiatives. Fashion and makeup have become important vehicles for expressing resistance, which has meant ever-increasing employment opportunities in the ranks of the despised moral police who patrol the streets of urban centres in Iran (Hoodfar, forthcoming).

The political space and debate devoted in the Middle East to the issue of clothing, and in particular the veil, indicate that the latter is far more than just a head cover. In many ways the veil remains a most potent political and social tool. If it is true that a picture is worth a thousand words, the image of veiled women can account for literally hundreds of political speeches, whether as a symbol of opposition to the state, an expression of particular religious currents, a symbol of patriarchy and misogynist tradition, a declaration of Muslim identity in primarily non-Muslim society or a reassurance to one's family that one's respect for Muslim mores remains strong despite unconventional activities and circumstances. It is from this perspective that I examine the use of the veil in the daily lives of Muslim women generally, before turning to the politics of veiling in Canada.

THE VEIL IN PRACTICE

Although in Western literature veiling is often presented as a uniform and static practice going back over a thousand years, the veil itself has had many variations and has been subject to changing fashion throughout history and in modern times. Moreover, like other articles of clothing, the veil may be worn for multiple reasons. It may be worn to beautify the wearer (Chatty, 1996; Wikan, 1982), much in the way makeup beautifies Western women; to demonstrate respect for conventional values (Abu-Lughod, 1986; Hoodfar, 1991); or to hide the wearer's identity (Fernea, 1965). Today, veiling typically consists of a long, loosely fitted dress of any colour combination worn with a scarf wrapped in various fashions so as to cover all the hair. Nonetheless, the imaginary veil that comes to the minds of most Westerners is an awkward black cloak that covers the whole body, including the face, and which is designed to prevent women's mobility (Dickey, 1994).[8] Throughout history, however, except for among the elite, women's labour was vital to the household economy and women's clothing of necessity ensured freedom of movement. Even a cursory survey of clothing habits in rural and urban settings, both in the Middle East and in other Muslim cultures, indicates that women's costumes, though all considered Islamic, cover the body to widely varying degrees (Rugh, 1986). The tendency of Western scholarly work and the colonial authorities to present a one-dimensional image of Islam, encompassing a seamless society of Muslims, precluded the exploration of the socio-economic significance of such variation, which is nevertheless widely evident, even in their own drawings and paintings.[9] Similarly, scholarly study of Islamic beliefs and culture has focused on Islamic texts, but generally overlooks the actual variations in the way Islam has been and is being practised.

THE RESEARCH

Until the mid-1980s, when veiling began attracting attention in Europe and North America, debate and concerns regarding veiling seemed to be limited to the Middle East, particularly in relation to Iran, Egypt and the Gulf countries. Outside this region, what has made veiling so perplexing to many non-Muslims over the past fifteen years or so is the apparent fact that many of the young women in Europe and North America who have taken up the veil have been raised, if not in fact born, in the "West." The controversies surrounding the veil and the sometimes hostile attitude towards veiling and veiled women, combined with the insistence of the Diaspora Muslim community in presenting the veil as an Islamic symbol of Muslim identity, have given birth to a political battle where few combatants or onlookers have bothered to re-examine their assumptions about the veil or its implications for the women who wear it. The following data and discussion examine the politics of contemporary veiling from the perspective of Muslim women within the Canadian social and political context.

Given the intimate nature of the data this research required, and given the importance of age hierarchy in most Muslim cultures (Hoodfar, 1995), anthropology by proxy was the most suitable research method. A research team was formed consisting of twelve Muslim women of different ages, both veiled and unveiled, with diverse cultural origins and trained in anthropology and other social sciences. Several workshops were also organized at McGill and Concordia universities in Montreal, as well as in mosques in Ottawa and Toronto, to discuss the concerns of Muslim women. In light of these discussions, I prepared a guideline for interviews. Each of the research assistants then interviewed some ten young women from among their own friends and relatives. Each in-depth interview lasted two to eight hours, often extending over several sessions. We also carried out some interviews with the parents of our respondents.

The respondents ranged in age from fifteen to thirty-three, with the large majority between the ages of nineteen to twenty-three. In the tradition of anthropology, I rely in this paper on representative statements from the interviewees, or quote from my notes, where, as a rule, the informant's statements are recorded in the first person. At times, I have added explanatory phrases in order to situate the discussion, especially for non-Muslim readers who may be unfamiliar with the particular context to which the quotes are referring.

However, several important points must first be made. On examining the data it quickly became apparent that Somalis and Iranians occupy opposite poles with respect to their views on Muslim communities and Muslim women. The Iranians, who for the most part left Iran to escape the impositions of the Islamic Republic and in particular compulsory veiling, were very critical and skeptical of the veil and Islam (at least as interpreted by the Iranian regime) having anything to offer the Muslim community and in particular women. Interestingly, this group of Iranian women included a few supporters of the regime at the time studying in Canada—women who, while having a stronger religious inclination, nonetheless believe that Islam needs revision and reinterpretation if it is to survive and remain relevant to Muslims.

At the other extreme, the Somali women, many of whom had come to Canada as refugees escaping years of civil war and upheaval, had turned to Islam and the Muslim community for support upon their arrival. As a symbolic gesture to confirm their allegiance to the Muslim community, the Somalis abandoned some traditional practices and especially traditional costumes in favour of modern "Muslim" clothing.[10] Since the Somali population is relatively small and new in Canada, without its own community centres or other formal organizations to support the newcomers in adjusting to their new home, for many Somalis emphasizing their membership and participating in the Muslim community is a means of coping with a new culture and social system. Mosques and the Muslim community provide support and a sense of belonging, crucial "for their mental health," as one Somali community worker put it. Given the ethnic divisions that exist among Muslims in Canada, absorption of newly arrived Muslim immigrants plays a critical role in the construction of a common, hybrid Muslim identity that transcends ethnic and cultural boundaries to assert a "Muslim" community and Islamic mores in Canadian society (Waardenburg, 1988). Given this context, a detailed comparative analysis of these two Muslim cultural groups—Iranians and Somalis—deserves special consideration and historical conceptualization, a task that lies beyond the scope of this paper. Thus, except for highly pertinent and representative material, I have not focused greatly on this section of data.[11]

VEILING IN CANADA

The data revealed several compelling and very surprising results, some of which totally contradicted many commonly held assumptions, as well as some of my own preconceptions. The first of these to be disproven concerned the family backgrounds and cultural origins of the majority of young veiled university students and graduates. I had assumed that one major reason for the increase in the number of veiled Muslim women stemmed from changes in Canadian immigration policy. Until 1967 it would have been difficult for most people from Muslim countries, except those highly educated and wealthy (as well as "Westernized"), to immigrate to Canada (Kelly 1998a). In more recent decades, however, some discriminatory measures have been removed, and, more importantly, the needs of the labour market have changed from requiring highly educated professionals to requiring skilled and semi-skilled workers. This would, in theory, have allowed more people with religious backgrounds—including families who continued to observe veiling practices—to immigrate to Canada. With the second generation of these more recently arrived families now at university, we observed the presence of young veiled women at universities and in the labour force. The data, however, indicates that only seven out of sixty-nine mothers on whom we have data wore the veil.

With the exception of two women, all Pakistani women wore their national clothing (*shalvar qamis*). Many of the others either wore the national long dresses (*jalabahs*) or opted for modest dresses, none of which necessarily incorporate the veil. These mothers may be described as being rather conventional. Not the daughters, nor the mothers, nor the Muslim community consider such outfits to constitute veiling, except when a modern scarf is worn along with the traditional costume. Generally speaking, among our sample, a considerable number of young, veiled women came from more conventional backgrounds, that is, families that observed their heritage culture's norms and values—particularly as these related to male and female interactions—rather than from more religious families. The distinction, though perhaps a subtle one for North Americans whose understanding has been shaped by persistent colonial images of Muslims, is nonetheless considerable for Muslims. The data, as I shall demonstrate below, indicate that young Muslim women employ this distinction to reject those aspects of their parents' culture, which they see as incompatible with their view of Islam, rather than appearing to deny their ethnic roots or their parents' values.

In Canada, and particularly in Quebec, many feminists and Quebec nationalists who have advocated banning the veil in public schools claim that young women are forced by their families to wear the veil, and that banning it will free young women from such oppression. However, among the participants in this study, we did not find any evidence to support such claims. Moreover, one very unexpected finding was that many young women had to fight with their parents—who in many cases had come to Canada to give their daughters "better opportunities"—for the right to wear the veil. Furthermore, while some mothers felt powerless to deny their daughters' decision to veil, they themselves did not associate veiling with Islam. Other parents reluctantly accepted their daughters' decision and continued to hope that the young women would "come to their senses" and give up the veil. Two fathers, after failing to convince their daughters not to veil, refused to talk to them for several months. Another father told me:

> I had to accept her choice; there was nothing I could do. I convinced myself that at least I did not have to fear that she is running around with unsuitable company, getting drunk or worse, coming home with the news of an out-of-wedlock pregnancy. But it was not easy. My father and his generation fought to remove the veil and free women and bring them into public life. Now how can I explain that my daughter, two generations later and in Montreal, chooses to take up the veil? Just as well that my father is not alive to see this.

I had also hypothesized that if women attended religious gatherings in mosques they might have been encouraged to take up the veil. However, many of the veiled women, particularly in Montreal, did not visit mosques for prayer or other religious activities. In fact, it emerged that weekend Qur'an lessons were not generally held in mosques. Some of the women said they had started attending mosque infrequently, but only some years *after* they began veiling. Many of the university students in the sample did frequent the university prayer room—where such a room existed—to rest, socialize with other Muslim women or to pray. Their reasons for not going to mosque varied: the Toronto women said the mosques were too far away; in Montreal the women claimed the mosques were not "real," that they were dirty or that the Imam knew only the Qur'an and old-fashioned *fiqh* (Islamic jurisprudence), but nothing about issues pertinent to Muslims living in North America. One young woman said:

> I understand why our grandmothers did not go to the mosques [in many Arab countries women did not traditionally go to mosque but prayed at home. This situation has been changing rapidly in most of the Arab world since the mid-1970s], if the mosques were as dirty and unwelcoming as they are here, with men standing at the door to tell you, "pull your scarf down and cover your hair" or something like that, just to reiterate their power over you as men. They forget that at the very least in the house of God they should obey the Qur'anic injunction and not look and examine

a woman's physical appearance. You know, something worse about men in the mosque here is that so many women who go there get offers of marriage within a few minutes of their arrival. These places in Montreal are not real mosques. I have been in Egypt and Jordan. I know how a mosque is supposed to be. When there is a real mosque here, I will go all the time.

After further conversation, she smiled and said with a twinkle in her eye:

Maybe me and a few other women will set up Montreal's first real mosque, just like we have set up our own Muslim women's group, which has worked well for the last two years. Why not? We will let men in only on Fridays and only in the back!

Our own and other more recent data indicate that young women are increasingly attending mosque (Haddad, 2002; Meshal, 2003). There has also been an increase in the number of mosques and Islamic religious centres, discussion groups, youth camps and Internet sites where women, particularly younger ones, can participate in discussion and debate.[12] Some of the more established mosques organize talks, often in Arabic, on issues of interest to the various Muslim communities. Women also participate in social activities, including picnics and organized outings. As well, the Muslim community has become more politicized since the Gulf War and the conflict in Bosnia, from which Muslims were forced to flee for their lives. Montreal mosques, in particular, have become community centres as well as places of worship, as have many mosques in Toronto.

When we asked our veiled informants why they chose to veil, the majority said the veil was part of their religion and that they wanted to be good Muslim women. Only four out of fifty-nine veiled women claimed the veil to be part of their Arab or Muslim identity and not an Islamic requirement. Another woman said she was not really religious, and that she was not really sure if Islam required women to wear the veil, since neither of her grandmothers, both from very religious backgrounds, had ever taken up the practice. But she felt that in the context of North America the veil enabled her to be a "person" rather than an object of male scrutiny. A closer reading of the interview transcripts regarding women's decisions to take up the veil reveals a somewhat different story, however. Beyond personal or religious convictions, there seem to be several overlapping reasons influencing them to adopt the custom. Some are individual in nature, while others stem from a communal impetus.

One common factor precipitating the decision to veil involved restrictive parents. Most girls said that once they reached the age of thirteen or fourteen, their parents were reluctant to let them visit their friends, particularly if the friends were not Muslim or were of a different cultural background. This was particularly objectionable to the young women, whose brothers by contrast enjoyed great freedom. Also frustrating was the disparity they observed between themselves and their Canadian or Quebecoise friends, whose freedom and autonomy increased rather than diminished as they became teens. Increasing restrictions placed on Muslim girls as they entered the teenage years was common even among more educated and generally more "modernized" parents.

Even when they were younger the women had recognized that their parents had their best interests and protection at heart, though they may not have agreed with their methods. Parental fears concerning drinking, sexual activity and possible pregnancy are even more pronounced among Muslim parents; the consequences of such actions for Muslim women, who must according to religious law marry Muslim men, and generally from within their own community, are inevitably disastrous. The interviewees noted that a woman whose reputation is questionable will have a difficult time finding a husband. Nevertheless, despite understanding their parents' concerns, many girls found themselves in conflict at home.

Under such circumstances the veil offers a means to mitigate parental and social concerns. Many of the women said that if they had realized how veiling could alleviate such parental fears, they would have taken it up even earlier. Reem, for instance, is seventeen and is very grateful for the peace and quiet that she has finally found in her heart and home since she began veiling:

I was two and my brother five when we came from Pakistan to Canada. We had other relatives here in Quebec, which was good, since it meant we were not lonely. My parents were both educated and professional and seemed to adjust to life here. We had friends of all sorts and played with them in the alley. The only thing different about us was that we had funny names, ate different food and my parents played different music, which sometimes became the subject of jokes among our friends, but nothing severe. After I turned twelve my parents did not want me to visit my Canadian friends and more and more I had to stay home. I hated it because all my childhood friends had started to go to cinema and picnic with each other, but I had to stay home. Worse was that now I was expected to wear traditional clothing except when I was going to school, and God forbid if I wanted to try wearing a little makeup, because all hell would break loose in our house. If I was half an hour late from school, my mother would be out in the street looking for me, and then there was hell to pay for days. This was very hurtful for me, because I didn't understand it. Even if my mother had lived that way in Pakistan, it didn't mean that I should live like this in Canada. After all, what was the point of coming to Canada if we were going to behave the same? What bothered me most and made it harder for me to put up with all these restrictions was that they did not apply to my brother because he was a boy. Of course, he was not as free as most of his friends, but the difference between my life and his was considerable. Sometimes he felt sorry for me and took me out. Other times, to hurt me, as siblings do, he would remind me that as a Muslim woman I have to be housebound and in my place. I had big fights with my parents and life was miserable. As news of my disagreement with my parents spread, other Pakistani families did not want to visit us, or if they did, they left their daughters at home for fear of being influenced by me. So my life became lonelier. It was during this time that one of our relatives took up the veil. Like me she had had problems at home. She said that since she started wearing the veil, she feels so much happier and freer. It is as though she has suddenly matured in the eyes of her parents and everyone else. Now she is allowed to drive, to go to her friends or to have them come home. We talked and I spent more time with her. My parents were happy that I was spending time with a good Muslim girl. Then I decided to take the veil and my life has changed. It is true that I cannot have boyfriends and do some of the things my school girlfriends do. But I never wanted to do those things anyway. I know that I am a Muslim and I cannot have sexual relations before marriage. Now my parents respect me. I go to Qur'anic classes, I spend time with my friends, and not all of them are Muslim; some are Hindu and one is a Christian of Indian origin. I also have some Muslim-only get-togethers. Since I have my licence now, I can even have the car when I want it, something I never thought my parents would allow me. My brother respects me too. I do not know what happened. But I know that now that I wear the veil, no one in my family and community disrespects me. I wish I had taken it even earlier.

An articulate nineteen-year-old Palestinian woman told me:

The veil has freed me from arguments and headaches. I always wanted to do many things that women normally do not do in my culture. I had thought living in Canada would give me that opportunity. But when I turned fourteen, my life changed. My parents started to limit my activities and even telephone conversations. My brothers were free to go and come as they pleased, but my sister and I were to be good Muslim girls. Even the books we read became subject to inspection. Life became intolerable for me. The weekends were hell. Then as a way out, I asked to go to Qur'anic classes on Saturdays. There I met with several veiled women of my age. They came from similar backgrounds. None of them seemed to face my problems. Some told me that since they took the veil, their parents know that they are not going to do anything that goes against Muslim morality. The more I hung around with them, the more convinced I was that the veil is the answer to all Muslim girls' problems here in North America. Because parents seem to be relieved and assured that you are not going to do stupid things, and your community knows that you are acting like a Muslim woman, you are much freer. Now I am happy, and since I go to Islamic study group, I have learnt a lot. From studying *true Islam* [emphasis added], and comparing notes with Muslims from other countries like Egypt and Syria, I have also realized that so much of what our parents impose on us in the name of Islam is not Islam but it is their cultural practice. So I can discuss with them and sometimes I succeed in changing their minds.

These narratives were typical of many young women who took up the veil towards the end of high school or upon entering university. In a sense, they had recognized the effectiveness of the veil in communicating certain values. By taking up the veil, they symbolically but clearly announced to their parents and their community that, despite their unconventional activities and involvement with non-Muslims, they retain their Islamic mores and values. They are modern Muslim women who want to be educated and publicly active, but not at the cost of their moral principles.

Some women said that since donning the veil, it had become easier to interact with men, both Muslim and non-Muslim:

Previously, it was always the worry that maybe there would be a misunderstanding, that someone might think I was propositioning them [men], or that if someone sees me talking or walking with a man, they might think he is my boyfriend, and that of course is not good for one's reputation in the community. Since taking the veil these worries about talking with classmates or colleagues have disappeared.

Veiling also makes it clear to Muslim and non-Muslim men that the veiled women are not available for dating. The veil is a powerful means of communicating all these messages without uttering a word, and with this understanding, it is not surprising that women have discovered and adopted it.

There are other reasons behind the choice to veil or to adopt other perceived Islamic symbols, including religious language. In most Muslim cultures, parents have considerable influence in the choice of their child's spouse. This practice is usually justified with reference to Islam. While sons may have a voice in matters of marriage, in many contexts girls have limited opportunities to speak out, though passing on their wishes and feelings through close relatives is one of these. In the North American context, however, this channel is very limited because there are fewer aunts and uncles who can discreetly elicit a girl's views and advocate on her behalf in conversation with her parents. In their zeal to protect their daughters' reputations, some parents marry their daughters off against their wishes, sometimes at a young age when it is harder to resist. Islam, however, expressly gives all adult men and women the right to choose their spouse, though in some branches of Islam a first-time bride needs her father's consent as well. By increasing their Islamic knowledge of matters such as these, and through appearing to be serious and committed to Islam, many women have successfully resisted unwanted marriage arrangements without alienating their parents. Farida's story describes such a situation:

When I was seventeen my father wanted to arrange a marriage for me to a guy from Pakistan. He had talked about this match before, but I had not taken it seriously. I knew that he worried I might fall in love and want to marry a person they wouldn't find acceptable. But since I had demonstrated my commitment as a student, and had taken the veil, I thought he was reassured. However, he went ahead with the marriage arrangements, and persisted despite my objections. I tried to get our relatives and friends here in Canada involved, but it did not work. It only made him more insistent. He thought my objection was in itself proof that I was becoming too Canadian. He said for generations girls in his family had married whomever their fathers had chosen, and he was not about to allow a sixteen-year-old to break centuries of Islamic tradition. So I went and studied Islamic books, sought knowledgeable people's views and prepared my arguments with references to Qu'ran and Islamic texts. I told my mother that I had talked to the Imam, who said that if I were married against my wishes, in the eyes of God the marriage would not be valid. I want to study, and if my father pushes me into marriage, according to Islam he has condemned me to a sinful life. I told her that a marriage without my consent, which is my Islamic right, is not an Islamic marriage. The same way as my marriage without my father's consent is also un-Islamic. I told my mother if he forces me into this marriage, he has to carry the sin as I do not give my consent. I let all the friends and neighbours know my views; I also criticized their imposing outdated culture on us in the name of Islam. I told my parents and others that their mistake is that they have never bothered to read and learn Islam for themselves. Everyone was impressed by my knowledge of Islam and many young women became interested in having a discussion group. The marriage was called off on the pretense of me wanting to continue my education. My father, who saw that even in the heat of the debate I never denied his authority and rights as a father, did not hold this against me and I have heard him saying that he was proud of me. My using Islam as the basis of my rejection of the marriage, without reference to my right under Canadian law or the like, made it easier for my father to save face among his friends. After all, as you said earlier, Islam enjoys a much higher order of legitimacy than any laws and traditions. I have heard my mother pointing out to her friends, with some pleasure, that the world has turned upside down and they have ended up learning their religion from their Canadian children rather than from their Muslim parents back home.

Farida further explained that many young Muslim women increase their opportunities within their families and communities, and secure greater respect, by studying Islam and its diverse interpretations. In many ways, young Muslims in Canada view modernity and Islam as being fully compatible. Their education, along with their much broader contacts with Muslims of diverse ethnic backgrounds, has allowed them to separate cultural traditions and norms from what they view as religion and, more importantly, to privilege those interpretations of Islam that are more acceptable to them—a choice that their parents, having been brought up in a mono-Muslim culture and given only limited access to religious education, in most cases did not have.

It is important to note that many young women have witnessed unhappy marriages and sometimes divorce among Muslim friends and relatives who married against the wishes of their parents, and this has deterred them from discarding traditional practices and the support of their families and culture. We heard many secondhand stories of love marriages not blessed by parents, which turned out to be disastrous for the Muslim women involved. Our interviewees seemed to believe that using Islamic arguments to oppose certain restrictions or practices seems to be a much more effective and appropriate strategy than defiance. As one woman pointed out, veiling and learning about Islam has enabled young Muslim women to have their cake and eat it too. They have the freedom to do much of what they want, and also have the support and protection of their families.

Fatemeh is a good illustration of this. Aged twenty-three and very happy with her life, she recently completed a degree in chemistry in Toronto and has worked for a few years, but is planning to pursue graduate studies. She told me:

I wanted to go to university and there was no university in our area. In any case I wanted to go and live by myself and experience that kind of life as well. Everyone said I was crazy, that my parents would never let me do that. My older brother left for university in London, Ontario, and there was no problem. Then it was my turn, but my father said it was out of the question, particularly because I wanted to go to Toronto, and not where my brother was. I stayed home for one year. During that year I took the veil and studied religious text and the more I read and thought about it, the more I felt I was suffering unjust discrimination that had no Islamic basis. In Islam parents are obliged to educate both their daughters and sons. I applied for university again and insisted on my Islamic rights and criticized my parents for misunderstanding Islam. Finally, they agreed. I guess they realized that I am so strong in my religious beliefs that, although in our little town it was not easy, I chose to wear the veil of my own free will. So they did not have to worry about my reputation or that I won't be able to find a good Muslim husband, or that I will fall in love with a non-Muslim, or start drinking or any of the things our Muslim parents are worried about. So my father came with me to Toronto, found me a place to live and I went to university. After my brother graduated, everyone moved to Toronto and I moved back home. Now I am my father's favourite child. I am a committed Muslim and a highly educated modern woman. I am very respectful of my parents as is my Islamic duty. Moreover, the Muslim community also thinks highly of me, because I am very active in community matters. To the community, I represent the best of Canada and Islam and modernity, so many urge their daughters to see me as a role model.

Some of the young women defend veiling, though they themselves do not veil. They suggest that much of the fuss in non-Muslim Canadian society over veiling, such as debates about banning veils from public schools, stems from anti-Muslim sentiment. They point out that wearing strange and unconventional clothing, tattooing, and piercing noses, lips and eyebrows—practices that many students engage in—go unremarked. Nahed, age sixteen, asked:

Why is it that nobody is worried that these individuals, who are much more numerous in Canada than veiled women, might be oppressed? Or that they may be mutilating their bodies? We know that the fuss is all about their prejudices against Islam and the Muslim community. It makes me so angry that sometimes I feel like taking the veil to spite them.

In many ways Muslims themselves wish to deny the expressive power of the veil. I suggested therefore to Nahed that, while society may understand what is being communicated by radical hairdos and body-piercing, perhaps this same society does not quite understand or is worried about the message the Muslim community is sending through veiling. Nahed thought for a moment and said, "I don't think so. I do not see them trying to understand it. They are just using it as an excuse to vilify the Muslim community. Maybe you are philosophizing too much. I do not see much goodwill out there, just a lot of hypocrisy."

Many girls who don't veil, but have friends who do, recognize the benefits of hanging around with veiled friends. Afsaneh, a sixteen-year-old Iranian, complained about the restrictions her parents imposed when she turned thirteen, but said things had improved since she became friends with two Arab girls who wear the veil. Prior to this she couldn't go out with friends or even to a movie, while her three brothers had a fine time participating in sports clubs, travelling and staying with friends. Since meeting her two friends at school, she is allowed to go out with them, and they visit each other. I asked her why she thinks things have changed. She replied:

> It is obvious. Although my parents are not very strict Muslims and in fact came to Canada to escape the daily oppression of the Islamic regime of Iran, they don't approve of many things here in Canada. They worry about things that all parents, but particularly Muslim parents, worry about—that I will start drinking, that I will get a boyfriend or get into sexual relations. That would, in their minds, ruin my reputation and my future chances of marriage. But if I am hanging around with veiled women and go out with them to cinema or stay at their home, they know that I am not getting into trouble. More importantly, the community sees me with the veiled women, so they know that I am a virtuous young woman and not after finding a boyfriend and all things they consider evil.

I asked Afsaneh why she did not take the veil herself, since it would probably offer her even more freedom. She replied:

> Oh no. For one thing, though I defend the right of women to wear the veil, I don't see it as a necessary part of Islam. I know that at the time of the Prophet, people did not wear these kinds of clothes and these things are all made up to control women. Look at what is happening in Iran [referring to compulsory veiling and codification of *shary'ah* laws that have rendered women second-class citizens]. Moreover, my parents would not want me to wear the veil because it probably would restrict the chances of me finding a husband in the Iranian community, something they desire for me. You know Iranians, having experienced the Islamic Republic that forced women to wear a veil instead of encouraging both men and women to avoid clothes that are seductive, this has turned a lot of people, including religious people like my parents, against the veil. But my parents wish me to hang around with good Muslim women.

It is clear from Afsaneh's statement, and other similar cases, that in the context of Canada, where women can choose whether or not to veil, veiling can be an indicator of a woman's commitment to Islamic mores. Despite her parents' ambivalence towards veiling, which they associate with the oppressive regime in Iran, they approve of Afsaneh's friendships with veiled women. This underscores the symbolic value of the veil as an effective vehicle for communicating a multiplicity of immediate visual messages.

There were other issues regarding identity and belonging that induced some of the younger women to begin veiling. Some felt isolated at school as they matured, and their parents increasingly restricted their participation in various school activities, which invariably led to social exclusion. Activities such as gym class and swimming strained relations between the female Muslim students and their schoolmates. Parents sent letters excusing their daughters from swimming lessons on the basis that Muslim women should not reveal their bodies to unrelated men. This frequently made them the subject of discussion and occasionally of ridicule, even at times from teachers. The Muslim girls always wore tracksuits for gym. Though other students wore similar attire, some interviewees said it was only the Muslim girls who were the butt of jokes in this regard. They were made to feel like outsiders, not quite up to the standards of Canadian society. In this situation, taking up the veil was a means of turning the tables, actively asserting identity as opposed to being identified as different by exclusion or ostracism. By choosing to veil, they defined themselves, establishing their own collective to the exclusion of others. Seventeen-year-old Ziba from Pakistan explains:

> We came from Pakistan and since we had many friends and relatives, we lived near them. Financially we were not so badly off and that made it easier. Although we did not intermingle much with non-Indian-Canadians, I very much felt at home and part of the wider society. This, however, changed as I got older and clearly my life was different than many girls in my class. I did not talk about boyfriends and did not go out. I did not participate in extracurricular activities. Gradually, I began feeling isolated. Then my cousin and I decided together to wear the veil and made a pact to ignore people's comments, that no matter how much hardship we suffered at school, we would keep our veils on. One weekend we announced this to our surprised parents. They were perplexed that their fifteen- and sixteen-year-olds had decided to take such a drastic measure without consulting them. At that time, there were not very many Pakistani women in Montreal who wore the modern veil. Most women wear our traditional clothes. Our parents consented, though they did not think we would stick with it. But we did. At first it was difficult. At school people joked and asked stupid questions, but after three months they took us more seriously and there was even a little bit of respect. People no longer invited us to their parties, knowing we could not go, and we did not have to apologize or explain. The teachers did not try to convince our parents that swimming is compulsory. We even got a little more respect when we talked about Islam in our classes, while before our teacher dismissed what we said if it didn't agree with her casual perceptions. Now I have no problem wearing the veil, even though I do like to let my hair loose, but the trade-off is worth it.

In order to reduce their isolation at school or university, some of the women organized social groups and rotating parties, and actively involved themselves in community activities, a trend that has continued to increase since 1996. Others started Muslim clubs and societies in their educational institutions wherever none were already in place.

The interviewees with a post-secondary education, especially in the social sciences, as well as those who were more politically inclined, presented feminist arguments in support of the veil. They argued that Canadian society and the Occident as a whole have turned women into sexual objects, their half-naked bodies used to sell everything from toothbrushes to sports cars. In the West, a woman's breasts, waist, hips and clothing are supposed to conform to an ideal standard of beauty. Therefore, they argued, women preoccupy themselves with achieving these standards instead of improving their minds and becoming confident and useful members of society. The veil, according to these young women, even with all its problems, removes women to some degree from these preoccupations. It relieves the emphasis on their bodies, enabling them to participate in public life as people rather than as bodies.

Further discussion with this group of veiled women revealed that their arguments have developed following their decisions to veil and their need to defend their choice. In the process, they became more aware of feminist concerns and gender politics in the broader society as well as within the Muslim community. Tahera, for instance, a youngish-looking twenty-three-year-old trying to keep her slippery scarf on her head, explained:

> Perhaps the reasons I took the veil are not the same as the reasons I continue to wear it. Maybe I don't see it as much as a religious requirement. I will continue to wear the veil as a way of trying to cope and be what I want to be in this society. This scarf, that to so many appears such a big deal, at least has made others aware of Islam, and of my identity within the Canadian society, instead of looking at me and judging me for my figure and looks. This alone is sufficient reason to wear the veil, particularly since it reinforces my identity and that of Muslim community.

Questions of identity, and the demonization of Islam and Muslims in Canada and in the West in general, do play a role in the decision of some women to take up the veil. This was especially notable in Montreal following the Gulf War. Mona, always beautifully dressed in light, understated colours, including matching veil, was born in Montreal to an Egyptian family and was raised in that city. In 1994, almost two years after having adopted the veil, she told me:

> I would never have taken up the veil if I lived in Egypt. Not that I disagree with it, but I see it as part of the male imposition of rules. I believe that Muslims should try to bring order to their sexual urges and not be seductive, and not disrupt the social order. But the veil puts all the responsibility on women's shoulders. The double standard frustrates me. But since the Gulf War, seeing how my veiled friends were treated, I made a vow to wear the veil to make a point about my Muslimness and Arabness. I am delighted when people ask me about my veil and Islam, because it gives me a chance to point out their prejudices concerning Muslims.

I asked her what kinds of questions people ask her and how she responds. Mona replied:

> They ask all sorts of stupid questions and, of course, occasionally an intelligent one too. They ask me why I wear the veil since I live in Canada. I tell them I want to exercise my democratic rights, just like they do. I tell them that democratic rights are not enjoyed by everyone in other parts of the world. And I ask them if the governments of Quebec or Canada are so different from Khomeini's Iran, when they try to ban veiling in public schools or expel veiled students from schools. I ask them how many students would have to leave school if we were to expel all those who wore the cross, since that is also a religious symbol. Some ask whether I feel discrimination as a

woman, since men don't have to wear the veil. I say yes, but I have yet to hear that people have raised a public outcry about Jewish men suffering discrimination or oppression because they have to wear *kippah* and Jewish women do not. Or I tell them it can't be worse than seeing women's naked bodies at the sex shops and in all sorts of ads and maybe they should put their energies to solving those problems instead of worrying whether my veil is a form of oppression. Others ask me if the veil interferes with my hearing. I say yes it does, but I still manage to be at the top of the class and get A+ in all my courses, while many who don't wear the veil flunk.... Every day something new happens. The other day some woman in the metro, after chatting with me a bit, said, "You with such beauty, how can you bring yourself to wear the veil?" I smiled and told her it is so people can see beyond my physical beauty and realize that I want to be a person.

Mona even suggested to me at this point that if I really wanted to instigate discussion about Islam, Muslim women and Arabs, I should go out veiled. This would generate all kinds of opportunities for me personally to experience people's perceptions and attitudes, and to get into arguments!

When I asked Mona if she didn't miss her sexuality, and whether she truly wanted to be considered exclusively in non-sexual terms, she admitted that while she would like to be admired for her beauty and femininity as well, the price in this society is too high:

> There is no in between, at least when you are young. Our society forces you to be either a person or a woman and object of desire. So for now and as long as I have the courage, I would rather be a person.

When I pointed out that even with a veil she is, and is perceived to be, a woman, being that the veil is an exclusively female garment actually symbolizing femininity, Mona said:

> Right! Of course, I am a woman, but instead of people judging whether I have a nice body and whether my clothes are fashionable, they think of my veil. They discuss the veil. Similarly the men know that even though I am a woman, I am telling them [to] see me otherwise. Do not think of my body, but of me as a person, a colleague and so on.

Some of the veiled informants, who view the veil primarily as a political statement, use the veil specifically when they feel it important to reinforce their Arab or Muslim identities, and do not necessarily practise veiling regularly. The reception accorded to this type of "selective veiling," which is increasing within the Muslim community as well as within society at large, would be interesting to examine, though our attention was drawn to this practice only towards the end of our field research.

Among the women we interviewed was a group that recognized how veiling and other perceived religious practices had the potential to give them power over those normally exercising power over them. In a group discussion held at a mosque in Toronto, Samira, twenty-two, whose parents are of Indian and Syrian extraction, told me that her life had changed since she took the veil. As the eldest daughter in her family and her entire kin group in Canada, all her senior relatives felt they could tell her what to do and where to go. She explained:

> By the time I took notice of everyone's wishes, I was practically a prisoner. School was my only escape. Then I joined a group of women who had religious meetings and eventually I took the veil. Quite a revolution in the family despite their claim to being good Muslims. No one was veiled in my family and all were very lackadaisical about their prayers and fasting. Then it was my turn. I gave them lectures on Islam every time I got an opportunity and reminded them how they wanted me to be a good Muslim, and not do this and that. Now I have become one, and one of the duties of a good Muslim is to encourage others to practise their religion correctly and seriously. They really dislike that I, a young woman, do this. They never knew anything about Islam and just understood their cultural practices as Islam and forced them on us. Now they have to listen to me. The other day there was a big celebration in our house. Some thirty people in their best clothes were there and my mother had made a very nice dinner. She put the food on the table and announced that all should go to eat. I objected that we should not eat before praying, and that with the whole family together we all have to say a collective prayer. I knew that nobody wanted to do it. My mother was worried about her food being cold and tasteless. The girls and boys were worried about their clothes getting creased [because they had to kneel on the floor], but nobody dared object to such a legitimate religious request. We did the prayer. My father, who was the eld[est] member, led the prayer and then we ate. Most people did not talk to me much after that, but what does it matter? They all had to do as I asked.

While historically unequal power relations have often been justified in the name of religion and Islam, women are now discovering that they too can use Islam to assert their will. Studying Islam, and in particular taking the veil (a public pronouncement of piety), subverts the veil as a symbol of patriarchal control and redefines it as a marker of status and as a tool of emancipation, empowerment and, in some cases, a means of exerting power over those generally considered to have ultimate control, as illustrated in Samira's case. Many of the younger women we interviewed recognized this, and were able to demonstrate to their parents that cultural practices and values are not synonymous with Islam. According to our informants, it is not as easy for sons to use this strategy of introducing new views to their families based on the study of Islam. This reversal of influence in families, where traditionally males are significantly more influential than females, seems to stem from the power of the veil in the context of Canadian society, which publicly denotes women as religious. Many women are aware that the respect and power they gain in this way stem from the assumption that veiling in North America requires more courage and commitment than veiling in Cairo, Lahore or elsewhere in the Muslim world.

The data indicate other reasons as well underlying the decision to veil, particularly among those aged twenty-three to thirty, the most educated cohort in our sample. This segment included economists, accountants, computer scientists, fashion designers and social workers, who by conventional standards are successful professionals, fully integrated into Canadian society. However, despite this, many of them felt true contentment was to be found as homemakers and mothers, with time to enjoy their children. They were not interested in competitive struggles in the workplace, vying for insignificant promotions. They did not necessarily want to direct all their energies towards their careers, and felt that Islam allowed them this luxury by designating men as family providers, contrary to the Western feminist perspective, which sees the ideal of "man, the breadwinner" as one of the sources of Muslim women's oppression. Fatema explained in this connection how she rediscovered Islam and took the veil:

> Now I have a job with good money, but I see how much headache this job has, and while I was studying so hard to get here, I have lost many chances of a good marriage. Now men come and say you pay for this and that, or that I should keep working full-time after I have children. Well, these are not the kind of husbands I want. Not that I don't want to work, but for them to expect me to do so, it means they don't want to accept responsibility in life. I want a man who accepts his Islamic responsibility and provides for his family. Gradually I wised up and returned to my religion. The more I study the rights of women in Islam, the more I feel that as Muslim women, we are given the best opportunities. I wonder why we were so eager to throw this out for the vague feminist promise of equality. I have tried it, and I do not want to be a man, competing for a promotion and an increase of a $100 or so in my paycheque. I want to be a woman and enjoy my womanhood. As I became more aware of Islam and women's rights, I became more convinced of taking up the veil. Now that I am veiled, it is not a surprise when I tell a suitor I don't want to work outside home once I'm married, that I want to be a wife and a mother and devote myself to my family. I have studied and hold a good job, so men know that I am able to earn a good living, but I choose to be a homemaker. I think this is the nature of a woman as it has been said in Qu'ran. We [women] are kind and delicate and loving. Why should I want to change this state rather than enjoy it? Anyway, I don't see the point of fighting against nature.

By taking the veil, Fatema is publicly announcing her Islamic views pertaining to her expectations of a husband. This symbolic communication also indicates who may or may not be an appropriate suitor. Our informants were also aware that according to Islam, their husbands are bound to provide for them at the minimum level to which they are accustomed. This generally dissuades economically unsuitable men from presenting themselves as marriage candidates. Wearing the veil establishes basic values and expectations from the outset, and marriage negotiations take place within this framework of conventional values. This is not to say that all Muslims are in absolute agreement over these values, but the parameters of debate are set.

The return to Islamic values, which is communicated by many women through wearing the veil, may involve other motives too. Many Muslim women in North America with advanced education and other credentials have difficulty in finding a suitable husband. Muslim women can marry only Muslim men, while men can marry women of other faiths. Thus the Muslim community loses some potential husbands to other communities. As well, some men would rather go back to their countries of origin and marry "authentic" Muslim women (Aswad, 1991; Cainkar, 1991). This means that the pool of potential husbands becomes even smaller. On the other hand, many Muslim women raised in North America are not prepared to marry men from their parents' country of origin, because of the different expectations concerning the role of women and wives. Thus, many women past the age of thirty feel they may not get a chance to marry. This is unfortunate and even unacceptable from the point of view of both unmarried women and their communities, who consider marriage and raising a family an Islamic duty. Thus a few women in the sample chose to become second wives, justifying their decision on Islamic grounds.

Sherene, a university graduate who spent some time in the workforce, came to Canada when she was five years old. In retrospect she believes that if she had followed a more Islamic path, her life would have been much better. She did finally return to Islam, as she recounts here in the story of her marriage:

> When I was young I had many suitors. I was rather beautiful. But I wanted to take full advantage of Canadian society, so I rejected them all. I went to university and then got myself a job. I was successful and had money and dressed very smartly. But I was lonely. There were no longer that many suitors and I could not accept non-Muslims. I had a couple of marriage offers from men from home, but I could not see myself marrying someone who had not lived in North America and does not know English, and probably only wants to marry me because he wants to come abroad. Otherwise such men would choose women from home who would not question their position as head of household. I knew I would be asking for trouble if I married that way. On the other hand, I wanted to have a home and children. Finally I met my husband, who is married and has three children. He proposed to me and I accepted. I think it is better to marry as a second wife of a good Muslim man than to marry a non-Muslim or not marry at all. Now I have a child and I am very happy with my husband.

Sherene's situation prompted a group discussion of polygyny, again a subject beyond the scope of this chapter. Of relevance to the issue of veiling is the consideration of how her family and her community would have reacted had she not been a veiled woman, well versed in religious reasoning and justifying her decisions within the framework of Islam. As far as Canadian law is concerned, she is an unmarried woman with a child; yet in the eyes of her community, she has fulfilled her Islamic duty in a prescribed fashion. Although many women did not approve of polygyny and did not quite feel it was fair for the first wife, nonetheless Sherene was not marginalized despite the fact that she moved within the same circle as her co-wife, a situation unthinkable within a secular Muslim community. Clearly, many women examine their Islamic rights in consideration of how to best serve their own particular situations.

SUMMARY AND CONCLUSION

In this paper, I argued against a one-dimensional treatment of veiling as an unchanging practice symbolizing oppressive patriarchy in Muslim societies. I suggested we must examine veiling in a broader framework, situating the veil within the history of clothing as a vehicle for political and social expression and action. A cursory review of the history of clothing and dress codes of Europe and the Middle East since the Middle Ages disabuses any simple, functionalist or materialist perspective of clothing as a socially neutral response to biological and climatic needs. Historically, clothing has carried significant communicative power. Clothing frequently indicates age, gender, social class, ethnicity and religion. It can mark (or blur) social boundaries, forge or destroy alliances. Clothing is used by the powerful to reinforce power, while the underclasses, through the appropriation and manipulation of clothing, can shift the balance of power and challenge the status quo. In short, clothing has been and continues to be a potent vehicle of symbolic communication.

Framing the veiling debate in a context broader than the conventional, dichotomous one of religion–Islam–patriarchy versus individual freedom of choice provides a more comprehensive understanding of this practice. It cautions us, for instance, against transposing an Iranian or Saudi Arabian notion of the compulsory veil onto the Egyptian or European or Canadian context, where we must understand veiling as a voluntary act with a multiplicity of motives and meanings. This broadening of the discussion will help us view a veiled woman not as a passive subject, but as an active agent involved in redefining her position and options in the contemporary context of her life.

The veil in Canada plays a crucial role of mediation and adaptation for many young Muslim women, something the literature has totally overlooked. Often the veil has allowed Muslim women to participate in public life without compromising values and hard-won cultural and religious rights. In a North American context, adoption of the veil symbolizes women's religiosity and commitment to Islamic mores, while allowing them to resist patriarchal values and cultural practices imposed elsewhere in the name of Islam. In a similar fashion, veiled women can argue for their Islamic right to choose their spouse and resist arranged marriages without compromising family and community support. And veiling, along with a self-taught knowledge of Islamic practices, is used by some women to counter the control of male and senior family members and as a way of exercising considerable power themselves by preaching proper religious observance.

Wearing the veil has defused parents' resistance to their daughters' leaving home for university, entering the labour market and engaging in other activities in the public domain that are considered unconventional for Muslim women. The reason for this is that wearing the veil is a clear statement to parents and the wider Muslim community that these women are not relinquishing Islamic mores in favour of "Canadianness." Rather, they are publicly asserting their Muslim-Canadian identity. In effect, the veil has helped many Muslim women not only to practise their religion, but also to take advantage of what Canada, their new home, has to offer. The veil has thus been instrumental in helping Muslim women adapt to the wider Canadian society. Hence it is not the veil or Islam that has prevented the Muslim community from being fully integrated into Canadian society; rather, it is, to a significant degree, the colonial image of Muslims and the veil, along with the continuous demonizing of Islam, that has proved a major obstacle to such integration. As the data indicates, the continued negative portrayal of Islam and Muslims in the West has, in fact, motivated some women to take up the veil. They do so not only because of their personal religious beliefs, but also out of a wish to assert openly the presence of the Muslim community.

Clearly, veiling means different things in different social contexts. While the veil was invented and perpetuated within a patriarchal framework as a means of controlling women, more often than not women have appropriated this same artifact to loosen the bonds of patriarchy. It is the lack of recognition of women's agency and the tendency to view women as passive victims that has flawed the current debate, distorted the image of veiled women and promoted the divide between those who do and those who do not wear the *hijab*.

NOTES

1. For a history of clothing since Egyptian times, see Crawley (1931) and Payne (1965). For a summary of definitions and categorization of dress, see Barnes and Eicher (1992), and Lindisfarne-Tapper and Ingham (1997).

2. Military uniform is perhaps one of the best examples of these functions. The uniform is designed to set its personnel apart from the public while creating an impression of physical solidity, thus psychologically reinforcing the military physical presence and power. For example, it is reported that one reason the Ottoman military initially resisted a modern uniform was that its tight fit made soldiers less imposing (Wheatcroft, 1993). Generally speaking, wearing a uniform creates a sense of belonging; however, the hierarchical nature of the military institution is maintained through creating subtle, and sometime not so subtle, details and differences to indicate and reinforce the rank of the wearer.

3. However, women's attempts to change the colour of the veil in Iran at the turn of the twentieth century created a public outcry, although no legal reaction (Bamdad, 1977:Chapter 2).

4. One estimate puts the number of publications at 60,000 books—excluding articles and shorter writings—between 1800 and 1950 (Nader, 1989).

5. Of course, this is not to say that historically there haven't been other attempts to control women's dress and clothing, but only that these attempts were not made in the name of Islam (see, for example, Ahmed, 1992:118).

6. Islam in fact supports education for both males and females; indeed, today many governments, including conservative ones such as those of Iran and Saudi Arabia, are promoting female education as Islamic. For example, since the revolution, the walls of all adult literacy classes in Iran are decorated with posters reiterating words of the Prophet, which advocate learning for all Muslims, especially his famous command to Muslim men and women to go even to China (which was, in the time of the Prophet, the farthest centre of intellectual activity) in search of knowledge.

7. Iran was, however, the only country that actually made veiling illegal and used the police to enforce the law.

8. In 1991, I conducted an informal survey among my Western acquaintances and students; they invariably described the veil as this all-enveloping black robe. Some added that it is designed to prevent or hamper women's mobility. Dickey's (1994) study yielded very similar results.

9. More recently, some of the Islamist political groups have adopted the same strategy of presenting one "Islam" and one transnational culture, each group championing its particular version of Islam and Islamic attire, which is claimed to be the only authentic version.

10. We can note that it was with some regret that most of these women made this change, feeling (and rightly so, I believe) that few other clothing styles in the world can match the beauty of Somali tra-

ditional clothing. Others continue to wear their traditional clothing under the cover of their "Muslim" costume.

[11] I hope to examine in more detail the data collected from thirty-five interviews (of nineteen Iranian and sixteen Somali women) in a separate paper where I can do justice to the particular situations of these two Muslim ethnic groups.

[12] We do not have comparable data on this particular trend for Ottawa, as this area was not in the interviews conducted there.

REFERENCES

Abu Lughod, Leila. 1986. *Veiled Sentiments: Honour and Poetry in a Bedouin Society*. Berkeley: University of California Press.

Ahmed, Leila. 1992. *Women and Gender in Islam: Historical Roots of a Modern Debate*. New Haven: Yale University Press.

Alloula, Malek. 1986. *The Colonial Harem*. Trans. Myrna Godzich and Wlad Godzich. Minneapolis: University of Minnesota Press.

Aswad, Barbara C. 1991. "Yemeni and Lebanese Muslim Immigrant Women in Southeast Dearborn, Michigan." In *Muslim Families in North America*, ed. Earle Waugh, Sharon McIrvin Abu-Laban, and Regula B. Qureshi, 256–281. Edmonton: University of Alberta Press.

Badran, Margot. 1995. *Feminists, Islam and Nation: Gender and the Making of Modern Egypt*. Princeton: Princeton University Press.

Baker, Patricia L. 1997. "Politics of Dress: The Dress Reform Laws of 1920/30s Iran." In *Languages of Dress in the Middle East*, ed. Nancy Lindisfarne-Tapper and Bruce Ingham, 178–192. London: Curzon.

Bamdad, Badr ol-Moluk. 1977. *From Darkness into Light: Women's Emancipation in Iran*. Trans. and ed. F.R.C. Bagley. Smithtown, NY: Exposition Press.

Barnes, Ruth, and Joanne B. Eicher. 1992. *Dress and Gender: Making Meaning in Cultural Contexts*. New York: BERG.

Berkes, Niyazi. 1964. *The Development of Secularism in Turkey*. Montreal: McGill University Press.

Brewer, Jahm, and Roy Porter. 1993. *Consumption and the World of Goods*. London: Routledge.

Cainkar, Louise. 1991. "Palestinian-American Muslim Women: Living on the Margins of Two Worlds." In *Muslim Families in North America*, ed. Earle Waugh, Sharon McIrvin Abu-Laban, and Regula B. Qureshi, 282–308. Edmonton: University of Alberta Press.

Chatty, Dawn. 1996. *Mobile Pastoralists: Development Planning and Social Change*. New York: Columbia University Press.

Crawley, E. 1931. *Dress, Drink and Drums*. London: Methuen and Co.

Dickey, Melissa. 1994. "Images of Muslim Women in Occidental Consciousness: Reality vs. Fiction." Honours thesis, Department of Sociology and Anthropology, Concordia University.

Esposito, John. 1988. *Islam: The Straight Path*. New York: Oxford University Press.

Fandy, Mamoun. 1998. "Political Science without Clothes: The Politics of Dress or Contesting the Spatiality of the State in Egypt." *Arab Studies Quarterly* 20(2):87–104.

Fernea, Elizabeth. 1965. *Guests of the Sheik: An Ethnography of an Iraqi Village*. New York: Anchor Books.

Haddad, Yvonne, ed. 2002. *Muslims in the West: From Sojourners to Citizens*. New York: Oxford University Press.

Hassan, Riffat. 1994. *Selected Articles*. Montpellier, France: Women Living under Muslim Laws.

Hendrickson, Hildi. 1996. *Clothing and Difference: Embodied Identities in Colonial and Post-colonial Africa*. Durham, NC: Duke University Press.

Herald, Jacqueline. 1981. *Renaissance Dress in Italy 1400–1500*. London: Bell and Hyman.

Hewer, Christopher T.R. 1992. "Muslim Teacher Training in Britain." *Muslim Education Quarterly* 9:21–34.

Hoodfar, Homa. 1991. "Return to the Veil: Personal Strategy and Public Participation in Egypt." In *Working Women: International Perspectives on Labour and Gender Ideology*, ed. Nanneke Redclift and M. Thea Sinclair, 104–124. London: Routledge.

_____. 1995. "Situating the Anthropologist: A Personal Account of Ethnographic Fieldwork in Three Urban Settings: Tehran, Cairo, and Montreal." In *Urban Lives: Fragmentation and Resistance*, ed. Vered Amit-Talai and Henri Lustiger Thaler, 206–226. Toronto: McClelland & Stewart.

_____. 2000. "Iranian Women at the Intersection of Citizenship and Family Code: The Perils of 'Islamic Criteria.'" In *Women and Citizenship in the Middle East,* ed. Joseph Suad, 287–313. Syracuse: Syracuse University Press.

_____. (forthcoming). *Everyday Forms of Resistance in Iran*. Montpellier, France: Women Living under Muslim Laws.

Kabbani, Rana. 1986. *Europe's Myths of Orient: Devise and Rule*. Bloomington: Indiana University Press.

Keddie, Nikki, and Beth Baron. 1991. *Women in Middle Eastern History: Shifting Boundaries in Sex and Gender*. New Haven: Yale University Press.

_____, and Lois Beck. 1978. *Women in the Muslim World*. Cambridge: Harvard University Press.

Kelly, Patricia. 1998a. "Muslim Canadians: Immigration Policy and Community Development in the 1991 Census." *Islam and Christian-Muslim Relations* 9(1):83–102.

Lindisfarne-Tapper, Nancy, and Bruce Ingham, eds. 1997. *Languages of Dress in the Middle East*. London: Curzon.

Mabro, Judy. 1991. *Veiled Half-Truths: Western Travellers' Perceptions of Middle Eastern Women*. London: I.B. Tauris & Co.

Meshal, Reem A. 2003. "Banners of Faith and Identities in Construct: The Hijab in Canada." In *The Muslim Veil in North America,* ed. Sajida Sultan Alvi, Homa Hoodfar, and Sheila McDonough, 72–104. Toronto: Women's Press.

Mernissi, Fatima. 1991a. *The Veil and the Male Elite: A Feminist Interpretation of Women's Rights in Islam*. Trans. M.J. Lakeland. Reading, Mass.: Addison-Wesley.

Nader, Laura. 1989. "Orientalism, Occidentalism and the Control of Women." *Cultural Dynamics* 2(3):323–355.

Paidar, Parvin. 1995. *Women and the Political Process in Twentieth-Century Iran*. Cambridge: Cambridge University Press.

Parkington, A. 1992. "Popular Fashion and Working Class Affluence." In *Chic Thrills: A Fashion Reader*, eds. J. Ash and E. Wilson, 145–161. Berkeley: University of California Press.

Payne, Blanche. 1965. *History of Costume: From the Ancient Egyptians to the Twentieth Century*. New York: Harper and Row.

Perrot, Philippe. 1994. *Fashioning the Bourgeoisie: A History of Clothing in the Nineteenth Century*. Trans. Richard Bienvenu. Princeton: Princeton University Press.

Quataert, Donald. 1997. "Clothing Laws, State and Society in the Ottoman Empire, 1720–1829." *International Journal of Middle East Studies* 29(3):403–425.

Rugh, Andrea. 1986. *Reveal and Conceal: Dress in Contemporary Egypt*. Syracuse: Syracuse University Press.

Shahshahani, Soheila. 1995. *A Pictorial History of Iranian Headdresses*. Tehran: Modabber Press.

Sponsler, Clair. 1992. "Narrating the Social Order: Medieval Clothing Laws." *Clio* (Spring):280.

Waardenburg, Jacques. 1988. "The Institutionalization of Islam in the Netherlands, 1961–86." In *The New Islamic Presence in Western Europe*, eds. T. Gerholm and Y.G. Lithman, 8–31. London: Mansell.

Webb, Wilfred Mark. 1912. *The Heritage of Dress*. London: Times Book Club.

Wheatcroft, Andrew. 1993. *The Ottomans: Dissolving Images*. London: Penguin Books.

Wikan, Unni. 1982. *Behind the Veil in Arabia: Women in Oman*. Chicago: University of Chicago Press.

CHAPTER 14

ABORIGINAL SPIRITUALITY AND THE LEGAL CONSTRUCTION OF FREEDOM OF RELIGION

Lori G. Beaman

> I was at my grandfather's house, and he was sitting down, getting his pipe ready early in the morning and here was Father Sialm knocking on the door. They opened the door, and he came in, and he saw my grandfather with the pipe. Father Sialm grabbed the pipe and said "This is the work of the devil!" And he took it and threw it out the door on the ground. My grandfather didn't say a word. He got up and took the priest's prayer book and threw it to the ground. Then they both looked at each other, and nobody said one word that whole time. (Esther, in *Black Elk Lives*, 2000:137)

Religious freedom is a constitutionally protected right in both Canada and the United States.[1] Yet the ideal of freely expressing religious beliefs seems to be more attainable for some groups than for others. As the courts in both countries construct an increasingly narrow view of what constitutes religion worthy of protection, religious minorities such as North America's First Nations[2] peoples are more likely to be excluded from, than included in, First Amendment and Charter of Rights and Freedoms protection. Legislation designed specifically to protect Aboriginal peoples is either "toothless," such as the American Indian Religious Freedom Act,[3] or considered unconstitutional, as was the Religious Freedom Restoration Act. This paper uses some key Supreme Court decisions in both Canada and the United States to explore Aboriginal spirituality and the legal construction of freedom of religion.

In the following pages I argue that Aboriginal spirituality is legally constructed outside of the boundaries of religious freedom.[4] Three explanations for this are examined: First, the religious landscape is dominated by mainstream Christianity, resulting in a narrow interpretation of religion and religious freedom. Second, legal claims are framed in the rhetoric of individual rights that ignores the systemic disadvantages suffered by Aboriginal peoples. In Canada, where group rights and the correcting of systemic disadvantage are constitutionally possible, Aboriginal claims are framed as treaty rights in relation to hunting and fishing, or as rights relating to Aboriginal title, resulting in the minimization or marginalization of issues concerning religious freedom. Finally, the legal construction of Aboriginal spirituality continues the legacy of European colonizers that treats First Nations peoples as an "abnormal" group to be either tolerated or accommodated by the benevolent "normal" majority.

One of the challenges posed by an analysis of Aboriginal spirituality and its place in a constitutional schema that protects religious freedom is grasping just how wide the conceptual gulf is between the world view of the Aboriginal and that of the colonizer.

The difference between the two is significant. As I write this, I am conscious of the limitations of language—"difference" implies "different from," with Native Americans inevitably being constructed as "the other." This is not my intention. A couple of years ago I was doing some reading and work in the area of Aboriginals and the legal construction of property ownership in an effort to find out how Aboriginal peoples thought about property ownership. I read through some obvious sources, but could find nothing dealing specifically with ownership. I eventually realized that for Aboriginals, ownership was tied up in daily life to the extent that its categorization was not part of that cultural experience. I had been trying to use the categories of the colonizer to understand Aboriginal life. I have encountered similar difficulties as I have tried to understand Aboriginal "religion." Like many North Americans, my socialization has imbued in me a sense of religion that is limited to churches, congregations and Sunday attendance. Native spirituality cannot adequately be understood in these terms. Perhaps the most challenging aspect of Native spirituality to grasp is its all-pervasiveness. Certainly a number of religions provide their believers with a world view that is both prescriptive and explanatory or interpretive, but the sacralization of the life-world remains almost the exclusive terrain of Native Americans. Esther Black Elk-DeSersa explains: "Our religious way is a way of life. It's not a church or an organization. It's the way we live and what we believe in our hearts. We never write anything down—no prayers are written down.... That's the way Indians believe—our bible is this whole world. Everything is supposed to be sacred...."[5] Religious practices, then, are a part of social life, and continuing rather than commemorative in nature.[6] In other words, the articulation of the sacred is an ongoing process that emphasizes balance rather than dominance.

Aboriginal spirituality is perhaps better described as Aboriginal spiritualities. As a "lived religion," Aboriginal spiritual practices and beliefs vary from tribe to tribe and across geographic boundaries, reflecting the daily lives of its practitioners.[7] Added to the variety of Native American religious experiences is the influence of the religions of European colonizers, manifested in the tendency of many Native Americans to practise a combination of traditional and Christian religion.

UNDERSTANDING THE RELIGIOUS LANDSCAPE

In order to understand the ways in which the law responds to Native American claims for religious freedom, it is important to consider briefly the religious terrain of North American society. Despite much ado about religious pluralism, there is a Christian hegemony[8] that largely determines the manner and extent to which religious minorities are able to express their beliefs. Reginald Bibby identifies a pervasive religious conservatism in North America demonstrated by the intergenerational transmission of religious traditions, which, in the United States, are most likely to be mainstream Protestantism, or, in Canada, mainstream Protestantism and Roman Catholicism. In other words, the religion of one's parents is likely to be one's own religion, even if one's habits do not reflect traditional measures of religiosity, such as regular church attendance. This in turn translates into particular notions about what constitutes the religious "normal," ideas that are reflected in the legal construction of religion. While

Bibby argues that there is a "general softening of attitudes toward other religious groups"[9] by Canadians, he does acknowledge that tolerance zones and comfort zones may be different. Bibby sums it up this way: "In a nation of close to thirty million people, less than five thousand individuals are identifying with religions including New Age, Scientology, and Theosophy. Such data suggests that Canada has an extremely tight 'religious market' dominated by Catholic and Protestant 'companies.' New entries find the going extremely tough."[10] Although not a "new" entry, Aboriginal spirituality stands outside of the Christian mainstream, and, as such, joins the ranks of minority religious groups whose freedom to express their beliefs is tenuous.

The ways in which academics translate the negotiation of religion in so-called public debate, an area of inquiry generally designated as, simply, "church–state relations," have been centred around two primary positions that are echoed in, or are perhaps echoes of, court decisions relating to religious rights. Briefly, these positions are the "accommodationist" and the "separationist," although scholars such as Ted G. Jelen and Clyde Wilcox introduce more complex versions of the typology.[11] Succinctly and perhaps simplistically, accommodationists argue for the public (or state) accommodation of religion to varying degrees. Separationists believe in the metaphorical wall of separation (between church and state) as the best way to ensure religious freedom. Caught in the crossfire of these two positions are groups like North America's First Nations peoples. What neither "side" acknowledges is that each position fails to protect religions on the margins. A strict separationist stance acknowledges that allowing religion into the public square is likely to reinforce mainstream Christian domination, but frequently fails to grapple with the pervasiveness of the hegemonic force of Protestantism. In other words, some religious minorities have been so marginalized that they may need state protection or support that differs from what is offered to mainstream religion. Accommodationists allow for greater participation of religion in the public square in theory without recognizing that there is a Christian hegemony that silences or muffles all but the strongest voices. Ignoring this is like leaving religious freedom to a "survival of the fittest" mode, in which those religious groups with the most resources survive and thrive.

The main problem that both "sides" either ignore or under-address revolves around the systemic disadvantages faced by religious minorities. This is especially true in the United States, where the liberal rhetoric of individualism overshadows the recognition of disadvantages faced by groups. That rhetoric is a powerful foundational element of U.S. Establishment Clause jurisprudence that "views groups as mere aggregations of individual thinkers—aggregations that are formed primarily to advance and balance the interests of the individual members."[12] "Special" treatment for disadvantaged groups such as Native Americans is thus rejected as running counter to a belief that individuals should be treated equally, with "equally" being defined very narrowly.

In Canada, the separationist-accommodationist typology and its analysis is not particularly helpful. There is no constitutional separation of church and state, and therefore the separationist-accommodationist dichotomy has little explanatory or analytical value. Yet the process of legal marginalization of minority religious groups in Canada is similar to what happens in the United States, and the result would appear to be very similar as well. Native Americans on both sides of the border (a border which, incidentally, has little meaning to them) are legally constructed as the "other."

CASE STUDIES

Case law represents an important public forum in which discussions about the boundaries of rights and freedoms take place. This does not mean that case law is the only locus of negotiation for these freedoms (indeed, only a small portion of cases are heard at the Supreme Court level). In this section I will consider a few recent and important decisions that are representative of the manner in which the courts have considered Aboriginal claims to religious freedom. In the United States, perhaps the most important Supreme Court decision on Aboriginal free exercise is *Employment Division* v. *Smith*, in which the Supreme Court rejected free-exercise claims of two drug rehabilitation organization employees who had ingested peyote for sacramental purposes. The two were subsequently denied state unemployment compensation because they had been dismissed "with cause." By stating that the respondents were seeking to place themselves beyond the reach of the criminal law, the Court framed the issue so as to raise the "special treatment" alarm that the pervasive liberal rhetoric of U.S. civil society so adamantly opposes. Oddly, in its opinion, the Court uses the very diversity of the U.S. religious landscape to justify sameness of treatment:

> "Precisely because we are a cosmopolitan nation made up of people of almost every conceivable religious preference," *Braunfeld* v. *Brown*, and precisely because we value and protect that religious divergence, we cannot afford the luxury of deeming presumptively invalid, as applied to the religious objector, every regulation of conduct that does not protect an interest of the highest order.[13]

Yet what the Court does not acknowledge is that by framing as "exemptions" or "special treatment" the legal claims of religious minorities to exercise their basic right of religious freedom, the Court makes it more likely that religious groups will be denied protection for their religious beliefs and practices. The *Smith* decision is viewed by many as a blow to free exercise across the board, its implications extending beyond Native Americans to any minority religious group whose beliefs (and practices) collide with those of the mainstream religion as it is protected by the state.[14] Such constitutional battles represent very dramatic and public constructions of Aboriginal religious freedom.

A more insidious surveillance and limiting of Aboriginal religious practices occurs at the administrative level, as illustrated by the decision in *United States* v. *Hugs*.[15] In that case, the ninth circuit court of appeals upheld the conviction of two Crow Indian Tribe members for violation of the Bald and Golden Eagle Protection Act. Eagles and eagle parts are an important part of most religious ceremonies for Native Americans. While there is an elaborate system of permissions and a central warehouse of eagle parts (the National Eagle Repository), the very fact of having to request permission to practise their religion "and subsequently having FWS (United States Fish and Wildlife Service) investigate the request to determine if the reported religious ceremony is legitimate, the inefficiency and delay of BGEPA permit process impose a formidable burden on Native American Religious practice."[16] Such intensive state monitoring of the religious activities of a particular group is troubling, as is the subjecting of their ability to worship to "administrative whim."[17] A similar "administrative" type of limitation is illustrated by *Bowen v. Roy*, in which the United States Supreme Court stated, "the Free Exercise Clause simply cannot be understood to require the Government to conduct its own internal affairs in ways that comport with the religious beliefs of particular citizens."[18] In that case, a Native-American father objected to the assigning of a social security number to his daughter.

The other significant body of cases related to Native Americans is those dealing with land claims and the protection of sacred space. Native American claims dealing with sacred space have consistently been minimized in the interests of compelling state interests. Unfortunately, those cases too have resulted in a diminished interpretation of freedom of religion. In the 1988 case of *Lyng v. Northwest Indian Cemetery Protective Association*, the Supreme Court rejected a claim by several tribes that would have halted the construction of a highway through sacred burial grounds. The Court defined the Free Exercise Clause as only prohibiting governmental actions coercing a moral choice. Thus, by characterizing the issue in this way, the Court was able to ignore the devastating effect of land development on sacred spaces of Aboriginal peoples. George Linge summarizes the situation this way: "By flooding a valley, or a canyon, for example, or by building a road through a high alpine area, the government has made it impossible in practice for Indians to exercise their religion."[19]

These cases represent a significant source of tension: whereas debate over the performing of various sacraments or rituals may continue between the dominant religious community and various minority communities, it is the difference over the meaning of land that presents the most perplexing dilemmas in the confrontation between Native American religious communities and the dominant culture.[20] The profound differences between colonizer and Native American understandings of land, and humans' relationship to it, are impossible to overstate, and result in the desecration of sacred Aboriginal sites for the convenience of the colonizer.

In Canada, there has been a plethora of cases involving Aboriginal rights, particularly since 1982 when the Canadian Charter of Rights and Freedoms came into force. However, only two of these post-Charter cases have focused explicitly on either religion or Aboriginal spirituality. In a 1985 decision, *R. v. Jack*, the appellants, two Coast Salish Indians living in British Columbia, were convicted of hunting out of season in contravention of the Wildlife Act. Elizabeth Jack needed deer meat for a burning ceremony for her great-grandfather. Her husband and her brother shot a deer not on an Indian reserve, cleaned it and then were apprehended with the carcass in their trunk. There was no dispute over the facts—the trial judge granted them an absolute discharge. Both members of the band and an "expert" anthropologist gave evidence about the ceremony. The sincerity of the religious beliefs of the accused was not challenged. At the time of the offence the Charter had not been enacted, the Canadian Bill of Rights was not pleaded; and the legal basis of the defendants was somewhat unclear, but amounted to an invocation of religious freedom as a fundamental principle of law. The

Court was able to uphold the conviction by separating the killing of the deer from the ritual itself:

> There was some evidence that the type of food to be burned was of significance and that raw deer meat was required in this case but no evidence as to the circumstances or methods of obtaining it, except by theft, which would render the meat unsuitable. There was no evidence that the use of defrosted raw deer meat was sacrilegious as is alleged in the appellants' factum.

The Court continues on in its reasoning, stating,

> If he had shot two deer on the same spot, in the same manner, at the same time, one deer for a burning and one for food, there is no indication that any one of them was more suitable for one purpose than the other.

The Court effectively distills the ritual into bits and privileges the "expert" evidence that the killing of a deer was not part of the essence of the sacred ceremony. Tradition surely did not include the use of meat that had been stored in a deep-freeze, but because the tradition is not articulated in that way, but merely practised that way, the killing of the deer, in the Court's view, has no legal justification.

A later case, R. v. Sioui, involves members of a Huron band of Aboriginals who cut down trees, camped and built fires as part of their customs and rituals. The rituals were carried out within the boundaries of a provincial park. The Supreme Court of Canada overturned their conviction, finding that the activities were protected by a 1760 treaty, and that the "activities with which the respondents are charged do not seriously compromise the Crown's objectives in occupying the park." Interestingly, despite the religious or spiritual emphasis of the activities, the actions of the group are seen to be protected by treaty, rather than under the s.2(a) protection of religious freedom under the Charter of Rights and Freedoms. While treaty rights are an important part of the preservation of Aboriginal culture, the minimization of religious freedom ignores the centrality of spiritual meaning in Aboriginal life, especially as it relates to place. The recognition of Aboriginal spirituality as falling within the parameters of s.2(a) protection is important, but thus far the Supreme Court of Canada has been able to avoid addressing it directly.

In Canada there has been a tendency to characterize issues concerning First Nations activities in two ways—either as treaty rights related to hunting and fishing or as issues related to Aboriginal title. Freedom of religion or spirituality is less likely to be cited as a basis for claims. Thus cases include questions of religion or spirituality, but the legal issues are often not framed in terms of the Charter protection of religious freedom. For example, in Dick v. The Queen (an illegal hunting case) the Court states: "They [the Indian band] described their lives and the significance of the rituals of food gathering,"[21] raising the question of "whether there are activities that Indians undertake as Indians that fall within a central core of Indianness that cannot be touched by provincial legislation."[22] Both of these statements touch on spirituality but do not directly acknowledge its central role in either the case or the daily lives of First Nations peoples. Instead, the case is framed in terms of hunting and fishing rights. Similarly, in *Delgamuukw*,[23] the Supreme Court acknowledges the spiritual connection between the Wet'suwet'en people and their land as evidenced through a collection of sacred oral tradition or stories. Again there is discussion of a core of "Indianness." Yet the case is framed around establishing the existence of Aboriginal title. The result of this tendency to characterize issues outside of a religious freedom framework is a desacralizing of Aboriginal life such that spirituality becomes an ancillary issue, reflecting a common perception of North American society that relegates spirituality and religion to the "private" realm. It also commodifies Aboriginal expressions of spirituality by quantifying the amount and value of fish, wildlife and property involved in the various rituals and practices.

In both Canada and the United States, the courts isolate Native Americans as an "exception," to be accommodated according to the interests of the state. In *Smith*, the "war on drugs" is the dominant narrative; in *Sioui*, the state interests in preserving a park for "common" use is the measure of accommodation; in *Lyng*, highway construction is given priority over a sacred burial site. In none of these cases is there recognition of Aboriginal spirituality as an important freedom or right to be protected in a manner consistent with the constitutions of the United States and Canada, both of which suggest that religious freedom is every citizen's entitlement.

DISCUSSION: THE LEGAL CONSTRUCTION OF RELIGIOUS BOUNDARIES

Why are the boundaries around what counts as religion and what is protected as religious freedom so rigid? There are three explanations I would like to explore. First, there is an underlying Protestantism in the United States, and an underlying Protestantism/Roman Catholicism in Canada, that dominates conceptualizations of religion. Religious beliefs, religious organizations and religious practices are framed according to Christian standards. For example, as a result of what B.C. Gordon-McCutchan describes as an "edifice complex,"[24] it is often difficult for those who do not share the Aboriginal life experience to understand the notion of sacred space.[25] Christians think of sacred space primarily in terms of buildings; Aboriginals do not.[26] Further, as Echo-Hawk argues, "It is undoubtedly difficult for a culture with an inherent fear of 'wilderness' and a fundamental belief in the 'religious domination' of humans over animals to envision that certain aspects of nature can be sacred."[27]

Within the problem of Christian hegemony there are important subtexts. What is the relationship between law and First Nations peoples? How does the law support Christian hegemony? As we have seen in the brief discussion of case law above, the law sets narrow boundaries around the interpretation of religious freedom when considering Aboriginal religious practices. A second subtext is the relationship between mainstream churches and marginalized groups. This is complex and nuanced, and frequently varies from denomination to denomination. On occasion, seemingly divergent religious groups become collaborators in their mutual pursuit of the preservation of freedom of religion. For example, in *Adler*, Jewish and fundamentalist Christian parents joined together to argue for state financial support for denominational schools. In the battle for Blue Lake, a sacred space for Taos Indians, the National Council of Churches advocated publicly on behalf of the Indians.[28]

A second difficulty in expanding the boundaries of religious definition may relate to the framework within which claims are made in North American society. Rhys Williams and Timothy Kubal identify three rhetorics that are successfully used by groups in making social-legal rights claims. Covenant rhetoric is based on the notion of society as a moral community in a relationship with a higher authority, in which individuals owe a duty to the collective. Even though this model includes a language of collectivity, ultimately it is the individual who must act, and be acted upon. Stewardship rhetoric involves a collective duty towards preservation for the future. It has roots in both the Judeo-Christian tradition, in which humans are expected to act in the best interests of creation, and in environmental movements—particularly, as Williams and Kubal note, deep ecology. Contractual rhetoric focuses on the social contract that is tied to notions of justice and rights, and protects individuals from infringement by the community (see Holland, 1992 for a full discussion of contractual approaches to religious liberty). The social contract allows the individual to have maximum freedom to act according to his or her desires. As Williams and Kubal point out, none of these models involves a language of collective rights. Claims based on collective rights have met with little support in the United States.[29]

Rhys H. Williams and Timothy J. Kubal, in fact, use the example of claims made by Native Americans and the relative hostility with which they are received. They point out that the basis on which Native American claims are denied is usually articulated in contract-based language: "Protesters state that recognizing collective rights violates the equality before the law that is guaranteed to individuals."[30] Certainly, claims to sacred space are articulated in collective terms. Thus Native Americans are doubly disadvantaged in these claims: the space they identify as sacred does not resonate with the religious views of the Christian mainstream, and the manner in which their claims are articulated fall outside of the acceptable framework for rights claims in the United States.

A third limitation to the permeation of boundaries is the colonizing discourse that pervades any negotiation of space, in its broadest possible sense, between First Nations peoples and the colonizers. Shelagh Day and Gwen Brodsky make an argument about the framing of religious rights in the context of accommodation and undue hardship relating to employment law as it has developed in Canada through Supreme Court case law.[31] They argue that inherent in the employer's duty to accommodate—the employee is the dichotomy of "sameness/difference," with the implicit understanding that "different" means "inferior." Such a position reinforces the power differential between religious minorities and the majority. In this model, the benevolent majority permits the religious freedom of the minority as long as it does not cost too much. Employment cases are often framed as individual claims, and thus minority accommodation is unlikely to cost much. But Native American claims are frequently group claims that are perceived to infringe upon the economic interests of the majority. If religious freedom continues to be framed as a privilege to be accommodated, then minority religious groups will continue to be legally marginalized.

In his discussion of Aboriginal spirituality in Canadian prisons, James Waldram also notes this tendency to accord formal equality by referencing mainstream religion as the norm against which Aboriginal spirituality is measured:

> Conceptually, equating Aboriginal spirituality with Christian faiths is Eurocentric. It implies that these faiths are the standard to which Aboriginal spirituality, and presumably any other non-Christian religion, is to be compared. Such an approach, in addition to being culturally and morally repugnant, necessarily limits the availability of the Aboriginal services to those that have Christian parallels. Hence "equality" is, in effect, inequality.[32]

Christianity thus remains the constitutionally referenced baseline or "normal" against which other religions or spiritual practices are referenced.

A corollary to the problem of colonizing discourse is the distinct world views of each group. To reiterate the point made at the beginning of this essay, the ways in which Native Americans see their world are often quite different from the lenses used by the colonizers. Inevitably, though, the colonizing discourse is privileged, following the blueprint established by Columbus when he wrote in 1492 about Native inhabitants:

> They ought to be good servants and of good intelligence ... I believe that they would easily be made Christians because it seemed to me that they had no religion. Our Lord pleasing, I will carry off six of them at my departure to Your Highnesses, in order that they may learn to speak.[33]

Colonziers carried out this "enlightenment" project in a number of ways, not least of which was the establishment of residential schools that saw the destruction of much of First Nations culture in the name of Christian charity, whose leaders are described by James Sakej Youngblood Henderson as "cultural serial killers."[34] Native spirituality was recognized early on as the source of Aboriginal strength, and thus colonizers set out to destroy it.[35]

Jo-Anne Fiske explores the intersection of colonizing discourses and patriarchal constructions of the "good woman" in her discussion of the ways in which the Aboriginal girl was portrayed as the "untamed savage" to be normalized according to European standards through the residential school. Fiske contrasts this with the virgin nun, who was entrusted with the colonizing project of the transformation of the Aboriginal girl: "The notions of extreme virtue invested in the virgin female placed her beyond the male gaze and therefore outside of secular scrutiny, giving school staff unquestioned dominion over the children."[36] Dominion included destruction of language and any spiritual expressions outside of Christianity. We know that European cultural nihilism extended to Aboriginal boys, men and women as well, but Fiske's work is a powerful statement about the brutality of the attempted destruction of Aboriginal culture, which involved a collaborative effort by church and state.

Walter Echo-Hawk argues that separation of church and state seems to have been ignored in the state treatment of Aboriginals. "The government placed entire reservations and Indian nations under the administrative control of different denominations to convert the Indians and separate them from their traditions."[37] The collusion of religion and government in the attempted destruction of Aboriginal culture reveals the existence of a Christian hegemony that is embedded in U.S. civil society. In Canada, a similar collaboration occurred, but its significance is altered by the lack of constitutional separation of church and state. State support for Christian initiatives to "tame" the "savages" are a striking example of the predominance of a Christian hegemony that is perhaps less blatant today, but still pervasive. In both Canada and the United States, the courts have failed to give a meaningful interpretation to freedom of religion cases involving First Nations peoples, thus continuing the colonization project. Allison Dussais argues that this continuation is no accident, but is, in fact, simply a reiteration of old attitudes in present-day form.[38]

CONCLUSION

The point of the constitutional protection of religious freedom is to prevent privileging one group's religious beliefs and practices over another. And yet the practical working out of these protections reveals a systemic discrimination against religious groups outside of the Christian mainstream. In the case of the First Nations peoples of North America, the marginalization of religious freedom is part of a larger colonizing project that sought to destroy a culture. Case law would suggest that there are boundaries beyond which rights language will not offer protection to First Nations peoples. This does not mean that First Amendment protections of the United States Constitution or the s.2(a) protections of the Canadian Charter of Rights and Freedoms cannot offer protection. But thus far the range of interpretation of religious freedom has remained primarily within the dominant Christian narrative of European colonizers. It is therefore of the utmost importance that the claims of religious freedom by First Nations peoples be taken very seriously, and their denial be rare rather than commonplace. The role of Aboriginal spirituality is linked to the preservation of a culture—it "protects an ecology, a unique cognitive space, an endangered linguistic consciousness and a way of life."[39]

While Native Americans have suffered devastating blows to their culture at the hands of European colonizers and their descendants, it is important to recognize them as agents while acknowledging their victimization. To paraphrase Michel Foucault, such power relations contain the seeds of resistance.[40] Christian hegemony must be viewed in the context of conflict, struggle and resistance, a process that continues today among North American First Nations peoples through the use of law, and sometimes through acts of defiance.[41] It is through these resistances that Aboriginal spirituality has persisted. Hopefully, like Black Elk, in throwing the prayer book on the ground, Aboriginals will continue to resist until the constitutional protection of freedom of religion is offered in a meaningful way.

NOTES

1 In the United States, the First Amendment of the Constitution prohibits the government from making any law "respecting an establishment of religion" or from interfering with the "free exercise" of religion. In Canada, section 2(a) of the Charter of Rights and Freedoms guarantees Canadians "freedom of religion."

2 I use multiple terms interchangeably in this essay to reflect the differences between the language used in the United States and Canada, and the terms used by Aboriginals in writing and speaking about themselves. First Nations is a term that is used in Canada, and not, it would seem in the United States. As to who is considered to be First Nations, this is very much contested terrain. Government definitions at one time excluded women who married "non-Native" men from receiving benefits under the Indian Act. In addition, the Metis have had to fight for recognition by the state. In short, these boundaries are constantly shifting, depending upon the results of power struggles for recognition. Amongst First Nations themselves, again, definitions as to who is "really" Aboriginal vary and change, depending upon the context. For a discussion of the legal parameters and implications of these terms, see Thomas Isaac, "The Power of Constitutional Language: The Case against Using 'Aboriginal Peoples' as a Referent for First Nations," *Queens Law Journal* 19(2)(1993):415.

3 See Eric Mazur, *The Americanization of Religious Minorities Confronting the Constitutional Order* (Baltimore, MD: The Johns Hopkins University Press, 1999), 108, for a discussion of the effectiveness of the American Indian Religious Freedom Act. See also Patricia Byrnes, "Freedom of Whose Religion?" *Wilderness* 58(1994): 27; Steve Talbot, "Desecration and American Indian Religious Freedom," *Journal of Ethnic Studies* 12(1985):1–18.

4 The exclusivist approach by law in relation to Aboriginal spirituality is accomplished in a number of ways, as will become evident in the following pages. By specifically (quasi-) criminalizing activities such as hunting out of season, the law effectively prohibits some Aboriginal rituals. In other cases, the law monitors and controls such activities (see the discussion of the use

of eagle parts later in this essay). Such criminalization has an historical context that is outside of the parameters of this essay, but includes, for example, the prohibition of the Sundance. Aboriginal spirituality is far enough removed from mainstream concepts of religion that it is also simply not covered by law. The all-encompassing nature of Aboriginal spirituality is a major challenge to the dominant view of religion. Finally, Aboriginal spirituality is pushed outside of the boundaries of legal protection when "more important" social needs are identified, such as highways or the need to control illicit drugs. This point is also developed later in this essay.

5 Hilda Neihardt and Lori Ulect, *Black Elk Lives* (Lincoln, NB: University of Nebraska Press, 2000), 92.

6 Talbot, "Desecration and American Indian Religious Freedom," 2.

7 For a collection that illustrates the diversity of Native American spiritualities, see Lawrence E, Sullivan, ed., *Native Religions and Cultures of North America: Anthropology of the Sacred* (New York: Continuum, 2000).

8 For more detailed discussions of "mainstream Protestant culture," see Philip E. Hammond, *With Liberty for All: Freedom of Religion in the United States* (Louisville, KY: Westminster John Knox Press, 1998), and Mazur, *The Americanization of Religious Minorities*. For a compelling discussion of the minimization of discrimination against religious minorities as "incidental," see H.N. Hirsch, "Let Them Eat Incidentals: RFRA, the Rehnquist Court, and Freedom of Religion," in *Obligations of Citizenship and Demands of Faith: Religious Accommodation in Pluralist Democracies*, ed. Nancy L. Rosenblum (Princeton, NJ: Princeton University Press, 2000), 285, who states the problem simply: "America is a deeply and overwhelmingly Protestant country."

9 Reginald Bibby, "On Boundaries, Gates, and Circulating Saints: A Longitudinal Look at Loyalty and Loss," *Review of Religious Research* 41 (1999):160.

10 Reginald Bibby, "Canada's Mythical Religious Mosaic: Some Census Findings," *Journal for the Scientific Study of Religion* 39(2000):237.

11 Ted G. Jelen and Clyde Wilcox, "Conscientious Objectors in the Culture War?: A Typology of Attitudes toward Church–State Relations," *Sociology of Religion* 58(1997):277–287.

12 Robert A. Holland, "A Theory of Establishment Clause Adjudication: Individualism, Social Contract, and the Significance of Coercion in Identifying Threats to Religious Liberty," *California Law Review* 80(1992):1632.

13 *Employment Division of Oregon v. Smith*, 485 U.S. 660(1990) at 888.

14 See James D. Gordon, III, "Free Exercise on the Mountaintop," *California Law Review* 79(1991): 91–116; Mazur, *The Americanization of Religious Minorities*.

15 *United States v. Hugs*, 109 F 3d 1375 (9th Cir 1997).

16 Matthew Perkins, "The Federal Indian Trust Doctrine and the Bald and Golden Eagle Protection Act: Could Application of the Doctrine Alter the Outcome in *U.S. v. Hugs*?" *Environmental Law* 30(2000):4.

17 Walter R. Echo-Hawk, "Native American Religious Liberty: Five Hundred Years after Columbus," *American Indian Culture and Research Journal* 17 (1993):44.

18 *Bowen v. Roy*, 476 U.S. 693(1986).

19 George Linge, "Ensuring the Full Freedom of Religion on Public Lands: Devils Tower and the Protection of Indian Sacred Sites," *Environmental Affairs Law Review* 27(2000):315.

20 Mazur, *The Americanization of Religious Minorities*, 112.

21 *Dick v. The Queen*, 1985 2 SCR 309, 43.

22 *Ibid.*, 45.

23 *Delgamuukw*, [1997] 3SRC 1010.

24 R.C. Gordon-McCutchan, "The Battle for Blue Lake: A Struggle for Indian Religious Rights," *Journal of Church and State* (Autumn 1991):785–797.

25 See also Mark S. Cohen, "American Indian Sacred Religious Sites and Government Development: A Conventional Analysis in an Unconventional Setting," *Michigan Law Review* 85(1987):771–808; Joshua D. Rievman, "Judicial Scrutiny of Native American Free Exercise Rights: *Lyng* and the Decline of the *Yoder* Doctrine," *Boston College Environmental Affairs Law Review* 17(1989):169–199.

26 One of the anonymous reviewers of this essay pointed out that Christianity "claims more sacred-

ness than just buildings—it focuses on a whole way of life." Admittedly, the boundaries are not always as clear as I have portrayed them here; however, many Christians do associate sacred space primarily with the church building.

27 Echo-Hawk, "Native American Religious Liberty: Five Hundred Years after Columbus," 41.

28 Gordon-McCutchan, "The Battle for Blue Lake: A Struggle for Indian Religious Rights."

29 Williams's argument may have much less weight in Canada, which has constitutionally enshrined the notion of collective rights in the Charter of Rights and Freedoms.

30 Rhys H. Williams and Timothy J. Kubal, "Movement Frames and the Cultural Environment: Resonance, Failure, and the Boundaries of the Legitimate," in *Research in Social Movements, Conflicts and Change* 21(1999):241.

31 Shelagh Day and Gwen Brodsky, "The Duty to Accommodate: Who Will Benefit?" *The Canadian Bar Review* 75(1996):433–473.

32 James Waldram, *The Way of the Pipe: Aboriginal Spirituality and Symbolic Healing in Canadian Prisons* (Peterborough, ON: Broadview Press, 1997), 17.

33 Echo-Hawk, "Native American Religious Liberty: Five Hundred Years after Columbus," 33.

34 James Sakej Youngblood Henderson, "The Struggle to Preserve Aboriginal Spiritual Teachings and Practices," in *Religious Conscience, the State, and the Law: Historical Contexts and Contemporary Significance*, eds. John McLaren and Harold Coward (Albany, NY: SUNY Press, 1999), 180.

35 Monique Fordham, "Within the Iron Houses: The Struggle for Native American Religious Freedom in American Prisons," *Social Justice* 20(1993):165; Waldram, *The Way of the Pipe: Aboriginal Spirituality and Symbolic Healing In Canadian Prisons*.

36 Jo-Anne Fiske, "Ordered Lives and Disordered Souls: Pathologizing Female Bodies of the Colonial Frontier," in *New Perspectives on Deviance: The Construction of Deviance in Everyday Life*, ed. Lori G. Beaman (Scarborough, ON: Prentice Hall Allyn and Bacon, 2000), 238.

37 Echo-Hawk, "Native American Religious Liberty: Five Hundred Years after Columbus," 35.

38 Dussais, "Ghost Dance and Holy Ghost."

39 Henderson, "The Struggle to Preserve Aboriginal Spiritual Teachings and Practices," 169.

40 Michel Foucault, *Discipline and Punish: The Birth of the Prison* (New York: Pantheon, 1977).

41 See Rebecca Kugal, "Religion Mixed with Politics: The 1836 Conversion of Mang'osid of Fond du Lac," *Ethnohistory* 37(1990):126, who documents the case of Mang'osid, a Minnesota Ojibwa leader who converted to Christianity as a political strategy.

CHAPTER 15

AT THE INTERSECTION OF ECOFEMINISM AND RELIGION:

DIRECTIONS FOR CONSIDERATION

Heather Eaton

INTRODUCTION

Ecological feminism has developed from many directions and locations, and with differentiated links between feminism and ecology and between women and nature. Religious discourses are taking ecofeminist analyses into their folds. As a whole, however, religious ecofeminist perspectives are uneven. In this article, I suggest seven hermeneutics that might strengthen religious ecofeminist discourses as well as develop connections among the various viewpoints towards larger horizons, and specifically ones that link theory with concrete and material life-conditions.

What is the state of the question of the intersection of ecology, feminism and religion? How can we continue to develop the mutual insights such that this intersection can bear more "traffic," moving in a favourable direction? For the purposes of this article, the guiding question is: "What hermeneutics will assist in the development of adequate ecofeminist religious conversations that are sufficiently comprehensive to be of genuine transformative value?"

Although I work within the complex ecological, political, racial and social landscape which is Canada, I do not pretend to speak for "the Canadian context." I also do not purport to speak about Canadian ecofeminist theology(ies), as such a discourse does not exist in any organized manner. There are feminist academics and activists who work on ecological issues, theologians who address feminism and/or ecology (albeit very few who connect the two) and there are myriad women's groups and movements that seek to create links among women, spirit and earth. It is only recently that these have begun to work together.

Over the years I have tracked the emergence of "ecofeminism," a term that shelters hosts of differentiated links between feminism and ecology, and between women and nature. I have studied these as they have arisen in different parts of the world and in diverse social locations. Ecofeminism has come gradually to mean an assortment of ecological and feminist concerns, approaches, political goals and orientations, best understood by way of its genealogy.[1] Thus, it is evident that I am able to speak only from a partial and limited awareness of both the vastness of what ideas, ideals and analyses have entered the ecofeminist intersection, as well as of the countless material transformations that are concretizing the discourse.

As ecofeminism developed and seeped into religious awareness, I observed several general hermeneutics emerging within the ecofeminist religious efforts. I surmised that, viewed as a whole, they might be helpful in strengthening the religious ecofeminist discourses in general, and, in specific ways, in creating connections among the various voices claiming an ecofeminist perspective.[2] Listed, these are:

1. an in-depth awareness of the logic of domination; the interlocking patterns of oppressions and the critical theories of liberation informing ecofeminist theory(ies);
2. a recognition of the multi and interdisciplinary character, indeed of the breadth and depth of ecofeminist analyses, and of the need to collaborate to gain new insights;
3. critical appraisals of the destructive and liberating elements within religious traditions, especially with respect to the oppressed and the earth;
4. an appreciation of the exchange between science and religion, and the need for religions, and specifically Christianity, to take evolution seriously;
5. a rigorous understanding of the extent of the ecological crisis;
6. openness to the insights of the myriad religious traditions, especially those that have developed a high degree of sensitivity to the natural world, and a willingness to be transformed by the dialogue;
7. commitment to politically relevant and engaged work in tandem with an awareness of the strained material realities of women of the South, and the need for religious voices to be active within the political and governmental arenas.

In what follows I will discuss each of these hermeneutics, affirming the transformative potential of ecofeminist theologies, noting certain limitations, and proposing future directions. The main thrust is to orient ecofeminist theology to larger horizons of reflection and critical analysis, with a specific view to forging strong links between theory and praxis in ecofeminist religious—predominantly Christian—discussions. The critical relationship between theory and practice is a central preoccupation of feminist and liberation theories—meaning, a commitment to concrete changes in a situation that will contribute to liberation at all levels of experience.[3] This requires a consciousness of the highly mediated dialectic of and dynamic interplay between theory and praxis. It is this dialectic that requires attention in the intersection of ecofeminism and religion. The larger goal of this conversation is to situate ecofeminist theologies within a notion of a practical theory of liberation. This implies a practical property to, and an awareness of the political dimensions of, theory. If ecofeminist religious theories hold transformative value, then these hermeneutics offer possible directions for future consideration.

1. An In-Depth Awareness of the Logic and Practices of Domination; The Interlocking Patterns of Oppressions and the Critical Theories of Liberation Informing Ecofeminist Theory(ies)

Ecofeminist philosophers have reflected extensively on the theoretical substructure of the patterns of domination that are characteristic of Euro-Western societies. This matrix of domination and oppression has identifiable roots in anthropocentrism, androcentrism, misogyny, hierarchy, naturism[4] and even in the emergence of organized agriculture.[5] These are linked theoretically through conceptual frameworks characterized by hierarchical dualisms, that propagate an ideological and material logic of domination.[6] Ecofeminists claim that race, class, gender, sexual orientation, colonialism and ecological exploitation are mutually sustaining patterns.

More specifically, the predominant ecotheology issue within Christianity is usually the extreme anthropocentrism that has permeated not only the teachings but the religious imagination and religious experiences. Ecofeminist theologians detect and critique both the andro- and anthropocentrism of the Christian traditions. However, do ecofeminist theologians attend sufficiently to the above-mentioned pervasive nature of domination? Is there a connection made between the analysis of domination and theories of liberation?

Liberation theologies are one method of orienting theology to the issues of the world: one interpretation of Christianity that brings the ethical core to the centre of theology. The hallmark of liberation theologies is a dedication to reality, and reality is concrete and historically bound.[7] Social ethicist Beverly Harrison says that an analysis is theological only if it attends to the concrete and interconnected webs of social relations.[8] Liberation theologies are a challenge to other theological methods, and one that needs to be used if ecofeminism is to be transformative. Dorothee Sölle sends a clear warning to theologians in her delineations among neo-conservative civic religion, helpless liberalism and a theology of liberation. Only the latter, radical liberation theologies, are not in complicity with the systems of domination.[9] Only liberation theologies can claim to be politically transformative and liberative, especially for those most oppressed, and only if they stay connected to the everyday world. "Everyday violence is common rather than rare. It is the violence that is intertwined with, and therefore configures, people's everyday lives of public or private work, sustenance, recreation, and intimate relations."[10]

The blatant, subtle and elusive forms of violence experienced by women are a familiar feminist topic, in terms of experiences, structural forms and theoretical underpinnings. There are insights from feminists who reflect why and how the "everyday world is problematic," and how unexamined divisions exist between the "everyday world" and the abstracted and academic reflection on this same world. The work of Canadian sociologist Dorothy Smith, influenced by numerous streams of thought in addition to Marx, Mannheim and feminist critical theory, carefully exposes how even radical liberation analysis can be disconnected from the everyday world. It can indirectly support what she calls "the relations of the ruling apparatus."[11] It is the ongoing work of critical theorists that offers assistance in developing an acute awareness of the relations between theory and praxis.[12] The challenge to those connecting ecofeminism and religion is threefold: to be cognizant of the logic and issues of domination; to reflect within a liberationist methodology; and to remain connected to the problematic of the everyday world.

2. A Recognition of the Multi- and Interdisciplinary Character, Indeed of the Breadth and Depth, of Ecofeminist Analyses, and of the Need to Collaborate to Gain New Insights

Although it is difficult to be fully aware of the breadth of ecofeminism, to speak for ecofeminist perspectives one needs to be aware, in general, of the variations encompassed by the term. The reality is that ecofeminism is many things and has many origins. One difficulty for academics is that ecofeminism is not theoretically consistent. For some this means that it is hopelessly contradictory and they abandon the term.

From the 1960s to the present, ecofeminist connections were arising out of the environmental and feminist movements as well as from anti-militarist, peace, anti-nuclear and anti-racist initiatives. Women were working in areas such as toxic waste, health, media, art, urban ecology, theater, energy, political transformation and spirituality. These activist groups, academics and socially engaged citizens formed the base from which, over time, ecofeminist perspectives emerged into the international arena. Academics began writing about ecofeminism from many disciplines (philosophy, sociology, science, anthropology, economics, et cetera), and from different parts of the world. From religious perspectives, women from Christian, Jewish, Goddess, Wiccan, Buddhist, Indigenous and womanist traditions were claiming the term.[13] They were studying how human/women-nature relations have been understood, excavating resources from their traditions, and creating alternative interpretations. Approaches and issues were plural.

Ecofeminism spans a wide genre of styles. There are collections that are uneven with respect to sources, parameters of discussion, or cultural, historical or political issues. A price has been paid in the loss of clarity and precision, generalizations and uneasy alliances. Ecofeminism continues to be haunted due to the combination of ecofeminism, essentialism and religion (usually Goddess), or spirituality (multiform). One ongoing problem is the amount of commentary on, and in particular critiques of, ecofeminism, with an obvious disregard for the actual discourse. The number of authors who associate ecofeminism with an essentialist connection between women and nature, either lauding or denouncing it, is irksome to the vast majority of ecofeminists who reject essentialism.[14] But ecofeminism is not situated only in academia, and the differentiations are central to its ethos. It is worth considering whether the internal ecofeminist debates reflect more a desire for ideological purity than the need for auto-critiques. It may also be helpful to remember that there has never been an idea or intellectual position that has not changed through history, and that does not appear in many forms.[15]

It is important to be cognizant of *ecofeminism* as an umbrella term, an analysis, a symbol for a change of consciousness, or a vision or insight into alternative ways of understanding, organizing and relating to the world. It can be context specific. One could say that ecofeminism is experienced, interpreted and appropriated in different ways depending upon the social situation. Ecofeminists reflecting from religious perspectives need to enlarge their horizon of understanding of the expanse of ecofeminism in order to adequately bring an ecofeminist critique into their tradition. In addition, most of ecofeminist discourses are developing outside of religious conversations. Therefore, it is necessary to be aware of the general lines of development in ecofeminist theory and praxis.

3. Critical Appraisals of the Destructive and Liberating Elements within the Religious Traditions, Especially with Respect to the Oppressed and the Earth

It is essential to be candid and conscientious about the negative legacies of religious heritages. Although it is too simplistic to capitulate to Lynn White's denunciation of Christianity, it is also naive to simply "green" Christianity without coming to terms with the legacy of Christian cultures and their predatory praxis towards nature. It is, in part, this critical appraisal of the past that creates a necessary hermeneutic of suspicion of proposals made for the future. How is this best accomplished? Three options will be discussed.

First, there is a need to examine the effects of Christianity on cultures and their ecological integrity as it has traversed the world. Is there an ecological pattern to the inculturation of Christianity? How have the pre-existing ecological practices been absorbed?

The second is by way of Dorothee Sölle, who insists that we develop and clarify "again and again" the distinction between the oppressive and liberating elements of—and have a critical awareness of the destructiveness that has resulted from—theology and religious traditions. For example, she reminds us that the Christian doctrine of creation has had three oppressive consequences: (1) the total otherness of God and God's dominion over men, women, animals and the earth; (2) an idea of a godless, lifeless earth; and (3) human loneliness, presumed to be the *a priori*, incontrovertible essence of the human condition. She acknowledges that the ecological catastrophe has its roots, in part, in the Christian tradition. "If we are to develop a new understanding of creation," she writes, "then we need a critical awareness of the destructiveness of our faith."[16]

A third way to develop this critical appraisal is in dialogue with a sociology of knowledge: that is, that the type of one's sociopolitical participation determines how the thinker formulates the problems, and hence limits solutions. In any attempt to address or redress the ecological crisis, it is imperative to acknowledge the socially situated roots of thought. As Karl Mannheim says, we need to "dig up the soil out of which the varying points of view emerge."[17] There is a need to be aware of our eco-social location, as ecotheologian Larry Rasmussen remarks, because this affects directly the approach to ecotheological issues.[18]

It is possible to point to the proliferation of ecotheology publications continuing conversations that seem to lack awareness or analyses about the relations between religious ideas and ideals, the political strata from which they emerge and to whom they speak, and the specific cultural context. Several publications rewrite central Christian symbols (creation, sacraments) and orient them to stand for empowerment and earth ethics. Some even call forth "She Who Is," and still do not make the connections with the past, and possible future, cultural and political destructiveness. The more (eco)feminist theologies are detached from cultural realities—from knowing the evidence and from the "frail global networks of accountability," as says Catherine Keller—the greater the chance will be that we are promoting liberal, albeit graceful, theologies with little or no political responsibility.[19] It helps to remember that political discussion penetrates more profoundly into the existential foundation of thinking than the kind that addresses the various "points of view" and examines only the theoretical relevance of an argument.[20]

4. An Appreciation for the Exchange between Science and Religion, and the Need for Religions, and Specifically Christianity, to take Evolution Seriously

Several key ecofeminist theologians have written on the significance of the dialogue between science and religion. Anne Primavesi, Sallie McFague, Rosemary Radford Ruether, Eleanor Rae and Catherine Halkes are among those who explicitly are engaging Christianity and ecofeminism in conversations with earth science and cosmology.[21] One reason is that the evolutionary discourse of science puts into relief the religious beliefs and assumptions about nature and what it means to be human. As mentioned above, the hegemonic Christian world view is a profoundly human-centred ideology. Without a dialogue with science it is effortless to develop anthropocentric ecological ethics that continue to see the earth as a set of resources having no intrinsic value or sacred independence.

To see the earth primarily as a whole, and humanity as an integrated element is no easy task for many Christians. In fact, ecofeminist Anne Primavesi writes that "the fears inspired by the loss of the theological anthropocentricity, or even the suspicion of its loss, explain why ecotheology seems to have lost its appeal for some theologians."[22] Theologian John Haught argues that much of the reluctance of theology to address ecological issues in depth stems from a prior reluctance to think about evolution and its relationship to God.[23] The biblical-redemptive story rather than the creation-evolutionary story has been chosen as the primary context of understanding and finding meaning in life. The Christian faith, therefore, has set aside the earth and its magnificence as the primary religious reality. Because a sense of the divine is encouraged to be derived extensively from biblical sources, an awareness of the revelation of the divine in the natural world has been all but lost for many Euro-Western Christians. The excessive concern for the redemptive processes has concealed the realization that the disintegration of the natural world is also the destruction of the primordial manifestation of the divine.[24] As a result there is a diminished Christian awareness of a sacred indwelling presence in the natural world.[25]

At the core of the problem is a theological paradigm that radically (from the root) separates humanity from the earth. This separation permeates the entire theological tradition, including eschatology, teleology, anthropology, Christology and ethics. As Mary Grey writes, "An ecofeminist theology of creation demands a radical re-thinking of all our cosmic, cultural and vital reference points."[26] It is a crisis of Christian world views.

Sallie McFague suggests that a common creation story could become the beginning of an

> evolutionary, ecological, theological anthropology that could have immense significance transforming how we think about ourselves and our relations and responsibilities toward other human beings, other species, and our home, planet Earth.[27]

Nancy Howell proposes that the intricacies of "relationship" are an appealing model by which to consider an ecofeminist cosmology.[28] To conceive of Christianity in light of an evolutionary cosmology calls for substantial re-evaluations of the self-understanding and foundational assertions of theology, and would broaden the historical framework beyond biblical and human history.[29]

5. A Rigorous Understanding of the Extent of the Ecological Crisis

Some ecotheology writers, obviously addressing the "generic" ecological crisis, do not seem to know many specifics. This is important because to speak of a generic ecological crisis is to ignore the contextual specificities as well the range of issues involved. Ecofeminist Karen Warren, who has written extensively on the theoretical aspects, also argues for the need to be aware of the ecological crisis in specific terms such as water, forestry, soil erosion, agriculture and pollutants.[30]

Numerous resources are available, including the annual *State of the World Report*, the GEO 2000 (Global Environment Outlook 2000: United Nations Environment Programme), various accounts from the United Nations and countless meticulous reports that give considerable data as to the evidence of the ecological crisis. Awareness of the crisis will always be limited. But to address ecotheology or ecofeminist theology and discuss only feminism or theology, as happens at times, or to omit how this will relate to or alleviate an aspect of the ecological crisis, weakens the possibility of actual transformation.

For example, in his book *Christian Faith and the Environment: Making Vital Connections*,[31] Brennan Hill includes little data about the ecological crisis. He discusses the familiar classical subjects: Scripture, Christology, sacraments, the church, and so on. While these concerns are not negligible, one gets the impression that all that needs to happen is that we change our thinking on religious tenets. The ecological crisis is addressed within the purview of theology. It seems to be disconnected from the facts of the ecological crisis. Hill's book is not unique in this regard. A different problem is the absence of ecotheological discourses in theology in general, feminist or otherwise. At the annual American Academy of Religion, less than 1 percent of papers deal with ecology. It is also not uncommon for entire faculties of theology, while perhaps acknowledging the ecological crisis, to fail to teach pertinent courses or make personal lifestyle changes. Yet what could be more pertinent for the present and the future? It seems to be difficult for theologians to make these connections at a deep level. To be aware of the specifics of the ecological crisis is, in my view, one way to make connections that will stick.

Continuity needs to occur between theological symbols, such as water, earth or air, and the actual conditions of these elements. For example, Marq de Villiers, in *Water* (a book that won the prestigious Canadian Governor General's Award), reports on the truly dire situation of water in many parts of the world.[32] He examines such issues as weather patterns, desertification, irrigation, dams and aquifers. He surveys the "politics of water" emerging in China, United States, Canada, the Middle East and India. He concludes that the only prognosis for the future is radical change now, or the arrival of pervasive, desperate and violent situations in the very near future. During the year 2000, the proliferation of private, multinational companies seeking water rights "troubled the waters" even further. Theologically, it makes little sense to write about the "waters of life" when the problems surrounding water are acute and highly political. Thomas Berry writes, "[I]f water is polluted it can neither be drunk nor used for baptism. Both in its physical reality and its psychic symbolism it is a source not of life but of death."[33]

Another example of the need for ecological awareness can be drawn from the complex issues of biotechnology, considered here to be a subset of the larger ecological crisis.[34] Apart from a few, such as Celia Deane-Drummond, theologians are late getting on the scene. Yet, biotechnology has become an integral part of life. It is deeply embedded in the cultural projects and practices, and is part of the social, political and religious landscapes. There is a great need to map the "real world" of biotechnology,[35] and to identify all the levels of reality in which biotechnology is structured and operative. From the major religious traditions there is no consensus on virtually any biotechnological issue. Religious positions are pluralistic in their sources, premises, modes of argument and conclusions.[36] The religious voice often addresses the ethical questions, and is one of the voices scrambling to develop ethical paradigms equipped to address the current biotechnological ventures. Still, most biotechnology goes unnoticed by the religious communities, with the exception of the Humane Genome Project—on which there is little agreement—and medical ethics. The impetus for reflection is not usually that biotechnology is an inherently religious issue. Rather it is because of the public outcry over antifreeze protein genes from flounder injected into tomatoes, chicken genes in potatoes, firefly genes in corn, hamster genes into tobacco … the list is endless.

Canadian ethicist Margaret Somerville has written on what she calls the problems of doing ethics in science time.[37] Science time is fast, and accelerating. Ethics time is slow. Ethics requires time, pondering and discerning: time to learn the facts, to understand the values, to discern the implicit and explicit assumptions, the motivations and aims, the risks and consequences, and ultimately to ask the question of the public or common good. The level of ethical conversation needed to address biotechnology has never before been required. Old principles and precepts cannot contain the issues.[38]

Theologians need to attend to the data of the ecological crisis in order to respond adequately. If it is possible to recover a sense of the mystery of the divine in nature, we may heal our sight and stand in reverence of the great "biotechnology" of the earth processes, unadorned by human correctives. A deep and nourishing sensitivity towards life engenders reverence, and this is a profound resource for religious awareness and activism. If we are committed to transformation, not just of the theological systems, but of the world/earth, then we must attend to ecological situations.

6. An Openness to the Insights of the Myriad Religious Traditions, Especially Those That Have Developed a High Degree of Sensitivity to the Natural World, and a Willingness to Be Transformed by the Dialogue

It is urgent that the Christian tradition not only engage in interreligious dialogue, but interpret itself in light of the world's religions as one thread within a tapestry of revelations.[39] The exclusive and semi-inclusive Christian attitudes towards most major religions continue to support an idea of Christian supremacy, albeit from subtle to blatant.[40] A viable option is the emerging pluralist–correlational model for a theology of religions.[41] Although still in the initial stages of systematic articulation, this model proposes a shift from Christocentrism to theocentrism, a shift that many feminists and ecofeminists have advocated. It is a way to preserve an/the essential meaning of Christianity and releases the binds that prevent a genuine appreciation of other religious perceptions.[42]

For ecofeminists, the rigidity of Christianity is problematic on many fronts.[43] There are limitations in reworking a Christianity that has accumulated misogynist notions and anti-ecological stances. The discontinuity required from core elements of many traditions from both the ecological and feminist evaluations is daunting. There is a tension between how far a tradition can be stretched and be reinterpreted, and the need for new religious sensitivities which can respond to the socio-ecological plight. To some extent, this tension mirrors the ambivalence of many feminists towards patriarchal religions: tensions between those who modify existing systems, those who continue the analytic (deconstruction) work and those who create new traditions. It is, however, in the interreligious dialogue, especially by feminists or ecofeminists, that these issues come blazing to the fore.[44]

Nonetheless, it is possible to identify the transformative and prophetic insights of distinct traditions, and affirm the particular values that will assist collaborative responses to the socio-ecological crises. This process, described by Mary Evelyn Tucker and John Grim as that of critical understanding, requires empathetic appreciation and creative revisioning to understand the multilayered symbol systems in world religions.[45] The central task, from an ecofeminist perspective, is to align religious efforts, and the spectrum of cosmologies, myths, symbols, rituals, values and ethical orientations, and self-understanding within the rhythms and limits of the natural world.

7. A Commitment to Politically Relevant and Engaged Work in Tandem with an Awareness of the Strained Material Realities of Women of the South, and the Necessity of Religious Voices to Be Active within the Political and Governmental Arenas

There is a growing need for theologians to be politically and socially engaged, and there are more efforts in this direction.[46] As Mahatma Gandhi is noted for saying, "Those who think religion has nothing to do with politics, do not know the nature of religion." Yet there continue to be theological discourses with apolitical appearances.

As Rosemary Radford Ruether has pointed out, there is a myopia in Northern ecofeminism due to its emphasis on theory while not making concrete connections with women at the bottom of the socioeconomic system. She writes,

> we must recognize the ways in which the devastation of the earth is an integral part of an appropriation of the goods of the earth whereby a wealthy minority can enjoy strawberries in winter, while those who pick and pack the strawberries lack the money for bread and are dying from pesticide poisonings.[47]

Northern ecofeminism can fall prey to cultural escapism, illusions and irresponsibility with an excessive emphasis on theory, and is in need of correctives of this myopia. It may be that the problem is greater than myopia, and is located in a distortion in method and starting points, inadequate interlocutors and a failure to attend to the world.[48] This renders ecofeminist theology not only powerless to face the real issues it is addressing, but worse still, indirectly participating in the destruction of the world while creating beautiful theories about alternative futures.

While we need to attend to the perversions and rectifications of various religious interpretations and methods, the accelerating ecological crisis and the strained material relationships between women and the natural world intensifies. The methodology of the liberationist traditions is useful, although as Ivone Gebara indicates, one cannot emulate Latin American liberation theologies in developing an ecofeminist theology, as they are generally neither feminist nor ecological. With the exception of Leonardo Boff, most Latin American liberation theologians have not examined and modified the Christian-based patriarchal anthropology and cosmology.[49] Within an ecofeminist liberationist theological perspective links can be forged between social justice and eco-justice. In general, however, ecofeminist theology takes its cues from ecofeminist *theory* in which the ideological issues are prevalent and steers away from the global ecofeminist discourse on the material connections. This translates into the fact that, thus far, few theologians who take the ecological-feminist matrix seriously have addressed issues such as militarism, bio, agro or reproductive technologies, multinational corporations and globalization, debt and trade, free-trade zones, life-form patents, and so on. In short, they have not moved into the realm of the global political arena.

CONCLUSION

If, as Einstein says, problems cannot be solved at the level of consciousness in which they were created, then business as usual cannot continue. It is not simply that as theologians we need to rearrange our theological thinking and discourse. We also need to understand the dialectic between religion and culture in order for religion to become an active political player. One could say that, at least in this part of the world, the religious right is active politically—which is true. In fact, it is virtually the *only* religious voice that is sufficiently loud to be heard. This is not helpful, as their agenda, in North America at least, is usually pro-military, anti-environmental protection, anti-evolution, pro-family values (read "women return to the home"), limited reproductive freedom, and little state intervention in business. This cannot continue. Other religious perspectives need to be in the arena.

This paper has explored seven different hermeneutics that could enlarge the horizon of ecofeminist theologies in order to increase their effectiveness. The presupposition of this article is in line with the Marxist maxim "Philosophers have only interpreted the world, in various ways; the point, however, is to change it." The critical relationship, and oftentimes breach, between theory and practice needs to be restored. These hermeneutics, or directions for consideration, are oriented towards this restoration, in the vein of liberation theories and theologies. Although no one can be truly knowledgeable, it is nonetheless important to be aware of the significance of a diverse range of issues that have an impact on the discourse one is addressing. There are many others that were not mentioned here. Perhaps, as suggests Mary Grey, it is time to hear from those writing directly out of their own struggles, and not from those of us trying to include their voices.[50] The conversation continues, in tandem with the deterioration of earth and health, and efforts to prevent further decline. Ecofeminist efforts could become a significant social, political, religious and ecological force to reckon with. Let us hope so!

NOTES

[1] Noël Sturgeon, *Ecofeminist Natures: Race, Gender, Feminist Theory and Political Action* (New York: Routledge, 1997), 24–48.

[2] Heather Eaton, "The Edge of the Sea: The Colonization of Ecofeminist Religious Perspectives." *Critical Review of Books in Religion* 11(1998): 57–82.

[3] See Marsha Hewitt, *Critical Theory of Religion: A Feminist Analysis* (Minneapolis: Fortress Press, 1995), 5.

[4] Karen J. Warren defines naturism as "the domination or oppression of nonhuman nature," in "The Power and Promise of Ecological-Feminism," *Environmental Ethics* 12(1990):125–146 (132).

[5] For example, see Gerder Lerner, *The Creation of Patriarchy* (Oxford: Oxford University Press, 1986):48–53.

[6] Warren, The Power and the Promise of Ecological-Feminism, 133.

[7] Beverly Harrison and Carol Robb, *Making the Connections: Essays in Feminist Social Ethics* (Boston: Beacon, 1985), 145.

[8] Harrison and Robb, *Making the Connections*, 245.

[9] Dorothee Sölle, *The Window of Vulnerability: A Political Spirituality* (Minneapolis: Fortress Press, 1990), 133–141.

[10] Bat-Ami Bar On, "Everyday Violence and Ethico-Political Crisis," in Bat-Ami Bar On and Ann Ferguson, eds., *Daring to Be Good: Essays in Feminist Ethico-politics* (New York: Routledge, 1998), 45–52 (45).

[11] Dorothy Smith, *The Everyday World as Problematic: A Feminist Sociology* (Toronto: University of Toronto Press, 1987).

[12] Humanities Press (New Jersey) publishes a series entitled Key Concepts in Critical Theory in which three references are particularly useful: Carolyn Merchant, ed., *Ecology* (1994); Kai Nielsen and Robert Ware, eds., *Exploitation* (1997); and Carol Gould, ed., *Gender* (1997). See also Hewitt, *Critical Theory of Religion*.

[13] Carol Adams, ed., *Ecofeminism and the Sacred* (New York: Continuum, 1993).

[14] Ecofeminism had been criticized for the essentialism and apolitical spiritualities which are assumed to permeate the discourse. Janet Biehl's book, *Finding Our Way: Rethinking Ecofeminist Politics* (Montreal: Black Rose, 1991), is an influential misrepresentation of ecofeminism. See also Mary Mellor, *Breaking the Boundaries: Towards a Feminist Green Socialism* (London: Virago, 1992); Joni Seager, *Earth Follies: Coming to Feminist Terms with the Global Environmental Crisis* (New York: Routledge, 1993).

Raymond Murphy, *Rationality and Nature: A Sociological Inquiry into a Changing Relationship* (Boulder: Westview, 1994), pp. 184–192; Laura Westra, *An Environmental Proposal for Ethics: The Principle of Integrity* (Lanham, MA: Roman and Littlefield, 1994), 161–170; and Luc Ferry, *The New Ecological Order* (trans. Carol Volk; Chicago: University of Chicago Press, 1995), which offers a complete distortion of ecofeminism (108–126).

15 Karl Mannheim, *Ideology and Utopia: An Introduction to the Sociology of Knowledge* (trans. Louis Wirth and Edward Shils; London: Kegan Paul, Trench, Trubner and Co., 1936), 69.

16 Dorothee Sölle, *To Work and to Love: A Theology of Creation* (Philadelphia: Fortress Press, 1984), 20.

17 Mannheim, *Ideology and Utopia*, 43.

18 Larry Rasmussen, *Earth Community, Earth Ethics* (Maryknoll, NY: Orbis Books, 1996).

19 This is further developed in Heather Eaton, "Ecofeminism and Globalization," *Feminist Theology* (May 2000):41–55. See Catherine Keller, "Seeking and Sucking: On Relation and Essence in Feminist Theology," in Rebecca Chopp and Sheila Greeve Davaney, eds., *Horizons in Feminist Theology* (Minneapolis: Fortress Press, 1997), 56–66.

20 Mannheim, *Ideology and Utopia*.

21 Anne Primavesi, *Sacred Gaia: Holistic Theology and Earth Systems Science* (London: Routledge, 2000); Sallie McFague, *The Body of God: An Ecological Theology* (Minneapolis: Fortress Press, 1993); Rosemary Radford Ruether, *Gaia and God: An Ecofeminist Theology of Earth Healing* (San Francisco: HarperSanFrancisco, 1992); Eleanor Rae, *Women, the Earth, the Divine* (Maryknoll, NY: Orbis Books, 1994); Catharina Halkes, *New Creation: Christian Feminism and the Renewal of the Earth* (Louisville, KY: Westminster/John Knox Press, 1991).

22 Anne Primavesi, "Ecology's Appeal to Theology," *The Way* 40 (January 2000):60–71 (63).

23 John Haught, *The Promise of Nature: Ecology and Cosmic Purpose* (New York: Paulist Press, 1993), 32. Although an evolutionary paradigm will not de facto reorientate theology. For example, versions of the strong anthropic principle are used to indicate that humans are indeed the pinnacle of creation.

24 These views would be similar to those of Thomas Berry, *The Great Work* (New York: Bell Tower, 1999).

25 For a further discussion of this, see Heather Eaton, "Biotechnology: Theological and Ethical Resources," in *Biotechnology and Genetic Engineering: Current Issues, Ethics and Theological Reflections, Taskforce on the Churches and Corporate Responsibility* (Toronto: United Church of Canada, 2000), 64–82.

26 Mary Grey, "Ecofeminism and Christian Theology," *The Furrow* 51(September 2000):481–490 (486).

27 McFague, *The Body of God*.

28 Nancy Howell, *A Feminist Cosmology: Ecology, Solidarity and Metaphysics* (Amherst, NY: Humanity Books, 2000).

29 See Haught, *God After Darwin: A Theology of Evolution* (Boulder: Westview, 1999); Haught, *Promise of Nature*, 32–35; Primavesi, *Sacred Gaia*.

30 Karen J. Warren, "Taking Empirical Data Seriously: An Ecofeminist Philosophical Perspective," in Karen J. Warren, ed., *Ecofeminism: Women, Culture, Nature* (Bloomington: Indiana University Press, 1997), 3–20.

31 Brennan Hill, *Christian Faith and the Environment: Making Vital Connections* (Maryknoll. NY: Orbis Books, 1998).

32 Marq de Villiers, *Water* (Toronto: Stoddard, 1999).

33 Thomas Berry. "Economics as a Religious Issue," *Riverdale Papers* X(1985):1–24 (4).

34 For an in-depth discussion of this material see the collection *Biotechnology and Genetic Engineering: Current Issues, Ethics and Theological Reflections*. See also Celia Deane-Drummond, *Theology and Biotechnology: Implications for a New Science* (London: Geoffrey Chapman, 1997).

35 I am borrowing this term from Ursula Franklin, *The Real World of Technology* (Toronto: Anasi Press, 1992), taken initially from C.B. MacPherson, *The Real World of Democracy* (Toronto: Canadian Broadcasting Corporation, 1965), 12.

36 "Religious Perspectives," in *Cloning Human Beings: Report and Recommendations of the National Bioethics Advisory Group* (Rockville, MD: June 1997), 39–61.

37 Margaret Somerville, Doing Science in Ethics Time, personal communication.

38 The problem is amplified exponentially in an information age where biotechnology can have an instant global use and impact. Developments occurring in one geographic location are implemented elsewhere. If restrictions exist in one country, the project is relocated. Ethics tends to be geographically and cultural bound. Biotechnology is not.

---

39 Thomas Berry, "The Catholic Church and the Religions of the World," *Riverdale Papers* X(1985): 1–15 (6).

40 See Paul Knitter, *One Earth: Many Religions: Multifaith Dialogue and Global Responsibility* (Maryknoll, NY: Orbis Books, 1995).

41 Knitter, *One Earth: Many Religions.*

42 Ecofeminist theologians often call for a relativising of the hegemonic understanding of Christianity in the face of world religions. For a recent and elegant view of this, see Brazilian ecofeminist theologian Ivone Gebara, *Longing for Running Water: Ecofeminism and Liberation* (Minneapolis: Fortress Press, 1999).

43 See Rosemary Radford Ruether, "Ecofeminism: The Challenge to Theology" and Heather Eaton, "Theology and Ecofeminism: Challenges, Confrontations and Reconstructions," in Dieter Hessel and Rosemary Radford Ruether, eds. *Christianity and Ecology* (Harvard: Harvard University Press, 2000), 97–112, and 113–124, respectively.

44 For example see Arvind Sharma and Katherine K. Young, eds., *Feminism and World Religions* (New York: SUNY, 1999). In this collection, ecological issues are rarely mentioned. For a multi-religious ecofeminist conversation, see Carol J. Adams, ed., *Ecofeminism and the Sacred.*

45 Mary Evelyn Tucker and John Grim, "Overview: The Nature of the Environmental Crisis" (Introductory Paper for the Series of Conferences on *Religions of the World and Ecology*), 6–7. This ten-volume series is published, with edited collections on each of the ten major world religions (Harvard University Press). Mary Evelyn Tucker and John Grim, with hosts of consultants from numerous disciplines, have created a Forum on Religion and Ecology to promote the conversation in educational settings, public policy, research and outreach. See divweb.harvard.edu/cswr/ecology.

46 I am struck by several Canadian theologians who work and write overtly within political spheres. Two examples are former National United Church Moderator, Lois Wilson, now a government senator, who recently published *Nuclear Waste: Exploring the Ethical Dilemmas* (Toronto: United Church Publishing House, 2000), and Tony Clarke, *Silent Coup: Confronting the Big Business Takeover of Canada* (Toronto: James Lorimer and Co., 1997), and who recently co-authored with Maude Barlow *Global Showdown: How the New Activists Are Fighting Global Corporate Rule* (Toronto: Stoddart, 2001). The latter two work for the Council of Canadians, a national left-leaning lobby group active on international issues of water, biotechnology and globalization. www.canadians.org

47 Rosemary Radford Ruether, *Women Healing Earth: Women on Ecology, Feminism and Religion* (Maryknoll, NY: Orbis Book, 1996), 5.

48 For a developed discussion of this, see Eaton, "Ecofeminism and Globalization," 41–55.

49 Mary Ress, "Cosmic Theology: Ecofeminism and Panentheism. An Interview with Brazil Feminist Ivone Gebara," *Creation Spirituality* (Nov./Dec. 1993):9–13.

50 Personal conversation, 12 March 2001.

CHAPTER 16

THE POLITICS OF THE BODY IN CANADA AND THE UNITED STATES

John H. Simpson

I

In recent years a number of issues, controversies and popular discourses bearing on the control, use, display and maintenance of the body have entered public arenas. In some cases matters pertaining to the body sustain social continuity by intensifying the link between traditional values and practices (Ellison and Sherkat, 1993). In other cases they signal new social directions by challenging established institutions (Schneirov and Geczik, 1997). Occasionally body-related matters are implicated in conflicts in the global system of action.[1]

Where the body is now a subject of public attention and controversy especially in the West, it has also become an object of wide-ranging theoretical speculation (Bell, 1972; Butler, 1993; Foucault, 1979, 1981, 1988; Frank, 1991; Giddens, 1992; Mellor and Shilling, 1997; O'Neill, 1985, 1989; Shilling, 1993; Synnott, 1993; Turner, 1984, 1992, 1996). This development stands in marked contrast to the near absence of the body as a thematized unit of analysis in classic sociological theory and the variable but generally persistent suppression of the "mode of desire" (Turner, 1984) during the period of industrial capitalism and high modernity (Simpson, 1993).

High modernity (*c.* 1800–1965) was marked by the enactment of an ascetic ideology summarized in the Cartesian slogan "I think, therefore I am." The conceptual separation of mind and body, the subordination of the body to the mind, and the dominance of reason in action were the principle elements of the Cartesian myth. "Practical" Cartesianism in the form of instrumental means–ends rationalization subordinated nature and people to Western technology and civilization (Turner, 1996: 10). The need to control bodies and reproduce them in order to sustain the entrepreneurial/industrial capitalist mode of production was undergirded by the ideologies and practices of ascetic Protestantism and those of Roman Catholicism as well in some circumstances (Simpson, 1993). They were joined by the tendency in scientific medicine to treat the body as a stimulus–response "machine" (thus, reinforcing high modernity's separation of mind and body), the use of the state's powers of organization, surveillance and repression to form and control bodies as social units (Foucault, 1979;

cf. Lyon, 1994a), and the rise of the patriarchal nuclear family—a unit separate but integral to the workplace and "designed" for the reproduction and socialization of bodies and their maintenance through consumption (Shorter, 1977; *cf.* Garrett, 1998).[2]

The decade of the 1960s marked a definitive behavioural and ideological move against the restrictive cultural and institutional patterns of high modernity (Gitlin, 1987; Levitt, 1984; Roszak, 1969). There was a turn that deconstructed the repressed body and increased tension between embodied and "minded" forms of modern action. The dominance of the mind over the body was relaxed. The moral apparatus of bourgeois industrial capitalism seemed to lose its grip (Simpson, 1998a; Turner, 1996:2). Youth in the West embraced a visible counterculture of sexual permissiveness, the use of mind-altering substances, new forms of popular musical expression and a rejection of the regimented industrial order of work. Sex, drugs, and rock and roll became the talismans of the post-Second World War baby-boom generation.

At the same time various social movements sought to advance the economic, political and social rights of students, minorities and the marginalized, including women, gays and lesbians, and the disabled (Buechler and Cylke, 1997; Herzog, 1998; Eiesland and Saliers, 1998). These movements also promoted nuclear disarmament, an end to the cold war and the halt of the U.S.- (and Soviet-) sponsored "hot" conflict in Vietnam. Together the counterculture and the sociopolitical movements of the 1960s formed a metonymous complex that combined progressive—often utopian—social and moral purposes with free expression of the body in a symbolic "package" that was widely disseminated in the media. The modern sensibility of duty and suppression of the body gave way to a postmodern mood of right and expression of the body. The modern emphasis on the immanence of the mind and self in action was joined and countered by a new emphasis on embodied forms of action. The body became part of the self project (Mellor and Shilling, 1997). The "somatic" society was born (Turner, 1996).

No single factor accounts for the body-oriented sociocultural shifts in the West that took off in the 1960s and worked themselves out in subsequent decades, often in interaction with new developments such as the advent of AIDS. Multiple causes and multiple outcomes are entwined in complex patterns where causes and outcomes are interchangeable. Factors implicated in the changing times include new forms of work focused on services, information, communication and transportation, an increase in the participation of women in the workforce, the development of highly reliable methods of birth control, second- and third-wave feminist social analysis, critiques of the patriarchal model of family and work, and the rise of consumer capitalism.

The changes of the 1960s are encoded in the shift across the West from a strong emphasis on economic and political security or material values to a recognition of postmaterialist values that foreground individual expression, participation in decision making, and the preservation and enhancement of nature rather than its domination and exploitation (Englehart, 1990). At the most general level of interpretation this shift can be viewed as a new moment in the construction, meaning and relationship between what Talcott Parsons (1979) writing late in his life described as the "hot spots" of civilization: the institutions that embed economic and reproductive exchanges and their media—money and sex. The enactment of postmaterialist values and the concomitant rise of body-oriented action are consistent with Parsons's analysis of the reconfiguration of norms pertaining to work and the family that have occurred at crucial junctures in the evolution of Western civilization. However, as Englehart (1990) observes—and as Parsons, no doubt, would have agreed—general trends and movements are subject to national particularisms and peculiarities. Cross-national differences in the configuration of institutions and variations in the cultural resources embedded in the social systems of nation-states can act as "filters" or gates that shape the flow of movements in ways that produce "local" versions and responses to general trends (cf. Simpson, 1996, 1998b). Thus, while there has been a culture shift in the West that is traceable to the events and the generational sensibility of the 1960s, there are variations across the nation-states of the West in terms of such matters as the impact of consumer culture and the political expression of body-related issues.[3]

The purpose of this chapter is to "tease out" comparisons between Canada and the United States regarding the impact of the somatic society in North America. Where the shift to postindustrialism in the context of economic globalization has generated a diffuse set of work-related social problems (Barlow, 1990, 1995), the mitigation and solution of these problems tends to proceed within the established frameworks of the welfare state and its reconfiguration in late capitalism. Body matters, on the other hand—especially abortion and homosexuality—have become sources of sharp division and ongoing unsettled, intense bitter conflicts in the public arenas of North America (Jelen and Chandler, 1994; Rayside, 1998). These conflicts are implicated in relations between the institutions of church and state where law, ethics and morals may collide. Furthermore they are implicated in controversies and practices within denominations (O'Toole et al., 1991) and in the expression of religion and morals in the everyday lives of ordinary citizens (Simpson, 1998a). Arguably, then, body matters are "leading indicators" of social tensions and changes in late modernity. The right to work and a fair wage—the central domestic concerns of the parents of the baby-boom generation—have been supplemented (if not replaced) by body-oriented issues in the public arenas of North America.

Data discussed below provide a base for a consideration of the emergent relations between church, state, and the body in the somatized societies of North America. In the first instance attention is directed to the demographic roots of controversy over body matters. Consideration of attitudes towards a variety of body issues in the Canadian and U.S. populations follows. Third, general attitudes are examined in Canada and the United States regarding linkages between religion and politics, that is, the nexus where battles over the body tend to be joined.

II

Religious demography provides the baseline indicator of the likelihood that controversies pertaining to the body will arise in a national jurisdiction. Although patterns of church–state relations and the organization of politics (Martin, 1978) may affect the intensity of body-oriented controversies, the number of carriers of the ingredients for body-oriented conflicts is the best initial estimate of the likelihood that body politics will occur in a population. Since the mid-1970s concerns regarding abortion, sexual orientation, personal "purity" and control of the body have been expressed and pursued as political issues by some within the domain of sectarian Protestantism (Simpson, 1983).[4] A supporting hand has been lent by some Roman Catholics where Roman Catholicism lacks a determinative majority and where the issue of abortion has become publicly salient (Cuneo, 1989).

No European nation-state has the provocative population characteristics that have led to politicized body controversies: a sizable component of sectarian Protestants with Roman Catholics in a minority position. A comparison of the U.S. and Canadian populations in that regard is instructive. Canada is a near-majority Catholic country (46 percent) at the aggregate national level. The United States, on the other hand, is a Protestant country (57 percent). Proportionately, there are nearly twice as many Catholics in Canada as there are in the United States, and for every Baptist in Canada there are nearly eight in the United States. About 13 percent of the American population and 20 percent of the Canadian population is mainline Protestant, and there are about twice as many Protestant others (neither Baptist nor mainline) in the United States as there are in Canada.

Not every Baptist or other sectarian Protestant is a carrier of the ingredients of a body-oriented politics or so-called moral majority-type politics (Simpson, 1983). Furthermore, some mainline Protestants are carriers of body-oriented politics and the category of Protestant Other contains both carriers and non-carriers. Nevertheless, the religious demography of the United States underwrites body-oriented public controversy, but the religious composition of the Canadian population does not support politically oriented body conflicts to the same degree.[5]

Some interesting comparisons can be drawn between the foregoing remarks and results from the Canada/U.S. Religion and Politics Survey (CUSRPS) (Angus Reid, 1996a).[6] Earlier surveys by the American National Survey of Religious Identification (NSRI, see Kosmin and Lachman, 1993) and Statistics Canada (1991 Census) elicited religious identity or affiliation as a response to a set of unfiltered alternatives to the question, "What is your religious identity/affiliation?" CUSRPS, on the other hand, posed the following filter question to respondents: "Do you ever think of yourself as part of a religious tradition? For example, do you consider yourself as Christian, Jewish, Muslim, other non-Christian, agnostic or atheist, nothing in particular, or something else?" Only those who answered "Christian" were probed for a specific denominational response. The figures from NSRI and the 1991 Census of Canada indicate the proportion of Christians in the U.S. (86 percent) and Canadian (83 percent) populations. The percentage of respondents in each country who said they were Christian in response to the CUSRPS filter is 76 percent in the United States and 68 percent in Canada. Also, there are estimates based on the CUSRPS survey for the percentage of Catholics in the Canadian population (33 percent) and the U.S. population (21 percent) and the percentage of Baptists in the two populations as well (Canada, 1.4 percent; United States, 16 percent).

There are differences—in some cases substantial differences—between the CUSRPS estimates and estimates from the Census of Canada and NSRI. According to CUSRPS, both Canada and the United States are less Christian and less Catholic than indicated by the other sources. Also, CUSRPS provides an estimate of fewer Baptists in Canada and the United States than the other sources do. However, the estimated proportion of sectarian Protestants in each country—using Baptists as a rough indicator—adheres to the familiar pattern of fewer sectarian Protestants in Canada than in the United States.[7]

The religious demography of a country is a baseline indicator of its capacity for body-oriented politics. An exploration of the distribution of orientations and attitudes towards body-oriented matters sharpens the assessment of the likelihood of such politics. Writing in the wake of Ronald Reagan's election in 1980, George Marsden (1980) noted that U.S. fundamentalism had re-emerged as a political force in the United States. Many themes and causes were the same as during the first fundamentalist era, according to Marsden, including a call to return to evangelical-Victorian mores with an emphasis on "personal holiness as evidenced especially by avoidance of barroom vices" (p. 228). Marsden also recognized that there were new issues, including opposition to the women's movement and abortion, that had drawn some sectarian Protestants into the public arena.

In the context of the rise of the new Christian right as a force in the U.S. public arena in the late 1970s, Marsden's references to both "barroom vices" and new issues such as abortion raise the question of support in the U.S. population for old and new body-oriented issues. Barroom vices encompass drinking alcoholic beverages and the use of tobacco. Viewed from within the frame of the conservative Protestant interpretation of Romans 12:1 ("I beseech you therefore, brethren, by the mercies of God, that ye present your bodies a living sacrifice, holy, acceptable unto God"), drinking and smoking pollute the body, thereby rendering it unholy and unacceptable to God. Thus, smoking and drinking are—at least from a sectarian Protestant perspective—religiously implicated body-oriented matters. They are the old body issues in the public arenas of North America.

How do the old body issues fare today in the U.S. population as a basis for politics? Changing American attitudes towards barroom vices are instructive. According to the NORC General Social Survey (GSS) (see www.norc.uchicago.edu/homepage.htm) there is clearly no basis in the U.S. population for a politics of prohibition. What was killed in 1933 remains dead. In 1993 only 28 percent of the respondents indicate that they are abstainers. Even among those respondents classified as fundamentalists, 53 percent say that they use alcohol; 72 percent of religious liberals say that they drink.

While the U.S. population is not "on side" in terms of the "classic" Protestant body issue of abstention from alcohol, tobacco use presents a somewhat different picture. Only 27 percent of the respondents indicated that they are smokers. Among those classified as fundamentalists, 26 percent say that they smoke. Among religious liberals the figure is 31 percent. The most reasonable interpretation of these findings is that smoking has ceased to be a "spiritually focused" body issue in the United States and has become a consensual health-related matter. A barroom vice has been transformed into a health-risk factor.

Where barroom vices have lost their once formidable public clout as signifiers of religious practice and Protestant respectability (Gusfield, 1963), new body issues have taken their place. However, these issues have little if anything to do with the use of practices to mark distinctions, differences, status levels and mobility patterns in the society (Simpson, 1985b). Rather, at the heart of the issues is a concern regarding the moral strength and continuity of U.S. society. That concern has been precipitated in such issues as prayer in the schools, abortion, homosexuality and controversies regarding women in the labour force.

The focus in this chapter is on the explicitly body-oriented issues that are part of the complex of concern: sexual orientation and abortion. But extramarital sex is also relevant, a matter that has contemporary saliency in the U.s. public arena in light of allegations regarding the extramarital sexual behaviour of President Bill Clinton. In 1977 about 60 percent of Americans rejected abortion on demand (Simpson, 1983). That figure drops to 55 percent in 1993, with sampling error (probably) accounting for most of the difference. Clearly, the U.S. population is divided on the issue of abortion on demand, with a small majority siding with the politicized Protestant sectarian position.

In 1977 about 68 percent of the NORC GSS respondents took the view that homosexual relations between consenting adults were "always wrong" (Simpson, 1983). In 1993 the figure is virtually the same: 66 percent. Again, the U.S. population sides with the politicized new Christian right position on the issue.

In 1993 77 percent of the GSS sample indicated that extramarital sex is "always wrong." That represents a slight increase (again, probably attributable to sampling error) over the 1977 figure of 73 percent (Davis, 1982). Americans are less conflicted in their attitudes towards extramarital sex (77 percent strongly disapprove) than they are regarding either abortion on demand (55 percent reject it) or homosexual relations (66 percent strongly disapprove).

There is a bimodal pattern in the distribution of attitudes towards homosexual relations (66 percent say that they are "always wrong," 22 percent say that they are "not wrong at all") and abortion on demand (45 percent approve, 55 percent disapprove). On the other hand, the distribution of attitudes towards extramarital sex is highly skewed in the direction of disapproval. There is no sizable "rump" at the approval end of the distribution. All other things being equal, bi-modal distributions of attitudes in populations underwrite conflict. Because there is no division in the population that provides a basis for conflict (most Americans disapprove of extramarital sex), the skewed distribution of attitudes towards extramarital sex, paradoxically, may have strengthened President Clinton's hand in the controversy regarding his extramarital sexual behaviour. There is no sizable response rate at the approval end of the scale to underwrite a plausibility structure for conflict.

The fact that a new body-oriented politics entered the U.S. public arena in the late 1970s in reaction to social somatization is consistent with the religious demography of the United States and patterns of orientation in its population to abortion and homosexuality. The religious demography of Canada does not favour a U.S.-style politics of body issues. Is it the case that attitudes in the Canadian population to body issues also discourage body-oriented public controversies?

Data for assessing that question are not available in a Canadian equivalent of the NORC General Social Survey. Estimates provided here are taken from Bibby's (1993) Project Can90, the 1984 Canadian National Election Survey (Lambert et al.), and CUSRPS. Of the three sources of data, only Project Can90 has items that match the NORC GSS questions pertaining to abortion on demand and homosexual relations between consenting adults. Cross-tabulations (truncated) of those items with the self-reported importance of religion appear in Bibby (1993: 87). Bibby's cross-tabulations can be compared with cross-tabulations of the abortion and homosexual relations items in the NORC GSS with the self-reported strength of religion.

Among the Project Can90 respondents indicating that religion is very important in their lives, 15 percent approve of abortion on demand, and 17 percent approve of homosexual relations. Among the respondents reporting that religion is not important at all in their lives, 46 percent approve of abortion on demand and 40 percent approve of homosexual relations. Among U.S. respondents reporting high religious strength, 30 percent approve of abortion on demand and 23 percent say that homosexual relations are not wrong at all. Among those who report low religious strength, 54 percent approve of abortion on demand and 27 percent approve of homosexual relations.

While caution should be exercised in interpreting the figures, it would appear that Canadians tend to be more conservative than Americans regarding abortion on demand and somewhat more liberal regarding homosexual relations. These patterns are consistent with general differences in the religious demography of the countries. Canada is more Catholic than the United States. The United States is more Protestant and has more sectarian Protestants in its population than Canada. As a rule Catholics are more conservative regarding abortion and somewhat more liberal in their views of homosexuality than sectarian Protestants.

The homosexuality items in the surveys mentioned above elicited judgments from respondents regarding the moral status of homosexual behaviour. Where question wording shifts to the performance of public roles, interesting differences emerge between Canada and the United States. In 1984, Canadians' attitudes towards homosexuals in the school classroom and Americans' attitudes towards homosexuals teaching in post-secondary institutions of learning suggested that Canadians are more "edgy" than Americans regarding the presence of homosexuals in teaching roles.

In deciding whether that conclusion is justified it should be borne in mind that the 1984 NORC General Social Survey question can be interpreted as an indicator of attitudes towards civil rights and, specifically, the desirability of freedom of expression in a venue (the post-secondary classroom) where ideas are supposed to receive free rein. While the question may evoke some thoughts about the risk of corrupting the morals of youth, it is more likely—given the marked emphasis on the norm of free speech in American society—to raise the question of the extent to which limits should be imposed on the expression of "dangerous ideas." The question in the 1984 Canadian National Election Survey, on the other hand, may have evoked the putative risks involved in exposing school-age children to homosexuals. In that case the emphasis is not on free speech but rather on the potential for child abuse and the recruitment of "innocent youngsters" to a deviant lifestyle.

The best direct evidence for differences between Canada and the United States in the matter of body issues is found in the CUSRPS data obtained in response to an open-ended question regarding issues that should receive the greatest attention of leaders. As Table 16.1 indicates, no Canadian respondents mentioned either abortion or moral issues and pornography as matters that should receive "first call" on leaders' attention. Only 1 percent of Canadian respondents mentioned moral issues and pornography at all. On the other hand, both abortion and moral issues were each mentioned by 3 percent of the U.S. sample as the most important issue facing leaders, and 6 percent and 5 percent, respectively, thought that leaders should pay attention to those matters.

Table 16.1 also provides figures regarding the issues that Canadians and Americans thought were most important in 1996. For Canadians it was jobs and unemployment. For Americans it was crime/violence and education/schools. Comparisons between these figures and the numbers for abortion and moral issues are instructive. Clearly, abortion and moral issues were hardly on the public agenda in Canada at all in 1996. Jobs and unemployment were. In the United States, on the other hand, there was less consensus regarding what was important, and abortion and moral issues were reasonably close in importance to those issues that were deemed to be the most important (crime and education). In general theoretical terms, the numbers in Table 16.1 indicate that social control or system maintenance (crime/violence/education/schools/abortion/moral issues) were perceived by the U.S. public as problematic in 1996. In Canada, on the other hand, adaptation or survival in the form of jobs and the reduction of unemployment were significant public concerns.

CUSRPS respondents were also asked to indicate the importance of different public goals arranged in two sets of three priorities each. The priorities in each set tap orientations towards a social-control goal (raising moral standards; preserving and promoting the family), a materialist goal (maintaining law and order; building a healthy economy), and a postmaterialist goal (giving people more say in government; protecting the environment).

In each set of priorities, the social-control goal was chosen more often by Americans, with the materialist goal second and the postmaterialist goal third. The pattern of choices among Canadians is more complex. In the first set, the postmaterialist and materialist goals were chosen at virtually the same rate, with the social-control priority ranking third. In the second set of priorities, the materialist goal ranks first, the social-control goal second and the postmaterialist goal third. In both sets of priorities, Canadians were less likely to endorse social-control goals than Americans.

Where matters pertaining to social control or system maintenance can be thematized in public arenas in terms of personal morality, they can also be thematized in terms of the discourse of rights. The responses of Canadians and Americans to items in the CUSRPS survey pertaining to the rights of gays and lesbians and the regulation of abortion are as follows. A majority of respondents in both countries endorse the proposition that gays and lesbians should have the same rights as other citizens and that the government regulation of abortion infringes the rights of women. The pattern of implication in the discourse of rights—at least in the cases of homosexuality and abortion—is virtually the same in Canada and the United States. Why?

The idea of human rights has been interpreted as a fundamental element in the "social ontology" of the West (Thomas *et al.,* 1987; *cf.* Huntington, 1996:220–250). The idea of human rights, in other words, is an institutionalized element in the culture of the West. It is a taken-for-granted feature of Western civilization and, as such, is endorsed and valued throughout the West. That, of course, does not mean that practices with respect to rights are necessarily the same across nation-state jurisdictions

TABLE 16.1: ISSUES THAT SHOULD RECEIVE GREATEST ATTENTION FROM LEADERS IN 1996–

First Mention (+), Total Mentions (++)

	Canada (%)		United Stales (%)	
Issue	+	++	+	++
Jobs / unemployment	27	46	–	–
National unity / Quebec's future	18	41	–	
Economy / recession	14	24	–	–
Deficit / debt / govt spending	12	23	–	–
Health care / medicare	6	16		
Crime / violence	–	–	9	20
Education / schools	–	–	9	20
Deficit / debt / govt. spending	–	–	8	15
Defence	–	–	8	17
Economy / recession	–	–	8	15
Drugs	–	–	7	15
Health care		–	6	14
Abortion	*	*	3	6
Moral issues / pornography	*	1	3	5

* Less than 1%

Source: CUSRPS

within Western civilization. However, it does mean that the idea of human rights tends to be accepted by at least substantial pluralities of citizens in nation-states across the West. It is not surprising, then, that Canadians and Americans are similar in terms of their willingness to recognize and endorse the idea of human rights in the case of abortion and homosexuality.

Notwithstanding the institutionalization of the idea of human rights in the West, differences exist across national jurisdictions in the enactment of human rights in everyday practices and orientations. In the matter of body issues these differences are mediated in part by religion, religiosity, and linkages between religion and politics. As a rule, variation across jurisdictions in the level of tension and conflict regarding abortion and homosexuality is directly proportional to the level of religiosity and the linkages between religion and politics: the higher the level of religiosity and the stronger the links between religion and politics, the higher the level of tension where abortion and homosexuality are thematized as matters of public concern.

The CUSRPS study also shows that, compared with Americans, Canadians consider religion to be less important in their lives. Fewer indicate that they are affiliated or active in religious organizations, there is a lower rate of activism in religious organizations in Canada, and more Canadians than Americans indicate that one need not go to church to be a "good Christian." In general, religion is somewhat less important to people in Canada than it is to those in the United States, and Canadians are less involved in religion than Americans.

Regarding linkages between religion and politics, fewer Canadians than Americans indicate that religion is important to their thinking about politics. Fewer Canadians believe that it is essential that traditional Christian values play a role in politics and that Christians should get involved in politics to protect their values. More Americans than Canadians feel close to the Christian right.

III

The data adduced above constitute a sketch of certain responses in Canada and the United States to the rise of the somatic society, responses that can be framed in the first instance within demographic contrasts. With proportionately more Roman Catholics and mainline Protestants than the United States, Canada is a "churchly'" society. The United States, on the other hand, with its large proportion of non-mainline Protestants, is a sectarian society. The strident politicization of abortion and homosexuality in the U.S. political arena that began in the late 1970s is ultimately attributable to the sectarian Protestant emphasis on individual moral purity linked to an ideology associating national strength with individual beliefs and behaviour (Falwell, 1980). That, of course, does not mean that Roman Catholics and others, as well, were not "on side" particularly on the matter of abortion. Nevertheless, the emergent body-oriented sociomoral politics of the late 1970s and its development in the 1980s had its base in Protestant sectarianism (Nesmith, 1994). Furthermore, apart from the presence in the U.S. public arena of the sensibility of sectarian Protestant personal moral purity (assuredly not uncontested), it is difficult to imagine that the extramarital adventures of President Clinton would have become a public and political affair in the 1990s.

Where the U.S. response to the somatic society can be characterized as a grassroots reorganization of politics that brought Protestant sectarians back into the public arena, the responses in Canada have been different and more complex. In the first place, a sectarian Protestant sensibility has never had a hegemonic position in the Canadian public arena (Grant, 1973a). There have, of course, been sectarian Protestants who have played prominent roles in Canadian public life: Tommy Douglas, John Diefenbaker, Ernest Manning and, Preston Manning, the leader of the Reform Party of Canada. In each case, however, an emphasis on individual responsibility and personal purity remained a taken-for-granted private affair (the Mannings) or was expressed within a Tory (Diefenbaker) or socialist (Douglas) context championing social justice and collective integrity (Lipset, 1990).

Canada lacks the strident political voices and hard-bitten absolutism on body issues that have characterized the U.S.'s public arena since the late 1970s. In fact, the Canadian response to the advent of the somatic society has been significantly more positive than the U.S. response. While demography plays a role in differentiating the two countries in that regard, differences in relations between institutions and modes of political action are important as well.

Since its foundation as a nation-state, the United States has been a secularized country by virtue of the non-establishment clause in its Constitution. Secularization in this case refers to the relationship between church and state. Canada in that regard is not secularized to the same degree. There never has been a constitutional provision prohibiting the state's supporting presence in religious institutions and organizations in Canada. By the same token, the dominant church traditions in Canada have tended to be something other than centres of voluntary action playing roles in grassroots, interest-oriented politics. Rather, churches have laid claims on governments via elite accommodation. Thus, the leaders of governments and the leaders of churches have recognized and served each other's needs within the communicative circle of elite accommodation (Simpson and MacLeod, 1985; Hagan, forthcoming).

Prior to the Quiet Revolution, the "tightest" fit between church and government elites was found in Quebec, where there was not only a codetermination of the public agenda but also the presence of the Roman Catholic Church as a major agent in the provincially funded sectors of health, education and social services. In the Quiet Revolution, Quebec was rapidly and thoroughly secularized in an institutional sense. The politics of accommodation shifted from a religious to a linguistic base (Simpson, 1988).

In terms of body issues and the advent of the somatic society, Quebec has underwritten non-discrimination with respect to sexual orientation and publicly thematized the need for social benefits for same-sex couples. Abortion is available as it is elsewhere in Canada too. Quebec francophones have the lowest birth rate in Canada. Thus, the move of the Roman Catholic Church in Quebec from quasi-established to denominational status (cf. Greeley, 1972) has not only entailed the diminution of its role as a provider of health, education and social services, but has also transformed the church's teachings on body matters into voluntaristic norms that no longer have a determinative role in public space. The link between the everyday private practices of individuals and a public sense of normative requirements has been compromised as it invariably is where the Roman Catholic Church moves from a church-type status into denominationalism (cf. Swatos, 1979).

Where the Roman Catholic Church in Quebec is clearly not an advocate of a liberal position on body-oriented issues, it has not engaged in a vociferous politics of opposition to change. Ironically, its own children, the political elites of Quebec, secularized the institutions of the province. The church has not mobilized in any massive public way against them. On the other hand, Canada's largest Protestant denomination—the United Church of Canada—became proactive in response to the advent of the somatic society when it moved to allow the ordination of sexually active gays and lesbians in 1988. Viewed in the lens of history, there is some irony here.

As the bearer of the Methodist tradition, the United Church of Canada carried the norms of strict Protestant individual morality. The control of the sale of liquor still has the marks in many provinces of the Methodist or Protestant sectarian sensibility regarding drinking: a human weakness that should not be condoned and only barely tolerated where necessary. The Methodist stamp on Canadian society (outside Quebec) was pointedly symbolized and summed up in the ironic pejorative label "Toronto the Good," a city of churches where it was not possible to have "fun" on Sundays until long after the end of the Second World War (Morton, 1973).

Why did a bastion of "Toronto the Good"—the United Church of Canada—become the only large and nationally influential Christian Church in the world to ordain sexually active gays and lesbians? A key element was the earlier response of political elites to the advent of the somatic society. As former prime minister Pierre Elliott Trudeau put it in his well-known quip, "The state has no place in the nation's bedrooms" (Christiano, 1994:83). Trudeau's remark put the government on record as generally accepting of the implications of the somatic society. Trudeau's own lifestyle, as well, was publicly perceived as consistent with the sensibility of the 1960s, embodying as it did the outward signs of the permissive counterculture (Christiano, 1994:87–88). That brought a new element into play on the field of elite accommodation.

In the second place, while the United Church of Canada historically opposed the secular "fun" agenda of modernity, including drinking and gambling, it was the major Protestant Church sponsor of the social gospel in Canada—the movement to mitigate the worst human effects of industrial capitalism and the commodification of agricultural production (Allen, 1971). It was a party, in effect, to the founding of the Canadian welfare state through the political process of elite accommodation wherein the United Church of Canada was (and remains) a significant advocate for economic justice. As a "justice church," the United Church of Canada contains a rhetorical frame that allows it to respond to and assimilate new directions in the advocacy of justice.

The somatization of society in the wake of the 1960s was accompanied by a heightened global sense of right that underwrote the enlargement of justice in the Western ontology to include the "righting" of the bodies of the marginalized: women, gays and lesbians, people of colour, and the disabled. In that regard, the United Church of Canada expanded the scope of its justice mission when it "righted" and, thereby, "normalized" the bodies of gays and lesbians by extending ordination to them. That act was not only consistent with the history of the United Church of Canada as an advocate of justice, but also consistent with the accommodation of political and church elites that is still characteristic of the public sphere in Canada, even though religion is no longer as publicly important as it was before the Quiet Revolution and the secularizing trends that affected English Canada after the Second World War (Simpson, 1988).

IV

Clearly, body politics are alive and well today in the United States and in Canada. The furor in the United States regarding the extramarital affairs of former president Bill Clinton and the recent rage in Alberta over the Supreme Court of Canada's decision calling for the revision of the Alberta Human Rights Code to eliminate discrimination on the basis of sexual orientation underscore the presence of body politics. I have argued that contemporary body politics can be traced to the deconstruction of the disembodied mind—the turn against Cartesian dualism—that was enacted and symbolized by the generational revolt of the 1960s.

Although the generational revolt of the 1960s was an event that swept across the broad plain of Western civilization, it has worked itself out in various ways within the nation-states of the West. Religious demography, individual opinions and attitudes, and the extent and intensity of religious practice provide a different resource base for the politics of the body in Canada and in the United States. Furthermore, differences in the institutional and organizational features of the societies have an impact on political behaviour and agitation focused on body-oriented issues as well.

Both Canada and the United States have responded to the advent of the somatic society. Canada has moved in the direction of liberalization in a quieter and smoother way than the United States and it has moved further than the United States in institutionalizing rights at the state level for gays and lesbians. While abortion has been decriminalized in both countries, access to abortion has been limited in the United States by restrictions imposed through the welfare system. Abortion has also been subjected to intense protest accompanied by hostile—sometimes lethal—behaviour in the United States. Although there has been some collective agitation against abortion in Canada, it has not been as widespread nor as conflicted as in the United States (Ginsberg, 1993).

The institutions of religion in Canada and the United States have responded differently in mediating the impact of the somatic society. The response in the United States runs from civil, considered rejection of the ordination of gays and lesbians by most mainline Protestant churches to intense hostility to both abortion and homosexuality within the precincts of the new Christian right. In Canada, on the other hand, the response to the somatic society has been one of quiescence, isolated disapproval, or brave endorsement in the case of the United Church of Canada. Which of these directions will prevail in the twenty-first century remains to be seen.

NOTES

1 The Western press recently reported that in certain fundamentalist circles in Egypt "eggplants and gourds have been declared 'un-Islamic' since these vegetables can be stuffed, and the act of stuffing them might make women think of sex" (Roberts, 1998:D14). One imagines secular, Western cosmopolitans muttering, "And what do they think minarets symbolize?"

The body has its uses in national arenas too. The late Diana, Princess of Wales, arguably, found her body to be her best weapon in her "war" against the House of Windsor (Morton, 1995). Her "confession" on national television of infidelity as a response to the Prince of Wales's adultery aroused public sympathy. Her use of alternative therapies—herbal medicine, reflexology, acupuncture, colon irrigation—can be framed as a counter-systemic allegory of disdain for the restrictive conventions of the royal house. Alternative therapies challenge the authority of established medicine. Diana not only entered her body in the fray against the royal house via a public confession of her adultery, but also provided a sense of metonymic protest by subjecting her body to unconventional types of care. Her own well-publicized embodied ordeal, the affliction of bulimia, bolstered the body as a unit of action and site of problems in late capitalism.

2 Where the body was an object of positive action in high modernity, it tended to be treated as either a sexual force within a counter-systemic, collective context controlled by religious adepts or secular utopians, or an object to be cultivated and, perhaps, even sacrificed in accord with rigid, politicized aesthetic ideals. It was also viewed as a machine-like apparatus that required proper maintenance and repair.

Thus, forms of free love were practised in the highly regimented Oneida community in the United States (Stark and Bainbridge, 1997) and in avant-garde circles of the left as well (E. Wilson, 1982). The physical education movement followed an aesthetic ideal that, arguably, reached its apogee in the Third Reich's obsession with "perfect" bodies and its destruction of "grotesque" bodies (Segal, 1998). The ordered "disorder" of modern ballet occasionally evoked dramatic images of human sacrifice (Eksteins, 1989). The maintenance of the body-as-machine found expression among elites in the dietary and cleansing rituals of exclusive spas and sanatoria (Boyle, 1993). In all of the "revolts" against modernity's general tendency to sublate and forget the body there was a distinct, paradoxical element of suppressive control and a marshalling of the body in order to achieve an ideal, define a social boundary or mobilize for a cause. In high modernity the body was not a unit of voluntaristic expression.

3 Late capitalism produces a surfeit of goods and services serving wants that stretch far beyond the putative needs of populations at least as far as those needs were defined when industrial/entrepreneurial capitalism "reigned." The shift from an emphasis on production to consumption as the driving force of an economy has a somewhat different meaning where the memory and reality of class dominance in post-feudal societies persists as opposed to the circumstance where differences between classes tend to be only loosely connected, at least in a popular sense, with status and power differences. Thus, both the timing of the advent of relative affluence and increased consumption within a society and whether a society is postfeudal or liberal (in the Whig sense) affect the meaning of consumerism. For generations, Americans have had a sense of being a "people of plenty" (Potter, 1954). Furthermore, as Veblen (1908) pointed out long ago, consumption in the United States is a sign of simply having the means to consume. On the other hand, in post-feudal societies consumption occurs within the memories of sumptuary, class-bounded exchange. Consumption not only represents the possession of the means to consume, but also marks residual boundaries between classes that can be traced

to historical differences in the possession and use of the means of violence. Consumption in postfeudal societies is not, simply, a sign of the possession of the means to consume. These differences, then, may explain the ambivalent fascination of British (Featherstone, 1991) and continental theorists (Bourdieu, 1984) with the relatively recent advent of mass consumption in the United Kingdom and Europe and its links to perceived and constructed social differences and boundaries. The masses are now told via advertising that "It's *Your* Choice!" One imbued with the Whig sensibility and comfortably located "upscale" might respond: "So, what else is new? Isn't that the way it's always been?"

4 The term *sectarian Protestantism* as used herein refers to those Protestant traditions that have never had an established relationship with any state. In this usage Anglican, Episcopalian, Lutheran and Presbyterian are not sectarian Protestant traditions. Baptist, Pentecostal, Assembly of God and the like are sectarian Protestant traditions.

5 Differences between Canada and the United States in religious demography and other social features pertaining to religion were extensively explored in the *Canadian Journal of Sociology* 3, no. 2 (1978).

6 See Andrew Grenville's chapter in this volume for details regarding the design and sampling frames for the survey.

7 What is unusual and, perhaps, groundbreaking in the Angus Reid survey is the provision of the response categories "nothing in particular" and "something else" in filtering respondents to determine religious tradition. These categories usually do not appear in the range of responses to a survey query about religious identity or affiliation. A substantial proportion of respondents in both Canada (21 percent) and the United States (16 percent) chose one or the other of the categories. Thus, some of the "leakage" out of the Christian and Catholic categories detected by the CUSRPS survey can probably be accounted for by the provision of "nothing in particular" and "something else" as response categories. "Nothing in particular," especially, deserves further exploration as perhaps an indicator of diffuse, nonspecific religiosity particularly where it is offered alongside "no religion" as a response alternative.

REFERENCES

Allen, Richard. 1971. *The Social Passion: Religion and Social Reform in Canada.* Toronto: University of Toronto Press.

Angus Reid Group. 1996a. *Canada/U.S. Religion and Politics Survey.* Toronto: Angus Reid Group.

Barlow, Maude. 1990. *Parcel of Rogues: How Free Trade Is Failing Canada.* Toronto: Key Porter.

———. 1995. *Straight through the Heart: How the Liberals Abandoned the Just Society.* Toronto: HarperCollins.

Bell, Daniel. 1972. *The Cultural Contradictions of Capitalism.* 2nd ed. London: Heinemann.

Bibby, Reginald W. 1987. *Fragmented Gods: The Poverty and Potential of Religion in Canada.* Toronto: Irwin.

———. 1993. *Unknown Gods: The Ongoing Story of Religion in Canada.* Toronto: Stoddart.

Bourdieu, Pierre. 1984. *Distinction: A Social Critique of the Judgement of Taste.* Cambridge: Harvard University Press.

Boyle, T. Coraghessen. 1993. *The Road to Wellville.* New York: Viking.

Buechler, Steven, and F. Curt Cylke, Jr., eds. 1997. *Social Movements: Perspectives and Issues.* Mountainview, CA: Mayfield.

Butler, Judith. 1993. *Bodies That Matter.* London: Routledge.

Christiano, Kevin J. 1994. *Pierre Elliott Trudeau: Reason before Passion.* Toronto: ECW.

Cuneo, Michael W. 1989. *Catholics against the Church: Anti-Abortion Protest in Toronto, 1965–1985.* Toronto: University of Toronto Press.

Davis, James A. 1982. *General Social Surveys, 1972–1982: Cumulative Codebook.* Chicago: National Opinions Research Center.

Eiesland, Nancy L., and Don E. Saliers. 1998. "Barriers and Bridges: Relating the Disability Rights Movement and Religious Organizations." In *Human Disability and the Service of God.* Nashville: Abingdon.

Eksteins, Modris. 1989. *Rites of Spring: The Great War and the Birth of the Modern Age.* Toronto: Lester and Orpen Dennys.

Ellison, Christopher E., and Darren E. Sherkat. 1993. "Conservative Protestantism and Support for Corporal Punishment." *American Sociological Review* 58(1):131–144.

Englehart, Ronald. 1990. *Culture Shift in Advanced Industrial Society.* Princeton: Princeton University Press.

Falwell, Jerry. 1980. *Listen America!* Garden City: Doubleday.

Featherstone, Mike. 1991. *Consumer Culture and Postmodernism.* London: Sage.

Foucault, Michel. 1979. *Discipline and Punish: The Birth of the Prison.* Harmondsworth: Penguin.

———. 1981. *The History of Sexuality,* vol. 1, *An Introduction.* Harmondsworth: Penguin.

———. 1988. *The History of Sexuality,* vol. 2, *The Care of the Self.* Harmondsworth: Penguin.

Frank, Arthur. 1991. *At the Will of the Body.* Boston: Houghton Mifflin.

Garrett, William R. 1998. The Protestant Ethic and the Spirit of Modern Family. *Journal for the Scientific Study of Religion* 37(2):222–223.

Giddens, Anthony. 1992. *The Transformation of Intimacy.* Cambridge: Polity Press.

Ginsberg, Faye. 1993. "Saving America's Souls: Operation Rescue's Crusade against Abortion." In *Fundamentalism and the State: Remaking Policies, Economies, and Militance,* eds. Martin E. Marty and R. Scott Appleby. Chicago: University of Chicago Press.

Gitlin, Tod. 1987. *The Sixties: Years of Hope, Days of Rage.* New York: Bantam.

Grant, John Webster. 1973a. "At Least You Knew Where You Stood with Them: Reflections on Religious Pluralism in Canada and the United States." *Studies in Religion/Sciences Religieuses* 2 (4):340–351.

Greeley, Andrew M. 1972. *The Denominational Society*. Glenview and London: Scott, Foresman and Company.

Gusfield, Joseph R. 1963. *Symbolic Crusade: Status Politics and the American Temperance Movement*. Urbana: University of Illinois Press.

Hagan, John. 2001. *Northern Passage: The Lives of American War Resisters in Canada*. Cambridge, MA, and London: Harvard University Press.

Herzog, Alberta A., Jr. 1998. *An Analysis of the Disability Rights Movement within American Mainstream Protestantism at the Regional and Local Level*. Columbus, OH: Center for Persons with Disabilities in the Life of the Church.

Huntington, Samuel P. 1996. *The Clash of Civilizations and the Remaking of World Order*. New York: Simon and Schuster.

Jelen, Ted. G., and Martha A. Chandler, eds. 1994. *Abortion Politics in the United States and Canada*. Westport, CT: Praeger.

Kosmin, Barry A., and Seymour P. Lachman. 1993. *One Nation under God: Religion in Contemporary American Society*. New York: Crown.

Lambert, Ronald D., Steven D. Brown, James E. Curtis, Barry J. King, and John M. Wilson. *1984 Canadian National Election Survey*. See http://www/icpsr.umich.edu:80/ cgi-bin/archive.prl?path=ICPSR&num=8544.

Levitt, Cyril. 1984. *Children of Privilege: Student Revolt in the Sixties: A Study of Movements in Canada*. Toronto: University of Toronto Press.

Lipset, Seymour Martin. 1970. *Revolution and Counter-Revolution: Change and Persistence in Social Structures*. New York: Basic Books.

Lyon, David. 1994a. *The Electronic Eye: The Rise of Surveillance Society*. Minneapolis: University of Minnesota Press.

Marsden, George M. 1980. *Fundamentalism and American Culture: The Shaping of Twentieth Century Evangelicalism, 1870–1925*. New York: Oxford University Press.

Martin, David. 1978. *A General Theory of Secularization*. Oxford: Basil Blackwell.

Mellor, Philip A., and Chris Shilling. 1997. *Reforming the Body: Religion, Community and Modernity*. London: Sage.

Morton, Andrew. 1995. *Diana: Her New Life*. New York: Simon and Schuster.

Morton, Desmond. 1973. *Mayor Howland: The Citizens' Candidate*. Toronto: Hakkert.

Nesmith, Bruce. 1994. *The New Republican Coalition: The Reagan Campaigns and White Evangelicals*. New York: Peter Lang.

O'Neill, John. 1985. *Five Bodies: The Human Shape of Modern Society*. Ithaca: Cornell University Press.

———. 1989. *The Communicative Body*. Evanston: Northwestern University Press.

O'Toole, Roger, D.F Campbell, J.A. Hannigan, Peter Beyer, and John H. Simpson. 1991. "The United Church in Crisis: A Sociological Perspective on the Dilemmas of a Mainstream Denomination." *Studies in Religion/Sciences Religieuses* 20(2):151–163.

Parsons, Talcott. 1979. "Religious and Economic Symbolism in the Western World." *Sociological Inquiry* 49(2–3):1–48.

Potter, David M. 1954. *People of Plenty: Economic Abundance and the American Character*. Chicago: University of Chicago Press.

Rayside, David. 1998. *On the Fringe: Gays and Lesbians in Politics*. Ithaca: Cornell University Press.

Roberts, Paul Williams. 1998. The Politics of Islam. *Globe and Mail*, 25 July, D14–12.

Roszak, Theodore. 1969. *The Making of a Counter Culture: Reflections on the Technocratic Society and Its Youthful Opposition*. Garden City: Doubleday.

Schneirov, Mathew, and Jonathan Geezik. 1997. The Aesthetic of the Body and Public Life. Paper presented at the Annual Meeting of the American Sociological Association, Toronto, 9–13 August.

Segal, Harold B. 1998. *Body Ascendant: Modernism and the Physical Imperative*. Baltimore: Johns Hopkins University Press.

Shilling, Chris. 1993. *The Body and Social Theory.* London: Sage.

Shorter, Edward. 1977. *The Making of the Modern Family.* New York: Basic Books.

Simpson, John H. 1985a. "Federal Regulation and Religious Broadcasting in Canada and the United States: A Comparative Sociological Analysis." In *Religion/Culture: Comparative Canadian Studies*, eds. William Westfall, Fernand Harvey, and John H. Simpson. Ottawa: Association for Canadian Studies.

———. 1985b. "Status Inconsistency and Moral Issues." *Journal for the Scientific Study of Religion* 24(2):155–162.

———. 1988. "Religion and the Churches." In *Understanding Canadian Society*, eds. James Curtis and Lorne Tepperman. Toronto: McGraw-Hill Ryerson.

———. 1993. "Religion and the Body: Sociological Themes and Prospects." In *A Future for Religion? New Paradigms for Social Analysis*, ed. William H. Swatos. Newbury Park, CA: Sage.

———. 1996. "'The Great Reversal': Selves, Communities, and the Global System." *Sociology of Religion* 57(2):115–125.

———. 1998a. "Confessions, Outings, and Ordeals: Understanding Media in America." In *Religion, Mobilization, and Social Action*, eds. Anson Shupe and Bronislaw Misztal. Westport, CT: Praeger.

———. 1999b. "Selves and Stories: From Descartes to the Global Self." In *Character and Identity: The Philosophical Foundation of Political and Sociological Perspectives*, ed. Morton A. Kaplan. St. Paul: Paragon House.

———, and Henry MacLeod. 1985. "The Politics of Morality in Canada." In *Religious Movements: Genesis, Exodus, and Numbers*, ed. Rodney Stark. New York: Paragon.

Stark, Rodney, and William S. Bainbridge. 1985. *The Future of Religion: Secularization, Revival, and Cult Formation.* Berkeley: University of California Press.

Swatos, William H. 1979. *Into Denominationalism: The Anglican Metamorphosis.* Storrs, CT: Society for the Scientific Study of Religion.

Synnott, Anthony. 1993. *The Body Social.* London: Routledge.

Thomas, George, John W. Meyer, Francisco O. Ramirez, and John Boli. 1987. *Institutional Structure: Constituting State, Society, and the Individual.* Beverly Hills: Sage.

Turner, Bryan. 1984. *The Body and Society: Explorations in Social Theory.* Oxford: Blackwell.

———. 1992. *Regulating Bodies: Essays in Medical Sociology.* London: Routledge.

———. 1996. *The Body and Society: Explorations in Social Theory*, 2nd ed. London: Sage.

Weblen, Thorstein. 1908. *The Theory of the Leisure Class: An Economic Study of Institutions.* New York: Macmillan.

Wilson, Edmund. 1982. *The Thirties: From Notebooks and Diaries of the Period.* New York: Washington Square Press.

CRITICAL THINKING QUESTIONS

1. What preconceptions and difficulties do you think minority religions encounter as a result of a public expression of their faith? Why?
2. What limitations do we encounter when crafting legal definitions of religion?
3. What do you think the growth and existence of new religious movements signals about religious life in Canada?
4. Do you think churches should have a voice in issues such as same-sex marriage?

FURTHER READINGS

Barker, E. 1984. *The Making of a Moonie: Choice or Brainwashing?* Oxford: Basil Blackwell. This classic study was an important point in the development of the sociological study of new religious movements. Barker's theoretically grounded, fieldwork-based study concluded that those who joined the Moonies were not brainwashed, but were normal young people exercising agency around life choices. Her work sparked intense debate which continues to this day.

Côté, P., ed. 2001. *Frontier Religions in Public Space*. Ottawa: University of Ottawa Press. An excellent collection with pieces written from a variety of disciplinary perspectives, including sociology and political science.

Dawson, L., ed. 1998. *Comprehending Cults: The Sociology of New Religious Movements*. Toronto and New York: Oxford University Press. Dawson's book is an important contribution to the study of new religious movements. He takes an even approach in this theoretical discussion of the sociological exploration of new religious movements.

Kent, S. 2000. "Brainwashing and Re-Indoctrination Programs in the Children of God/The Family." *Cultic Studies Journal* 17:56–78. Stephen Kent finds himself on the cult side of the cult/new religious movement divide. He has done extensive research on new religious movements and argues that we need to be careful about minimizing the risks of involvement with such groups. His work is a good example of the issues taken up by scholars who focus on "cults."

Lippert, R. 1996. "The Construction of Satanism as a Social Problem in Canada." In L. Dawson, ed. *Cults in Context: Readings in the Study of New Religious Movements*, Toronto: Canadian Scholars' Press. Lippert's work examines the ways in which Satanism was worked up or socially constructed as a problem in the period 1980 to 1989. He uses interviews, content analysis of periodical and newspaper indices and a variety of other resources to develop his analysis of the working up of Satanism as a problem apart from the "objective reality."

Palmer, S. 2004. *Aliens Adored: Rael's UFO Religion*. New Brunswick: Rutger's University Press. This study is based on participant observation, interviews and review of documents and is Palmer's comprehensive analysis of this group from its beginnings to its current place in international news as a result of its cloning efforts. This book is an excellent example of a sociological study of a new religious movement, in the tradition of the work of Eileen Barker.

Richardson, J.T., ed. 2004. *Regulating Religion: Case Studies from Around the Globe*. New York: Kluwer Academic/Plenum Publishers. This massive collection is international in scope. It essentially surveys religious freedom around the globe, looking at the degree of freedom and the restrictions imposed in various countries around the world.

Robbins, T., and B. Zablocki, eds. 2001. *Misunderstanding Cults: Searching for Objectivity in a Controversial Field*. Toronto: University of Toronto Press. An extremely unusual collection in that it brings together scholars on both sides of the new religious movement/cult divide, some of whom are in dialogue with each other. This collection includes some theoretically sophisticated discussions of how sociologists conceptualize agency, a concept that is central to thinking about whether people who join cults are "brainwashed."

CONCLUSIONS

Arguably never before has the study of religion been so important in Canadian society. And yet, there seems to be a lag between the need for good sociological research and the carrying out of such research. At its very early stages this book was reviewed by some Canadian sociologists of religion. One comment several reviewers made was that the book was very Christian-centred—why was there not more information being considered on religious groups such as Sikhs, Muslims, Witches? So, my research assistants and I set to work, attempting to locate what we were assured existed. And yet, surprisingly, there is very little work in the sociology of religion on these groups. Within religious studies there is a great deal more, and to be sure there are some scholars with sociological training who work in Religious Studies departments, but there is a definite gap in our sociological knowledge about diverse religious groups, especially those from outside the Christian tradition. So, we drew from some work that was not clearly situated in sociology to augment our discussions as well as to challenge prevailing notions.

Obviously the organizing themes of this book—traditions, transitions, and innovations—are interrelated and cannot be as neatly separated as we have seen in the previous pages. The book has been designed to give an overview of the sociology of religion in Canada, but also to encourage a new direction in this field. First, we are in dire need of theoretical sophistication and a commitment to abandoning dogmatic adherence to theories that were developed to address the social and cultural climate of their times. This does not mean that we should abandon the theoretical tools of the past, but that we must learn to use them in a manner that enables us to understand the religious life of Canadians in global context.

Moreover, the sociological study of religion seems to be premised on an acceptance of secularization, or at the very least a continuous effort to refute it. This is intriguing given that most sociologists of religion have criticized this thesis for its simplicity. Yet when we employ simplistic measures we buy into a very narrow view of religion that dictates the conclusion of a more secular world. But what, in the end, does this tell us? The task remains to map the religious life of Canadians and the communities of which they are a part, whether local, regional, national, or global.

One of the perils of accepting some version of secularization, especially the notion of differentiation, is the tendency to accept the idea that religion is or has become privatized. The myth of privatization allows us to ignore the very public presence of religious discourse and the manner in which it shapes who has religious "voice." Does this mean that we want to eliminate religion from the public sphere? How would that look and is it even possible? And, of course, what exactly do we mean by "public" and "private"? These questions may lead us to conclude that the more important quest is to explore the ways in which religion is woven through social life. Ultimately, we need to move towards a view of religion that starts from questioning rather than knowing.

Further, we are in need of a methodological revamping that employs a nuanced approach to the study of religion. While surveys offer a valuable part of the sociological picture, in-depth studies of religious life in Canada are lacking. Moreover, surveys need to move away from strictly Christian conceptualizations of religion and religious life to capture the varieties of ways that people engage in religious practice and belief. In-depth studies of both mainstream Christians and religious groups on the margins are needed to provide a better sociological picture. This does not mean that it is possible to arrive at "the" picture, but that we need a better sense of the texture of religious life.

This collection represents some of the best work of sociologists of religion in Canada, but it is in no way comprehensive nor does it include all religious groups in Canada. Rather, it explores the major theoretical debates that affect how we see the religion–society relationship. These are relevant across religious beliefs and practices. The secularization debate, religious diversity, and religious freedom are issues central to the sociological exploration of religion and culture-society. I invite readers to use the concepts and perspectives introduced in this book to examine further their own areas of interest, and to contribute to the gap in sociological knowledge we presently experience about religion in Canada.

COPYRIGHT ACKNOWLEDGEMENTS

Roger O'Toole, "Religion in Canada: Its Development and Contemporary Situation" from *Social Compass*, 43(1). Copyright © Sage Publications, 1996. Reprinted by permission of Sage Publications.

Reginald W. Bibby, "On Boundaries, Gates, and Circulating Saints: A Longitudinal Look at Loyalty" from *Review of Religious Research*, 41. Copyright © Association for the Sociology of Religion/Religious Research Association, 1999. Reprinted by permission of The Religious Research Association.

David Seljack, "Resisting the 'No Man's Land' of Private Religion: The Catholic Church and Public Politics in Quebec" from *Rethinking Church, State, and Modernity: Canada Between Europe and America*. Copyright © University of Toronto Press, 2000. Reprinted by permission of University of Toronto Press.

Samuel H. Reimer, "A Look at Cultural Effects on Religiosity: A Comparison between the United States and Canada" from *Journal for the Scientific Study of Religion*, 34(4). Copyright © Blackwell Publishing, 1995. Reprinted by permission of Blackwell Publishing.

Peter Beyer, "Religious Vitality in Canada: The Complementarity of Religious Market and Secularization Perspectives" from *Journal for the Scientific Study of Religion*, 36(2). Copyright © Blackwell Publishing, 1997. Reprinted by permission of Blackwell Publishing.

Nancy Nason-Clark, "When Terror Strikes at Home: The Interface between Religion and Domestic Violence" from *Journal for the Scientific Study of Religion* 43(3). Copyright © Blackwell Publishing, 2004. Reprinted by permission of Blackwell Publishing.

William A. Stahl, "A Cultural Cartography of Science, Technology, and Religion" from *Handbook of Religion and Social Institutions*. Copyright © Kluwer Academic/Plenum Publishers, 2005. Reprinted by permission of Kluwer Academic/Plenum Publishers.

William Closson James, "Dimorphs and Cobblers: Ways of Being Religious in Canada" from *Studies in Religion/Sciences Religieuses*, 28(3). Copyright © *Studies in Religion/Sciences Religieuses*, 1999. Reprinted by permission of Wilfrid Laurier University Press.

William Shaffir, "Still Separated From the Mainstream: A Hassidic Community Revisited" from *The Jewish Journal of Sociology*, 39(1/2). Copyright © The Maurice Freedman Research Trust Ltd., 1987. Reprinted by permission of The Maurice Freedman Research Trust Ltd.

Siân Reid, "Two Souls in One Body: Ethical and Methodological Implications of Studying What You Know" from *The Pomegranate* 17. Copyright © Siân Reid, 2001. Reprinted by permission of Siân Reid and *The Pomegranate*.

Susan J. Palmer, "Caught Up in the Cult Wars: Confessions of a Canadian Researcher" from *Misunderstanding Cults: Searching for Objectivity in a Controversial Field*. Copyright © University of Toronto Press, 2001. Reprinted by permission of University of Toronto Press.

Lorne L. Dawson and Jenna Hennebry, "New Religions and the Internet: Recruiting in a New Public Space" from *Journal of Contemporary Religion*, 14(1). Copyright © Routledge, 1999. Reprinted by permission of Routledge.

Homa Hoodfar, "More than Clothing: Veiling as an Adaptive Strategy" from *The Muslim Veil in North America: Issues and Debates*. Copyright © Women's Press, 2003. Reprinted by permission of Women's Press.

Lori G. Beaman, "Aboriginal Spirituality and the Legal Construction of Freedom of Religion" from *Journal of Church and State*, 44. Copyright © *Journal of Church and State/ J.M. Dawson Institute of Church–State Studies*, 2002. Reprinted by permission of J.M. Dawson Institute of Church–State Studies.

Heather Eaton, "At the Intersection of Ecofeminism and Religion: Directions for Consideration" from *Ecotheology: Journal of Religion, Nature and the Environment*, 6(1/2). Copyright © Equinox Publishing Ltd., 2001. Reprinted by permission of Equinox Publishing Ltd.

John H. Simpson, "The Politics of the Body in Canada and the United States" from *Rethinking Church, State, and Modernity: Canada Between Europe and America*. Copyright © University of Toronto Press, 2000. Reprinted by permission of University of Toronto Press.